Indian Liberalism between Nation and Empire

This book analyses the political thought and practice of Gopal Krishna Gokhale (1866–1915), preeminent liberal leader of the Indian National Congress who was able to give a 'global voice' to the Indian cause.

Using liberalism, nationalism, cosmopolitanism and citizenship as the four main thematic foci, the book illuminates the entanglement of Gopal Krishna Gokhale's political ideas and action with broader social, political and cultural developments within and beyond the Indian national frame. The author analyses Gokhale's thinking on a range of issues such as nationhood, education, citizenship, modernity, caste, social service, cosmopolitanism and the 'women's question,' which historians have either overlooked or inserted in a rigid nation-bounded historical narrative. The book provides new enriching dimensions to the understanding of Gokhale, whose ideas remain relevant in contemporary India.

A new biography of Gokhale that brings into consideration current questions within historiographical debates, this book is a timely and welcome addition to the fields of intellectual history, the history of political thought, Colonial history and Indian and South Asian history.

Elena Valdameri is a postdoctoral researcher at the Chair for History of the Modern World, ETH-Zurich, Switzerland. She is a historian of modern South Asia, with specific interest and expertise in the history of political thought and the anticolonial movement.

Routledge Studies in South Asian History

For more information and a full list of titles published in this series, please visit: https://www.routledge.com/asianstudies/series/RSSAH

Indian Liberalism between Nation and Empire

The Political Life of Gopal Krishna Gokhale

Elena Valdameri

Routledge
Taylor & Francis Group

LONDON AND NEW YORK

First published 2022
by Routledge
4 Park Square, Milton Park, Abingdon, Oxon OX14 4RN

and by Routledge
605 Third Avenue, New York, NY 10158

Routledge is an imprint of the Taylor & Francis Group, an informa business

© 2022 Elena Valdameri

British Library Cataloguing-in-Publication Data
A catalogue record for this book is available from the British Library

Library of Congress Cataloging-in-Publication Data
A catalog record has been requested for this book

ISBN: 978-0-367-47032-6 (hbk)
ISBN: 978-1-032-21201-2 (pbk)
ISBN: 978-1-003-03742-2 (ebk)

DOI: 10.4324/9781003037422

Typeset in Baskerville
by KnowledgeWorks Global Ltd.

Contents

Acknowledgements

I have incurred many debts in writing this book and I would like to warmly thank all the individuals who have helped me with their intellectual generosity, inspiration and friendship. In particular, I want to thank Maria Framke, Parimala V. Rao, Joanna Simonow, Chandralekha Singh, Gagan Preet Singh, Massimiliano Vaghi, Lucio Valent and Carey Watt for having read and commented on drafts of my chapters. To my teachers, Michelguglielmo Torri and Harald Fischer-Tiné, my debts are infinite: with their intellectual passion and rigor, they have been a constant source of inspiration. The constant encouragement I have received especially from Harald has been crucial for carrying out this intellectual enterprise. Thanks are also due to my colleagues and friends at the Chair for History of the Modern World, at ETH Zurich.

I thank Dorothea Schaefter of Routledge for having believed in this project since our very first conversation. Very grateful thanks go to my copy editor Maria Paisley for her cheerful tolerance of my 'Italian' English and her great ability to transform my manuscript into a more coherent book.

Over the years, I have greatly benefitted from the professional help of the resourceful librarians and staff of the several archives where I pursued my research. Thanks are especially due to the people working at the Asian and African Studies at British Library, National Archives of India – in particular in the Private Section – Nehru Memorial Museum and Library, and the Gadgil Library at the Gokhale Institute of Politics and Economics (GIPE). Nanaji Shewale, the librarian at GIPE, deserves special mention because of the unconditional assistance he gave me.

My friends sustained me in so many ways that are too numerous to list. I want to thank, strictly in no particular order, Alessandra Zappatini, Sara Galvagni, Danila Berloffa, Denise Ripamonti, Joanna Simonow, Tim Eschke, Maria Framke, Sibilla Robutti, Mark Frost, Giorgio Bianchi, Anja Suter, Inna Zakharchenko, Nanda Moghe, Michele Torri, Erica Sereno, Walter Zacchini, Silvia Pizzetti, Irene Fumagalli, Giulia 'Pet' Marcolli, Daniele Ludovici, Agnese Riva, Giacomo Mastrorosa, Geeta Rai – who, besides being a dear friend, is also the best Hindi teacher one can think of –, Chandan Tiwary, Mihir Srivastava, Chandralekha Singh, Arijita Mukhopadhyay, and Chitra and Renu – the 'Home Ministers.'

Finally, my beautiful family continues to make just about everything possible: special thanks are for Laura, my sister, and Mattia, my brother-in-law. There are no suitable words to thank my *jivansaathi*, Davide Tadiello, for his love, companionship, unwavering support, endless patience and shared laughter.

It is my deepest regret that my words will not be read by my parents. This book is for my father, Angelo Valdameri, who passed away while I was writing it. It is to him that I owe my love for history.

Abbreviations

BL	British Library
CUP	Cambridge University Press
CWMG	Collected Works of Mahatma Gandhi
GIPE	Gokhale Institute of Politics and Economics
GP	Gokhale Papers
GSW	Gokhale Speeches and Writings
INC	Indian National Congress
NAI	National Archives of India
NMML	Nehru Memorial Museum and Library
OUP	Oxford University Press
PCGB	Proceedings of the Council of the Governor of Bombay Assembled for the Purpose of Making Laws and Regulations
PSS	Poona Sarvajanik Sabha
QJPSS	Quarterly Journal of the Poona Sarvajanik Sabha
SIS	Servants of India Society
SISP	Servants of India Society Papers
YMCA	Young Men Christian Association

Introduction

On a stroll through a garden located in Veer Nariman Road in south Bombay in 2014, a statue of Gopal Krishna Gokhale (1866–1915) caught my attention. I was in India to conduct archival fieldwork for my Ph.D., whose main focus was the very man represented by the statue before me. The makers of the white marble figure had inserted an inscription at the feet of the statue, next to a pile of books. It listed Gokhale's putative political agenda that supported his work as a leader of the Indian National Congress (INC): 'Universal education, national unity, equality of citizenship, and self-government.' I was immediately reminded of Robert Musil's writings about the invisibility of monuments.[1] Gokhale's statue was "conspicuously inconspicuous;" notwithstanding its assumed nation-building significance, it had become immune to public attention. And so has Gokhale. Despite the role he played in elaborating a political vision for India that would influence the development of Indian democracy, the leader of the so-called 'Moderates' has largely disappeared both from the Indian collective memory and from historiographical debates.

Against this background, it comes naturally to ask why Gokhale has been almost ignored by historians of late and, more importantly, if there are any lessons we can draw from making Gokhale a subject of critical historiographical inquiry again. If it is true that, as the Italian historian Benedetto Croce maintained, all history is contemporary history and the interest in the past originates from contemporary preoccupations,[2] then we must try to identify the problems and needs of the present that call for a serious re-assessment of Gokhale. In order to do so, it is imperative to briefly consider the specific sensitivities of the scholarship of South Asia regarding the historical evaluation of the anticolonial movement as well as to acknowledge the reorientations in the field of historiography that took place at the global level and to which historians of South Asia have contributed. Whereas the former helps explain why Gokhale has received only scant scholarly attention, the latter helps illuminate the raison d'être of this book.

DOI: 10.4324/9781003037422-1

Why Gopal Krishna Gokhale?

In the context of the newly independent Indian nation, following the establishment of state-sponsored institutions of teaching and research, history became a professional discipline. While questioning the constrained and distorted interpretations of colonial historiography, history writing became a pedagogical and cultural instrument for the new nation-state to support its nation-building endeavours: its main task was creating a 'useful' national historical narrative by glorifying India's march towards freedom.[3] Its unquestionable value in terms of historical research and understanding notwithstanding, this nationalist historiography tended to look at the Indian anticolonial movement in a teleological way, creating hierarchies of historical actors and moments according to their contribution to the grand narrative of the nation's march to independence.[4] In this view, 'Moderate' liberal early nationalism was considered an incomplete, half-hearted and elitist phenomenon, whose significance lies only in having preceded the allegedly authentic, legitimate version of Gandhi-led nationalism.

'Moderates' have not met with favour even outside the fold of nationalist history writing: they were blamed by Marxist historians for their bourgeois individualism and paternalism in the 1960s and 1970s;[5] they were considered 'collaborators' and more interested in getting a share of imperial power rather than achieving the welfare of the nation by the Cambridge school. Some exponents of post-colonial studies labelled them as passive victims of the Western cultural hegemony.[6] These perspectives must be credited with the merit of having put before us a more nuanced reconstruction of the anticolonial movement – something which had been largely obfuscated by the preceding homogenising tendencies of the nationalist historiography. They also pointed to the deep contradictions inherent in the efforts of liberal political elites of envisioning a national identity in colonial settings. Nonetheless, they failed to grasp the originality of the political visions of liberals – considered substantially 'derivative' from the European tradition of nationalism and therefore analytically redundant – and to acknowledge that their ideas were in fact often the by-product of creative borrowings from several sources and not simply imitative of 'Western' modernity.

The more recent crisis of credibility of liberalism,[7] too, seen by some as the ideological antecedent of today's unjust neoliberal global order, has further contributed to the marginal status of the intellectual and political agency of liberals in India, as well as to the consequent historiographical focus on radical anti-imperial figures.[8]

All this explains that, being an exponent of the 'Moderate' and liberal nationalism and compared to more radical anticolonial activists, Gokhale has long been considered a marginal historical actor in the struggle against British rule as well as a political figure lacking inventiveness.

All this notwithstanding, new historiographical trends – especially, but not only, in intellectual history – provide novel analytical lenses through which reconsidering a putatively unimaginative liberal like Gokhale seems worthwhile. In the last two decades, in fact, historiography has started paying closer attention to the circulation, transformation and adaptation of ideas, concepts and political models across geographical distances and political and cultural borders.[9] This development has resulted in a new sensitivity for the specificities of the historical, cultural and social contexts, as well as the need to overcome essentialist and reductionist interpretations that consider the different paths towards modernity as a unidirectional flow moving from the imperial metropolitan centre towards the colonised periphery. These perspectives of the past have treated and understood discourses of nationalism and nation-building programmes as part of wider, interconnected patterns.[10]

Several historians of South Asia have been leading this trend.[11] Breaking with territorial nation-bound narratives, their pioneering work has contributed to an analysis of the engagements and interactions of the different strands of the Indian national movement with the wider world. Conversely, their scholarship has enriched the field of the intellectual history of South Asia, showing that the Indian subcontinent has been part of a global public sphere since the early 19th century. Moreover, several of these new studies have reconsidered the important role of Indian political and intellectual elites, inserting them in a global arena, where they were engaged in a variety of international political networks and activities. Among these, the work by Christopher Bayly, *Recovering Liberties. Indian Thought in the Age of Liberalism and Empire* has been seminal in reconstructing the history of liberalism as a transnational phenomenon in which Indian liberals were deeply involved, as well as in highlighting the specific characteristics, internal contestations and evolution of liberal ideas and practices in India.

The emerging picture is that, far from being passive recipients of Western knowledge and ideology or "products of fields of power,"[12] Indian intellectuals and political thinkers were often not only mediators, but also producers of new ideas and knowledge which they skilfully combined with profoundly different intellectual traditions. In other words, they, like thinkers in other colonial settings, were ready to assimilate anything useful that came from other parts of the world. They were adapting different elements to their specific needs through a creative, original, and in several cases, highly ambiguous process of selective appropriation and synthesis.[13] In the effort to solve their problems as colonised people and to understand and change the world around them, public men from the subcontinent selectively appropriated Western concepts and ideas that helped them rediscover, reassess, criticise and reformulate their own cultural heritage and their social and political imaginaries. Western notions could represent normative ideals whose adoption was seen as useful for catching up with an idealised and imagined West,[14] or, conversely - in what was a common process of cultural differentiation and political resistance - negative models to reject in order to found a new polity that was more just, or culturally less alien, than those embodied by the Western nations.[15]

Building on this scholarship and engaging with these debates, this book is an attempt to investigate some aspects of G. K. Gokhale's political life that have been previously overlooked and examine them against the backdrop of transnational developments. In doing so, it combines theoretical discussions with a set of empirical case studies in ways that existing research does not do. The figure of Gokhale is thus used as a window onto several phenomena triggered by colonialism and globalisation in the late 19th and early 20th centuries. This study analyses, in particular, the envisioning of the Indian nation and the role of the state; the understanding of progress and modernity; the relationship between national and supranational sense of belonging; the significance of civil society associations in an authoritarian context. These are some of the issues upon which Gokhale reflected in the specific setting of 'British' India, but which can shine a light on the impact of foreign domination on intellectuals and political activists even in different colonial milieus. Such an examination of the political ideology elaborated by Gokhale can enrich also the understanding of the Indian anticolonial movement as being forged since its early phase by external influences and global constellations, which Gokhale himself called the 'mysterious forces.'[16]

Gokhale lived in the period of "flux and cosmopolitanism" that characterised high imperialism[17] and was among those Indian intellectuals and politicians who reflected upon the past, present and future of their society under the impact of colonial domination. This book demonstrates that this moment of intellectual shifts and political tensions in the subcontinent is reflected in Gokhale's political views and vision of the Indian nation. Through the foundation of the Servants of India Society (SIS), a social service association aimed at fostering nation building through civic activism and voluntarism, he called for greater Indian participation in the 'moral and social uplift' of those segments of society that were perceived as weak and 'backward.' Although he was not a diasporic intellectual in the Benoy Kumar Sarkar[18] or Shyamji Krishnavarma[19] or Taraknath Das[20] mould and not even an intellectual *stricto sensu*, Gokhale too had a 'global reach' and was indeed very active on the international stage in his effort to give India a voice. In England and South Africa, his appeals contributed to unveiling the deep contradictions of the 'benevolent' British Empire, so that liberals in the metropolitan countries were sensitised by liberals from the colonies.[21] Being a member of a non-Western globally oriented intellectual and political elite that emerged in the late 19th and early 20th centuries and being aware of the ever-denser global interconnections, Gokhale imagined and discussed the world as a single unified space. His global consciousness provided him with the ability to link local or national questions with larger contexts, whereas his liberal nationalism presented universalist/extraterritorial affiliations – something that reminds us that "Indian liberalism was both wider in scope, and more specific in its remedies, than what is commonly called nationalism."[22] At the same time, trying to render a deeper and more nuanced understanding of Gokhale's political thought, this book seeks to explore the contradictions and ambivalences that characterised his liberal nationalism. It argues that, while some of these limitations are inherent in liberalism, others were shaped by the specific constraints of Indian socio-political conditions as well as by the transition to a new imperialism increasingly underpinned by racism and white supremacy. The analysis pursued in the following four chapters reveals that the abstract language of universalism adopted by the Indian liberal had to come to terms with the increasingly exclusionary impulses of the 'modern' nation. His inclusivist ideas and discourse of national diversity faltered in the face of the 'emergence' of political minorities such as the Muslim community or the so-called Depressed Classes, perceived as a potential threat for the nation-in-the-making. Also, the unease felt about India's 'uneducated masses' and the perceived need to make them disciplined raises legitimate questions about how truly liberating his national vision was. Hence, the story this book tells moves beyond dichotomising views about the 'success' and 'failure' of liberal nationalism as well as narratives of Gokhale as the champion of democracy and freedom or, conversely, of elitism. What it does instead is consider to what extent the nation envisaged by Gokhale engendered structures of dominations and opened up opportunities of emancipation.

Overall, what I intend to do in this book is to demonstrate that Gokhale's political vision is relevant today both from the historical and political viewpoint. Historically, it matters because it offers a reappraisal of a crucial moment of the political and intellectual history of modern India. Politically, it still raises questions of relevance to the present-day engaged intellectual. In fact, political ideologies generated in colonial contexts provide us with enlightening debates and discussions on issues whose significance cannot be ignored in today's world, such as constructions of citizenship, secularism, human rights and global justice.[23] Therefore, rather than focusing on what is most 'authentic' in Indian political thought, it is interesting to look at whether political ideas in modern India underwent changes in form and content, regardless of their place of origin and their original doctrine, how they became significant in a particular temporal and geographical frame, how they interacted with other similar or different ideas in other contexts and, finally, what impact they have had in the socio-political realities of the postcolonial nation-state.[24]

I believe that a close investigation and re-interpretation of Gokhale's political vision can offer insight into intellectual history from two main perspectives. It contributes to constructing the complex web of global and local connections that informed epistemes in colonial India by challenging misleading cultural essentialisms which draw clear-cut boundaries between 'East' and 'West.' With this in mind, this study adopts shifting scales of observation that alternate from the regional to the national and the supranational levels according to the issues analysed. Furthermore, a critical engagement with Gokhale can enhance our understanding of that liberal, secular and republican progressivism that, despite its flaws and limits, was crucial in the ideological foundation of Indian democracy and that, in today's India, is increasingly jeopardised by the rise of Hindu nationalism.

Thematic foci and chapter preview

Exploring Gokhale's political thought, as I have already stressed, is not an end in itself, and the objective of this book is to explore some of the larger themes with which he was confronted during his period of intellectual and political activity. In order to do so, four main thematic foci define the structure of this book and are developed in four corresponding chapters: liberalism, nationalism, cosmopolitanism and citizenship. All were crucially important elements in Gokhale's vision, and all were, in different ways, affected by processes of cultural and epistemic transference as well as shaped by the specific intellectual and socio-political context of 'British' India. The foci, however, should not be considered watertight compartments, as each, although predominant in a specific chapter, intersects to a variable extent with the others too. For that reason, the four foci effectively provide a comprehensive analysis of Gokhale's political views and practices while examining and engaging with the debates over the various issues. Given its strong influence on Gokhale's intellectual formation, liberalism is the focus of the first chapter, as the following section elaborates. Nevertheless, since it informed Gokhale's understanding of nationalism, cosmopolitanism and citizenship, liberalism is also the thread that connects all chapters.

Liberalism

A rich and sophisticated literature has over the years highlighted how *liberalism*, with its focus on abstract universal rights and principles of neutrality, has made invisible inequalities of power such as relations between genders or social classes.[25] The scholarship dealing with colonial settings has shown that liberalism revealed its most exclusionary face and became a powerful ideological weapon in the hands of the colonial rulers who justified their domination with the 'difference' and 'inferiority' of the colonised.[26] These insights have undeniably contributed to revealing the uncomforting liberal attitudes towards hierarchy, exploitation and domination and therefore to render a more nuanced account of liberalism than the monolithic 'other' of totalitarianism.[27]

At the same time, as scholarship on the intellectual history of colonial India has illustrated – Bayly's work *in primis* – the liberal tradition of arguments in favour of individual freedom became a valuable resource for Indian intellectuals, social reformers and political activists in which they rooted their notions of liberty, social progress and their rightful claims for equal citizenship and political freedom, creating their own versions of liberalism, which were more suitable for the particular conditions that prevailed on the subcontinent.[28] In a process of selective appropriation, Victorian liberal ideas were picked up and purged of their derogatory language about the 'uncivilised' in order to serve the agenda of colonised Indian elites to claim greater rights. In other words, liberal ideas provided Indians with a 'respectable' and ready-made method which, from John Locke onwards, had been used in the West to refute both the paternalistic and the despotic conception of sovereign power, and therefore to condemn the abuse of power against citizens. This was undoubtedly a vantage point to reveal the political inconsistency of British rule. Thus, in the context of 'British' India, the Janus-faced liberalism was both an imperial doctrine and a powerful intellectual instrument for the Indian intelligentsia.

This development began with the formation of an Indian civil society and public sphere especially after the 1820s, which allowed the creation of a rich associational culture, the circulation of ideas as well as the production and dissemination of new knowledge, and the development of press and literature in English and the 'vernaculars.'[29] Like its Western configurations, Indian liberalism was not a coherent body of political philosophy. It was internally contested and subjected to changes due to the impact of events, influenced by competing ideologies and philosophies, challenged by the ideological urgency to establish 'Indian' cultural differences. Despite its diversity, the main objectives of liberalism in India were the attainment of a constitutional order that would increasingly grant representation, the safeguard of the individual from the illiberal colonial state as well as the incorporation of concepts of personal freedom and autonomy within the particular structures of cultural and religious communities.[30]

The sociological characteristics of the social groups who received, discussed and transformed liberal ideas and who later on would be responsible for the birth of the nationalist movement were one of the main factors that made the emergence of liberalism possible in India.[31] As a matter of fact, traditionally, in Indian society there were social groups specialised in bureaucratic activities, mostly belonging to Hindu high castes, but with scarce economic means. With the rise of the colonial state and the simultaneous destruction of the most important regional powers, the members of these castes began working for the new rulers while acquiring their language. Through English,[32] they came in contact with the most liberal culture of the time, which, with all its limits, emphasised the values of the bourgeoise liberal democracy and the principles of representation. Giving priority to the preservation of social harmony and hierarchy while discouraging mass upheavals, liberal values and ideals, such as the advancement at a gradual and controlled pace or the distrust towards the masses, recurring themes in authors like Edmund Burke or John Stuart Mill, gained ground not least because they corroborated, in part, the ethos of the high castes.[33] From these caste groups came the great majority of political activists, socio-religious reformers, journalists, economists, writers, scholars and intellectuals that took the lead in creating the associational culture and publicist environment which functioned as platforms for transnational intellectual and cultural exchange, facilitated by the diffusion of print culture and a 'vernacular public sphere.'[34] To one of these social groups – like the great majority of Western India's intelligentsia – Gokhale belonged.

Taking into account these historical developments, the first chapter provides the biographical gist of the book. It illustrates Gokhale's attainment of a Western education and his exposure to liberal ideas and attendant discourses of rights and liberties. It analyses the would-be INC leader's early activities as teacher, journalist and political activist, with special focus on the vibrant political atmosphere of Poona. In doing so, this initial chapter considers Gokhale's relationship with Tilak, Agarkar and Ranade, as well as his first commitments as a representative of the Poona Sarvajanika Sabha (PSS) and Deccan Sabha, and as a volunteer during the plague in 1899. While providing biographical details, it reveals how Gokhale's ideas and lived experiences were strongly intertwined and co-constitutive.

Nationalism

Liberalism was also instrumental in providing the explicit political expression of Gokhale's *nationalism*, which is the second thematic focus of this book.

New treatments of nationalism have convincingly argued that there is nothing highly distinctive in nationalist ideology: nationalism is defined as a complex and varied pattern of thought, with blurry outlines and which needs to host another thicker ideology to be able to provide answers for political problems.[35] In other words, nationalism acquires a given conceptual distinctness according to the ideological frame in which its beliefs are inserted. The meaning of national identity, the definition of national culture, the criteria which define members of the national community and who really counts among them – all this is a contested terrain greatly dependent on the type of nationalism being articulated.

One question is relevant to the present study. Can nationalism be liberal? Can liberalism be nationalist? Until today, these are debated issues among scholars of political thought. The primary consideration of the ongoing discussions revolving around the relationship between liberal and national ideals and values is that nationalism is theoretically committed to the significance of the particular,[36] whereas liberalism, with its emphasis on universally applicable liberties and the free movement of individuals, renders the ties of national identity less significant.[37] By and large, liberal nationalism has often been seen as theoretically naïve as well as ideologically incoherent, and therefore destined to fail. But more than ideological incoherence, which, as history has shown, does not necessarily exclude effective political results, the success or failure of liberal values and ideals in translating the overarching national imaginary into a concrete political agenda is politically contingent and determined by specific historical and empirical factors rather than by philosophical questions.[38] Put differently, assuming the irreconcilability between the liberal principle and nationalism implies a teleological understanding of nationalism as necessarily transforming itself into a conservative, chauvinist or racist ideology. We know, however, that at the beginning of the 19th century, nationalism was not yet marred by its divisive and bellicose potential.[39]

With the American and French Revolutions and their attendant assumption that political communities, in order to count as credible and legitimate, had to constitute themselves as nation-states,[40] nationalism became one of the dominant modern socio-political imaginaries.[41] The normative idea that the state had to take the form of the nation-state became an increasingly established one in the world – including colonial India – endorsed by the principle of self-determination of peoples and nation that gained even further currency after the First World War.[42] In the specific settings of 'British' India, the process of consolidation and centralisation of the colonial state from the 1860s onwards involved the implementation of a set of institutional reforms aimed at making the colonial administrative system more efficient. Mainly driven by the need to cope with growing economic difficulties, in reality these reforms of centralisation served only to increase the expenses of the colonial state, which, as a consequence, had to raise taxation while at the same time keeping the risk of social tensions under control. In other words, colonial authorities – with whom the memories of the 'Great Mutiny' were still very fresh – understood that the only way to counterbalance the discontent caused by increased taxes was by granting political concessions. Therefore, although reluctantly, the British rulers began taking very cautious steps towards the introduction of elective organs of self-government, initially at the municipal level,[43] through which Indians – a very small body mainly representing landed interests – could participate in the administration of local revenue and expense. While unable to resolve the continuous lack of economic resources for which it had initially been designed, the reform of the colonial state thus had the effect of creating at least some of the characteristics typical of a modern state by dramatically enhancing the intervention of the upper echelons of the colonial system at local levels.[44] Through this process, the colonial state became increasingly recognised as the main source of power and legitimacy even by the Indian (proto-)nationalists that questioned its illiberal nature.[45] However, unlike the modern states that had come into being in Europe, the gradual centralisation of the state in India was not accompanied by a process of social homogenisation and by a discourse of equality in terms of duties and rights: on the contrary, the system of representation co-existed with the classification of the Indian subject-citizens according to caste and ethnic-religious belonging.[46] Group identities were categorised and solidified via census operations, while concepts like majority, minority and 'backward' community were given new political significance that had far-reaching impacts on politics in the subcontinent.[47] The apparently credible colonial effort at creating an electoral system, although very exclusive, had to be counterbalanced by perpetuating vertical and horizontal social divisions, so as to prevent political solidarities as well as to justify the colonial argument claiming that the British presence was a fundamental factor in the avoidance of the balkanisation of India.[48]

In this context, the late 18th and 19th-century nationalist discourses that were undergirded with a strong sense of civic liberation and that emphasised the subjective element in belonging to the national community vis-à-vis putatively objective 'cultural' or ethnic traits – traits which were soon to become hegemonic factors in more radical and exclusive definitions of the nation all the world over – found 'ecological niches' in the visions of the Indian political activists that were working towards building a secular and plural nation.[49] So, the views of exponents of the American revolutionary tradition, like Thomas Paine, in particular with his *Common Sense*, and other liberal thinkers, such as the Italian Risorgimento Giuseppe Mazzini, became significant in contributing to the Indian political debate and to liberal politicians like Gokhale.[50]

These debates set the stage for the second chapter, which focuses on the analysis of the conceptualisation of the nation envisaged by Gokhale, especially after his coming to the national political fore following his election at the Imperial Council. Special attention is given to the several elements that constituted Gokhale's national vision, namely the role of the state, the meaning of Indianness, the vision of society and the task of the nation-builder, while highlighting the inherent contradictions in his efforts to strike a balance between being critical of and loyal to the British *Raj*. The chapter crucially demonstrates that Gokhale increasingly regarded nationalism as a form of civic religion that entailed the sacralisation of the nation. Finally, it examines Gokhale's dichotomising understanding of the educated elite and the ignorant masses, and analyses his stand towards the 'emergence' of the Muslim community as well as his increasing concern for the Depressed Classes.

Cosmopolitanism

The thematic focus lying at the core of the third chapter is *cosmopolitanism*. From the 1990s onwards, cosmopolitanism has stimulated lively discussions involving leading academics from different fields. The scholarship resulting from it has shown that with its long and complex history, cosmopolitanism is a protean concept, which has been given multiple meanings and definitions over time.[51] Sometimes qualified as 'rooted,' 'elite,' 'subaltern,' 'colonial,' 'third world,' 'actually existing,' etc., the term 'cosmopolitanism' has been marked by a considerable degree of theoretical and conceptual diversity and, at times, even by confusion.[52] Cosmopolitanism can be understood as the willingness to engage with the 'Other' through "the aesthetic and intellectual openness to diverse strivings, cultures and forms of reasoning."[53] It can be a political philosophy that makes us committed citizens at the local, national and transnational levels,[54] a moral obligation towards the less privileged[55] or the way social groups elaborate modes of living productively with each other.[56]

Historians of South Asia that have adopted the transnational lens to analyse the anticolonial movement have greatly contributed to these discussions.[57] They have explained cosmopolitanism as the global experiences, encounters and opportunities afforded to colonised peoples by the possibility of migration and mobility in the space of the empire and beyond,[58] as an ideology informed by the love of humanity and by the scepticism about narrow affiliations[59] or as the attitude of open-mindedness towards elements of thought coming from different cultural constellations.[60] Like liberalism, modernity or nationalism, cosmopolitanism too has been increasingly conceptualised as a multifaceted phenomenon and defined as both plural and particular as well as transcending its 'Western' normative origins of the so-called 'Enlightenment project.'[61]

The third chapter does not aim at further contributing to the discussions revolving around the abstract definitional questions of 'what is cosmopolitanism?' and 'who is a cosmopolitan?'. Existing literature and debates have perhaps reached the limits of their explanatory power by highlighting the plurality of cosmopolitanisms and substantially enhancing our understanding of intercultural encounters and conflicts at the global level. Here, cosmopolitanism is understood mostly, but not exclusively, in two ways, which, however, cannot be neatly separated as they are often overlapping and entangled. On the one hand, following Pratap Bhanu Mehta, we can define cosmopolitanism as a reflective consciousness,[62] presupposing a confrontation with alterity that is significant for critically engaging with one's self and status as a member of a certain cultural community. This definition pertains primarily to the field of cultural cosmopolitanism. On the other hand, and from a more political point of view, cosmopolitanism is seen as a worldview (and occasionally also a lived practice), although not necessarily predicated on a well-structured political project, that allows one to feel, think and act beyond the nation as well as to combine global awareness with local and specific forms of allegiance and identity.[63] A political cosmopolitanism implies also acknowledging the existence of universal norms of justice that should not be restricted to particular communities or polities but should be addressed to humanity in general.[64]

Keeping as reference points these definitions of cosmopolitanism, the third chapter asks whether, and to what extent, Gokhale may be considered a cosmopolitan. In addressing this question, it considers the global stage on which Gokhale was active as well as the wider connections and networks he built to give legitimacy and momentum to his political vision. More concretely, the chapter examines Gokhale's first encounter with Britishness and his subsequent political activism in the metropole, including his contribution to the 1911 Universal Races Congress and his engagement with the Moral Education League. In the final part, the chapter analyses the INC leader's active participation in the South Africa Indian question, highlighting the often-ambivalent relationship which existed between imperial affiliations and anticolonial endeavours.

Citizenship

The thematic focus around which the fourth and last chapter is organised is *citizenship*. Over the past 20 years, scholars from different disciplines have made a compelling case for the need to discuss citizenship beyond its putative primary link to the nation-state. The often-idealised universality of citizenship has been questioned and the status of citizens increasingly understood as contested, contingent and multi-layered. In highlighting that enjoying citizenship rights has not automatically translated into full integration or equality, the scholarship on the role of ethnicity, class, religion and gender as factors of exclusion affecting entire societies (such as the colonised subjects) or sections of a given society has also generally contributed to challenging the conventional view of citizenship as an exclusively legal institution. Overall, it has become apparent that citizenship cannot be understood only as a legal status or as an abstract bundle of rights and obligations: citizenship also has a less normative dimension, which is underpinned by a set of behaviours, values and practices assigned to individuals and groups to signal their belonging.[65] These patterns determine who is a citizen and who is not while, more subtly, creating a hierarchy between citizens of the same polity, by differentiating between 'good' and 'bad' citizens. Citizenship then becomes an important lens through which investigating how standards of belonging and participation have been underpinned by political, social and cultural assumptions and, as such, have been characterised by continuous shifts, changes and negotiations throughout history. Besides offering a perspective on the processes of inclusion and exclusion, this approach to 'citizenship beyond the vote' is helpful to identify the role of the various political and social actors involved in such processes.[66]

Recent scholarship on citizenship in South Asia has interacted extensively with these theoretical debates.[67] A major contribution from studies of this region to the understanding of citizenship has been to grapple with the assumption that 'citizenship' is a term deeply rooted in the Western political tradition and, as such, might not be an entirely valuable prism with which to study conceptualisations and instantiations of citizenship in colonial and postcolonial contexts. In challenging West-centric projections and diffusionist interpretations, research has argued that citizenship in South Asia must be situated in colonial modernity *and* in precolonial contexts: in fact, the way India has experienced and developed its own approach to 'modern' citizenships has been influenced by both Western and/or colonial notions and practices as well as by precolonial 'indigenous' foundations of this institution which expressed at least some of the ideas associated with citizenship.[68] Also, it has been suggested that, in the appropriation, circumvention and subversion of endogenous and exogenous forms of citizenship, there existed multiple trajectories and entanglements not only within colonial India but also between colonial India and other parts of the world.[69]

In 'British' India, discussions on, and claims to, citizenship were far from considering territorial nationalism as the conventional base for the ascription of rights and obligations of citizenry. Even if to speak of citizenship in a colonial context might seem "conceptually implausible, legally dubious, and historically anachronistic,"[70] the aspiring political elite who gave voice to the early anti-colonial movement from the 1870s onwards intensely debated the question of belonging to a political community and the rights and obligations resulting from such a status. The ideas of citizenship emerging from these debates were initially barely circumscribed by the nation and, far from promoting exclusively "national" programmes, evinced local, regional, supra-national and cosmopolitan dimensions.[71]

Scholars of the Indian subcontinent have also explained the new attention paid to organised philanthropy and social service as part of discourses and practices of active citizenship from the early 20th century onwards. This new phenomenon, in which we can collocate the creation of Gokhale's SIS, was instrumental in countering the absence of a sympathetic and responsible state. It was part of a wider transnational trend: in fact, service for society became increasingly perceived in many parts of the world as a crucial instrument to enhance the well-being and 'efficiency' of the nation through the 'uplift' of its members. Profoundly influenced by eugenic ideas and by social Darwinist or Lamarckian thinking, it was spurred by anxieties about race degeneration which could be prevented by encouraging individual members of the nation to become 'manly,' dynamic and active citizens serving their own country. Such initiatives of active citizen-making, which in many ways resembled the colonial 'civilising mission,'[72] became prominent tools for activists in religious reform movements and more secular political leaders and social reformers, in order to present Indians as entitled to be an autonomous and sovereign people.[73] Aimed at bringing about a thorough transformation of Indian society, the various educational and political programmes sought to physically and morally 'improve' segments of the populace by spreading a sense of civic duty, an ethic of discipline and ideals of social service and co-operation. These civic constructions, when advocated by emancipatory elites, were less concerned with the state/citizen relation and more associated with membership and belonging to the community with a sense of public purpose. They were underpinned by moral values that often corresponded to autochthonous concepts that belonged to the cultural-religious domain of the Hindu upper-caste.[74]

Against this complex and multifaceted background of citizenship notions and practices, the fourth chapter shows that Gokhale understood citizenship not only as a legal/formal status including rights and duties, but also as the long-term process of becoming a citizen. This process implied an 'education into citizenship' which was tied to issues of moral authority and legitimacy and which made the attainment of citizenship potentially exclusionary. In explicating this question, the chapter examines the issues of political participation, social service and civic activism, welfare and education, namely elements that in different and similar ways served the purpose to 'put into practice' the nation that Gokhale envisioned. This final chapter argues that the civic construction articulated by the Indian liberal was underpinned by conservative elements and, at the same time, had the potential to create spaces for change and emancipation for the marginalised sections of Indian society.

Literature and sources

Before turning our attention to Gokhale's first steps in the public life of Western India, it is helpful to provide a short overview of the main existing literature on Gokhale and of the sources on which this study is based.

The most comprehensive (although dated) scholarly biography on Gokhale is B. R. Nanda's *Gokhale: The Indian Moderates and the British Raj*, first published in 1977, and later reprinted.[75] This is by far the most complete biography on Gokhale, based on a thorough perusal of archival sources, and rich in factual details. Nevertheless, and not surprisingly, despite being a valuable reconstruction of Gokhale's life as a political leader and as a man, Nanda's work is a product of its time: the spatial framework remains the narrow national enclosure and the history of nationalism substantially coincides with the history of the INC, whereas the complexities of Gokhale's political ideas are not always grasped.[76] Nanda appears to want to position Gokhale at the same level as Gandhi and Nehru, tracing a sort of ideological continuity between them. All this notwithstanding, this book undoubtedly remains the most reliable and comprehensive account of Gokhale's life and was a fundamental reference point for this study.

Another important – and dated – scholarly work is Stanley Wolpert's *Tilak and Gokhale: Revolution and Reform in the Making of Modern India*.[77] The author takes into account the simultaneous political careers of the two leaders hailing from Poona and creates a narrative in which they occupy antithetical positions. Tilak was socially conservative and perceived 'East' and 'West' as utterly incompatible. Therefore, he preferred promoting a reactionary social outlook vis-à-vis a modernity which was perceived as a direct by-product of colonial domination. Substantially, according to Wolpert, Tilak's strong traditionalism was tactical as it represented the ideological underpinning of his cultural nationalism. On the contrary, Gokhale, zealous student of European philosophy and political thought, adopted a relativistic approach to political and social issues; he blamed the backwardness of Indian society on Hindu orthodoxy and on the danger-ous overlapping of religious belief and social practice. The attainment of self-government was crucial for the progress of the nation, but not enough to liberate it from its social defects. The solution resided in the spread of education and initiatives of social reforms in order to 'improve' the masses. In a similar vein, Wolpert underlines the divergent views held by Tilak and Gokhale in terms of social questions, comparing their conflicting opinions about progress and evolution. By taking into account the conflicts over social reform, Wolpert's work problematises the equation Moderates/con-servatives and Extremists/revolutionaries. It offers analytical insights that help better appreciate the multiple levels on which Indian national leaders had to operate and the difficulties they faced in a society that was deeply affected by the influence of the colonial state – agent of modernisation on the one hand and responsible for the emergence of a 'traditional' India on the other. Yet, the weakness of Wolpert's study is that Gokhale is portrayed as the champion of modernity, while Tilak as the representative of tradi-tion. The outcome is a dichotomising oversimplification of the views and ideologies of the two nationalist leaders.

Although in this work Gokhale appears only *ex negativo*, Parimala Rao's *Foundations of Tilak's Nationalism: Discrimination, Education, and Hindutva*[78] is worth mentioning, since it pays a great deal of attention to the internal con-tradictions within Maharashtrian society that were then projected onto the national movement. The picture of Tilak that emerges from Rao's book is very different from the one of the nationalist 'hero' generally presented in the common historical narrative. In fact, Rao explains that Tilak's cultural nationalism was not only a strategical positioning against the colonial dom-ination. It was also – and more importantly – motivated by the will to restore the pre-colonial social structure in which Tilak and the other 'Extremists,' as part of the landed elite, enjoyed particular economic and social privi-leges, namely those same high-caste privileges that the 'Moderates' and the social reformers denounced as feudal and illiberal. However, the image of the 'Moderates' emerging from this study lacks nuance and the commonal-ities existing between the two parties are not acknowledged. Also, the scale of observation never transcends the national level.

Built on Christopher Bayly's *Origins of Nationality in South Asia: Patriotism and Ethical Government in the Making of Modern India*, the 2005 study by Carey Watt, *Serving the Nation: Cultures of Service, Association, and Citizenship*, too, is relevant to the present book. The author shows the important connections that existed in the early 20th century between the process of nation-build-ing and the social service, charitable and philanthropic activities ani-mated by several organisations founded by 'Moderate' political activists. Gokhale's SIS is among the associations explored. The book reassesses the political significance of 'Moderate' activists showing that their effort to build civil society organisations actually empowered Indians, creating for them opportunities of participation in activities that were politically and socially relevant and which hollowed out the colonial state of its moral authority. The insights from this work have been particularly valuable for the fourth chapter of the present study.

The most important primary sources for the analysis of Gokhale's ideology are his private papers and the collection of the *Speeches and Writings of Gopal Krishna Gokhale* (GSW). Gokhale's papers, kept in the National Archives of India (NAI) in Delhi, are a valuable collection, from which one can see Gokhale's vision from a 'backstage' perspective; the perception that Gokhale had of the other leaders of the INC and of the anti-colonial movement; his concerns about painful and complex issues such as the Hindu-Muslim question or the conditions of Indian indentured laborers in South Africa, etc. It is also interesting to see how certain clashes between Indian political figures were not brought to the political fore by Gokhale in order to keep the credibility of INC intact, nor to leave it vulnerable to British attacks. Moreover, among the recipients of Gokhale's correspondence, throughout the full span of his life, were several British individuals that, often linked to the INC, were sympathetic towards the Indian cause. That Gokhale acquired wide visibility and became a 'homme public' far beyond the borders of India and Great Britain is evinced by the numerous letters that he received from Indian individuals and organisations scattered throughout the space of the Empire, appealing to Gokhale so as to find in him a supporter of their battles.

The GSW are even more valuable in reconstructing Gokhale's political vision, because it is in the discursive space that concepts of the nation or notions of good citizenship are circulated and given authoritative voice. The GSW were published in the 1960s – although previous partial editions had already been published, even during Gokhale's lifetime[79] – by the publishing house of the SIS. They are divided into three volumes – economic, political and educational – according to the main topics addressed.[80] The collection includes speeches in English and English translations of speeches in Marathi directed to different kinds of audiences, from the members of the Imperial Legislative Council, to Indian students and British organisations interested in the Indian cause.

In addition, the SIS Papers, kept at the Nehru Memorial Museum and Library (NMML) in Delhi, are crucial to reconstructing the activities of the association founded by Gokhale, its evolution and internal fissures. This collection contains mainly reports of the activities of the SIS and correspondence between its members and between members and other figures. A few early letters by Gokhale are also included.

I have also consulted official publications such as the Reports of the INC, the Imperial Legislative Council debates, the Proceedings of the Bombay Legislative Council as well as colonial reports of specific commissions, etc.

Ultimately, I have integrated these sources with numerous private papers and speeches of individuals and archives of various organisations that were in touch with Gokhale and the SIS. I have also perused periodicals and newspapers of the time, for example, the *Times of India*, the *Hindu*, the *Bombay Chronicle*, the *Times*, the *Mahratta*, the *Indian Social Reformer*, the *Indian Opinion*, the *Indian Sociologist*, the *Modern Review*, the *Servant of India*, as well as the *Reports of Native Papers*. The *Sudharak*, or *Reformer*, and the *Quarterly Journal of the Poona Sarvajanika Sabha* have been useful in order to scrutinise the young Gokhale's views on many issues.

It should finally be mentioned that several biographies of Gokhale, written mostly by his disciples and friends, have proved to be valuable secondary sources. Most of these works, not surprisingly, are of a hagiographic and apologetic character; they do not provide references for their sources and can therefore hardly be considered scholarly contributions. Yet, they must be given credit for having reconstructed some aspects of Gokhale's political and private life, which could not otherwise be told by the archival material.[81]

Notes

1. Robert Musil held that "monuments are so conspicuously inconspicuous. There is nothing so invisible as a monument" (Robert Musil, 'Monuments', in *Posthumous Papers of a Living Author*, Penguin, New York 1978, p. 61).
2. Benedetto Croce, *La storia come pensiero e come azione*, Bari, Laterza 1938, p. 5.
3. On the history writing in independent India, see among others Supriya Mukherjee, 'Indian Historical Writing since 1947', in A. Schneider and D. Woolf (eds.), *The Oxford History of Historical Writing: Volume 5: Historical Writing Since 1945*, OUP, Oxford 2011, pp. 515–538; Michael Gottlob, *History and Politics in Post-colonial India*, OUP, Delhi 2011, pp. 1–80. On Jawaharlal Nehru's historiographical production and on the lasting influence he exerted in terms of the understanding of the history of India, see Georg G. Iggers, Q. Edward Wang and Supriya Mukherjee, *A Global History of Modern Historiography*, Pearson Education Limited, Edinburgh 2008, pp. 237–238; V.G. Kiernan, "Nehru the Historian", *World Affairs: The Journal of International Issues*, Vol. 2, n. 2 (1993), pp. 9–15.
4. Of course, the official 'national' history and the hierarchies in terms of historical actors and moments vary according to the different political agendas that drive the (re)writing of history. For example, the forces of Hindu nationalism have tried to marginalise even figures like Nehru and Gandhi, while appropriating as their own the ideas of lesser-known freedom fighters. The appropriation of the revolutionary Shyamji Krishnavarma by the Hindu nationalist Bhartiya Janata Party is a telling example of this process (see Harald Fischer-Tiné, *Shyamji Krishnavarma: Sanskrit, Sociology, and Anti-Imperialism*, Routledge India, New Delhi 2014, esp. pp. 187–190).
5. The most influential work in the Marxist field is A.R. Desai, *Social Background of Indian Nationalism*, Bombay 1948. For a recent Marxist critique of the Moderates, see Sanjay Seth, 'Rewriting Histories of Nationalism. The Politics of "Moderate Nationalism" in India 1870-1905', in Sekhar Bandyopadhyay (ed.), *Nationalist Movement in India: A Reader*, OUP, New Delhi 2009, pp. 30–48.
6. C.A. Bayly, *Recovering Liberties: Indian Thought in the Age of Liberalism and Empire*, CUP, Delhi 2012 (first published 2011), p. 343.

7. For an insightful discussion on the meaning of liberalism today, see the third chapter of Duncan Bell, *Reordering the World: Essays on Liberalism and Empire*, Princeton University Press, Princeton 2016, pp. 62–90.

8. See among others, Ali Raza, *Revolutionary Pasts: Communist Internationalism in Colonial India*, CUP, Cambridge 2020; Michael Silvestri, *Policing 'Bengali Terrorism' in India and the World: Imperial Intelligence and Revolutionary Nationalism, 1905-1939*, Palgrave Macmillan, Cham 2019; Kama Maclean, J. Daniel Elam and Christopher Moffat (eds.), *Writing Revolution in South Asia: History, Practice, Politics*, Routledge, Abingdon and New York 2017; Kama Maclean, *A Revolutionary History of Interwar India: Violence, Image, Voice and Text*, Penguin, UK 2016; Fischer-Tiné, *Shyamji Krishnavarma*; Satadru Sen, *Benoy Kumar Sarkar: Restoring the Nation to the World*, Routledge, New Delhi and New York 2015; Kris Manjapra, *M.N. Roy: Marxism and Colonial Cosmopolitanism*, Routledge, London, New York and New Delhi 2010. It should be noted, however, that liberal ideas could be useful to articulate radical worldviews too: Shyamji Krishnavarma is just one telling example among many others. According to Bayly's broad definition of liberalism, liberal ideas tinged, in different measure, all political positions (Bayly, *Recovering Liberties*, p. 245).

9. Samuel Moyn and Andrew Sartori, 'Approaches to Global Intellectual history', in S. Moyn and A. Sartori (eds.), *Global Intellectual History*, Columbia University Press, New York 2013, pp. 3–30.

10. For a discussion on the transnationalisation of historical perspectives at the global level, see, for example, Sven Beckert and Dominic Sachsenmaier (eds.), *Global History, Globally: Research and Practice Around the World*, Bloomsbury, London and New York 2018. See also the recent, already considered a classic, Sebastian Conrad, *What is Global History?*, Princeton University Press, Princeton and Oxford 2016.

11. A useful introduction is Shruti Kapila, 'Preface', *Modern Intellectual History*, Vol. 4, n. 1 (2007), pp. 3–6 and the 'Afterword' by Bayly, pp. 163–196. All the articles in the special issue are representative of the abovementioned trend. Among many others, important works include: Uday Singh Mehta, *Liberalism and Empire: A Study in Nineteenth-Century British Liberal Thought*, University of Chicago Press, London 1999; Leela Gandhi, *Affective Communities*, Duke University Press, Durham 2006; Thomas R. Metcalf, *Imperial Connections: India in the Indian Ocean Arena, 1860-1920*, University of California Press, Berkeley 2008; Jennifer Reagan-Lefebvre, *Cosmopolitan Patriotism in the Victorian Empire: Ireland, India and the Politics of Alfred Webb*, Palgrave Macmillan, Houndmills and New York 2009; Sugata Bose and Kris Manjpara (eds.), *Cosmopolitan Thought Zones: South Asia and the Global Circulation of Ideas*, Palgrave Macmillan, Basingstoke and New York 2010; Manjapra, *M.N. Roy*; C.A. Bayly, *The Birth of the Modern World, 1780-1914: Global Connections and Comparisons*, Blackwell, Oxford 2004; Bayly, *Recovering Liberties*; Andrew S. Sartori, *Liberalism in Empire: An Alternative History*, University of California Press, Berkley 2014; Fischer-Tiné, *Shyamji Krishnavarma*; Tony Ballantyne and Antoinette Burton, *Empires and the Reach of the Global 1870-1945*, Harvard University Press, Harvard 2014; Kris Manjapra, *Age of Entanglement*, Harvard University Press, Cambridge, MA 2014; Sen, *Benoy Kumar Sarkar*; Ali Raza, Franziska Roy and Benjamin Zachariah (eds.), *The Internationalist Moment: South Asia, Worlds, and World Views 1917-39*, Sage, New Delhi 2015; Michel Louro, *Comrades against Imperialism: Nehru, India, and Interwar Internationalism*, CUP, Cambridge 2018;.

12. Burke A. Hendrix and Deborah Baumgold (eds.), *Colonial Exchanges: Political Theory and the Agency of the Colonized*, Manchester University Press, Manchester 2017, p. 9.

13. Hendrix and Baumgold (eds.), *Colonial Exchanges*, Introduction, pp. 1–19.
14. Hagen Schulz-Forberg, 'Introduction: Global Conceptual History: Promises and Pitfalls of a New Research Agenda', in idem (ed.), *A Global Conceptual History of Asia, 1860–1940*, Pickering & Chatto, London 2014, pp. 1–24. For an early perspective on nationalism in India, and more broadly in Asia, as a fruitful synthesis of Western and Asian epistemes, notions and practices see the work by Italian historian Giorgio Borsa, in particular *Le origini del nazionalismo in Asia Orientale*, (edited by G. C. Calza), Università di Pavia, Pavia 1965, and *La nascita del mondo moderno in Asia Orientale. La penetrazione Europea e la crisi delle società tradizionali in India, Cina e Giappone*, Rizzoli, Milan 1977. What is noteworthy about Borsa's scholarship is the fact that, more than fifty years ago, it started challenging Eurocentric as well as Asiacentric interpretations of history.
15. Ante litteram efforts of 'provincializing Europe' were very often the outcome of a process of interaction and exchange with Western ideas and debates. See Harald Fischer-Tiné, "<Deep Occidentalism>? Europa und <Der Westen> in der Wahrnehmung hinduistischer Intellektueller und Reformer ca.1890–1930", *Journal of Modern European History*, Vol. 4 (2006), pp. 171–203 for Hindu reformers and intellectuals and Cemil Aydin for Occidentalism and Islamism in Turkey in the 20th century (Cemil Aydin, "Between Occidentalism and the Global Left: Islamist Critiques of the West in Turkey", *Comparative Studies of South Asia, Africa and the Middle East*, Vol. 26, n. 3 (2006), pp. 446–461).
16. 'East and West in India', in R.P. Patwardhan and D.V. Ambekar (eds.), *GSW, Vol. II, Political*, Deccan Sabha, Asia Publishing House, Poona 1966, p. 383.
17. C.A. Bayly, 'Liberalism at Large: Mazzini and Nineteenth-century Indian Thought', in C.A. Bayly, Eugenio F. Biagini (eds.), *Giuseppe Mazzini and the Globalisation of Democratic Nationalism (1830-1920)*, OUP for the British Academy, 2008.
18. Sen, *Benoy Kumar Sarkar*.
19. Fischer-Tiné, *Shyamji Krishnavarma*.
20. Maria Framke, "Shopping Ideologies for Independent India? Taraknath Das's Engagement with Italian Fascism and German National Socialism", *Itinerario*, Vol. 40, n. 1 (2016), pp. 55–81.
21. On this, see, for example, Nicholas Owen, 'Alliances from Above and Below: The Failures and Successes of Communist Anti-Imperialism in India, 1920-34', in Yann Béliard and Neville Kirk (eds.), *Workers of the Empire Unite: Radical and Popular Challenges to British Imperialism, 1910s to 1960s*, Liverpool University Press, Liverpool 2021, pp. 81–114; Priyamvada Gopal, *Insurgent Empire: Anticolonial Resistance and British Dissent*, Verso, London 2019; Nicholas Owen, *The British Left and India: Metropolitan Anti-Imperialism, 1885-1947*, OUP, New York 2007, esp. chapter 1, pp. 22–48, chapter 2, pp. 49–77 and chapter 3, pp. 78–105.
22. Bayly, *Recovering Liberties*, p. 1.
23. 'Introduction', in Margaret Kohn and Keally McBride, *Political Theories of Decolonization: Postcolonialism and the Problem of Foundations*, OUP, Oxford and New York 2011, pp. 3–13.
24. See Gurpreet Mahajan, *India: Political Ideas and the Making of a Democratic Discourse*, esp. chapter 1, Zed Books, London 2013.
25. The literature reflects the complexity of the debate, and for paucity of space, it is not possible to refer to it at length. Suffice it to say that a classic critique is the one elaborated by Harold J. Laski in the 1930s who, inspired by Marxist analysis, saw liberalism as a sovrastructural manifestation of the bourgeois society since it pretended to express universal claims and to create conditions for the freedom of all human beings, whereas it expressed exclusively

particular needs, granting freedom only to a small minority. Overall, liberalism remained premised on differences such as religion, property, education, birth and the like (Harold J. Laski, *The Rise of European Liberalism*, London 1936). A more recent critique of liberal movement and society coming from the same side of the political spectrum is Domenico Losurdo, *Controstoria del liberalismo*, Laterza, 2005. Feminist scholars, too – divided on whether liberalism can sustain equality and liberty for all – have elaborated sophisticated and diverse critiques of the liberal ideology. See among others, Wendy Brown, *States of Injury: Power and Freedom in Late Modernity*, Princeton University Press, Princeton 1995; Catharine A. MacKinnon, *Toward a Feminist Theory of the State*, Harvard University Press, Cambridge 1989; Carole Pateman, *The Sexual Contract*, Stanford University Press, Stanford 1988; Martha C. Nussbaum, *Sex and Social Justice*, OUP, New York and Oxford 1999; Susan Moller Okin, 'Humanist Liberalism', in Nancy L. Rosenblum (ed.), *Liberalism and the Moral Life*, Harvard University Press, Cambridge and London 1989, pp. 39–53. A helpful historical perspective on feminism and liberalism is provided by Linda M. G. Zerilli, 'Feminist Critiques of Liberalism', in *The Cambridge Companion of Liberalism*, pp. 355–380.

26. See, among others, Barbara Arneil, "Liberal Colonialism, Domestic Colonies and Citizenship", *History of Political Thought*, Vol. 33, n. 3 (2012), pp. 491–523; Karuna Mantena, *Alibis of Empire: Henry Maine and the Ends of Liberal Imperialism*, Princeton University Press, Princeton 2010; Jennifer Pitts, *A Turn to Empire: The Rise of Imperial Liberalism in Britain and France*, Princeton University Press, Princeton 2005; Jeanne Morefield, *Covenants without Sword: Idealist Liberalism and the Spirit of Empire*, Princeton University Press, Princeton 2004; Uday Singh Mehta, *Liberalism and Empire*, University of Chicago Press, Chicago 1999.

27. Duncan Bell, 'What is Liberalism?', in *Reordering the World: Essays on Liberalism and Empire*, Princeton University Press, Princeton 2016, esp. pp. 81–90.

28. See Andrew Sartori, *Liberalism in Empire: An Alternative History*, University of California Press, Oakland, 2014; Rochana Bajpai, 'Liberalism in India: A Sketch', in B. Jackson and M. Stears (eds.), *Liberalism as Ideology: Essays in Honour of Michael Freeden*, OUP, New York 2012, pp. 53–76.

29. On civil society in colonial India, see Neelandri Bhattacharya, 'Notes Towards a Conception of the Colonial Public', in Rajeev Bhargava and Helmut Reifeld (eds.), *Civil Society, Public Sphere and Citizenship: Dialogues and Perceptions*, Sage, New Delhi 2005, pp. 130–156.

30. Bayly, *Recovering Liberties*, p. 212. For the emergence of new kinds of public spheres and their intertwining with the histories of literature and languages at the time of colonialism, see the excellent contribution by Hans Harder, 'Languages, Literatures and the Public Sphere', in Harald Fischer-Tiné and Maria Framke (eds.), *The Routledge Handbook of the History of Colonialism in South Asia*, Routledge, Abingdon 2022, pp. 412–423. See also the concluding part in Bhikhu Parekh, 'Limits of the Indian political imagination', in V.R. Mehta and T. Pantham (eds.), *Political Ideas in Modern India: Thematic Explorations*, Sage, Delhi, Thousand Oaks, London 2006, pp. 437–458, here 455.

31. Bayly, *Recovering Liberties*, pp. 26–41. Michelguglielmo Torri, "'Westernised Middle Class', Intellectuals and Society in Late Colonial India", *Economic and Political Weekly*, Vol. 25, n. 4 (1990), pp. 2–11 explains how these educated Indians were intellectuals in the Gramscian sense.

32. A few years before, in 1837, English had substituted Persian as the official language for the administration of the *Raj*.

33. The distrust towards the masses was not exclusive to the early phase of Indian nationalism. For example, as argued by Ranajit Guha, Gandhi was afraid and

felt contempt for the Indian masses and he harshly criticised what he called 'mobocracy.' This word is, in Guha's view, "lifted directly out of the lexicon of elitist usage" (Ranajit Guha, 'Discipline and Mobilize', in Partha Chatterjee and Gyanendra Pandey (eds.), *Subaltern Studies VII: Writings on South Asian History and Society*, OUP, New York 1992 pp. 69–120).

34. See Bayly, *Recovering Liberties*, chapter 5; Rama Sundari Mantena, "Vernacular Publics and Political Modernity: Language and Progress in Colonial South India", *Modern Asian Studies*, Vol. 47, n. 5 (2013), pp. 1678–1705; Vasudha Dalmia, *The Nationalization of Hindu Traditions: Bharatendu Harishchandra and Nineteenth Century Banaras*, OUP, New Delhi 1997; Francesca Orsini, *A Hindi Public Sphere*, OUP, New Delhi 2003; Veena Naregal, 'Vernacular Culture and Political Formation in Western India', in Abhijit Gupta and Swapan Chakraborty (eds.), *Print Areas: Book History in India*, Permanent Black, Delhi 2004.

35. Philip Spencer and Howard Wollman, *Nationalism: A Critical Introduction*, Sage, London 2002; David Brown, "Are There Good and Bad Nationalisms?", *Nations and Nationalism*, Vol. 5, n. 2 (1999), pp. 281–302; Andrew Vincent, 'Nationalism', in Michael Freeden et al. (eds.), *The Oxford Handbook of Political Ideologies*, OUP, Oxford and New York 2013 and, in the same volume, Manfred B. Steger, 'Political Ideologies in the Age of Globalisation', pp. 219–221.

36. Andrew Vincent, *Nationalism and Particularity*, CUP, Cambridge 2002.

37. Andrew Vincent, "Liberal Nationalism: An Irresponsible Compound?", *Political Studies*, Vol. 45, n. 2 (1997), pp. 275–295; Paul Kelly, 'Liberalism and Nationalism', in Steven Wall (ed.), *The Cambridge Companion to Liberalism: Cambridge Companions to Philosophy*, CUP, Cambridge 2015. This is the reason why, for example, promoters of nationalist politics have been calling for language and tradition protection policies against the challenge of a cosmopolitanism-oriented liberalism (see Margaret Moore, *The Ethics of Nationalism*, OUP, Oxford 2001, especially chapter 3).

38. See Kelly, 'Liberalism and Nationalism', p. 34.

39. Although dated, the work of Yael Tamir, *Liberal Nationalism*, Princeton University Press, Princeton 1993, provides thought-provoking arguments on the compatibility of liberalism and nationalism. For a more recent contribution to the debate, see the political essay by Jill Lepore, *This America: The Case for the Nation*, Liveright, New York 2019. The author argues in favor of revitalizing liberalism as a weapon to fight the populist forms of nationalism that threaten American values of liberty and equality.

40. See, for instance, Liah Greenfeld, 'Is Modernity Possible without Nationalism?', in Michel Seymour (ed.), *The Fate of the Nation-State*, McGill-Queen's University Press, Montreal 2004, pp. 31–51.

41. For a definition of social imaginaries, see Charles Taylor, *Modern Social Imaginaries*, Duke University Press, Durham and London 2004, pp. 23–26.

42. For an insightful discussion, see Partha Chatterjee, "Empires, Nations, Peoples: The Imperial Prerogative and Colonial Exceptions", *Thesis Eleven*, Vol. 139, n. 1 (2017), pp. 84–96. See also by the same author, *The Black Hole of Empire: History of a Global Practice of Power*, Princeton University Press, Princeton and Oxford 2012, pp. 273–276.

43. The principle of election at the municipal level was introduced for the first time in 1868 in the North Western Provinces (Francis Robinson, "Consultation and Control: The United Provinces' Government and its Allies, 1860–1906", *Modern Asian Studies*, Vol. 5, n. 4 (1971), pp. 313–336, here 325) and then gradually extended to other Indian provinces until 1882 when a resolution by the Viceroy Lord Ripon enacted it over all British India. It goes without saying that both the right to vote and, even more, the right to be elected were strongly limited by strict property criteria.

44. David Washbrook, 'India 1818-1860, The Two Faces of Colonialism', in A. Porter (ed.), *The Nineteenth Century (The Oxford History of the British Empire, Volume III)*, OUP, Oxford, 1999), pp. 395–421; Hayden J. Bellenoit, *The Formation of the Colonial State in India*, Routledge Abingdon and New York 2017, chapter 5; Sabyasachi Bhattacharya, *The Colonial State: Theory and Practice*, Primus Books, Delhi 2016, esp. chapters 3 and 5; Michelguglielmo Torri, *Storia dell'India*, Laterza, Roma e Bari 2000, pp. 443–451; David Washbrook, "Law, State and Agrarian Society in Colonia India", *Modern Asian Studies*, Vol. 15, n. 3 (1981) to name just a few.

45. For a discussion on political discourses of good government and forms of patriotisms before and after the establishment of British colonial rule, see Christopher A. Bayly, *Origins of Nationality in South Asia: Patriotism and Ethical Government in the Making of Modern India*, OUP, Delhi 1998. On the colonial state, see Bhattacharya, *The Colonial State*. On the relationship between state and society in India, see Sudipta Kaviraj, *The Imaginary Institution of India: Politics and Ideas*, Columbia University Press, New York 2010, esp. pp. 9–38 and 210–233.

46. It must be noted that from the second half of the 19th century, the moral mission of liberal imperialism to improve native society was opposed by an anti-liberal ideology of empire which endorsed the preservation of traditional society as the new alibi of empire. These opposed views coexisted as "oscillations internal to the structure of imperial ideology" (Karuna Mantena, *Alibis of Empire*, p. 185). For a discussion on this, see also Partha Chatterjee, "The Curious Career of Liberalism in India", *Modern Intellectual History*, Vol. 8, n. 3 (2011), pp. 687–696. On liberal imperialism, see also Peter Robb, *Empire, Modernity and India: Liberalism, Modernity and the Nation*, OUP, New Delhi, 2007.

47. Among a rich and sophisticated literature, see Arjun Appadurai, 'Number in the Colonial Imagination', in Carol A. Breckenridge and Peter van der Veer (eds), *Orientalism and the Postcolonial Predicament: Perspectives on South Asia*, University of Pennsylvania Press, Philadelphia 1993, pp. 114–135; Susan Bayly, *Caste, Society and Politics in India from the Eighteenth Century to the Modern Age*, CUP, Cambridge 1999; Nicholas B. Dirks, *Castes of Mind: Colonialism and the Making of Modern India*, Princeton University Press, Princeton 2001; Laura Dudley Jenkins, *Identity and Identification in India*, Routledge, London 2003; Christophe Jaffrelot, *India's Silent Revolution: The Rise of the Lower Castes in North India*, Permanent Black, New Delhi 2003 and from the same author, *Religion, Caste and Politics in India*, Primus, Delhi 2010.

48. Bhattacharya, *The Colonial State*, chapter 5.

49. The phrase "ecological niche" is from C.A. Bayly, "Rammohan Roy and the Advent of Constitutional Liberalism in India, 1800-1830", *Modern Intellectual History*, Vol. 4, n. 1 (2007), p. 41.

50. For a global history of liberalism in India, reference has already been made to Bayly, *Recovering Liberties*.

51. Carol A. Breckenridge, Sheldon Pollock, Homi K. Bhabha, Dipesh Chakrabarty (eds.), *Cosmopolitanism*, Duke University Press, Durham and London 2002, pp. 1–14. See also Garrett W. Brown and David Held (eds.), *The Cosmopolitanism Reader*, Polity, Cambridge and Malden 2010.

52. Steven Vertovec and Robin Cohen, 'Introduction: Conceiving Cosmopolitanism', in Steven Vertovec and Robin Cohen (eds.), *Conceiving Cosmopolitanism: Theory, Context and Practice*, OUP, Oxford 2002, p. 20.

53. Pranab Bhanu Mehta, "Cosmopolitanism and the Circle of Reason", *Political Theory*, Vol. 28, n. 5 (Oct. 2000), pp. 619–639, here 622.

54. Ulf Hannerz, "Cosmopolitan and Locals in World Culture", *Theory, Culture and Society*, Vol. 7, n. 2–3 (1990), pp. 237–251; Bruce Robbins and Pheng Cheah (eds.), *Cosmopolitics*, University of Minnesota Press, Minneapolis 1998, pp. 98–117.

55. Martha Nussbaum, 'Patriotism and Cosmopolitanism', in Martha Nussbaum and Joshua Cohen (eds.), *For Love of Country: Debating the Limits of Patriotism*, Beacon, Boston 1996, pp. 21–29.

56. Robert J. Holton, *Cosmopolitanisms: New Thinking and New Directions*, Palgrave Macmillan, Houndmills and New York 2009.

57. For an overview, see Mohinder Singh, 'Cosmopolitanism: A Review of Literature in Indian Political Thought', in Pradip Kumar Datta, Sanjay Palshikar and Achin Vanaik (eds.), *Indian Political Thought: Volume 3, ICSSR Research Surveys and Explorations: Political Science, Volumes 1-4*, OUP, New Delhi 2013, pp. 151–182.

58. Nico Slate, *Colored Cosmopolitanism: The Shared Struggle for Freedom in the United States and India*, Harvard University Press, Cambridge, MA 2012; Robert John Holton, "Cosmopolitanism or Cosmopolitanisms: The Universal Races Congress of 1911", *Global Networks*, Vol. 2, n. 2 (2002), pp. 153–170; Sugata Bose, *A Hundred Horizons: The Indian Ocean in the Age of Global Empire*, Harvard University Press, Cambridge, MA 2006; Leela Gandhi, *Affective Communities: Anticolonial Thought, Fin-de-Siècle Radicalism, and the Politics of Friendship*, Duke University Pres, Durham 2006; Fischer-Tiné, *Shyamji Krishnavarma*.

59. Rustom Barucha, *Another Asia: Rabindranath Tagore and Okakura Tenshin*, OUP, New Delhi 2006; Christian Geulen, 'The Common Grounds of Conflict: Racial Visions of World Order 1880-1940', in Sebastian Conrad and Dominic Sachsenmaier (eds.), *Competing Visions of World Order: Global Moments and Movements, 1880-1930s*, Palgrave Macmillan, New York 2007, pp. 69–96.

60. See the concept of 'cosmopolitanism of sentiment' in Mehta, *Liberalism and Empire*; for the cosmopolitan attitude of an intellectual that never left the Indian subcontinent, see Dilip Menon, 'A Local Cosmopolitan: Kesari Balakrishna Pillai and the Invention of Europe for a Modern Kerala', in Sugata Bose and Kris Manjapra (eds.), *Cosmopolitan Thought Zones*, pp. 131–156; instead, for the significance of German culture in Bengal, see Andrew Sartori, "Beyond Culture-Contact and Colonial Discourse: 'Germanism' in Colonial Bengal", *Modern Intellectual History*, Vol. 4, n. 1 (2007), pp. 77–93.

61. Among the vast and diverse scholarship that has attempted to identify alternatives to Western cosmopolitan formations, see, for example, Peter Van der Veer, "Cosmopolitan Options", *Etnográfica*, Vol. 6, n. 1 (2002), pp. 15–26; David Hollinger, *Post Ethnic America*, Basic Books, New York 1995; Arjun Appadurai, *Modernity at Large*, University of Minnesota Press, Minneapolis 1996; Holton, *Cosmopolitanisms*; Hannerz, 'Cosmopolitan and Locals in World Culture'. For a discussion on the post-colonial critique of liberal cosmopolitanism, see David Harvey, *Cosmopolitanism and the Geographies of Freedom*, Columbia University Press, New York 2009, pp. 37–50.

62. Mehta, 'Cosmopolitanism and the Circle of Reason'.

63. Kwame Anthony Appiah, "Cosmopolitan Patriots", *Critical Inquiry*, Vol. 23, n. 3, (Spring, 1997), pp. 617–639.

64. See among many others, Thomas Pogge, "Priorities of Global Justice", *Metaphilosophy*, Vol. 32, n. 1/2 (January 2001) and Seyla Benhabib, *The Rights of Others: Aliens, Residents and Citizens*, CUP, Cambridge 2004 and from the same author, 'The Philosophical Foundations of Cosmopolitan Norms', in Seyla Benhabib and Robert Post (eds.), *Another Cosmopolitanism*, OUP, New York 2006.

65. The literature on these issues is vast and, for reasons of space, cannot be exhaustively referenced here. A useful publication that deals with the most relevant debates on citizenship, although with a largely West-centric focus, is Ayelet Shachar, Rainer Bauböck, Irene Bloemraad and Maarten Peter Vink (eds.), *The Oxford Handbook of Citizenship*, OUP, Oxford 2017; the introduction

of Anupama Roy, *Mapping Citizenship in India*, OUP, New Delhi 2010 provides a concise but insightful discussion on how understandings of citizenship have changed over the past few decades.

66. See, among others, Martijn Koster, Rivke Jaffe and Anouk de Koning (eds.), *Citizenship Agendas in and beyond the Nation-State*, Routledge, Abingdon and New York 2019; Matthew Grant, "Historicizing Citizenship in Post-war Britain", *The Historical Journal*, Vol. 59, n. 4 (2016), pp. 1187–1206; Olsen, Stephanie. *Juvenile Nation: Youth, Emotions and the Making of the Modern British Citizen, 1880–1914*, Bloomsbury, London 2014; Michael Freeden, 'Civil Society and the Good Citizen: Competing Conceptions of Citizenship in Twentieth-century Britain', in Jose Harris (ed.), *Civil Society in British History: Ideas, Identities, Institutions*, OUP, Oxford 2003.

67. A very useful and insightful introduction to the complex question of citizenship in India is Anupama Roy, *Citizenship in India*, OUP, New Delhi 2016.

68. For a survey of pre-colonial political institutions which expressed ideas of rights, obligations and participation that are now generally associated with citizenship, see David Washbrook, "Forms of Citizenship in Pre-Modern South India", *Citizenship Studies*, Vol. 23, n. 3 (2019), pp. 224–329; James Jaffe, "The Languages of Petitioning in Early Colonial India", *Social Science History*, Vol. 43, n. 3 (2019), pp. 581–597; Rosalind O'Hanlon, "In the Presence of Witnesses: Petitioning and Judicial 'publics' in Western India, c. 1600-1820", *Modern Asian Studies*, Vol. 53, n. 1 (2019); Nicholas B. Dirks, *The Hollow Crown: Ethnohistory of an Indian Kingdom*, CUP, Cambridge 2007; C.A. Bayly, *Origins of Nationality*; Lucy Carroll, "Colonial Perceptions of Indian Society and the Emergence of Caste(s) Associations", *The Journal of Asian Studies*, Vol. 37, n. 2 (1978), pp. 233–250.

69. For example, Edward Vickers and Krishna Kumar (eds.), *Constructing Modern Asian Citizenship*, Routledge, London 2015.

70. Niraja Gopal Jayal, *Citizenship and its Discontents, an Indian History*, Harvard University Press, Cambridge, MA 2013, p. 27.

71. Frederick Cooper, *Citizenship, Inequality, and Difference: Historical Perspectives*, Princeton University Press, Princeton 2018; Mark Frost, "Imperial Citizenship or Else: Liberal Ideals and the India Unmaking of Empire, 1890–1919", *The Journal of Imperial and Commonwealth History*, Vol. 46, n. 5 (2018), pp. 845–873; Isabel Hofmeyr, 'Seeking Empire, Finding Nation: Gandhi and Indianness in South Africa', in Joya Chatterji and David Washbrook (eds.), *Routledge Handbook of the South Asian Diaspora*, Routledge, London 2013; Sukanya Banerjee, *Becoming Imperial Citizens Indians in the Late-Victorian Empire*, Duke University Press, Durham and London 2010.

72. Among others, Sanjay Seth, "Nationalism, Modernity, and the 'Woman Question' in India and China", *The Journal of Asian Studies*, Vol. 72, n. 2 (2013), pp. 273–297; Prashant Kidambi, 'From "Social Reform" to "Social Service"', in Carey A. Watt and Michael Mann (eds.), *Civilizing Missions in Colonial and Postcolonial South Asia: From Improvement to Development*, Anthem Press, London 2011, pp. 217–240 and in the same volume, Carey Watt, 'Philanthropy and Civilizing Mission in India, c. 1820 – 1960. States, NGOs and Development', pp. 271–316; Jayal, *Citizenship and its Discontents*, pp. 109–135; Mohinder Singh, 'Spectres of the West: Negotiating a Civilizational Figure in Hindi', in Margrit Pernau et al. (eds.), *Civilizing Emotions: Concepts in Nineteenth Century Asia and Europe*, CUP, Cambridge 2015, p. 193.

73. It is important to note that this phenomenon was border crossing and involved several transnational actors like Christian missionaries, INGOs and foundations, who could not be easily situated in the colonial or anticolonial field (see, for example, Harald Fischer-Tiné, "Fitness for Modernity? The YMCA and Physical-Education Schemes in Late-Colonial South Asia (circa 1900–40)",

Modern Asian Studies, Vol. 53, n. 2 (2019), pp. 512–559; Melanie Oppenheimer and Nicholas Deakin (eds.), *Beveridge and Voluntary Action in Britain and the Wider British World,* Manchester University Press, Manchester 2011; Harald Fischer-Tiné, 'Global Civil Society and the Forces of Empire: The Salvation Army, British Imperialism, and the "prehistory" of NGOs (ca. 1880-1920)', in Conrad and Sachsenmaier (eds.), *Competing Visions of World Order,* pp. 29–67.

74. Carey A. Watt, *Serving the Nation: Cultures of Service, Association, and Citizenship in Colonial India,* OUP, New Delhi 2005, *passim.* Even after the expansion, although limited, of franchise with the 1909 Morley-Minto Reforms, the concept of citizenship espoused by social and political commentators was not exclusively linked to the right to vote but continued to encompass an idealised set of moral and emotional qualities which were dispensed to the wider population through different channels.

75. See the omnibus edition, B.R. Nanda, *Three Statesmen: Gokhale, Gandhi and Nehru,* OUP, New Delhi 2004. Along with *Gokhale: The Indian Moderates and the British Raj,* it includes also *Mahatma Gandhi: A Biography* (first published 1958) and *Jawaharlal Nehru: Rebel and Statesman* (first published 1995). More recently, in 2015, Nanda's biography of Gokhale has been reprinted individually by Princeton University Press.

76. Bipan Chandra's *The Rise and Growth of Economic Nationalism in India, Economic Policies of Indian National Leadership 1880-1905* (People's Publishing House, New Delhi 1966) develops along these lines and is apologetic of the INC. Nevertheless, the book is helpful because it examines in detail the wide range of economic issues discussed by the early leadership of the anticolonial movement. It was the economic critique of the British imperialist economic policies that provided the INC with a solid ideological apparatus.

77. Stanley A. Wolpert, *Tilak and Gokhale: Revolution and Reform in the Making of Modern India,* OUP, New Delhi 1989 (first published 1961).

78. Parimala V. Rao, *Foundations of Tilak's Nationalism: Discrimination, Education, and Hindutva,* Orient Blackswan, New Delhi 2010.

79. Gopal Krishna Gokhale, *Speeches of the Honourable Mr. G. K. Gokhale,* G.A. Natesan, Madras 1908 and *Speeches of Gopal Krishna Gokhale,* G.A. Natesan, Madras 1916.

80. *GSW, Vol. I Economic,* edited by R.P. Patwardhan and D.V. Ambekar, Asia Publishing House, Poona 1962; *GSW, Vol. II Political,* edited by R.P. Patwardhan and D.V. Ambekar, Asia Publishing House, Poona 1966; *GSW, Vol. III Educational,* edited by D.G. Karve and D.V Ambekar, Asia Publishing House, Poona 1967.

81. Among these works see, for example, R.P. Paranjpye, *Gopal Krishna Gokhale,* Aryabhushan Press, Poona 1918; T.K. Shahani, *Gopal Krishna Gokhale: A Historical Biography,* R.K. Mody, Bombay 1929; Srinivasa Sastri, *My Master Gokhale: A Selection from the Speeches and Writings of V. S. Srinivasa Sastri* (edited by T.N. Jagadisan), Model Publications, Madras 1946; T.R. Deogirikar, *Gopal Krishna Gokhale,* Publications Division, Gov. of India, Delhi 1992 (1964).

References

Appadurai, Arjun. 'Number in the Colonial Imagination', in Carol A. Breckenridge and Peter Veer (eds.), *Orientalism and the Postcolonial Predicament: Perspectives on South Asia,* University of Pennsylvania Press, Philadelphia 1993, pp. 114–135.

——. *Modernity at Large: Cultural Dimensions of Globalisation,* University of Minnesota Press, Minneapolis 1996.

Appiah, Kwame Anthony. "Cosmopolitan Patriots", *Critical Inquiry*, Vol. 23, n. 3 (1997), pp. 617–639.

Arneil, Barbara. "Liberal Colonialism, Domestic Colonies and Citizenship", *History of Political Thought*, Vol. 33, n. 3 (2012), pp. 491–523.

Bajpai, Rochana. 'Liberalism in India: A Sketch', in B. Jackson and M. Stears (eds.), *Liberalism as Ideology: Essays in Honour of Michael Freeden*, OUP, New York 2012, pp. 53–76.

Banerjee, Sukanya. *Becoming Imperial Citizens: Indians in the Late-Victorian Empire*, Duke University Press, Durham and London 2010.

Barucha, Rustom. *Another Asia: Rabindranath Tagore and Okakura Tenshin*, OUP, New Delhi 2006.

Bayly, C.A. "Rammohan Roy and the Advent of Constitutional Liberalism in India, 1800-1830", *Modern Intellectual History*, Vol. 4, n. 1 (2007), pp. 25–41.

——. "Afterword", *Modern Intellectual History*, Vol. 4, n. 1 (2007), pp. 163–196.

——. 'Liberalism at Large: Mazzini and Nineteenth-Century Indian Thought', in C.A. Bayly and Eugenio F. Biagini (eds.), *Giuseppe Mazzini and the Globalisation of Democratic Nationalism (1830-1920)*, OUP, Oxford 2008, pp. 355–374.

——. *The Birth of the Modern World, 1780-1914: Global Connections and Comparisons*, Blackwell, Oxford 2004.

——. *Recovering Liberties, Indian Thought in the Age of Liberalism and Empire*, CUP, Delhi 2012 (first published 2011).

——. *Origins of Nationality in South Asia: Patriotism and Ethical Government in the Making of Modern India*, OUP, Delhi 1998.

Bayly, Susan. *Caste, Society and Politics in India from the Eighteenth Century to the Modern Age*, CUP, Cambridge 1999.

Beckert, Sven and Dominic Sachsenmaier (eds.). *Global History, Globally: Research and Practice Around the World*, Bloomsbury, London and New York 2018.

Bell, Duncan. *Reordering the World: Essays on Liberalism and Empire*, Princeton University Press, Princeton 2016.

Bellenoit, Hayden J. *The Formation of the Colonial State in India*, Routledge, Abingdon and New York 2017.

Benhabib, Seyla. *The Rights of Others: Aliens, Residents and Citizens*, CUP, Cambridge 2004.

——. 'The Philosophical Foundations of Cosmopolitan Norms', in Seyla Benhabib and Robert Post (eds.), *Another Cosmopolitanism*, OUP, New York 2006.

Bhattacharya, Neelandri. 'Notes Towards a Conception of the Colonial Public', in Rajeev Bhargava and Helmut Reifeld (eds.), *Civil Society, Public Sphere and Citizenship: Dialogues and Perceptions*, Sage, New Delhi 2005, pp. 130–156.

Bhattacharya, Sabyasachi. *The Colonial State: Theory and Practice*, Primus Books, Delhi 2016.

Borsa, Giorgio *Le origini del nazionalismo in Asia Orientale*, (edited by G. C. Calza), Università di Pavia, Pavia 1965.

——. *La nascita del mondo moderno in Asia Orientale. La penetrazione Europea e la crisi delle società tradizionali in India, Cina e Giappone*, Rizzoli, Milano 1977.

Bose, Sugata. *The Indian Ocean in the Age of Global Empire*, Harvard University Press, Cambridge, MA 2006.

—— and Manjapra, Kris (eds.). *Cosmopolitan Thought Zones: South Asia and the Global Circulation of Ideas*, Palgrave Macmillan, Basingstoke and New York 2010.

Breckenridge, Carol A., Sheldon Pollock, Homi K. Bhabha and Dipesh Chakrabarty (eds.). *Cosmopolitanism*, Duke University Press, Durham and London 2002.

Brown, David. "Are There Good and Bad Nationalisms?", *Nations and Nationalism*, Vol. 5, n. 2 (1999), 281–302.

Brown, Garrett W. and David Held (eds.). *The Cosmopolitanism Reader*, Polity, Cambridge and Malden 2010.

Brown, Wendy. *States of Injury: Power and Freedom in Late Modernity*, Princeton University Press, Princeton 1995.

Carroll, Lucy. "Colonial Perceptions of Indian Society and the Emergence of Caste(s) Associations", *The Journal of Asian Studies*, Vol. 37, n. 2 (1978), pp. 233–250.

Chandra, Bipan. *The Rise and Growth of Economic Nationalism in India: Economic Policies of Indian National Leadership 1880-1905*, People's Publishing House, New Delhi 1966.

Chatterjee, Partha. *Nationalist Thought and the Colonial World: A Derivative Discourse?*, Zed Books, London 1986.

——. "The Curious Career of Liberalism in India", *Modern Intellectual History*, Vol. 8, n. 3 (2011), pp. 687–696.

——. *The Black Hole of Empire: History of a Global Practice of Power*, Princeton University Press, Princeton and Oxford 2012.

——. "Empires, Nations, Peoples: The Imperial Prerogative and Colonial Exceptions", *Thesis Eleven*, Vol. 139, n. 1 (2017), pp. 84–96.

Conrad, Sebastian. *What Is Global History?*, Princeton University Press, Princeton and Oxford 2016.

Cooper, Frederick. *Citizenship, Inequality, and Difference*, Princeton University Press, Princeton 2018.

Croce, Benedetto. *La Storia Come Pensiero e Come Azione*, Laterza, Bari 1938.

Dalmia, Vasudha. *The Nationalization of Hindu Traditions: Bharatendu Harishchandra and Nineteenth Century Banaras*, OUP, New Delhi 1997.

Deogirikar, T.R. *Gopal Krishna Gokhale*, Publications Division, Gov. of India, Delhi 1992 (first published 1964).

Desai, A.R. *Social Background of Indian Nationalism*, OUP, Bombay 1948.

Dirks, Nicholas B. *Castes of Mind: Colonialism and the Making of Modern India*, Princeton University Press, Princeton 2001.

——. *The Hollow Crown: Ethnohistory of an Indian Kingdom*, CUP, Cambridge 2007.

Fischer-Tiné, Harald. "Fitness for Modernity? The YMCA and Physical-Education Schemes in Late-Colonial South Asia (Circa 1900–40)", *Modern Asian Studies*, Vol. 53, n. 2 (2019), pp. 512–559.

——. *Shyamji Krishnavarma: Sanskrit, Sociology, and Anti-Imperialism*, Routledge India, New Delhi 2014.

——. 'Global Civil Society and the Forces of Empire: The Salvation Army, British Imperialism, and the "Prehistory" of NGOs (Ca. 1880-1920)', in Sebastian Conrad and Dominic Sachsenmaier (eds.), *Competing Visions of World Order: Global Moments and Movements, 1880-1930s*, Palgrave Macmillan, New York 2007, pp. 29–67.

——. "<Deep Occidentalism>? Europa Und <Der Westen> in Der Wahrnehmung Hinduistischer Intellektueller Und Reformer Ca.1890–1930", *Journal of Modern European History*, Vol. 4, n. 2 (2006), pp. 171–203.

Framke, Maria. "Shopping Ideologies for Independent India? Taraknath Das's Engagement with Italian Fascism and German National Socialism", *Itinerario*, Vol. 40, n. 1 (2016), pp. 55–81.

Freeden, Michael. 'Civil Society and the Good Citizen: Competing Conceptions of Citizenship in Twentieth-Century Britain', in Jose Harris (ed.), *Civil Society in British History: Ideas, Identities, Institutions*, OUP, Oxford 2003.

Frost, Mark R. "Imperial Citizenship or Else: Liberal Ideals and the India Unmaking of Empire, 1890–1919", *The Journal of Imperial and Commonwealth History*, Vol. 46, n. 5 (2018), pp. 845–873.

Gandhi, Leela. *Affective Communities: Anticolonial Thought, Fin-De-Siècle Radicalism, and the Politics of Friendship*, Duke University Press, Durham 2006.

Geulen, Christian. 'The Common Grounds of Conflict: Racial Visions of World Order 1880-1940', in Sebastian Conrad and Dominic Sachsenmaier (eds.), *Competing Visions of World Order: Global Moments and Movements, 1880-1930s*, Palgrave Macmillan, New York 2007, pp. 69–96.

Gokhale, Gopal Krishna. *Speeches of the Honourable Mr. G. K. Gokhale*, G.A. Natesan, Madras 1908.

——. *Speeches of Gopal Krishna Gokhale*, G.A. Natesan, Madras 1916.

——. *Gokhale Speeches and Writings (GSW), Vol. I Economic*, in R.P. Patwardhan and D.V. Ambekar (eds.), Asia Publishing House, Poona 1962.

——. *Gokhale Speeches and Writings (GSW), Vol. II Political*, in R.P. Patwardhan and D.V. Ambekar, Asia Publishing House, Poona 1966.

——. *Gokhale Speeches and Writings (GSW), Vol. III Educational*, in D.G. Karve and D.V. Ambekar (eds.), Asia Publishing House, Poona 1967.

Gopal, Priyamvada. *Insurgent Empire: Anticolonial Resistance and British Dissent*, Verso, London 2019.

Gottlob, Michael. *History and Politics in Post-Colonial India*, OUP, Delhi 2011.

Grant, Matthew. "Historicizing Citizenship in Post-War Britain", *The Historical Journal*, Vol. 59, n. 4 (2016), 1187–1206.

Greenfeld, Liah. 'Is Modernity Possible Without Nationalism?', in Michel Seymour (ed.), *The Fate of the Nation-State*, McGill-Queen's University Press, Montreal 2004, pp. 31–51.

Guha, Ranajit. 'Discipline and Mobilize', in Partha Chatterjee and Gyanendra Pandey (eds.), *Subaltern Studies VII: Writings on South Asian History and Society*, OUP, New York 1992, pp. 69–120.

Hannerz, Ulf. "Cosmopolitan and Locals in World Culture", *Theory, Culture and Society*, Vol. 7, n. 2-3 (1990), pp. 237–251.

Harder, Hans. 'Languages, Literatures and the Public Sphere', in Harald Fischer-Tiné and Maria Framke (eds.), *The Routledge Handbook of the History of Colonialism in South Asia*, Routledge, Abingdon 2022, pp. 412–423.

Harvey, David. *Cosmopolitanism and the Geographies of Freedom*, Columbia University Press, New York 2009.

Hendrix, Burke A. and Deborah Baumgold (eds.). *Colonial Exchanges: Political Theory and the Agency of the Colonized*, Manchester University Press, Manchester 2017.

Hofmeyr, Isabel. 'Seeking Empire, Finding Nation. Gandhi and Indianness in South Africa', in Joya Chatterji and David Washbrook (eds.), *Routledge Handbook of the South Asian Diaspora*, Routledge, London 2013, pp. 153–165.

Hollinger, David. *Post Ethnic America*, Basic Books, New York 1995.

Holton, Robert J. *Cosmopolitanisms: New Thinking and New Directions*, Palgrave Macmillan, Houndmills and New York 2009.

——. "Cosmopolitanism or Cosmopolitanisms? The Universal Races Congress of 1911", *Global Networks*, Vol. 2, n. 2 (2002), pp. 153–170.

Iggers, Georg G., Q. Edward Wang and Supriya Mukherjee. *A Global History of Modern Historiography*, Pearson Education Limited, Edinburgh 2008.

Jaffe, James. "The Languages of Petitioning in Early Colonial India", *Social Science History*, Vol. 43, n. 3 (2019), pp. 581–597.

Jaffrelot, Christophe. *India's Silent Revolution: The Rise of the Lower Castes in North India*, Permanent Black, New Delhi 2003.

——. *Religion, Caste and Politics in India*, Primus, Delhi 2010.

Jayal, Niraja Gopal. *Citizenship and Its Discontents, An Indian History*, Harvard University Press, Cambridge, MA 2013.

Jenkins, Laura D. *Identity and Identification in India*, Routledge, London 2003.

Kapila, Shruti. "Preface", *Modern Intellectual History*, Vol. 4, n. 1 (2007), pp. 3–6.

Kaviraj, Sudipta. *The Imaginary Institution of India: Politics and Ideas*, Columbia University Press, New York 2010.

Kelly, Paul. 'Liberalism and Nationalism', in Steven Wall (ed.), *The Cambridge Companion to Liberalism: Cambridge Companions to Philosophy*, CUP, Cambridge 2015.

Kidambi, Prashant. 'From "Social Reform" to "Social Service"', in Carey A. Watt and Michael Mann (eds.), *Civilizing Missions in Colonial and Postcolonial South Asia: From Improvement to Development*, Anthem Press, London 2011, pp. 217–240.

Kiernan, V.G. "Nehru the Historian", *World Affairs: The Journal of International Issues*, Vol. 2, n. 2 (1993), pp. 9–15.

Koster, Martijn, Rivke Jaffe and Anouk de Koning (eds.). *Citizenship Agendas in and Beyond the Nation-State*, Routledge, Abingdon and New York 2019.

Laski, Harold J. *The Rise of European Liberalism*, George Allen & Unwin Ltd., London 1936.

Lepore, Jill. *This America: The Case for the Nation*, Liveright, New York 2019.

Losurdo, Domenico. *Controstoria Del Liberalismo*, Laterza, Bari 2005.

Louro, Michel. *Comrades Against Imperialism: Nehru, India, and Interwar Internationalism*, CUP, Cambridge 2018.

MacKinnon, Catharine A. *Toward a Feminist Theory of the State*, Harvard University Press, Cambridge, MA 1989.

Maclean, Kama. *A Revolutionary History of Interwar India: Violence, Image, Voice and Text*, Hurst & Co, London 2015.

——. Elam, J. Daniel and Christopher Moffat (eds.), *Writing Revolution in South Asia: History, Practice, Politics*, Routledge, Abingdon and New York 2017.

Mahajan, Gurpreet. *India: Political Ideas and the Making of a Democratic Discourse*, Zed Books, London 2013.

Manjapra, Kris. *Age of Entanglement*, Harvard University Press, Cambridge, MA 2014.

——. *M.N. Roy: Marxism and Colonial Cosmopolitanism*, Routledge, London, New York and New Delhi 2010.

Mantena, Karuna. *Alibis of Empire: Henry Maine and the Ends of Liberal Imperialism*, Princeton University Press, Princeton 2010.

Mantena, Rama S. "Vernacular Publics and Political Modernity: Language and Progress in Colonial South India", *Modern Asian Studies*, Vol. 47, n. 5 (2013), pp. 1678–1705.

Margaret, Kohn and Keally McBride. *Political Theories of Decolonization: Postcolonialism and the Problem of Foundations*, OUP, Oxford and New York 2011.

Mehta, Pranab Bhanu. "Cosmopolitanism and the Circle of Reason", *Political Theory*, Vol. 28, n. 5 (2000), pp. 619–639.

Mehta, Uday Singh. *Liberalism and Empire: A Study in Nineteenth-Century British Liberal Thought*, University of Chicago Press, London 1999.

Menon, Dilip. 'A Local Cosmopolitan: Kesari Balakrishna Pillai and the Invention of Europe for a Modern Kerala', in Sugata Bose and Kris Manjapra (eds.), *Cosmopolitan Thought Zones*, pp. 131–156.

Metcalf, Thomas R. *Imperial Connections: Indian in the Indian Ocean Arena, 1860-1920*, University of California Press, Berkeley 2008.

Moore, Margaret. *The Ethics of Nationalism*, OUP, Oxford 2001.

Morefield, Jeanne. *Covenants Without Sword: Idealist Liberalism and the Spirit of Empire*, Princeton University Press, Princeton 2004.

Moyn, Samuel and Andrew Sartori. 'Approaches to Global Intellectual History', in idem (eds.), *Global Intellectual History*, Columbia University Press, New York 2013, pp. 3–30.

Mukherjee, Supriya. 'Indian Historical Writing Since 1947', in A. Schneider and D. Woolf (eds.), *The Oxford History of Historical Writing*, OUP, Oxford 2011, pp. 515–538.

Musil, Robert. 'Monuments', in idem, *Posthumous Papers of a Living Author*, Penguin, New York 1978.

Nanda, B.R. *Three Statesmen: Gokhale, Gandhi and Nehru*, OUP, New Delhi 2004.

Naregal, Veena. 'Vernacular Culture and Political Formation in Western India', in Abhijit Gupta and Swapan Chakraborty (eds.), *Print Areas: Book History in India*, Permanent Black, Delhi 2004.

Nussbaum, Martha C. *Sex and Social Justice*, OUP, New York and Oxford 1999.

——. 'Patriotism and Cosmopolitanism', in Martha Nussbaum and Joshua Cohen (eds.), *For Love of Country: Debating the Limits of Patriotism*, Beacon, Boston 1996, pp. 21–29.

O'Hanlon, Rosalind. "In the Presence of Witnesses: Petitioning and Judicial 'Publics' in Western India, c. 1600-1820", *Modern Asian Studies*, Vol. 53, n. 1 (2019), pp. 52–88.

Okin, Susan Moller. 'Humanist Liberalism', in Nancy L. Rosenblum (ed.), *Liberalism and the Moral Life*, Harvard University Press, Cambridge and London 1989, pp. 39–53.

Olsen, Stephanie. *Juvenile Nation: Youth, Emotions and the Making of the Modern British Citizen, 1880–1914*, Bloomsbury, London 2014.

Oppenheimer, Melanie and Nicholas Deakin (eds.). *Beveridge and Voluntary Action in Britain and the Wider British World*, Manchester University Press, Manchester 2011.

Orsini, Francesca. *A Hindi Public Sphere*, OUP, New Delhi 2003.

Owen, Nicholas. 'Alliances from Above and Below: The Failures and Successes of Communist Anti-Imperialism in India, 1920-34', in Yann Béliard and Neville Kirk (eds.), *Workers of the Empire Unite: Radical and Popular Challenges to British Imperialism, 1910s to 1960s*, Liverpool University Press, Liverpool 2021, pp. 81–114.

——. *The British Left and India: Metropolitan Anti-Imperialism, 1885-1947*, OUP, New York 2007.

Paranjpye, R.P. *Gopal Krishna Gokhale*, Aryabhushan Press, Poona 1918.

Parekh, Bhikhu. 'Limits of the Indian Political Imagination', in V.R. Mehta and T. Pantham (eds.), *Political Ideas in Modern India: Thematic Explorations*, Sage, Delhi, Thousand Oaks, London 2006, pp. 437–458.

Pitts, Jennifer. *A Turn to Empire: The Rise of Imperial Liberalism in Britain and France*, Princeton University Press, Princeton 2005.

Pogge, Thomas. "Priorities of Global Justice", *Metaphilosophy*, Vol. 32, n. 1/2 (2001), pp. 6–24.

Rao, Parimala V. *Foundations of Tilak's Nationalism: Discrimination, Education, and Hindutva*, Orient Blackswan, New Delhi 2010.

Raza, Ali. *Revolutionary Pasts: Communist Internationalism in Colonial India*, CUP, Cambridge 2020.

Raza, Ali, Franziska Roy and Benjamin Zachariah (eds.). *The Internationalist Moment: South Asia, Worlds, and World Views 1917-39*, Sage, New Delhi 2015.

Reagan-Lefebvre, Jennifer. *Cosmopolitan Patriotism in the Victorian Empire: Ireland, India and the Politics of Alfred Webb*, Palgrave Macmillan, Houndmills and New York 2009.

Robb, Peter. *Empire, Modernity and India: Liberalism, Modernity and the Nation*, OUP, New Delhi, 2007.

Robbins, Bruce and Pheng Cheah (eds.). *Cosmopolitics*, University of Minnesota Press, Minneapolis 1998.

Robinson, Francis. "Consultation and Control: The United Provinces' Government and Its Allies, 1860–1906", *Modern Asian Studies*, Vol. 5, n. 4 (1971), pp. 313–336.

Roy, Anupama. *Mapping Citizenship in India*, OUP, New Delhi 2010.

——. *Citizenship in India*, OUP, New Delhi 2016.

Sartori, Andrew S. "Beyond Culture-Contact and Colonial Discourse: 'Germanism' in Colonial Bengal", *Modern Intellectual History*, Vol. 4, n. 1 (2007), pp. 77–93.

——. *Liberalism in Empire: An Alternative History*, University of California Press, Berkeley 2014.

Schulz-Forberg, Hagen. 'Introduction: Global Conceptual History: Promises and Pitfalls of a New Research Agenda', in idem (ed.), *A Global Conceptual History of Asia, 1860–1940*, Pickering & Chatto, London 2014, pp. 1–24.

Sen, Satadru. *Benoy Kumar Sarkar: Restoring the Nation to the World*, Routledge, New Delhi and New York 2015.

Seth, Sanjay. 'Rewriting Histories of Nationalism. The Politics of "Moderate Nationalism" in India 1870-1905', in Sekhar Bandyopadhyay (ed.), *Nationalist Movement in India: A Reader*, OUP, New Delhi 2009, pp. 30–48.

——. "Nationalism, Modernity, and the 'Woman Question' in India and China", *The Journal of Asian Studies*, Vol. 72, n. 2 (2013), pp. 273–297.

Shachar, Ayelet and others (eds.). *The Oxford Handbook of Citizenship*, OUP, Oxford 2017.

Shahani, T.K. *Gopal Krishna Gokhale: A Historical Biography*, R.K. Mody, Bombay 1929.

Silvestri, Michael. *Policing 'Bengali Terrorism' in India and the World: Imperial Intelligence and Revolutionary Nationalism, 1905-1939*, Palgrave Macmillan, Cham 2019.

Singh, Mohinder. 'Spectres of the West: Negotiating a Civilizational Figure in Hindi', in Margrit Pernau and Helge Jordheim (eds.), *Civilizing Emotions: Concepts in Nineteenth Century Asia and Europe*, CUP, Cambridge 2015.

——. 'Cosmopolitanism: A Review of Literature in Indian Political Thought', in Pradip Kumar Datta, Sanjay Palshikar and Achin Vanaik (eds.), *Indian Political Thought: Volume 3, ICSSR Research Surveys and Explorations: Political Science, Volumes 1-4*, OUP, New Delhi 2013, pp. 151–182.

Slate, Nico. *Colored Cosmopolitanism: The Shared Struggle for Freedom in the United States and India*, Harvard University Press, Cambridge, MA 2012.

Spencer, Philip and Howard Wollman. *Nationalism: A Critical Introduction*, Sage, London 2002.

Srinivasa Sastri, V.S. *My Master Gokhale: A Selection from the Speeches and Writings of V. S. Srinivasa Sastri* (edited by T.N. Jagadisan), Model Publications, Madras 1946.

Steger, Manfred B. 'Political Ideologies in the Age of Globalisation', in Michael Freeden (ed.), *The Oxford Handbook of Political Ideologies*, OUP, Oxford and New York 2013, pp. 214–231.

Tamir, Yael. *Liberal Nationalism*, Princeton University Press, Princeton 1993.

Taylor, Charles. *Modern Social Imaginaries*, Duke University Press, Durham and London 2004.

Torri, Michelguglielmo. *Storia dell'India*, Laterza, Roma e Bari 2000.

——. '"Westernised Middle Class', Intellectuals and Society in Late Colonial India", *Economic and Political Weekly*, Vol. 25, n. 4 (1990), pp. 2–11.

van der Veer, Peter. "Cosmopolitan Options", *Etnográfica*, Vol. 6, n. 1 (2002), pp. 15–26.

Vertovec, Steven and Robin Cohen. 'Introduction: Conceiving Cosmopolitanism', in idem (eds.), *Conceiving Cosmopolitanism: Theory, Context and Practice*, OUP, Oxford 2002.

Vickers, Edward and Krishna Kumar (eds.). *Constructing Modern Asian Citizenship*, Routledge, London 2015.

Vincent, Andrew. "Liberal Nationalism: An Irresponsible Compound?", *Political Studies*, Vol. 45, n. 2 (1997), pp. 275–295.

——. *Nationalism and Particularity*, CUP, Cambridge 2002.

——. 'Nationalism', in Michael Freeden (ed.), *The Oxford Handbook of Political Ideologies*, OUP, Oxford and New York 2013.

Washbrook, D.A. "Law, State and Agrarian Society in Colonial India", *Modern Asian Studies*, Vol. 15, n. 3 (1981), 649–721.

——. 'India 1818-1860, The Two Faces of Colonialism', in A. Porter (ed.), *The Nineteenth Century (The Oxford History of the British Empire, Volume III)*, OUP, Oxford 1999, pp. 395–421.

——. "Forms of Citizenship in Pre-Modern South India", *Citizenship Studies*, Vol. 23, n. 3 (2019), pp. 224–329.

Watt, Carey A. 'Philanthropy and Civilizing Mission in India, c. 1820', in Carey A. Watt and Michael Mann (eds.), *Civilizing Missions in Colonial and Postcolonial South Asia: From Improvement to Development*, Anthem Press, London 2011, pp. 271–316.

——. *Serving the Nation: Cultures of Service, Association, and Citizenship in Colonial India*, OUP, New Delhi 2005.

Wolpert, Stanley A. *Tilak and Gokhale: Revolution and Reform in the Making of Modern India*, OUP, New Delhi 1989 (first published 1961).

Zerilli, Linda M.G. 'Feminist Critiques of Liberalism', in Steven Wall (ed.), *The Cambridge Companion to Liberalism: Cambridge Companions to Philosophy*, CUP, Cambridge 2015, pp. 355–380.

1 Liberalism

> I do not ask to see the distant scene: One step enough for me. *

This chapter explores the first stage of Gokhale's intellectual and political life, with a special focus on the cultural and political milieu of Poona – where Gokhale first became politically active, and which remained an important pivot to his private and public life. It illustrates Gokhale's attainment of a Western education and his exposure to liberal ideas and attendant discourses of rights and liberties. Gokhale's relationship with other thinkers and activists, especially Agarkar and Ranade, his early activities as a teacher at the Fergusson College and as a journalist, and his first public commitments as a representative of the Poona Sarvajanik Sabha (Poona All People's Society, PSS) and Deccan Sabha and as a volunteer in relief activities are analysed. It is shown that these years proved formative for Gokhale to engage with the liberal values and ideas that were circulating at the time and that would inform his political philosophy and conceptualisation of the nation.

The promises of a Western education

Gopal Krishna Gokhale was born in 1866 in a small village in the coastal Ratnagiri district in the Bombay Presidency.[1] His family, although belonging to the Chitpavan Brahman caste, had limited financial means. The Chitpavans, also defined as Poona, Deccan or Maratha Brahmans,[2] were a sub-caste group who had dominated Western India before the British took control of it and whose influence in the politics, education, literature, socio-religious reform and journalism of the region persisted during (and to a lesser extent even after) the colonial rule.[3]

Although often represented as a dominant elite by the British rulers, the Chitpavans did not form a social class, as among them there was no

---

* From the famous Christian hymn, "Lead, Kindly Light" composed by John H. Newman in 1833. Quoted by Gokhale in Gopal Krishna Gokhale, *Speeches of Gopal Krishna Gokhale*, edited by G.A. Natesan, Natesan & Co, Madras 1920, p. 620.

DOI: 10.4324/9781003037422-2

pattern of poverty or affluence.[4] Notwithstanding their high caste status, many were very poor.[5] Those classes who had traditionally constituted the great majority of the administrative personnel in the pre-colonial period and who, in the period under analysis, had scarce economic means were the more eager and predisposed to obtain a Western education at an advanced level.[6] This had become a precondition in order to have higher chances of upward social mobility and to be recruited in the lower ranks of the colonial bureaucracy.[7] As a matter of fact, being the immediate pre-British rulers of the Deccan and having overlapping roles as priests, landowners, estate managers, scholars and government servants,[8] Chitpavans were seen as a potential threat to the new establishment as well as unneglectable interlocutors whose expertise in terms of administration represented a tremendous resource the new rulers could tap into.[9]

While employment opportunities were undoubtedly a strong and concrete motivation that drove Chitpavans to acquire a Western education, for many of them – like those Indians from both high and low castes who had access to this kind of education – the 'new' knowledge available acquired significance much beyond instrumental reasons. It turned also into a political tool which empowered its receivers by enhancing their capability and adaptability to cope with a rapidly changing political and social order as well as, in several cases, to defy the discourse of superiority of the West.[10] It was through Western education that learned Indians became increasingly acquainted with the language of the 'universal' rights of liberalism. The colonial system of education introduced by the British directly and indirectly led to a new consciousness of the value of liberty, democracy and rule of law in India, bringing to light the enormous gap that existed between the British government in Great Britain and in India. Many would have agreed with the Poona social reformer Lokahitawadi Gopal Hari Deshmukh (1832–1892) that it was British rule that had opened the eyes of the Indian intelligentsia.[11]

Bombay and Pune were, for different and similar reasons, the most important urban centres of the region, from which the influence of new ideas gradually percolated into the inlands in various ways.[12] The port city of Bombay, which was also the seat of the colonial government in the Presidency and the economic heart of the British Raj, was a vibrant cosmopolitan metropolis. It had a long history of "predisposition towards the outside, empowered by connections and practices of its extraordinarily varied communities," which resulted in a modernity that was not only economic but also social and intellectual.[13] The prestigious Elphinstone College, established in 1834[14] and affiliated to the Bombay University after its foundation in 1856, played a major role in the spread of Western education. Among its early graduates there were men like M. G. Ranade, Dadabhai Naoroji, Badruddin Tyabji and Jamshedji Tata, whose influence in the social, political and economic fields in the second half of the century would not remain unnoticed. Poona was comparatively more resistant to change because of its recent political heritage as the seat of the Maratha state and because of its traditional core as the cultural hub of Sanskrit scholarship, in which Chitpavans stood out.[15] Here, one of the main 'incubators' of 'modernity' was the Deccan College. Initially named Poona Hindu College and reserved for the education of Brahmans, the Deccan College became, at least on paper, open to all castes[16] and started increasingly including 'useful' knowledge through subjects like English, natural and social sciences to the expenses of Hindu religious and classical learning.[17] This development gradually characterised curricula at matriculation, college and university levels all over the region.

Most religious and social reformers that were active in the Bombay Presidency – the vast majority of whom were Brahmins and Chitpavan *in primis* – had received their education from the Elphinstone and Deccan Colleges.[18] They belonged "to a small and select group possessed of a sense of mission and a belief in the possibility of effecting change" and were "caught up in the excitement of new ideas, in their discussion and in their spread."[19] Like the rest of India, they were engaged in the critique of social mores and in the socio-religious reforms projects in an effort to achieve what was perceived as the moral and material progress of their country. They were also promotors of the expansion of educational institutions in towns and villages through the establishment of private schools and colleges. Their activities directly or indirectly aimed at challenging the colonial discourse of 'inferiority' and 'backwardness' of Indian religions and civilisation vis-à-vis the Christian West, becoming tools of national awakening too. The richness and diversity of their intellectual elaborations and reform initiatives are evinced by the fact that 'traditional'/revivalist and 'modern'/progressive elements were combined in such complex ways that this dichotomy appears analytically unproductive.

The marginal class background from which Gokhale came – his father was a minor clerk in rural Kagal[20] – made him determined to take advantage of the possibilities opened by Western education. After attending elementary school in Kagal and then high school in Kolhapur, in 1881, he enrolled in Law from the Elphinstone College in Bombay. Perhaps not outstanding as a particularly gifted student – his biographers noted that he had an impressive memory though[21] – he was driven by an ambitious nature and considerable self-discipline. Gokhale finished his studies and comfortably graduated in law in 1884; he was apparently all set to pursue a typical *babu* career as a lawyer, like many of his caste fellows. Indeed, from the late 19th century due to the increasing complexity of regulations and litigation cases, the legal profession had become influential and much in demand. But for Gokhale, things would turn out rather differently and he would soon be overwhelmed by the vibrant social and political life of Maharashtra, and Poona in particular.

Teacher and journalist

Gokhale's entry in the milieu of social and political activism came about thanks to the combination of caste connections and his educational pedigree as an Elphinstone College graduate in 1885, when he was offered a position as an assistant master in the New English School in Poona, namely a 'native'-run educational institution. This high school had been created in 1880 by the eminent Marathi writer Vishnushastri Chiplunkar (1850–1882) with the help of the young and enthusiastic Bal Gangadhar Tilak (1856–1920) and Gopal Ganesh Agarkar (1856–1895), all Chitpavans, who wanted to offer a 'modern' kind of education but with cheaper fees than government schools, so that the less privileged might be reached.[22] The undergirding principle was that education for Indians had to be carried out by Indians. Given his budget restrictions, Gokhale accepted this job, because the salary, though meagre, could allow him to continue his studies in law at the Deccan College while teaching.[23] By the time Gokhale joined the New English School, this institution had seen a phenomenal success and the number of students, initially numbering 35, had exceeded 1,000 in the span of just a few years. This positive and unexpected development encouraged the founders of the school to create the Deccan Education Society in 1884, that is, a corporate body which would administer the institution and founding of new schools of all levels in the Presidency.[24] It was under the society's management that the Fergusson College was opened in Poona in the following year.

At the New English School, Gokhale taught English language and literature and started lecturing also in history and economics at the Fergusson College in 1885. While teaching economics, Gokhale developed an interest in mathematics. He published an arithmetic book that became widely used in schools and it provided the young teacher with financial security for the years to come.[25] T. K. Shahani, who was a student at the college when Gokhale was assistant master, wrote in the biography of his teacher that among the books that Gokhale had adopted in his history courses were Burke's *Reflections*,[26] from which Gokhale dwelled especially on the speeches on American taxation and conciliation; the trial of Warren Hastings; John Bright's speeches; Macaulay's *History of England*, Southey's *Life of Nelson* and other works that Gokhale deemed crucial to make students familiar with the history and ideas of the British people.[27] As Gokhale would say later, history was a subject of the utmost social value due to its role in awakening "love of free institutions" and interest in political questions among students of British history and more generally European history. This discipline was permeated "with ideas of the value and dignity of freedom, of constitutional liberty."[28] Thus, Gokhale's interest in history originated not only from the learned person's curiosity about the past, but also and more importantly from the political activist's concern for the present in which he lived. English history was seen as the unfolding of a successful and gradual struggle for civil liberties[29] and therefore inspiring for India too, whereas Irish history was a model of "steady work and disinterested sacrifice"[30] that, Gokhale hoped, would stimulate his students as future citizens of India. More generally, the cultural 'movements' that characterised the modern history of Europe, such as Enlightenment, Positivism and Risorgimento, could revivify Indian public life, providing a variety of solutions to social and political problems.

While teaching in Poona, Gokhale got in close contact with his colleagues Tilak and Agarkar, together with personalities such as Ranade (1842–1901) and the noted Sanskrit scholar Ramakrishna Gopal Bhandarkar (1837–1925) and retired civil servants that had embraced the cause of this small group of activists. It is significant that the newspapers *Kesari* ('lion,' in Marathi) and *Mahratta* (in English), which would go on to become mouthpieces of the Extremists, and the Arya Bhushan Press, which instead became the mainstay of the Moderates in Poona, were created at the same time as the school and were managed together, something which confirms the close connection between educational activities and the shaping of political public opinion.[31]

But divisions within the Deccan Education Society soon started to emerge. Rifts were not only based on different views regarding the management of the schools, but also and more importantly motivated by divergences in outlook on social questions, with on one side Tilak increasingly embracing socially conservative views and on the other side Agarkar and Gokhale supporting social reform against caste discriminations and in favour of spreading 'modern' rational views. This clash was reflected in the articles of both the *Kesari* and the *Mahratta* with often contradictory and confusing results.[32] The diverging ideological positions became particularly visible when issues that could potentially undermine extant patriarchies and social hierarchies were debated – the schooling of women and lower caste members being the starkest examples.

Initially, the clash involved Agarkar and Tilak. Gokhale had reached a certain degree of intimacy with both but he increasingly leaned towards Agarkar, a staunch rationalist, whose views he apparently found more similar to his own ones.[33] They shared the same views on the need to 'uplift' Indian society to bring it to the level of the more 'advanced' Western societies, on the role that the colonial government could play in helping their society 'emancipate' itself from the flaws of religious and irrational beliefs and on the importance of individual choices vis-à-vis the community. Conversely, since all measures of social reform were either directly sponsored by the colonial government or promoted by liberal Indians that did not want the immediate end of colonial domination, Tilak's "support of reactionary popular prejudice proved incidentally to be an attack against foreign rule, and was, therefore, at least an assertion of nationalism."[34] In other words, social reform was an expression of 'western' modernity and therefore meddling of colonial domination, whereas the traditional and indigenous realm was correlated with the 'national' and needed to be safe-guarded as it defined Indianness/Hinduness.[35] Moreover, the advent of the non-Brahman movement in the region made Brahmans like Tilak feel that Brahminism was under attack from several sides.[36]

In 1888, Agarkar and Gokhale created their own Anglo-Marathi newspaper, the weekly *Sudharak*, or *The Reformer*, and severed their con-tacts with what became Tilak's newspapers.[37] Agarkar was chief editor, whereas Gokhale was in charge of the English section.[38] From his cor-respondence, it is clear that Agarkar was deeply concerned about "the shabby writing in the *Mahratta* and the *Kesari* of the past two years" which had tarnished the image of the New English School both in the eyes of "thoughtful natives and European gentlemen" and questioned the "peaceful means of bringing about intellectual moral and physical regen-eration of a country."[39] The *Sudharak* was meant to address these faults and "reach the poorest class of readers in order that the ideas of reform contained therein should be dinned into the ears of thousands of men every week" and "gradually come to be generally liked and adopted."[40] The significance of a newspaper went beyond that of mere means of com-munication: it was a civic virtue.

Working side by side with Agarkar deeply influenced Gokhale's out-look on social issues. This political apprenticeship was as important for Gokhale as the one 'at Ranade's feet.' Agarkar was in fact very independent minded, an agnostic who was convinced that society could be improved only through reason and its reform had nothing to do with the spiritual-re-ligious realm. He drew significantly from Herbert Spencer's ideas on pro-gress and evolution and believed that western education and individual freedom were useful means to reform Indian society, the caste system and 'retrograde' social practices that were currently justified by obscurantist traditions. Spencer's evolutionary racial theory,[41] which compared biolog-ical organisms with societies, was crucial in convincing Agarkar about the interdependence between political institutions and types of society. He was convinced that in order to implement political reforms, the social structure had to be changed first. In the pages of the *Sudharak*, Agarkar explained these Spencerian organicist theories as well as the evolution of the concept of God and religious institutions, or recommended readings like 'Prison Ethics,' which influenced his own views on prison management.[42] Agarkar did not perceive the British rule as the ruin of India or Hindu society, as Tilak and other cultural nationalists did, at least at the rhetorical level. On the contrary, in his view, the colonial state, with all its flaws, was based on rational principles and thus responsible for bringing about the social change that he saw as necessary for the survival of society.[43] This was at var-iance with Spencer's anti-statism as well with his strong disagreement with the imperial project.[44] But, according to Agarkar, the theory of the mini-mal state advocated by Spencer could not be applied to an underdeveloped country like India, where the state had yet a big role to play.[45]

The masthead of the *Sudharak*, published every Monday, explained the purpose of the paper as being "devoted to the discussion of social, ethical and political subjects." Its motto was "What ought to be spoken will be spoken, and what is possible will be done." The perusal of the English section of the newspaper is a fascinating source if we are to follow the development of Gokhale's thought on issues which would remain significant for him in the future. The newspaper dealt with diverse questions, a sign of the will to sensitise the readers on multiple fronts. Some supported the agenda of the recently created Indian National Congress (INC), such as the request to introduce simultaneous examinations in India and Great Britain to ease Indians' access to the Indian Civil Service;[46] the reliance on the British Liberal Party as a preferred interlocutor to further the Indian cause; the need to extend Indian representations on local boards and councils. From other articles, we can already recognise Gokhale's faith in the local boards as fundamental platforms, where citizens could be trained to work together and share the same political culture, or his advocacy to protect the poor from the 'rapacious exactions' of government and landlords. It is also interesting to see how, at this early career stage, he was against separate representations for minorities[47] and reservations for recruitments in the provincial service on the basis of caste and class belonging.[48] The 'uplifting' of womankind appeared often among the pages of the reformist newspaper. This is hardly surprising as the 'woman question' had already kindled vivid interest, fostered anxious debates and stoked acrimony and fights between different factions by mid-19th century. From the 1850s onwards, the issue of educating women – although on different levels and for different purposes according to their caste and class – was a pressing one and thence topical in journals and magazines.[49] It provoked mixed feelings in terms of the amount of liberty that women should be granted. The question of mobility too, made easier throughout the subcontinent by the introduction of railways, was a matter of concern: the fact that women travelled on their own, although in most cases for joining religious pilgrimages, raised anxieties about their sexual safety and decency. The main point of discussion was to what extent change in women's lives was acceptable and which dose of independence and mobility could be matched with publicly acknowledged respectability.[50] The flourishing and circulation of mass print in India from the second half of the 19th century reflected this atmosphere of uncertainty and was consequential for women too. In fact, a huge variety of print material in the vernacular languages targeted specifically women and were aimed at regulating their behaviour, manners, clothing, thoughts, etc.[51] The position of the *Sudharak* was quite clear, being overall in line with the social reformers' beliefs: it advocated educating women and assigning them their "just position in human society."[52] An article, penned by Gokhale in 1893, for instance, urged fellow reformers to introduce compulsory primary education for both girls and boys. It praised the intervention of a woman called Hardevi, who encouraged female education during the 1892 National Social Conference in Allahabad by writing that "a Hindu lady addressing such a large gathering was an elevating sight."[53] Despite commending women's activism in the public sphere, Gokhale's understanding of women's 'just position' in society remained fraught with ambiguities. It is indicative of this that in the preface which Gokhale wrote in 1910 to the book by Ramabai Ranade (1862–1924), Ranade's wife, entitled *Ranade: His wife's Reminiscences*, we can read a passage that is worth quoting in its entirety:

> It is important to refer to one or two things which cannot but make a deep impression on the minds of the readers. A deep love between husband and wife is often found in Western society. That is a relationship of equality. But even when there is a similar deep love, that the wife should devote herself wholly to the service of the husband and consider this as the fulfilment of her life, is a special characteristic of the women of the East and particularly of India. This characteristic is the fruit of the culture and tradition of thousands of years and here in these pages we have a beautiful specimen of it. This fundamental characteristic remains unaffected in women like Vahinibai [literally 'sister-in law', affectionately indicating Ramabai], although the pattern of their life may be modified by new education, new ideas and new environment.[54]

Even the supported female education, then, was not intended to question patriarchy in the household: devotion to the husband – the *devpati* – was one of the norms of true womanhood, a belief shared by progressive and conservative forces.[55] 'Modernity' for women was tolerated only if consistent with an essentially Indian 'tradition.'[56] We cannot deny that Gokhale's viewpoint, although not addressing the question of gender inequalities in marital relationships nor the private/public sphere distinction, represented an advancement, even if a limited one. Compared to Brahmanical patriarchal notions that considered the domestic space as the only legitimate domain for 'authentically' Indian women and saw 'modern' education as unnecessary, if not dangerous, for them, Gokhale's views about women's role in society were progressive.[57] For example, when Ranade and Bhandarkar opened the first High School for Girls[58] in Poona in 1885, Tilak wrote in the *Mahratta* that "it is the fair sex that has to play a prominent and a difficult part in the work of increasing the human species"[59] and thus education disturbed women's 'biological' tasks and caused a national loss.[60] Gokhale did not agree with such crude views, but at the same time it is not possible to tell with certainty if he was driven by merely abstract humanitarian principles when dealing with women's issues or if, on the contrary, his convictions had a real impact on his private life. Not much is known about his married family life. As custom decreed and authoritative religious codes recommended, Gokhale married when he was 14. Unfortunately, though, his wife, Savitribai, suffered from an incurable illness[61] and Gokhale married another woman, Radhabai, in 1887, while his first wife was still alive.[62] From this second marriage, he had two daughters, of whom only Kashibai, the eldest, survived. It is difficult to say whether Gokhale was a "loving husband" – whatever this may mean – as Shahani[63] and Nanda write,[64] because there are no elements in Gokhale's correspondence to reconstruct his private life, his view on gender roles in the family, or to know how he felt about his child marriage and abandonment of the first sick wife. These life episodes, especially the second marriage which happened when Gokhale was already an adult and close to the environment of social reform, are telling of the contradictions of belonging to two different and not always communicating epistemic worlds. It is nevertheless interesting to note that Gokhale exchanged letters with several women who were active in the public sphere, Indian and non-Indian, such as the British nurse and social reformer Florence Nightingale, Swami Vivekananda's disciple Sister Nivedita, women's rights advocate Cornelia Sorabji, the poetess, feminist and political activist Sarojini Naidu, and the Bengali suffragette Mrinalini Sen, whose opinion he seemed to value and by whom he appeared to be deeply fascinated. More importantly, in supporting the Special Marriage Bill in 1912, Gokhale advocated free choice and interracial marriages vis-à-vis arranged ones.[65]

The clash between Gokhale (and Agarkar) and Tilak, which was later reflected on the political level and came to represent the two factions of the 'moderates' and 'extremists,'[66] continued deepening until it became irretrievable in 1890, when Gokhale was elected secretary of the PSS. Since this post was, according to Tilak, incompatible with the Deccan Education Society membership, Gokhale's election became the pretext which led to the rupture.[67] The PSS, a voluntary political body founded in 1870 whose members intended to act as mediators between the people and the colonial authorities, had become one of the most important constituting bodies of the INC in 1885.[68] It functioned as a democratic association consisting of representatives who had to prove that their mandate was wanted by at least 50 adult men from any caste or community. As was the case for the INC, however, the majority of the members of the PSS were part of the professions and were mostly Hindus and Brahmins.[69] Among the founding members were Ganesh Vasudev Joshi (1828–1880) and Ranade, two influential figures in the circles of social reformers and political activists of that period. Joshi was a lawyer and economist who greatly contributed to framing an elaborate critique of the economic policies of the British *Raj*. He defended the interests of peasants through the Sabha and was the first to publicise *khaddar*, that is, the hand-spun cloth, vis-à-vis the British textile manufactures in order to provide jobs to the rural poor and to oppose the abolition of the tariff on British imports introduced in 1870. He was also the lawyer of Vasudev Balwant Phadke, the man who mobilised Deccan peasants against the colonial tax collectors in 1876–1877.[70]

Ranade, while pursuing an official career as judge – he reached the peak of his career in 1895 when he became High Court Justice in Bombay – was also an erudite scholar and active in issues of social reform. With his second wife Ramabai[71] he played a prominent role in the creation of schools of different levels for girls and non-Brahman students. Due to his initiative, the National Social Conference, which he himself had founded in 1887, was held alongside the annual gatherings of the INC, so that, in his view, political and social reform could interact and advance together. Ranade was also among the earliest members of the Prarthana Samaj, whose purposes were similar to those of the Brahmo Samaj created by Rammohan Roy in Calcutta.[72] Aimed at purifying Hinduism from its "practical immoralities" – caste was "the greatest monster we have to kill"[73] – and at fostering inter-religious dialogue, the society was inspired by the Bhakti tradition, especially by the 17th-century saint Tukaram, as well as by Theism.[74] Ranade considered the Samaj as protestant (i.e. radical) as the saints of Maharashtra had been.[75] Like other reformists, Ranade did not idealise the past, but relied on historical interpretations that could validate projects of social reformation. His biography of Shivaji,[76] for example, emphasized the peaceful and cooperative coexistence of all castes in the 17th-century Maratha state as a characteristic of Maharashtrian cultural greatness and as a model of 'national unity' to follow in the future.[77]

Besides their work as social reformers, Joshi and Ranade contributed, like Dadabhai Naoroji (1825–1917), to broadening and systematising the economic analyses elaborated by the early economists, highlighting the predatory nature of British rule.[78] In particular Ranade was very active in debates with the colonial administration on several issues which, with a slight simplification, investigated and criticised the application of liberal political economy to India.[79] Gokhale became familiar with Joshi and Ranade's views, which exerted a strong and direct influence on him, especially their economic analysis, which resonated later in his budget speeches, both in the Bombay Legislative Council and in the Imperial one. Several of their most debated topics were followed up by Gokhale, such as the identification of the ever-increasing colonial land revenue assessment as the main cause of rural indebtedness, the intervention of the state to enhance India's economic potential, the priority of rights over ritual status, all aspects on which his vision of the nation was built. With both he maintained a long-lasting friendly and professional relationship.

The beginning of Gokhale's collaboration with the PSS corresponded *grosso modo* with the Age of Consent Bill controversy. The Bill was introduced by the colonial government in 1891 and aimed at increasing the minimum legal age limit for girls (married or unmarried) regarding sexual intercourse from 10 to 12 years. Mating with a girl below that age was equivalent to rape. Although the government measure was just cosmetic and did not really ameliorate the plight of girls, it roused a terrible wave of protest by the conservative sections of Indian society. This was particularly the case in the Bombay Presidency, where the Bill eventually became an Act in 1892. The Age of Consent became the terrain of a bitter ideological clash on which Tilak and his party, who saw it as a serious offence to the Hindu men's rights as well as to the shastric injunction – and thus an intolerable interference in Hindu religious matters by the colonial state – confronted the reformers. Granting women individual rights meant a threat for the entire Hindu community, according to the extremists.[80] For their part, the reformists, on the initiative of the Parsi journalist Behramji Malabari (1853–1912) who had written and circulated a treatise addressing the need of marriage reforms in 1884, had launched a campaign in favour of the legislative proposal.[81] The initiative sought the opinion from various public figures across India, such as Ranade, Jyotirao Phule (1927–1890), K. T. Telang (1850–1893), Bhandarkar and a more general public. Interestingly, however, women were not consulted. This was a significant omission given the fact that several women's organisations – religious and secular ones – as well as a well-developed women's press in Marathi were in existence in late 19th-century Maharashtra and through them a female collective voice, often at variance with male opinions, could be heard.[82] This "epistemic violence"[83] towards women's views was the reason for women's scepticism towards male reformism. Moreover, although reformers criticised the bill's limits in terms of protection for married girls, they supported it also on the basis of eugenic arguments and concerns for the collective good, showing a tendency to give in to 'nationalist' rhetoric when dealing with gender-related issues.[84] Even if disappointing for female activists, this was enough to rouse the anger of those who opposed state intervention in regulating marital reforms, either based on nationalist arguments or conservative beliefs. In Poona, a meeting organised by the reformers to address the people on the need for legal regulation of infant marriage was interrupted by a group of local 'rowdy' students, supporters of Tilak. The episode traumatised Gokhale and made him take a more definitive stand towards Tilak and his acolytes:

> The conduct of 'leading men' of Poona which culminated in the disgraceful rowdyism of Wednesday last had fairly sickened me. It has exercised a deciding influence on my wavering mind, and I am now most exceedingly anxious to be relieved of the necessity of keeping up any kind of connection with them (...). I am longing for the time when I shall have nothing to do directly with these people.[85]

This was a declaration of intent by Gokhale. The young politician realised Tilak's "matchless capacity for intrigue," that is, his ability to cater to Hindu traditional forces in order to foster his political aims, regardless the divisive potential of his course of action. Also, the first-hand experience of violence further opened Gokhale's eyes over not only the polarising potential of social reform, but over the strategic ways in which revivalism was adopted to thwart it.[86]

Learning at Ranade's feet

Not only was Gokhale's collaboration with the PSS the pretext which caused Tilak to leave the Society, it also marked a turning point in Gokhale's life and career. It was during the regular meetings of the PSS when Gokhale and the young men gathered around the leading figure of Ranade discussed relevant questions on society, economics and politics. During these formal meetings, which took place in the Sabha Rooms, situated in the still existing Nagarkar Wada in central Poona, the members drew petitions and appeals to the colonial government, having carried out thorough and systematic scholarly research and investigations among the people in order to evaluate the effects of government policies on the masses, especially in terms of famines and rural indebtedness. The PSS was in fact a fundamental nucleus of elaboration of the economic critique of colonialism from the perspective of a nationalist and self-sufficient economy: it also promoted the creation of societies aimed at reviving 'national' industry and arts and relief associations against famines.[87] The leaders of the PSS envisioned a model of national economic development vis-à-vis colonial and classical economy and contributed to providing the INC with a powerful ideological basis on which the territory, history and economy of the imagined nation were congruent.[88] Gokhale, who would become a central figure in the INC, played a prominent role on these terms through his budget speeches as a representative of the party. Following Ranade,[89] Gokhale too adopted Friedrich List's political economic views, which stressed the need of state intervention to compensate the damages created by the free market, much to the detriment of the poorest countries. Nevertheless, Gokhale was careful about applying dogmatically such notions to the particular colonial conditions of India, where state protection through the imposition of duties on imports could have ambiguous consequences, worsening the condition of the poor while making the rich even richer.[90]

Along with institutional meetings, the Sabha Rooms played host every evening to animated gatherings which, while of an informal character, were intellectually formative. The history and the political philosophy of the West were read and discussed and their possible relevance and application to Indian context were thoughtfully examined.[91] In several letters to friends – and in rather romantic tones – Gokhale recalled those meetings as the space where his *guru-chela* relationship with Ranade took shape and consolidated.

In the years between 1890 and 1896, Gokhale acted as editor of the *Quarterly Journal of the Poona Sarvajanik Sabha* (QJPSS) published in English.[92] He was personally trained by Ranade, who "sent him straight to original documents, made him work through masses of Blue Books; gave him petitions and memorials to draft which entailed long and laborious research; [Ranade] was unsparing in his demand for articles and memoranda on all manner of subjects of public interest."[93]

Besides containing proceedings of the Sabha, the QJPSS carried correspondence between government officials and other individuals, as well as an independent section where articles by scholars and experts on different topics or book reviews were published.

From this section we can understand which themes were particularly dear to the PSS and to Gokhale in this phase of his public life, which was coterminous with the turbulent period of administration of Lord Harris as Governor of the Bombay Presidency (1890–1895) – an administration defined by Gokhale as a regime that systematically defied public opinion and that revealed the ever-greater incompatibility between Anglo-Indian and Indian interests.[94] Apart from the constant presence of articles on socio-religious issues, such as the condition of peasantry or child marriage, there are several essays dealing with Hindu philosophy, which, while referring to the ancient 'Aryan customs,' did not refrain from questioning the Shastras whenever their prescription did not fit with the spirit of the times. The re-interpretation of the Hindu scriptures, in other words, served as a justification for the community to advocate changes in social customs and religious beliefs. The meaning of modernity in the Indian context was another debated issue, as well as the influence of Western ideas and capitalism.

A very interesting article published in 1893, 'The Exigencies of Progress in India,'[95] analysed the risks of accepting indiscriminately western civilisation, often entailing acquisitiveness and greed, conflict and social disaggregation. Modern civilisation was about "improving the station in life, subordinating romantic sentiments and prejudices of race and birth to the attainment of practical ends for the common welfare." This was a sideswipe at the colonial rulers and at their racist attitude as well as a warning against casteism and rising forms of exclusionary nationalisms. The same article criticised capitalism as well as progress towards unclear goals, but at the same time supported the need to industrialise India – a common trope – in order to achieve independence and material prosperity. Notwithstanding blistering attacks on the acquisitive nature of Western capitalism, the PSS was not in favour of redistributing land and opposed the restrictions over land acquisitions. Its members held that the only adequate measure to ameliorate the plight of the peasants was to encourage agricultural economy through investments carried out by the landowning classes.[96] Criticism of socialism was a recurring theme in the journal of the Sabha: marking the ideological distance from socialist ideas was definitely a safe way not to alarm the colonial authorities who were scared of the experiments which had taken place in France but also of the recent peasants' revolt in Maharashtra. At the same time, the Sabha did not advocate war between social classes (Ranade himself seemed to suggest that state socialism was driven by oligarchic interests just as free market was).[97] Also women's claims for emancipation and equality with men was a by-product of Western individualism where "everyone lives by himself, for himself."[98]

The article maintained the need to overcome a variety of Indian habits, practices and behaviours considered backward, non-modern, and incompatible with notions of national productivity and efficiency, such as the overpowering influence of religion, tradition and custom, the veneration of ancient past, as well as a general '*vis inertiae*' due to lack of system, method, precision and punctuality. It was the task of the educated classes, "natural leaders" to show to the masses the way towards modern life.[99] In line with Spencerian organicist ideas and drawing on Charles Henry Pearson's *National Life and Character* (1893), nations were compared to individuals, their past a premonition for their future – and this was not good news for India, because despite its ancient vibrant civilisation, its recent history had been characterised by foreign conquests and isolation. But English education, from primary to high, was already bearing its fruits by developing a spirit of inquiry and criticism and producing a 'practical man.' Quoting Burke and Hyndman and showing multidirectional epistemic reference points, the article engaged with topics and theories widely debated in the period, like efficiency – both national and individual – Hindu degeneracy, the need to spread education to the masses, a liberal historicism envisioning a march towards progress, 'universal' rights wiping the individual clean of cultural and community influences, etc. Evolution and degeneration were themes which Gokhale continued to deal with in the course of his career when reflecting about the possibilities of Indian politics.

Through the pages of both the *Sudharak* and the QJPSS, Gokhale did not spare Lord Harris strong criticism. The Governor was attacked especially for the introduction of the rules and regulations implementing the Council Act of 1892 in the Bombay Presidency which overrepresented European merchants and the Indian landowning classes, thus betraying the territorial principle of representation applied in Great Britain in favour of class interest. The concept underlying the argument was that of 'no taxation without representation': "The number of those who do not belong to any specially prominent class and yet who pay taxes and are bound by the laws of their legislature must in every country be overwhelmingly large, and the interests of such men can be safeguarded only by giving territorial representation."[100] Lord Harris was courting the "old aristocracy" to the detriment of the "educated Poona Brahmins," where 'educated' came to increasingly signify 'politicised' – positively for Indians and negatively for the British rulers. Although initially against any kind of reservations,[101] Gokhale would change his mind in future years, when the increasing tension between the Hindu majority and the Muslim minority required the former to ensure the latter political guarantees. Another major point of disapproval of the administration of Lord Harris was related to the Hindu-Muslim riots that broke out in the Presidency in 1893.[102] Criticism was directed to the Governor for not acting as an arbiter. According to the young journalist, the government had taken a biased stand in favour of Muslims while the Anglo-Indian press had been systematically engaged in the divisive activity of "sensitising" the Mohammedans on the potential danger of their religion "having the ranks of the Civil Service crowned with the Hindus."[103] Gokhale condemned also the polarising pro-Hindu meetings organised by Tilak as he thought that both communities – not particular sects or castes – under the guidance of the "educated classes" had to start a dialogue for peace.[104] Gokhale argued that, given the alarming circumstances, it was high time that "government should proclaim the equality of law and impartiality of justice to all classes, and not leave the thing to be done by the representatives of both sections."[105] He was referring disapprovingly to the conciliation boards created after the riots of 1893 and 1894 in Bombay. These included both Hindus and Muslims, who had been appointed by the 'natural leaders' and western-educated professionals and who represented their communities. Thus, the longstanding colonial idea that Indian society comprised (homogenous) communities was taken on by Indians themselves who appropriated these categories in their dealings with the state, as well as in the ways in which they addressed their own communities.[106] While perceiving the Ganapati festival[107] and, later on, the Shivaji festival – both transformed by Tilak into expressions of militantly anti-Muslim and anti-colonial protest after the outbreak of Hindu-Muslim violence[108] – as crystallising Hindu religious identity, Gokhale blamed the riots mainly on the Muslim community, "protagonists of a wave of religious enthusiasm,"[109] and the lower social strata. If the cow protection movement – which Gokhale saw uncritically as "preservation for agricultural cattle"[110] – was a cause, it was not enough to explain the course of the story. It was "the lower strata – ignorant and unemployed – unaffected as they are by the stream of progress, that are prone to rise en masse and turn their laziness into a regrettable activity." In the long run, Gokhale argued, the spread of education and employment would prove the best solution for preventing such "indolence and fierceness."[111] It seems that Gokhale – as we saw when referring to the Age of Consent Bill agitations – could explain violent outbursts only as expressions of fanaticism or rowdyism, revealing the persistence of prejudice towards Muslims[112] and, more generally, the denial of political consciousness for the masses.

Coming to the political fore

Being the secretary of the PSS, one of the most influential political associations of the time in India, allowed Gokhale to participate in the sessions of the INC as early as 1889. In that year, the INC met in Bombay and Gokhale, as one of the 59 delegates from Poona, delivered his two first speeches on that platform.[113] More important than these was a speech in which Gokhale addressed a meeting of the Bombay Graduates Association a few years later in 1896.[114] Here crucial issues regarding education were raised. Starting by crediting British rule as the introduction into India of "Western conceptions of duties of the rulers towards the ruled," Gokhale went on in less apologetic tones by showing the discrepancy between those conceptions and factual reality: he compared the poor performance of the colonial government in terms of educational policies to more advanced policies enacted in England and in other British colonies. He also refuted the colonial argument that increasing funds for primary education, to the spread of which Gokhale attributed a great deal of importance for the future of the country, meant reducing those for secondary and higher education. Moreover, Gokhale analysed what were, in his views, the reasons of young Indians' "intellectual decadence." First of all, there were huge lacunae in the examination system, which did not encourage critical thinking but only cramming. This was a problem that extended beyond the educational realm because it precluded a higher level of general intelligence through a thorough knowledge of literature, history and philosophy, fundamental to craft "better citizens." Another cause of degeneracy was the urgent need for outdoor games "which endures through life and where the foundation is laid of a manly vigorous type of character."[115]

Gokhale was hinting at a trope that would acquire increasing resonance in the years to come, namely the need to build up a physically fit collectivity. As a matter of fact, from the beginning of the 20th century, physical activity and outdoor games as tools to build character became almost a fixation among Indian educationists. Under the influence of globally circulating eugenicist ideas and Spencerian-organicist visions of society, the international physical culture movement made an impact on India and the body was increasingly perceived as a site for citizens-making. Physical fitness – and on a broader level the command of one's own body not only through exercise but also through cleanliness, nutrition and sexual abstinence – turned into an important aspect of one's integrity, self-control and discipline as well as a catalyst of socio-political transformation. The reinvigoration of the individual's physique was in fact soon considered a *conditio sine qua non* for a bottom-up regeneration of the collective national and communal body.[116]

Perhaps for these reasons, Gokhale himself expressed the desire to practise yoga regularly.[117] When in Calcutta as a member of the Imperial Legislative Council a few years later, he took up yoga classes but soon gave up.[118] We know from Gandhi that ever since he refused to commit to stay physically active. When Gokhale and Gandhi spent one month together in Calcutta, the would-be Mahatma was dismayed by Gokhale's 'bad' habit of not practising physical exercise. He asked Gokhale why he did not go for walks, suggesting that as the reason for his weak physical constitution. Gokhale replied that he had insufficient free time, but Gandhi maintained that being busy with public work was not a justification for neglecting physical exercise.[119] Unlike Gandhi, Gokhale apparently did not see the deep connection between his body, purpose and achievements.[120] In the late summer and autumn of 1914, just a few months before Gokhale's death the following February, the two were in London – Gokhale as a member of the Public Service Commission and Gandhi just about to return to India after 21 years in South Africa. Gokhale had spent some time in France treating his worsening physical problems, mainly due to a weak heart, whereas Gandhi was recovering from pleurisy. Both were concerned for the other's health. In Gokhale's view, Gandhi's ailment was due to his fruit and nut diet, while Gandhi attributed Gokhale's condition to his being overweight and insufficient exercise.[121]

There are a few other points of the 1896 speech that are worth considering as *pars pro toto* of Gokhale's political thought in this early period of his public life. One is the question of the use of the vernaculars at university level. Gokhale was among the signatories of a PSS petition submitted to the Senate of the Bombay University in 1890 favouring the introduction into the curriculum of composition and translation papers in Marathi and other vernaculars.[122] In his speech, Gokhale claimed that he had little faith in that proposal, which he supported only in principle. He, instead, proposed as an ideal option the setting up of separate vernacular universities which would grant, at least for some time, inferior degrees than the ones awarded by English-medium universities, with English and Sanskrit as compulsory second languages. It was a way to bridge the gap, both literally and figuratively, between the language of everyday life, of common sense, and scholarly knowledge, trying to deconstruct epistemic hierarchies. Nevertheless, the implied conviction that the vernaculars were not suitable for teaching and learning higher subjects entailed that "for a long time to come" those hierarchies were confirmed.

Moreover, in criticising the increase in military expenditure for the second Anglo-Afghan war (1878–1880) to the detriment of education, and in particular disapproving of the inflated allowances paid to frontier tribes, Gokhale commented that, in the eyes of the British Government, the "doubtful and enforced allegiance of these semi-barbarous tribes is of more consequence to the peace and glory of the Empire than the moral and intellectual elevation of the Indian people."[123] Although the condemnation of the war lay at the basis of his argument, Gokhale took part in the rhetoric of stigmatisation of the tribes as 'semi-barbarous,' thus showing the same cognitive horizon as the British rulers and creating a clear-cut differentiation between 'them' – the tribes – and 'us' – the Indian people.

One last issue emerges from this speech, that is, the call for the co-operation of private enterprise and charity with the government, reluctant to do more "in fulfilment of a sacred obligation," i.e., the development of education. In encouraging the need of private initiatives, Gokhale adopted the language of mystic devotion to the nation advocating sacrifice "on the altar of education" as a civic duty necessary to make the country "purified, regenerated, ennobled and strengthened." The use of this idiom would remain a constant feature in his nationalist discourse. Overall, Gokhale undoubtedly envisioned education instrumentally as a factor as well as an indicator of the material progress of a nation. However, he increasingly perceived mass education as a social right that would bring about equality of opportunity while at the same time, and central to the development of citizens' capacity "for discrimination between right and wrong," the self-realisation of the citizens of a democracy.[124] The state, therefore, was legally responsible as well as morally obliged to enforce mass education, even though Gokhale recognised the temporary need of charitable intervention in the presence of an irresponsible colonial government which, following the recommendations of the Hunter Commission (1882), had reduced public aid to higher education.

The PSS fell under the control of Tilak and his supporters in 1896 and ceased to be a democratic and secular body. In Gokhale's words, Tilak's aim in controlling the PSS was "to drive out of public life all workers who sympathise with the cause of social reform by discrediting them with the masses by all manner of means."[125] In the same year, reformers under the lead of Ranade and Gokhale created another body, the Deccan Sabha, whose meetings were held at Ranade's house. The new body proclaimed the "spirit of liberalism implied in freedom from caste, creed and regional prejudices and a steady devotion to all that seek to do justice between man and man."[126] Since the Sabha's foundation was coterminous with the outbreak of the famine in the Bombay Presidency in 1896–1897, its members soon found themselves busy as volunteers providing relief work.[127] They did not hesitate to coordinate and cooperate with the Bombay Government to carry out the measures required to provide relief to those affected by deprivation. They proved to be extremely efficient in collecting data from the villages in the affected areas, showing the specific needs of each village in reports to the government.[128] Some of the recommendations they made were finally accepted.[129]

The PSS and the Deccan Sabha gave Gokhale a 'stage' for rehearsing in public life and the opportunity to meet British liberal politicians and activists who sponsored the Indian cause and were more or less officially active within the INC. It was Gokhale's responsibility to address Allan Octavian Hume, General Secretary of the INC, and William Digby, secretary of the British Committee of the INC, when they visited Poona in 1892 and 1893 respectively.[130] Both these occasions contributed to Gokhale's coming to the fore not only among the Bombay group of Pherozeshah Mehta, D.E. Wacha and Dadabhai Naoroji, but also at the national level.

The address for Hume – in fact a high-sounding eulogy that Hume himself described as "very extravagant" – is of some interest, being one of the early speeches Gokhale made. Besides praising Hume's work, Gokhale listed what, in his opinion, had been the main results of the INC since its recent creation. The Congress had welded together "all the influences in the country which were struggling scattered to create throughout India a sense of common nationality." Those influences had come into existence along with the presence of the British rule in the subcontinent, especially thanks to "the wise and large-heartedly policy" of statesmen and politicians like the Marquess of Ripon, John Bright, Henry Fawcett, Charles Bradlaugh and, one century earlier, Edmund Burke – names that had become "household words with the people." India could now "breathe and feel like one nation" while public opinion was generally more informed about the main political questions being debated. Moreover, after the formation of the INC, English politicians too had been provided with a new machinery and were now anxious to fulfil their duty to the people of India.[131]

Even considering the strongly hagiographic nature of the speech and the fact that Gokhale uses the misnomer 'people' to indicate what actually was a minority of educated classes, it is still possible to pinpoint some elements that would continue to be significant in Gokhale's political thought, as will be seen further on. In the first place, belonging to the same nation was not an innate feeling in a people but the consequence of a voluntary and active process. In this process, not only did British rule play an essential role in uniting a very diverse country under the same administration, but also liberal ideas were crucial in leading to the emergence of a sense of nationality due to their emphasis on the abstract equality of men. At the same time, by endorsing British liberals, Gokhale seemed to suggest that Indians had a great deal to take from them, but not much to give, mainly because of Indians' lack of public spirit.[132] Although this last position would oscillate in the following years as Gokhale increasingly recognised India's merits too, the strong reliance on British liberalism remained a weakness among the Moderates that the Extremists were able to increasingly exploit.[133]

Amidst 'the stormy and uncertain sea of public life'

It was, again, as a representative of the Deccan Sabha, that Gokhale was selected to give evidence before the Royal Commission on Expenditure in London in 1897, chaired by Lord Welby, to investigate the financial relationship between England and India.[134] Whereas Gokhale's work in Great Britain will be analysed in the third chapter, here it is worth focusing on a paper that Gokhale presented, during that same trip, at an educational congress to which he was invited to speak by the Women's section on female education in India. The congress was part of an exhibition held at Earls Court in London, called the Victorian Era Exhibition. Gokhale's paper is very telling about his views on women.[135] He began with historicist arguments, based on Romesh Chunder Dutt's *Civilisation in Ancient India* and on fairly typical revivalist views of the time. [136] According to these, women had held "an honoured place" in society in the past, they were intellectual partners of their husbands and did not lead a secluded life. For these reasons, Gokhale argued, education and "enlightened" freedom[137] were the "rightful inheritance of Indian women," which would restore them to their past dignity and free their mainly religious mind from the bondage of caste and custom, from the hold of religious notions on aspects of everyday life and from resistance to change and innovation. Thus, whereas male education was predicated on the secular ideas of future progress underpinning liberalism, women's entitlement to education was based on an idealised Hindu tradition.[138] While advocating the raising of marriage age and considering, in line with utilitarian views, female education as the benchmark of the true well-being of every nation, Gokhale made no mention of patriarchal power relations precluding women's choices, but expressed in very optimistic tones male "indifference and toleration" towards girls' education in India. More importantly, invoking the need of a "*proper* curriculum for girls" [italics is mine], he also maintained that it was necessary "to take note of the different surroundings of boys and girls in Indian Society in determining the course of instruction, and to make some concession even to popular prejudices on the subject."[139] Gokhale therefore missed the fundamental point that "the different surroundings of boys and girls" were precisely those social relations shaped by patriarchy and defining the gender stereotypes and norms which underpinned arguments of women's inferiority. Also, it is striking that among the individuals and organisations committed to female education in India, Gokhale did not refer to the pioneering work done by any woman, not even Pandita Ramabai and her Sharada Sadan (Home for Learning), which had been based in Poona since 1890 and which Gokhale knew very well. Furthermore, the Sadan's curriculum was broadly in line with state-run schools for boys.[140] Was it a Freudian slip? Or was it a voluntary omission aimed at not displeasing Ranade who had dissociated himself from the Sadan? In any case, in Gokhale's words, the history of education in colonial India was mainly a male-made story. Last but not least, although Gokhale depicted female education as a question of utmost importance in front of a British audience, he had not made reference to the issue in the 1896 speech he gave at the meeting of the Bombay Graduates Association, probably because he was aware of the fact that education for girls and women was still a taboo for many in Maharashtra. Gokhale thus showed a capacity to adapt his tone strategically to cater to different audiences. His cautious attitude was guided by the principle of gradualism, that is to carry out activities "on the lines of least resistance" to make them more practical and more acceptable to the public – a principle that more broadly defined the social reform movement in the Bombay Presidency.[141]

No sooner had Gokhale returned to Poona from London in July 1897, he had to face a deeply personal and political humiliation, which commonly became known as the 'apology incident.' When he left India in March, plague had already broken out in Poona. The Government had taken strict measures to fight the epidemic, passing the Epidemic Disease Act that enabled provincial governors to prescribe regulations to control the disease, such as forced house perquisitions and the transfer of infected persons to hospitals. Disobedience was punished under the penal code. Colonial authorities were thrown into a state of panic as the plague "became the focus of the most terrible anxieties which India evoked in the British imagination,"[142] whereas medical aid was given administrative power as never before.[143] The anti-plague measures were carried out in Poona mostly by British soldiers, whose conduct roused many to complain to the press, especially against strangers violating the *zenana*, the domestic space reserved for women. The general resentment against operations perceived as brutal and inflexible eventually led to the assassinations of the ICS Plague Commissioner in Poona, Mr. Rand, and Mr. Ayerst, an officer of the British Army, by the Chapekar brothers who belonged to an anti-reformist and anti-British quasi-military group. Tilak's expression of sympathy towards the murderers was the cause of his arrest and imprisonment for one year[144] – a "great national calamity," Gokhale wrote from London to Joshi.[145] While still in London, during an interview with the *Manchester Guardian*, Gokhale mentioned that he had received reports from people and newspapers he fully trusted in Poona describing the misconduct of British soldiers during the plague relief operation. These reports were empathetic towards Hindu and Muslim susceptibility to the encroachment of their domestic peace and seclusion. In particular, Gokhale denounced the rape of two women and the suicide of one of them. Nevertheless, once back in India, Gokhale could not substantiate his declarations, as his correspondents were unable to provide evidence for the facts they had described in their reports.[146] He therefore decided to submit an unreserved apology in front of the Government, causing his unpopularity both in India and England.[147] This humiliating event threatened Gokhale's professional integrity and pushed him into a deep depression. However, the recrudescence of the epidemic the following year galvanised him to take part in voluntary work, leading a team of volunteers in service of the plague-stricken people, with the aim to mitigate the public discontent stirred by the health measures. That same year, Lord Sandhurst, the Governor of Bombay from 1895 to 1900, commended Gokhale's voluntary work commenting that "there is no more hard-working, generous and sympathetic worker amongst the plague volunteers than Professor Gokhale."[148] Gokhale also decided to be inoculated against the plague to set an example to those people afraid of the side effects that the vaccination could have.[149] The vaccine, discovered by Waldemar Haffkine in 1897 and showing limited efficacy, was not made compulsory by the colonial authorities[150] but was encouraged en masse. Tilak condemned the inoculation as "half-baked scientific discoveries" tested on "poor and tolerant" Indians.[151] Appointed member of the Poona Plague Commission, Gokhale did not underestimate the risks involved in the inoculation process, required to be carried out by experts, and suggested that the serum dose could be decreased to diminish its potential negative effects.[152] At the same time, while colonial assumptions blamed Indian custom and habits as well as poverty and conditions of filth for the spread of the plague,[153] Gokhale took a more constructive stand. He reiterated the urgent need of sanitary improvement such as the extension of good water-supply, drainage, medical relief, construction of hospitals and dispensaries as long-term objectives that could prevent the spread of epidemics. During his Budget speeches both in the Bombay Legislative Council and, later, in the Imperial Legislative Council, Gokhale demanded central government intervention in support of local boards, responsible for sanitation initiatives but lacking adequate financial resources.[154]

The election to the Bombay Legislative Council in December 1899, in all likelihood, helped dispel the clouds of depression from Gokhale's mind. The District Local Boards of the Central Division of the Presidency elected him non-official member of that body, giving him preference over a candidate belonging to Tilak's faction.[155] Gokhale remained a member for two years before joining the Imperial Council. The membership in the Bombay Council amplified his public voice and was undoubtedly a training ground for his future work in Calcutta. The support from G. V. Joshi, especially helpful in providing Gokhale with financial data, was constant in these years. The short time spent on the provincial council was intense: two consecutive famines and the plague affected Maharashtra and subjected the region to a period of economic depression. Gokhale attacked the colonial administration without compromise for the inefficacy of famine relief operations. Moreover, famine relief was not combined with the temporary suspension of revenue collection, as prescribed in the Famine Code, although this had been done in the Central Provinces.[156] Gokhale also inquired into the conditions of "relief workers," denouncing their economic ill-treatment, especially in Khandesh and Gujarat, where the wage was below the minimum established by the Famine Code.[157] A few years later, during a famine in the United Provinces in 1907–1908, the response of the recently created Servants of India Society (SIS) provided relief to the famine-affected – a field of activity that remained important for the associations in the years to come.[158] Similarly, Gokhale's scathing opposition to the Land Revenue Amendment Bill, introduced in the council in 1901 aimed at amending the Land Revenue Code of 1879 by restraining land transferability with a view to reduce rural indebtedness, revealed the huge vulnerabilities to which the *ryot* would be exposed. It also unmasked the rulers' real motives behind the bill. According to the colonial administration, the main reason for rural indebtedness was the peasant's alleged innate incapability of thrift and self-reliance. This behaviour led peasants to mortgage their land to the village *mahajan* and in many cases to finally sell it. Gokhale was well-prepared to dispute the government views due to previous years of study at the PSS, which, as seen, took a great deal of interest in the matter of rural indebtedness. Quoting the Deccan Riots Commission of 1875 and the Deccan Agriculturalists' Relief Commission of 1891–1892, he proposed, as a short-term measure, greater flexibility in terms of revenue collection, advocating an assessment of land based on net produce and not on potential productive capacity. He further proposed the need to enact a general suspension of revenue collection, not one based on individual investigations, in times of crop failure.[159] The real solution was "non-agricultural industries to relieve the pressure of surplus population on soil, a better organization of rural credit, an abatement of the state demand where it is excessive."[160] However strong the arguments against the amendments and notwithstanding the public outcry both in India and England, the bill was passed.[161] Gokhale took part in the protest walkout of the Indian members, led by Mehta, from the Council. He did so reluctantly though, publicly declaring that only his strong sense of duty pushed him to dissociate completely from the bill and to follow his colleagues.[162] In the future, however, especially after meeting Gandhi, he would support far more radical methods of protest, such as passive resistance.

Gokhale's performance in the Bombay Legislative Council created a positive impression on the anti-colonial field generally and on Pherozeshah Mehta in particular, so much that, when the latter resigned from his post at the Imperial Legislative Council in 1901, he supported Gokhale's request to be accepted as a possible candidate and exerted his influence to ensure that the young politician replaced him.[163] The beginning of Gokhale's work at the Supreme Council in 1902, which lasted up to the end of his life, marked also his retirement from the Fergusson College; the legislative work made impossible the teaching commitment there. When he took leave from the college after almost 20 years of service, Gokhale gave a most eloquent speech during a public celebration held in his honour. The speech was in many ways a prelude to the constitution of the SIS and even 30 years afterwards was still included in university textbooks for its nation-building significance.[164] In that speech, Gokhale said that he was ready to sacrifice his comfortable life at the college to embark "on the stormy and uncertain sea of public life," aware of the "few rewards and many trials and discouragements" ahead.[165] That sea was made even more 'uncertain' by Ranade's death in early 1901, an event which left "a sudden darkness" in Gokhale's life.[166] This loss, as well as the brutal administration of the Viceroy Lord Curzon (1898–1905), undoubtedly accelerated Gokhale's political maturity, something which enabled the nationalist leader to elaborate the idea of national emancipation predicated not only on political freedom, but also on a slow but steady progress towards social and economic freedom.

Conclusion

This chapter has shown that Gokhale's belonging to a social group which was deeply affected by the socio-economic developments produced by the colonial domination played a significant role in determining the trajectory of his early life and political career. Taking advantage of the opportunities provided by his Western education, Gokhale could engage at first hand as a member of the 'educated classes' in the lively cultural and political environment of Poona. The years of teaching at the Fergusson College and the collaboration with Agarkar and Ranade were a period of intense study and intellectual growth, during which Gokhale was open to fresh and manifold influences. In those years, through his journalism and political activism, the would-be leader of the INC worked towards developing a public increasingly sensitive to the liberal language of rights, as well as to moral sentiments and values that were seen as contributing to Indian society becoming a liberated one. Those early activities functioned as a training ground as well as a springboard for his future political ambitions: they gave him visibility well beyond the political scene of Poona and Western India.

From the account and analysis of this chapter, aspects of Gokhale's political views have emerged that would remain significant in the course of his public life, as the following chapters show in a more detailed way. First of all, it emerged that liberalism was central to Gokhale's vision for different reasons. Values coming from the liberal tradition were considered instrumental to the transformation of Indian society in terms of finding a new balance between individual and community, namely limiting the effects of social and cultural factors on individuals' freedom and lived experience without engendering sudden social disruptions. In this sense, the added value of liberal ideas lay also in the fact that they were easily compatible with the conservative Brahminical social outlook. Liberal ideas and values were also useful to refute both the paternalistic and the despotic conception of sovereign power and therefore to question the abuses of power of the colonial state. But liberalism was not only about the absence of social constraints and state violence, it also contained constructive elements and inspired a concrete state project that rested on a constitutional political system which would gradually represent the Indian people. It was therefore an effective ammunition for shooting at the political inconsistency of the British rulers and the perfect language in which to frame discourses of political and civil rights.

The call for the intervention of the state as a factor of socio-economic change, crucial for India to catch up with the more 'advanced' societies of the West, is another recurring theme in Gokhale's political vision. At the same time, however, as already seen in this chapter, since the initial phase of his political career, Gokhale promoted civic activism through voluntarism; to this he committed in the first person, as a means not only to compensate for the limited responsibility of the colonial state for the welfare of its subjects, but also to control and direct colonial state policy. We see here *in nuce* two aspects that would remain central not only for Gokhale but also, broadly speaking, to the following decades of Indian history. The first is the discourse about the need to balance (colonial) state power with the initiatives within civil society. The second is that civil society, which would become increasingly animated by rich associational cultures, allowed participation in initiatives of social relevance that fostered inclusion and membership of a nation in the making and conferred a sense of moral superiority to those who took part in them.

Finally, it has already become visible what the following chapters of this book further explicate, namely that national emancipation as envisaged by

Gokhale was not only about modernization, understood as technological and economic improvement, but also about modernity as a project involving societal and political liberation. As seen ahead, these two aspects of nation building were closely intertwined, and both were functional to the goal of Gokhale's nationalist programme of preparing India for the long-term goal of freedom.

Notes

1. This administrative subdivision of 'British' India had Bombay as its capital and comprised most of today's Indian states of Maharashtra and Gujarat, parts of Karnataka, Pakistan's Sindh province and, for administrative reasons, the Aden colony and Zanzibar. Unless I refer explicitly to the contemporary state of the Indian Union, when I use the term 'Maharashtra' in this book, I generally mean the cultural region where Marathi was broadly spoken. This area, corresponding *grosso modo* with the Konkan, Pune and Nasik divisions of contemporary Maharashtra, included Bombay, the coastal Konkan districts and parts of the Deccan Plateau comprising important urban centres like Pune, Ahmednagar, Nasik, Satara and Khandesh.
2. Richard Cashman, *The Myth of the Lokamanya*, University of California Press, Berkeley 1975, p. 19.
3. On the social structure of Western India and on Chitpavans, see Gordon Johnson, 'Chitpavan Brahmans and Politics in Western India', in E.R. Leach and S.N. Mukherjee (eds.), *Elites in South Asia*, CUP, Cambridge 1970, pp. 95–118; Gail Omvedt, *Cultural Revolt in a Colonial Society: The Non Brahman Movement in Western India, 1873 to 1930*, Scientific Socialist Education Trust, Bombay 1976, pp. 76–78; Stewart Gordon, *Marathas, Marauders and State Formation in Eighteenth-Century India*, OUP, Oxford 1994; Veena Naregal, *Language Politics, Elites, and the Public Sphere*, Permanent Black, New Delhi 2001; Uma Chakravarti, *Rewriting History, The Life and Times of Pandita Ramabai*, Kali for Women, Delhi 1998, pp. 43–106. For the enforcement of caste boundaries under the Peshwai, see Sudha V. Desai, *Social Life in Maharashtra under the Peshwas*, Bombay Popular Prakashan, Bombay 1980, p. 40. See pages 30–61 of the same book for the specificities of caste in the region.
4. Rao, *Foundations of Tilak's Nationalism*, pp. 23–36.
5. Sumit Sarkar, *Modern India 1885-1947*, Palgrave Macmillan, New York 1989, pp. 66–76.
6. For the history of education, see among many others, Parimala V. Rao, "Myth and Reality in the History of Indian Education", *Espacio, Tiempo y Educación*, Vol. 6, n. 2 (2019), pp. 217–234; Sanjay Seth, *Subject Lessons: The Western Education of Colonial India*, Duke University Press, Durham and London 2007, pp. 159–182; Sabyasachi Bhattacharya (ed.), *The Contested Terrain: Perspectives on Education in India*, Orient Longman Limited, Hyderabad, India 1998. For a survey of the historiographical debates on education in India, see Catriona Ellis, "Education for All: Reassessing the Historiography of Education in Colonial India", *History Compass*, Vol. 7, n. 2 (2009), pp. 363–375; Tim Allender, "Understanding Education and India: New Turns in Postcolonial Scholarship", *History of Education*, Vol. 39, n. 2 (2010), pp. 281–288; Barnita Bagchi, "Connected and Entangled Histories: Writing Histories of Education in the Indian Context," *Paedagogica Historica*, Vol. 50, n. 6 (2014), pp. 813–821. For the continuities and discontinuities between pre-colonial and colonial school system as well as for a transnational perspective on the actors that

shaped the colonial educational system, see Jana Tschurenev, *Empire, Civil Society, and the Beginnings of Colonial Education in India*. CUP, 2019.

7. See Parimala V. Rao, 'Introduction', in Parimala V. Rao (ed.), *New Perspective on the History of Indian Education*, Orient Blackswan, New Delhi 2014, pp. 1–42; Chakravarti, *Rewriting History*, Chapter 2.

8. Kenneth Jones, *Socio-Religious Reform Movements in British India*, CUP, Cambridge 1989, p. 124.

9. Wasudeo Balwant Phadke, the author of a series of robberies and raids in the Deccan, was a Chitpavan. A few days before Phadke's arrest, Sir Richard Temple, the governor of Bombay, could not help expressing his anxiety in a letter to the Viceroy Lytton: "Barely sixty years have elapsed since the Chitpavans ceased to be rulers – the memory of all this is still to this day comparatively fresh in the minds of the Natives, fresher far than the memory of most of the great political events of Indian history. Now the Chitpavan tribe still exists in vigour and prosperity. They are inspired with national sentiment and with an ambition bounded only with the bounds of India itself" (Sir Richard Temple to Lord Lytton, 9 July 1879, Lytton papers, quoted in Nanda, *Gokhale*, p. 13.).

10. Gopal Ganesh Agarkar, close associate of Gokhale, is just one among many who, in these years, was not interested in the material benefits of an education in English. As soon as he got his Master's Degree in Law, he wrote to his mother asking her to abandon the hope that he would pursue a career in the service of the government and get a fat salary, as he was determined to live a poor man's life with the purpose of educating his countrymen who had less access to knowledge (P.M. Limaye, *The History of the Deccan Education Society*, Deccan Education Society, Poona 1935, p. 3).

11. Ravinder Kumar, 'The New Brahmans of Maharashtra', in D.A. Low (ed.), *Soundings in Modern South Asian History*, University of California Press, Berkeley 1968, pp. 95–130, here 110.

12. Anil Seal, *Emergence of Indian Nationalism, Competition and Collaboration in the Later Nineteenth Century*, CUP, Cambridge 1968, pp. 70–71; and Ellen McDonald, "City-hinterland relations and the development of a regional elite in nineteenth century Bombay", *Journal of Asian Studies* (Aug. 1974), pp. 583–584.

13. C.A. Bayly, 'Afterword: Bombay's "Intertwined Modernities" 1780–1880', in Michael S. Dodson and Brian Hatcher (eds.), *Trans-Colonial Modernities in South Asia*, Routledge, Abingdon and New York 2012, pp. 231–248, here p. 245.

14. The Elphinstone College was funded by well-off inhabitants of Bombay by public subscriptions in honour of the Governor Mountstuart Elphinstone.

15. On 'traditional' education in Poona and in the region at large, see Madhav M. Deshpande, "Pune: An Emerging Center of Education in Early Modern Maharashtra", *International Journal of Hindu Studies*, Vol. 19 (2015), pp. 59–96; Madhav M. Deshpande, 'Pandit and Professor: Transformations in the 19th Century Maharashtra', in Axel Michaels (ed.), *The PANDIT: Traditional Scholarship in India*, Manohar Publishers, Delhi 2001, pp. 119–153.

16. Despite government schools were in theory open to all castes, in reality, they were very unequally accessible, if not closed to the lowest ones. Besides Brahmans – both Chitpavan and Saraswat – there were other traditional 'literary' upper castes from which students mostly came, such as Prabhus, a scribal caste mainly found in Poona and Bombay, and, to a lesser extent and mainly in Bombay, from communities like Parsis and Goanese, which had undergone Western influence in the previous hundred years. Among those who had access to the higher levels of education, there were also few Muslims,

members of the aristocratic Shaikhs, legacy of the Muslim rule in the region before the 17th century. This pattern remained substantially unchanged even after the introduction by the Department of Education of fellowships for all castes in secular colleges and schools in 1859 (Jones, *Socio-Religious Reform Movements*, p. 137). In order to understand the colonial rule's positioning towards caste power relations and the patterns of dominance of the higher castes in educational institutions and new professions created by the British administration, I find very useful Chakravarti, *Rewriting History*, chapter 2. See also Ellen E. McDonald, "English Education and Social Reform in Late Nineteenth Century Bombay: A Case Study in the Transmission of a Cultural Ideal", *The Journal of Asian Studies*, Vol. 25, n. 3 (1966), pp. 453–470, here 454.

17. For the changes in the educational paradigms from the *Peshwai* to the colonial period, see Deshpande, "Pune: An Emerging Center of Education in Early Modern Maharashtra."

18. Raja Dixit, "Liberalism in Renascent India with special reference to J.S. Mill and Maharashtra" (draft paper), presented at Conference on *Motilal Nehru and his Times* at NMML, New Delhi, 16 and 17 January 2014; A.R. Kulkarni, 'The Drain Theory and Maratha Intellectuals in Nineteenth Century', in Kulkarni, A.R. and N.K. Wagle (eds.), *State Intervention and Popular Response: Western India in the Nineteenth Century*, Popular Prakashan, Mumbai 1999, pp. 115–129; Neeraj Hatekar, "Empire and the Economist: Analysis of 19th Century Economic Writings in Maharashtra", *Economic and Political Weekly*, Vol. 38, n. 5 (2003), pp. 469–479; J.V. Naik, 'Social Reform Movements in the Nineteenth and Twentieth Centuries in Maharashtra: A Critical Survey', in S.P. Sen (ed.), *Social and Religious Reform Movements in the Nineteenth and Twentieth Centuries*, Indian Institute of Historical Research, Calcutta 1979, pp. 284–285. On the emergence of the non-Brahman movement, see Rosalind O'Hanlon, *Caste, Conflict and Ideology. Mahatma Jotirao Phule and Low Caste Protest in Nineteenth-Century Western India*, Cambridge 2002 (first published 1985).

19. J.C. Masselos, *Towards Nationalism. Group Affiliations and the Politics of Public Associations in Nineteenth Century Western India*, Popular Prakashan, Bombay 1974, p. 79.

20. T.K. Shahani, *Gopal Krishna Gokhale: A Historical Biography*, RK Mody, Bombay 1929, p. 29.

21. V.S. Srinivasa Sastri, *Life of Gopal Krishna Gokhale*, Bangalore Printing and Publishing Co, Bangalore 1937, pp. 4–5. To have a good memory was a requirement of the education system in colonial India, where rote memorisation was one of the learning methods adopted by students to study all subjects through the English medium at high school and college levels. Out of their wider cultural and intellectual contexts, books in English became texts to learn 'by heart' (McDonald, "English Education and Social Reform," p. 456).

22. The fees could be as cheap as 30% less than government schools depending on the standard. Also, there were 15% of free studentships reserved for poor and deserving students, whereas in government schools the percentage was 5% (Limaye, *History of the Deccan Education Society*, p. 24).

23. Shahani, *Gokhale*, p. 46.

24. For a comprehensive history of the Deccan Education Society, see Limaye.

25. Gopal Krishna Gokhale, *Arithmetic for High Schools* (Revised and in part rewritten by V.B. Naik), MacMillan, London 1943. According to B.R. Nanda, the book, initially published by Arya Bhushan Press, was reprinted in 1896 by Macmillan and sold 312,000 copies (Nanda, *Gokhale*, p. 61).

26. Burke's well-known *Reflections on the French Revolution* became a very popular textbook in Indian colleges because the British considered it appropriate to

counteract the effect of the French revolutionary ideals thanks to its emphasis on gradual change and social order. But when Burke became the source of political inspiration in the national sense by virtue of his view on liberty, which to him was the birthright of humankind, Lord Curzon wanted to remove it from the texts of the Calcutta University, because [it was] 'dangerous food for the Indian students' (Suresh Chandra Ghosh, "The genesis of Curzon's University Reforms, 1899–1905" in Rao, *New Perspectives*, pp. 224–268, here 235, quoted from Curzon Papers, Letter from Curzon to Maclean, 14 February 1900, letter 44). Yet, the Senate of the University, still independent from governmental control before the reforms later introduced by Lord Curzon, refused the proposals in terms of textbooks advanced by the Viceroy and by the government (*Ibidem*).

27. Shahani, *Gokhale*, pp. 53–54.
28. Gokhale, "The Needs of India", Address at the New Reform Club, 15 November 1905, *GSW*, Vol. II, p. 334.
29. Gokhale suggested that the knowledge of English history could be an antidote against radical tendencies in India. In July 1911 during a debate on the revision of the Arts Course at the University of Bombay, according to which History ceased to be a compulsory subject in the curriculum, Gokhale rejected the view expressed by some English newspapers that the famous 1910 Nasik conspiracy case had been caused by the study of English history. On the contrary, he maintained that the Nasik incident took place *in spite of* it – a further proof being that in Bengal, where the majority of episodes of violent resistance took place, the study of history was not compulsory ("History Teaching in Bombay", *GSW*, Vol. III, p. 203).
30. Paranjpe, *Gokhale*, p. 17. See also Dinshaw Edulji Wacha, *Reminiscences of the Late Honourable Mr. G. K. Gokhale*, H. T. Anklesaria, Bombay 1915, pp. 6–10.
31. Paranjpe, *Gokhale*, p. 24.
32. Gokhale contributed occasionally to the *Mahratta*. For example, in 1886 he wrote a series on war in Europe.
33. Aravind Ganachari, *Gopal Ganesh Agarkar: The Secular Rationalist Reformer*, Popular Prakashan, Mumbai 2005.
34. Stanley A. Wolpert, *Tilak and Gokhale. Revolution and Reform in the Making of Modern India*, OUP, New Delhi 1989 (first published 1961), p. 38.
35. On these complex issues concerning the link between tradition and Hinduness/Indianness, see for example the introduction in Andrew Sartori, *Bengal in Global Concept History: Culturalism in the Age of Capital*, University of Chicago Press, London and Chicago 2008.
36. Sanjay Palshikar, 'Virtue, Vice and the Origins of Militant Nationalist Thought in Western India', in V.R. Mehta and Thomas Pantham (eds.), *Political Ideas in Modern India: Thematic Explorations*, Sage, Thousand Oaks 2006, p. 27. The most authoritative work on the non-Brahman movement and one of its early promoters, Jyotirao Phule is O'Hanlon, *Caste, Conflict and Ideology*.
37. A very bitter letter from Agarkar to Tilak dated 25 December 1888 shows that, besides ideological divergences, a strong clash of personalities had caused them to fall out (Agarkar to Tilak, 25 December 1888, Agarkar Papers, NMML).
38. The authorship of articles is not always certain, though.
39. Agarkar to Sadashiv Vishnu Bhagwat, 8 September 1888, Agarkar Papers. Sadashiv was Agarkar's uncle, whom Agarkar kept updated about the situation in the Deccan Education Society and about his own activities.
40. Letter from Agarkar to Sadashiv Vishnu Bhagwat, 7 April 1889, Agarkar Papers, NMML. In November 1889, the number of subscribers was around 2200: it was a remarkable achievement given the recent creation of the paper (letter from Agarkar to uncle, 25 November 1889).

41. On Spencer's and other Social Darwinists' influence on Indian intellectuals, see Bayly, *Recovering Liberties*, pp. 256–259; Harald Fischer-Tiné, *Shyamji Krishnavarma: Sanskrit, Sociology, and Anti-Imperialism*, Routledge, London and New Delhi 2014; Shruti Kapila, "Self, Spencer and Swaraj", *Modern Intellectual History*, Vol. 4, n. 1 (2007), pp. 109–27. Spencer's 'scientific' approach to social change, although purged of the racial aspects of natural selection, appeared to Indian intellectuals – both conservatives and radicals – as a plausible doctrine that explained the inevitability of changes that they saw as fundamental for their society to survive, such as social efficiency and evolutionism (see also Charles H. Heimsath, *Indian Nationalism and Hindu Social Reform*, Princeton University Press, Bombay 1964, p. 50).

42. Agarkar's writings in Marathi dealing with these topics have been collected in *Nibandh Sangraha* (Essay Collection) (edited by M.D. Altekar), Poona 1940.

43. Ganachari, *Agarkar*, p. 23 ff. See also Pratibha Bhattacharya, 'Overview of the Reformist Movement in Maharashtra with Special Reference to Lokahitavadi and Gopal G. Agarkar', in N.K. Wagle (ed.), *Writers, Editors, and Reformers*, pp. 166–172.

44. For Spencer's anti-imperialism, see Fischer-Tiné, *Shyamji Krishnavarma*, p. 127.

45. Rajendra M. Vora, 'Liberal Thought in Maharashtra from 1850 to 1920', unpubl. Ph.D. Dissertation, University of Pune 1974, p. 235.

46. A bill tabled by Dadabhai Naoroji, who in 1892 had become the first member of the British Parliament from South Asia, had been dropped in 1893 due to lack of support in the House of Commons.

47. *Sudharak*, Untitled, 22 May 1893. Dealing with the regulations defining the 1892 Indian Councils Act, Gokhale wrote that "In all countries where the principle of representation is in operation, it is the territorial principle and not that of class interests that is mainly adopted. The number of those who do not belong to any specially prominent class and yet who pay taxes and are bound by the laws of their legislature must in every country be overwhelmingly large, and the interests of such men can be safeguarded only by giving territorial representation. Minorities however important, ought to be taken into account after proper care is taken of the interests of the general public and we must therefore repeat that in choosing the principle of classes and interests, instead of the territorial principle, the Bombay Government have been guilty of an entire perversion of all right principles of representation."

48. *Sudharak*, Untitled, 3 June 1895.

49. Gail Minault, *Secluded Scholars: Women's Education and Muslim Social Reform in Colonial India*, OUP, Oxford 1998, chapter 3; Francesca Orsini, *The Hindi Public Sphere, 1920–40*, CUP, Cambridge 2002, chapter 4.

50. Charu Gupta, *Sexuality, Obscenity, Community. Women, Muslims and the Hindu Public in Colonial India*, Permanent Black, New Delhi 2001, pp. 140–150; Charu Gupta, 'Shiv Sharma Mahopdeshak: Women's Education. A Brief Commentary and Translation', in Charu Gupta (ed.), *Gendering Colonial India: Reforms, Print, Caste and Communalism*, Orient Blackswan, New Delhi 2012, pp. 360–369.

51. Anshu Malhotra, 'Bhai Sadhu Singh: Witches: That is the Siyapa of the Self-Willed Women A Brief Commentary and Translation by', in *Gendering Colonial India: Reforms, Print, Caste and Communalism*, pp. 354–359.

52. *Sudharak*, "Hindu society and reform", 16 October 1893.

53. *Sudharak*, Untitled, 2 January 1983.

54. *Ranade: His wife's Reminiscences*, translated by Kusumavati Deshpande. From Ramabai Ranade's Marathi Original *Amchya Ayushatil Kahi Athavani (Memoirs of Our Life Together)*, Publications Division, Ministry of Information and Broadcasting, Gov. of India, September 1963.

55. It is worth noticing that well educated women like Pandita Ramabai, founder of the Sharada Sadan, created not little discomfort even among reformers in Western India. While her initiative to educate Hindu high-caste widows at the Sharada Sadan (Home of learning) was initially well received by the reformers (and significantly enough, although only for a very short period, by the extremists too), the outstanding success of Pandita Ramabai's school – especially after it was shifted from Bombay to Poona in 1890 – made reformers like Ranade and Bhandarkar dissociate from the Sadan, whose activities were perceived as being in competition with theirs, especially those of the High School for Girls (see below). On this particular aspect, see Meera Kosambi, *Pandita Ramabai, Life and Landmark Writings*, Routledge, London 2016, pp. 189–190 and Padma Anagol, *The Emergence of Feminism in India, 1850-1920*. Routledge, Abingdon and New York 2016, pp. 37–50.

56. For a recent discussion on this, see Sanjay Seth, "Nationalism, Modernity, and the 'Woman Question' in India and China", *The Journal of Asian Studies*, Vol. 72, no. 2 (2013), pp. 273–297.

57. The recent work by Rachel Sturman, *The Government of Social Life in Colonial India. Liberalism, Religious Law and Women's Rights*, CUP, Cambridge 2012 shows that, although the family was increasingly conceived as a private sphere where the state should not intervene, it actually became critical as a political object with which the colonial state was concerned and operated to effectively act on social life. The family then was a realm of ongoing contestation between the colonial state and anticolonial politics, and not as Partha Chatterjee claims (Partha Chatterjee, "The Nationalist Resolution of the 'Women's Question'", in Kumkum Sangari and Sudesh Vaid (eds.), *Recasting Women: Essays in Indian Colonial History*, Rutgers University Press, New Brunswick, NJ 1990, pp. 233–253) a domain where Indian nationalists could retain their sovereignty versus the colonial power (see especially part II of the book, pp. 109–238 and pp. 24–27 of the introduction).

58. This is now the famed Huzurpaga school, which is still situated in Lakshmi road, on a piece of land donated by the princely state of Sangli. The school has trained several generations of female social reformers, political activists, scientists and intellectuals.

59. *Mahratta*, 'Higher Female Education', 24 August 1884.

60. On Tilak's sophisticated patriarchal arguments against female education, see Parimala V. Rao, "Women's Education and the Nationalist Response in Western India: Part I—Basic Education", *Indian Journal of Gender Studies*, Vol. 14, n. 2 (2007), pp. 307–316.

61. According to Shahani, it was a very serious and lethal form of anaemia, whereas Nanda writes that she had leprosy. Both Shahani and Nanda, and all subsequent Gokhale biographers, attribute to this re-marriage the decision made by Gokhale – fearing to be judged a laughingstock of Maharashtrian traditionalist society – not to pursue a career in social reform but in politics. Yet, this statement is not really substantiated by evidence, *a fortiori* given the efforts that Gokhale made to foster social reformism through the SIS and its sister association Seva Sadan. At the same time, it is undeniable that reformers were closely scrutinised to see whether they lived up to their ideals; in fact, the traditionalists were always ready to point to inconsistencies in their rivals' behaviour. For instance, the fact that Ranade, after the first wife's death, did not marry a widow as was urged by his reformist fellows, but an 11-year-old 'virgin,' tarnished his credibility and continued to weigh on his future actions. See Chakravarti, *Rewriting History*, p. 216.

62. Shahani, *Gokhale*, pp. 51–53.

63. Ibid., p. 76.

64. Nanda, *Gokhale*, pp. 65–66.
65. "Special Marriage Bill", 26 February 1912, Imperial Legislative Council, *GSW*, Vol. II, pp. 264–265. The Special Marriage Bill had been introduced by Bhupendra Nath Basu in the Imperial Legislature. It aimed at revising the Special Marriage Act of 1872 which excluded religious and caste barriers, legalised divorce and prohibited polygamy, but was limited only to those who did not profess any of the recognised religions of India. Bhupendra Nath Basu wanted to extend it to all Hindus (see Gupta, *Sexuality, Obscenity, Community*, pp. 138–140). It was opposed by the legislature and was rejected, despite the strong favour of, among others, Gokhale and, significantly, Muhammad Ali Jinnah. One of the arguments against the proposal was that it would cause the 'degeneration' of the Hindu race.
66. In Maharashtra, these two factions corresponded largely to Congressmen and cultural nationalists.
67. Limaye, *Deccan Education Society*, pp. 101–126.
68. See ahead.
69. Johnson, "Chitpavan Brahmans and Politics", p. 108.
70. Parimala V. Rao, "New Insights into the Debates on Rural Indebtedness in 19th Century Deccan", *Economic and Political Weekly*, Vol. 44, n. 4 (2009), pp. 55–61, here 56–57.
71. Ranade had been forced by the family to marry Ramabai – an illiterate 11-year-old girl – to prevent him from bringing shame to the entire family by marrying a widow, as several reformers had done. Ramabai became an original thinker and activist independently from her husband. See Anagol, *The Emergence of Feminism in India*, chapter 3, passim. For a discussion on the Hindu widow as central to the cultural encounter between coloniser and colonised, see Jyoti Atwal, *Real and Imagined Widows: Gender Relations in Colonial North India*, Primus Books, Delhi 2016, chapter 1.
72. Palshikar, 'Virtue, Vice and the Origins of Militant Nationalist Thought in Western India', pp. 30–31.
73. L.V. Kaikini, *The Speeches and Writings of Sir Narayan G. Chandavarkar*, MGPM, Bombay 1911, p. 72.
74. Only those who were willing to eat bread made by a Christian and drink water fetched by a Muslim – practices normally forbidden by caste prescriptions – could become members. Rao, *Foundations of Tilak's Nationalism*, p. 12.
75. M.G. Ranade, 'Hindu Protestantism', address delivered at the Prarthana Samaj Mandir in 1895, in *The Wisdom of a Modern Rishi. Writings and Speeches of Mahadev Govind Ranade with an address on Rishi Ranade by the Rt. Hon'ble V.S. Srinivas Sastri* (edited by T.N. Jagadisan), Rochouse and Sons Ltd., Madras 1942, pp. 81–87. In the same book, see also 'The Saints and Prophets of Maharashtra', pp. 88–107.
76. Mahadev Govind Ranade, *Rise of the Maratha Power*, Punalekar, Bombay 1900.
77. See also Philip Constable, "The Marginalization of a Dalit Martial Race in Late Nineteenth- and Early Twentieth-Century Western India", *The Journal of Asian Studies*, Vol. 60, n. 2 (2001), pp. 439–478, here 446.
78. Before them, Ramkrishna Vishwanath, Lokahitawadi Gopal Hari Deshmukh (1823–1892), and Krishna Shastri Chiplunkar (1824–1878), all conversant with western economic and political thought, produced works in Marathi on economics, formulating a sort of blue-print for the industrial development of the country. Vishwanath, in particular, in his *Thoughts on ancient and present conditions of Hindustan and the fitter consequences* (in Marathi, Bombay 1843) elaborated a critique of the economic nature of the *Raj*, which, while maintaining that the only way for India to be rescued was to develop a scientific and industrial culture, set the foundations for the more sophisticated 'drain

theory' developed by Naoroji. See A.R. Kulkarni, 'The drain Theory and Maratha Intellectuals in Nineteenth Century', in Kulkarni, A.R. and N.K. Wagle (eds.), *State Intervention and Popular Response: Western India in the Nineteenth Century*, Popular Prakashan, Mumbai 1999, pp. 115–129. See also Neeraj Hatekar, "Empire and the Economist: Analysis of 19th Century Economic Writings in Maharashtra", *Economic and Political Weekly*, Vol. 38, n. 5 (2003), pp. 469–479.

79. Sturman, *The Government of Social Life*, pp. 86–92, 171–195. See also *Ranade's Economic Writings*, ed. by Bipan Chandra, Gyan Publishing House, New Delhi 1990 and Rajendra Vora, 'Two Strands of Indian Liberalism: The Ideas of Ranade and Phule', in Thomas Pantham and Kenneth L. Deutsch (eds.), *Political Thought in Modern India*, Sage, New Delhi 1986, pp. 92–109.

80. See Chakravarti, *Rewriting History*, pp. 175–186. On the clash between Reformers and Extremists around the Age of Consent Bill see Rao, *Foundations of Tilak's Nationalism*, pp. 123–130. It is particularly interesting that while Tilak pretended that he was the leader of the Hindu orthodox opinion in opposing the bill, the Shankaracharya, who can be considered a sort of Pope for the Hindus, supported the reformers' views (p. 128). For an insightful theoretical perspective on women and rights, see also Tanika Sarkar, "A Prehistory of Rights: The Age of Consent Debate in Colonial Bengal", *Feminist Studies*, Vol. 26, n. 3 (2000), pp. 601–622. It is interesting to note the reflections by Tanika Sarkar on the use of the term 'consent,' which can be easily linked to the feminist critique of John Rawls' concept of choice and his perception of the family as a voluntary association. For a discussion on child-marriage legislation with a special focus on the construction of the child in colonial India, see Ishita Pande, *Sex, Law and the Politics of Age. Child Marriage in India 1891-1937*, CUP, Cambridge 2020.

81. For Malabari's initiative and more generally his engagement with the 'women's question,' see Harmony Siganporia, *I am the Widow: An Intellectual Biography of Behramji Malabari*, Orient Blackswan, Hyderabad 2018, pp. 135–199.

82. Anagol, *The Emergence of Feminism*, pp. 199–218. The work of Tarabai Shinde, daughter of a social reformer linked to Phule's Sathyashodak Samaj, is just one example – yet to be fully acknowledged – of Maharashtrian women's capacity to elaborate a feminist critique of gender relations and female oppression. It was published in 1882, that is before the Age of Consent debate started stirring the region. See *Stri Purusha Tulana* (translated and edited by Rosalind O'Hanlon as *A comparison Between Men and Women: Tarabai Shinde and the Critique of Gender Relations in Colonial India* with an Introduction, OUP, Madras 1994).

83. Gayatri Chakravorty Spivak, *A Critique of Postcolonial Reason: Toward a History of the Vanishing Present*, Harvard University Press, Cambridge 1999, pp. 266–267.

84. See Anagol, *The Emergence of Feminism*, pp. 207–208. The ubiquitous fear of the physical degeneration of the nation among reformers is obvious in Dayaram Gidumal, *The Status of Woman in India or A Handbook for Hindu Social Reformers*, Fort Printing Press, Bombay 1889.

85. Letter from Gokhale to G.V. Joshi, 3 March 1891, *GP*.

86. It was mainly because of Tilak's pressure that the Social Conference began to be held separately from the Congress sessions, from 1895 onwards.

87. Manu Goswami, *Producing India. From Colonial Economy to National Space*, University of Chicago Press, Chicago 2004, pp. 244–245.

88. Ibid., p. 11.

89. M.G. Ranade, 'Indian Political Economy', in M.G. Ranade (ed.), *Essays on Indian Economics: A Collection of Essays and Speeches*, Taraporevala Sons & Co., Bombay 1900, pp. 1–39.

90. See for example 'Import Duty on Sugar', in R.P. Patwardhan and D.V. Ambekar (eds.), *GSW*, Deccan Sabha, Asia Publishing House, Vol. I, Poona 1962, 9 March 1911, pp. 335–338 and *The Leader*, Editorial, 11 April 1911.
91. Shahani, *Gokhale*, p. 68.
92. From 1880, the Sabha started publishing also a journal in Marathi, the *Poona Sarvajanika Sabheche Masik Pustak* (Monthly Journal of the PSS) to reach out to the large Marathi-speaking public.
93. John Somerwell Hoyland, *Gopal Krishna Gokhale: His Life and Speeches*, YMCA Publishing House, Calcutta 1933, pp. 14–15.
94. "Five Years Administration of Lord Harris", *QJPSS*, April 1895, p. 2.
95. "The Exigencies of Progress in India", *QJPSS*, April 1893, Independent Section, pp. 1–27. Although the article's authorship has been generally attributed to Ranade on stylistic grounds (Ravinder Kumar, *Western India in the Nineteenth Century: A Study in the Social History of Maharashtra*. Abingdon: Routledge, Abingdon 2007 (1968), p. 287) – Ranade's name in fact does not appear – it could equally be authored by Gokhale, whose cultural references were already quite broad after years spent teaching at the Fergusson College and being in touch with Poona-educated elite. The themes dealt with in this article are the same that Gokhale will continue to cover in his future speeches and writings. There is therefore good reason to believe that it could have been written by him.
96. Johnson, "Chitpavan Brahmans and Politics", pp. 115–116.
97. "Indian Political Economy", *QJPSS*, October 1893, Independent Section, pp. 1–32.
98. 'The Exigencies of Progress in India', p. 9.
99. Ibid., p. 20.
100. *Sudharak*, 22 May 1893, and also "Further on", *Sudharak*, 5 June 1893, containing also excerpts of the PSS memorial presented to the government.
101. Gokhale saw certain limits in reservation policies which were not based on merit. Writing on a memorial presented by the Belgaum Sarvajanik Sabha about the rules for the recruitment in the provincial service, Gokhale expressed his agreement with the lines suggested by the local Sabha. According to Gokhale, "the service should be left open to open competition and promotion for lower grade irrespective of any distinction based on class or creed. Backward classes and classes in minorities should no doubt be encouraged by special privileges in all matters that concern their improvement moral and intellectual; but it will be always dangerous and destructive to push the principle so far as to justify their employment merely on grounds of caste and class" (*Sudharak*, 3 June 1895). Education was the way to overcome inequalities and privileges.
102. See J.C. Masselos, "The City as Represented in Crowd Action: Bombay 1893", *EPW*, Vol. 28, n. 5 (1993), pp. 182–190; S.A.A. Tirmizi, "The Cow Protection Movement and Mass Mobilization in Northern India 1882–93", *Proceedings of the Indian History Congress*, Vol. 40 (1979), pp. 575–580; Rao, *Foundations of Tilak's Nationalism*, pp. 194–195.
103. "Who is to Blame?", *Sudharak*, 21 August 1893. See also "The Bombay Government and the Bombay Riots", *Sudharak*, 15 January 1894.
104. *Sudharak*, 25 September 1893.
105. "Who is to Blame?", *Sudharak*, 21 August 1893.
106. Shabnum Tejani, *Indian Secularism: A Social and Intellectual History 1890-1950*, Permanent Black, New Delhi 2007, p. 53.
107. Ganapati was the regional version of the Shaivite elephant-headed god Ganesh. The urban mela, before Tilak revisited and politicised it, was mainly celebrated in the private domain by Hindu families.

108. See Cashman, *The Myth of the Lokamanya*, pp. 75–122; Gordon Johnson, *Provincial Politics and Indian Nationalism. Bombay and the Indian National Congress 1880–1915*, CUP, Cambridge 1973, pp. 84–90; Rao, *Foundations of Tilak's Nationalism*, pp. 158–167, 204–206.

109. "Fresh outbreak at Yeola", *Sudharak*, 12 February 1894.

110. "Mr Beck and the Mahomedans", *Sudharak*, 5 February 1894. It is true that the cow preservation movement started in the 1880s to preserve cattle for economic reasons. Nevertheless, it soon acquired socio-political connotations so much that protecting the cow – symbol of integrity and pureness in the collective imaginary of 'caste Hindus' – became a mark of respectability among Brahmans, commercial castes and even peasants with a strong element of exclusion of Muslims and untouchables (see Susan Bayly, *Caste, Society and Politics in India from the Eighteenth Century to the Modern Age*, CUP, New York 2001, pp. 219–220). By the time Gokhale wrote, he should have known the aggressive turn taken by the *Gaurakshini Sabhas* (the cow-protecting societies), whose activities contributed to the outbreaks of violence in much of North India in the 1890s. Having said this, it must be noted that Gokhale did not object to building slaughterhouses for the Muslim population, considering it their right ("Mofussil Municipalities Bill", Speech delivered at the Bombay Legislative Council, 12 February 1901, *GSW*, Vol. II, p. 124).

111. "The Racial Affrays", *Sudharak*, 14 August 1983.

112. See C.A. Bayly, "South Asian Liberalism under Strain c. 1900–14", Wiles Lectures (2007), www.s-asian.cam.ac.uk/wiles.html, p. 18.

113. See Nanda, *Gokhale*, pp. 66–71. These were not Gokhale's first public speeches, though. He had spoken at the Bombay Provincial Conference in November 1888 and few months later in 1889 at a meeting organised by the PSS to protest against the misrepresentation in the British press of the actions of the Bombay government.

114. "Education in India", General Meeting of the Bombay Graduates Association, 11 April 1896, GSW, Vol. III, pp. 158–176.

115. "Education in India", p. 169. On the question of character, manliness and games, see Harald Fischer-Tiné, "'Character Building and Manly Games': Viktorianische Konzepte von Männlichkeit und ihre Aneignung im frühen Hindu Nationalismus", *Historische Anthropologie*, Vol. 9, n. 3 (2001), pp. 432–455.

116. The literature, although mainly focusing on the male upper caste Hindu, is rich on this theme. It appears that physical education and fitness training became instrumental to the spread of civic ideals, norms, values, and patterns of behaviour. The underpinning conviction was that both bodily fitness and character were leading qualifications to become 'worthy' members of the nation/community in the making. See, just to name a few, Harald Fischer-Tiné, "Fitness for Modernity? The YMCA and Physical-Education Schemes in Late-Colonial South Asia (circa 1900–40)", *Modern Asian Studies*, Vol. 53, n. 2 (2019), pp. 512–559; Michael Philipp Brunner, "Manly Sikhs and Loyal Citizens: Physical Education and Sport in Khalsa College, Amritsar, 1914–47", *South Asia: Journal of South Asian Studies*, Vol. 41, n. 1 (2018), pp. 33–50; Carey A. Watt, "Cultural Exchange, Appropriation and Physical Culture: Strongman Eugen Sandow in Colonial India, 1904–1905", *The International Journal of the History of Sport*, Vol. 33, n. 6 (2016), pp. 1921–1942; Carey A. Watt, 'The Scouting Frontiers: The Boy Scouts and The Global Dimension of Physical Culture and Bodily Health in Britain and Colonial India', in Nelson R. Block and Tammy M. Proctor (eds.), *Scouting frontiers: Youth and the Scout Movement's First Century*, Cambridge Scholars Publishing, Newcastle 1999, pp. 121–142; Namrata R. Ganneri, 'The Debate on

"Revival" and the Physical Culture Movement in Western India (1900–1950)',
in Katrin Bromber, Birgit Krawietz and Joseph Maguire (eds.), *Sport across
Asia: Politics, Cultures, and Identities*, Routledge, New York 2011, pp. 121–143;
Mark Singleton, *Yoga Body: The Origins of Modern Posture Practice*, OUP, New
York 2010, chapters 4 and 5. Very important is Joseph Alter's work on the
reconfiguration of the modern Indian physical culture. See, for instance,
Joseph S. Alter, 'Yoga at the *Fin de Siècle*: Muscular Christianity with a Hindu
Twist', in John MacAloon (ed.), *Muscular Christianity in Colonial and Post-Co-
lonial Worlds*, Routledge, London and New York 2008, pp. 59–76; Joseph S.
Alter, "Physical Education, Sport and the Intersection and Articulation of
'Modernities': The Hanuman Vyayam Prasarak Mandal", *Journal of the History
of Sport*, Vol. 24 (2007), pp. 1156–1171.

117. In a note [5 February 1898, *GP* (file 203, 9)], he listed the goals he intended
to achieve in the future, that is, besides the practice of yoga, acquiring knowledge of modern and ancient history, modern and ancient philosophy, astron-
omy, geology, physiology and botany, psychology, and French; becoming
a member of the Bombay Legislative Council and of the Supreme Legislative Council and of the British Parliament "to do good to the country by all
means" in his power; becoming "a preacher of the highest philosophical religion to be spread all over the world." This last goal that Gokhale set for himself reminds us of Swami Vivekananda's commitment to spread Hinduism
and is quite striking if we consider the generally accepted image of Gokhale
as a secular politician. Vivekananda had become increasingly influential
after his success at the World's Parliament of Religions in Chicago in 1893
and there is evidence that his views had an effect on Gokhale (See chapter 2).

118. T.R. Deogirikar, *Gopal Krishna Gokhale*, Publications Division, Gov. of India,
Delhi 1992, p. 204.

119. Mohandas Karamchand Gandhi, *An Autobiography. The Story of My Experiments
with Truth*, Dover Publishing, Dover 1983, pp. 205–206. Gandhi would add "I
believed then and I believe even now, that, no matter what amount of work
one has, one should always find some time for exercise, just as one does for
one's meals. It is my humble opinion that, far from taking away from one's
capacity for work, it adds to it."

120. On this, see for example Nico Slate, *Gandhi's Search for the Perfect Diet: Eating
with the World in Mind*, University of Washington Press, Seattle 2019.

121. Ramachandra Guha, *Gandhi: The Years That Changed the World, 1914-1948*,
Random House Canada, Toronto 2018, p. 8. I am grateful to Carey Watt for
directing me to this publication as well as to the question of physical exercise
in Gandhi's autobiography.

122. See "The Re-admission of the Vernaculars into the University Curriculum",
in *QJPSS*, 1890, pp. 58–62.

123. "Education in India", p. 162.

124. "Financial Statement, 1901-02, Bombay Legislative Council", *GSW*, Vol. I,
p. 455. See chapter four for a more detailed discussion on this.

125. Gokhale to Naoroji, 3 September 1896, *GP*. Not bearing the influence that
Ranade wielded in political matters, Tilak thought he might strike at the root
of Ranade's influence, taking the PSS out of his hands. See Gokhale to G.V.
Joshi, 8 February 1896, *GP*. Gokhale was so much affected by the whole story
that he wanted to be relieved of all public responsibilities and lead an entirely
retired life (*Ibidem*). Tilak's imprudence in managing the activities of the PSS
led to a ban from the Government just after 12 months (Gokhale to Besant,
5 January 1915, *SISP*, NMML). The Deccan Sabha ceased to be active, though
still existing on paper, after Ranade's death in 1901 was revived again on the
occasion of the discussions around the Morley-Minto Reforms in 1908.

126. The Deccan Sabha Circular dated 4 November 1896, Deccan Sabha Papers, NMML.
127. From 1876–1878 and 1896–1897, recurring famines took place in India, for which colonial policies have been held responsible. See Mike Davis, *Late Victorian Holocausts: El Niño Famines and the Making of the Third World*, Verso, London 2007 and Joanna Simonow, 'Famine Relief in Colonial South Asia, 1858-1947. Regional and Global Perspectives', in M. Framke and H. Fischer-Tiné (eds.), *Routledge Handbook of the History of Colonialism in South Asia*, Routledge, London and New York 2022, pp. 497–509.
128. Gokhale and R.D. Nagarkar to James Monteath, 18 November 1896. Acting Chief Secretary, Deccan Sabha Papers, NMML.
129. J. Monteath to Gokhale and R.D. Nagarkar, 21 November 1896 and J. Monteath to Gokhale, R.D. Nagarkar and H.N. Apte, 14 December 1896, Deccan Sabha Papers, NMML.
130. For Digby's visit, see *QJPSS*, Vol. XV, n. 3 (1893), pp. 51–56.
131. "Poona's Farewell to A. O. Hume", *QJPSS*, Vol. XIV, n. 4 (1892), pp. 47–53.
132. Gokhale made this plain a few years later during a speech at the National Liberal Club in London when he said that Indian political reformers could only informally be considered allies of the Liberal Party in England as they had 'nothing to offer the Liberal Party in return of what it can do for us, except the gratitude and attachment of a helpless people, and this may not count for much in the eyes of many' ("England's Duty to India", 15 November 1905, *GSW*, Vol. II, p. 340).
133. Nicholas Owen, *The British Left and India. Metropolitan Anti-imperialism 1885–1947*, OUP, New York 2007, p. 61.
134. Other members of the Commission were D.E. Wacha for the Bombay Presidency, Surendranath Banerjea for Bengal and Subrahmanya Ayyar for Madras. See Nanda, *Gokhale*, pp. 88–102 for the Welby Commission and the positive reactions with which Gokhale was greeted.
135. "Female Education in India", *GSW*, Vol. III (1897), pp. 177–186.
136. The progressive historicism embraced by Indian intellectuals and political activists questioned the colonial discourse that depicted India as static and incapable of progress throughout history by arguing that in ancient times in the subcontinent, there had been at least some of the characteristics that were seen by the colonisers as essentially 'western.' See Bayly, *Recovering Liberties*, p. 347.
137. From the paper, it is not clear what kind of 'enlightened' freedom women should be entitled to. We can assume it meant 'moderate,' that is, embracing 'modernity' while at the same time remaining essentially 'Indian.' See above.
138. Although not dealing specifically with the question of education, most helpful is the discussion on the contraposition between male secular virtue and female *dharma* developed by Anupama Roy, *Gendered Citizenship. Historical and Conceptual Explorations*, Orient Blackswan, Hyderabad 2013, chapter 3, pp. 83–125.
139. "Female Education in India", p. 186.
140. Anagol, *The Emergence of Feminism*, p. 47.
141. Heimsath, *Indian Nationalism and Hindu Social Reform*, pp. 86–87 and 104–108.
142. Rajnarayan Chandavarkar, 'Plague Panic and Epidemic Politics in India, 1896–1914', in T.O. Ranger and Paul Slack (eds.), *Epidemics and Ideas: Essays on the Historical Perception of Pestilence*, CUP, Cambridge 1992, p. 111.
143. David Arnold, *Colonizing the Body: State Medicine and Epidemic Disease in Nineteenth-Century India*, University of California Press, Berkeley 1993, pp. 209–210.

144. On Tilak's connection with the Chapekars and on his arrest and trial, see Wolpert, *Tilak and Gokhale*, pp. 90–103. See also Sukeshi Kamra, "Law and Radical Rhetoric in British India: The 1897 Trial of Bal Gangadhar Tilak", *South Asia: Journal of South Asian Studies*, Vol. 39, n. 3 (2016), pp. 546–559.

145. Gokhale to G.V. Joshi, 15 September 1897, *GP*.

146. According to Shahani (*Gokhale*, p. 93), Gokhale's correspondents begged that their names not be revealed to the Government in connection with the reports.

147. For both Gokhale's interview and apology see "Plague Operations in Poona", *GSW*, Vol. II, pp. 160–172.

148. See "Plague Operations in Poona", p. 172.

149. Ranade to Gokhale, 29 August 1899, *GP*.

150. *Report of the Bombay Plague Committee*, Times of India Steam Press, Bombay 1898, p. 208.

151. *Kesari*, 25 September 1901, quoted in Nanda, *Gokhale*, p. 246.

152. Shahani, *Gokhale*, p. 101. As a non-official member of the Bombay Legislative Council, Gokhale suggested to the government that a medical commission be formed to investigate the alleged negative effects of the vaccine, but his advice was rejected (Proceedings of the Council of the Governor of Bombay Assembled for the Purpose of Making Laws and Regulations (hereafter PCGB), 1900, Vol. XXXVIII, p. 8).

153. Prashant Kidambi, "'An Infection of Locality': Plague, Pythogenesis and the Poor in Bombay, c. 1896–1905", *Urban History*, Vol. 31, n. 2 (2004), p. 251.

154. See for example, "Resources of Local Bodies", *GSW*, Vol. I, pp. 369–384.

155. For the electoral campaign, see Nanda, *Gokhale*, pp. 119–121.

156. "Financial Statement, Bombay Legislative Council", *GSW*, Vol. I, pp. 389–390. From the 1876 to 1878 famine onwards, the colonial state began to elaborate famine codes, the measures on which relief operations have since been based in independent India. See for example Amartya Sen, *Poverty and Famines: An Essay on Entitlement and Deprivation*, OUP, Oxford 1983.

157. PCGB, 1900, Vol. XXXVIII, pp. 9 and 47–48. The relief workers were famine-affected people who were provided by the colonial government with employment in public works, such as infrastructural projects, the construction of railways, roads and irrigation networks. In return for their labour, they received food and money. However, the meagre wage they were given was one of the reasons why so many people died in the times of famine. See Simonow, "Famine Relief", p. 499 and Stuart Sweeney, "Indian railways and famines, 1875–1914: Magic wheels and empty stomachs", *Essays in Economic & Business History*, Vol. 26 (2008), pp. 147–158.

158. For SIS relief work during famines, see Watt, *Serving the Nation*, pp. 172–176; N.M. Joshi, 'Relief work', in H.N. Kunzru (ed.), *Gopal Krishna Devadhar*, Servants of India Society, Poona 1939, pp. 133–150.

159. "Bombay Land Revenue Bill", *GSW*, Vol. I, p. 448 and the dissenting minute therein included p. 424.

160. "Bombay Land Revenue Bill", Dissenting Minute, *GSW*, Vol. I, p. 424.

161. See Nanda, *Gokhale*, pp. 124–128. William S. Caine (1842–1903), the Liberal MP and prominent temperance activist whom Gokhale met during his first journey to England and with whom he remained in contact ever since (see chapter four), was among those protesting in the House of Commons against the bill (R.C. Dutt to Gokhale, 15 and 30 August 1901, *GP*).

162. PCGB, 1901, Vol. XXXIX, p. 368. He wrote in a humble tone to Pherozeshah Mehta that he would rather be "in the wrong with you, than in the right by

myself" (V.S. Srinivasa Sastri, *My Master Gokhale: A Selection from the Speeches and Writings of V. S. Srinivasa Sastri* (edited by T.N. Jagadisan), Model Publications, Madras 1946, p. 258).

163. In his letter to Mehta, dated 15 January 1901, quoted in Nanda, *Gokhale*, p. 129, Gokhale skilfully combined the emotional jargon of self-sacrifice for the nation with a complimentary and charming style which could hardly leave a political leader like Mehta indifferent.

164. Sastri, *Life of Gokhale*, p. 36.

165. For the complete speech, see *GSW*, Vol. III, pp. 257–259.

166. Gokhale to G.V. Joshi, 19 April 1901, *GP*. Gokhale's wife, Radhabai, died the previous October as did the baby son to whom she gave birth. We find more references to Ranade's death in Gokhale's correspondence than to his wife's death, this being mentioned only in letters to Ranade and Joshi. The concern about having to take care of two young daughters is deeply felt in this correspondence.

References

Agarkar, Gopal Ganesh. *Nibandh Sangraha* (Essay Collection) (edited by M.D. Altekar), Agarkar Prakashan Mandal Poona 1940.

Allender, Tim. "Understanding Education and India: New Turns in Postcolonial Scholarship", *History of Education*, Vol. 39, n. 2 (2010), pp. 281–288.

Alter, Joseph S. "Physical Education, Sport and the Intersection and Articulation of 'Modernities': The Hanuman Vyayam Prasarak Mandal", *Journal of the History of Sport*, Vol. 24 (2007), pp. 1156–1171.

——. 'Yoga at the *Fin De Siècle*: Muscular Christianity with a Hindu Twist', in MacAloon, John (ed.), *Muscular Christianity in Colonial and Post-Colonial Worlds*, Routledge, London and New York 2008, pp. 59–76.

Anagol, Padma. *The Emergence of Feminism in India, 1850-1920*, Routledge, Abingdon and New York 2016.

Arnold, David. *Colonizing the Body: State Medicine and Epidemic Disease in Nineteenth-Century India*, University of California Press, Berkeley 1993.

Atwal, Jyoti. *Real and Imagined Widows: Gender Relations in Colonial North India*, Primus Books, Delhi 2016.

Bagchi, Barnita. "Connected and Entangled Histories: Writing Histories of Education in the Indian Context", *Paedagogica Historica*, Vol. 50, n. 6 (2014), pp. 813–821.

Bayly, C.A. 'Afterword: Bombay's "Intertwined Modernities" 1780–1880', in Michael S. Dodson and Brian Hatcher (eds.), *Trans-Colonial Modernities in South Asia*, Routledge, Abingdon and New York 2012, pp. 231–248.

——. "South Asian Liberalism under Strain c. 1900–14", Wiles Lectures (2007), www.s-asian.cam.ac.uk/wiles.html.

——. *Recovering Liberties, Indian Thought in the Age of Liberalism and Empire*, CUP, Delhi 2012 (first published 2011).

Bayly, Susan. *Caste, Society and Politics in India from the Eighteenth Century to the Modern Age*, CUP, New York 2001.

Bhattacharya, Pratibha. 'Overview of the Reformist Movement in Maharashtra with Special Reference to Lokahitavadi and Gopal G. Agarkar', in N.K. Wagle (ed.), *Writers, Editors, and Reformers: Social and Political Transformations of Maharashtra, 1830-1930*, Manohar, New Delhi 1999, pp. 166–172.

Bhattacharya, Sabyasachi (ed.). *The Contested Terrain: Perspectives on Education in India*, Orient Longman Limited, Hyderabad, India 1998.

Brunner, Michael P. "Manly Sikhs and Loyal Citizens: Physical Education and Sport in Khalsa College, Amritsar, 1914–47", *South Asia: Journal of South Asian Studies*, Vol. 41, n. 1 (2018), pp. 33–50.

Cashman, Richard. *The Myth of the Lokamanya*, University of California Press, Berkeley 1975.

Chakravarti, Uma. *Rewriting History, The Life and Times of Pandita Ramabai*, Kali for Women, Delhi 1998.

Chakravorty Spivak, Gayatri. *A Critique of Postcolonial Reason: Toward a History of the Vanishing Present*, Harvard University Press, Cambridge, MA 1999.

Chandavarkar, Narayan G. *The Speeches and Writings of Sir Narayan G. Chandavarkar* (D.V. Ambekar L.V. Kaikini), MGPM, Bombay 1911.

Chandavarkar, Rajnarayan. 'Plague Panic and Epidemic Politics in India', in T.O. Ranger and Paul Slack (eds.), *Epidemics and Ideas: Essays on the Historical Perception of Pestilence*, CUP, Cambridge 1992, pp. 1896–1914.

Chatterjee, Partha. 'The Nationalist Resolution of the "Women's Question"', in Kumkum Sangari and Sudesh Vaid (eds.), *Recasting Women: Essays in Indian Colonial History*, Rutgers University Press, New Brunswick, NJ 1990, pp. 233–253.

Constable, Philip. "The Marginalization of a Dalit Martial Race in Late Nineteenth- and Early Twentieth-Century Western India", *The Journal of Asian Studies*, Vol. 60, n. 2 (2001), pp. 439–478.

Davis, Mike. *Late Victorian Holocausts: El Niño Famines and the Making of the Third World*, Verso, London 2007.

Deogirikar, T.R. *Gopal Krishna Gokhale*, Publications Division, Gov. of India, Delhi 1992.

Desai, Sudha V. *Social Life in Maharashtra under the Peshwas*, Bombay Popular Prakashan, Bombay 1980.

Deshpande, Madhav M. 'Pandit and Professor: Transformations in the 19th Century Maharashtra', in Axel Michaels (ed.), *The PANDIT: Traditional Scholarship in India*, Manohar Publishers, Delhi 2001, pp. 119–153.

——. "Pune: An Emerging Center of Education in Early Modern Maharashtra", *International Journal of Hindu Studies*, Vol. 19 (2015), pp. 59–96.

Dixit, Raja. "Liberalism in Renascent India With Special Reference to J.S. Mill and Maharashtra" *(draft paper), presented at Conference on Motilal Nehru and His Times at NMML*, New Delhi, 16 and 17 January 2014.

Ellis, Catriona. "Education for All: Reassessing the Historiography of Education in Colonial India", *History Compass*, Vol. 7, n. 2 (2009), pp. 363–375.

Fischer-Tiné, Harald. "Fitness for Modernity? The YMCA and Physical-Education Schemes in Late-Colonial South Asia (Circa 1900–40)", *Modern Asian Studies*, Vol. 53, n. 2 (2019), pp. 512–559.

——. *Shyamji Krishnavarma: Sanskrit, Sociology, and Anti-Imperialism*, Routledge India, New Delhi 2014.

——. "'Character Building and Manly Games': Viktorianische Konzepte Von Männlichkeit Und Ihre Aneignung Im Frühen Hindu Nationalismus", *Historische Anthropologie*, Vol. 9, n. 3 (2001), pp. 432–455.

Ganachari, Aravind. *Gopal Ganesh Agarkar: The Secular Rationalist Reformer*, Popular Prakashan, Mumbai 2005.

Gandhi, Mohandas Karamchand. *An Autobiography: The Story of My Experiments with Truth*, Dover Publishing, Dover 1983.

Ganneri, Namrata R. 'The Debate on "Revival" and the Physical Culture Movement in Western India (1900–1950)', in Katrin Bromber, Birgit Krawietz and Joseph Maguire (eds.), *Sport Across Asia: Politics, Cultures, and Identities*, Routledge, New York 2011, pp. 121–143.

Ghosh, Suresh Chandra. 'The Genesis of Curzon's University Reforms, 1899–1905', in Parimala V. Rao (ed.), *New Perspectives on Indian Education*, Orient Blackswan, New Delhi 2014, pp. 224–268.

Gidumal, Dayaram. *The Status of Woman in India or A Handbook for Hindu Social Reformers*, Fort Printing Press, Bombay 1889.

Gokhale, Gopal Krishna. *Gokhale Speeches and Writings (GSW), Vol. I Economic*, in R.P. Patwardhan and D.V. Ambekar (eds.), Asia Publishing House, Poona 1962.

——. *Gokhale Speeches and Writings (GSW), Vol. II Political*, in R.P. Patwardhan and D.V. Ambekar (eds.), Asia Publishing House, Poona 1966.

——. *Gokhale Speeches and Writings (GSW), Vol. III Educational*, in D.G. Karve and D.V. Ambekar (eds.), Asia Publishing House, Poona 1967.

——. *Arithmetic for High Schools* (revised and in part rewritten by V.B. Naik), MacMillan, London 1943.

——. *Speeches of Gopal Krishna Gokhale*, in G.A. Natesan (ed.), Natesan & Co, Madras 1920.

Gordon, Stewart. *Marathas, Marauders and State Formation in Eighteenth-Century India*, OUP, Oxford 1994.

Goswami, Manu. *Producing India. From Colonial Economy to National Space*, University of Chicago Press, Chicago 2004.

Guha, Ramachandra. *Gandhi: The Years That Changed the World, 1914-1948*, Random House Canada, Toronto 2018.

Gupta, Charu. 'Shiv Sharma Mahopdeshak: Women's Education. A Brief Commentary and Translation', in Charu Gupta (ed.), *Gendering Colonial India: Reforms, Print, Caste and Communalism*, Orient Blackswan, New Delhi 2012, pp. 360–369.

——. *Sexuality, Obscenity, Community. Women, Muslims and the Hindu Public in Colonial India*, Permanent Black, New Delhi 2001.

Hatekar, A. Neeraj. "Empire and the Economist: Analysis of 19th Century Economic Writings in Maharashtra", *Economic and Political Weekly*, Vol. 38, n. 5 (2003), pp. 469–479.

Heimsath, Charles H. *Indian Nationalism and Hindu Social Reform*, Princeton University Press, Bombay 1964.

Hoyland, John Somerwell. *Gopal Krishna Gokhale: His Life and Speeches*, YMCA Publishing House, Calcutta 1933.

Johnson, Gordon. 'Chitpavan Brahmans and Politics in Western India', in E.R. Leach and S.N. Mukherjee (eds.), *Elites in South Asia*, CUP, Cambridge 1970, pp. 95–118.

——. *Provincial Politics and Indian Nationalism: Bombay and the Indian National Congress 1880–1915*, CUP, Cambridge 1973.

Jones, Kenneth. *Socio-Religious Reform Movements in British India*, CUP, Cambridge 1989.

Joshi, N.M.. 'Relief Work', in H.N. Kunzru (ed.), *Gopal Krishna Devadhar*, Servants of India Society, Poona 1939, pp. 133–150.

Kamra, Sukeshi. "Law and Radical Rhetoric in British India: The 1897 Trial of Bal Gangadhar Tilak", *South Asia: Journal of South Asian Studies*, Vol. 39, n. 3 (2016), pp. 546–559.

Kapila, Shruti. "Self, Spencer and Swaraj", *Modern Intellectual History*, Vol. 4, n. 1 (2007), pp. 109–127.

Kidambi, Prashant. "'An Infection of Locality': Plague, Pythogenesis and the Poor in Bombay, c. 1896–1905", *Urban History*, Vol. 31, n. 2 (2004), pp. 249–267.

Kosambi, Meera. *Pandita Ramabai. Life and Landmark Writings*, Routledge, London 2016.

Kulkarni, A.R. 'The Drain Theory and Maratha Intellectuals in Nineteenth Century', in A.R. Kulkarni and N.K. Wagle (eds.), *State Intervention and Popular Response: Western India in the Nineteenth Century*, Popular Prakashan, Mumbai 1999, pp. 115–129.

Kumar, Ravinder. 'The New Brahmans of Maharashtra', in D.A. Low (ed.), *Soundings in Modern South Asian History*, University of California Press, Berkeley 1968, pp. 95–130.

——. *Western India in the Nineteenth Century: A Study in the Social History of Maharashtra*, Routledge, Abingdon 2007 (1968).

Limaye, P.M. *The History of the Deccan Education Society*, Deccan Education Society, Poona 1935.

Malhotra, Anshu. 'Bhai Sadhu Singh: Witches: That is the Siyapa of the Self-Willed Women a Brief Commentary and Translation by', in Charu Gupta (ed.), *Gendering Colonial India: Reforms, Print, Caste and Communalism*, Orient Blackswan, New Delhi 2012, pp. 354–359.

Masselos, J.C. "The City as Represented in Crowd Action: Bombay 1893", *EPW*, Vol. 28, n. 5 (1993), pp. 182–190.

——. *Towards Nationalism. Group Affiliations and the Politics of Public Associations in Nineteenth Century Western India*, Popular Prakashan, Bombay 1974.

McDonald, Ellen E. "English Education and Social Reform in Late Nineteenth Century Bombay: A Case Study in the Transmission of a Cultural Ideal", *The Journal of Asian Studies*, Vol. 25, n. 3 (1966), pp. 453–470.

——. "City-Hinterland Relations and the Development of a Regional Elite in Nineteenth Century Bombay", *Journal of Asian Studies* (Aug. 1974), pp. 583–584.

Minault, Gail. *Secluded Scholars: Women's Education and Muslim Social Reform in Colonial India*, OUP, Oxford 1998.

Naik, J.V. 'Social Reform Movements in the Nineteenth and Twentieth Centuries in Maharashtra: A Critical Survey', in S.P. Sen (ed.), *Social and Religious Reform Movements in the Nineteenth and Twentieth Centuries*, Indian Institute of Historical Research, Calcutta 1979, pp. 284–285.

Nanda, B.R. *Three Statesmen: Gokhale, Gandhi and Nehru*, OUP, New Delhi 2004.

Naregal, Veena. *Language Politics, Elites, and the Public Sphere*, Permanent Black, New Delhi 2001.

O'Hanlon, Rosalind. "Contested Conjunctures: Brahman Communities and 'Early Modernity' in India", *The American Historical Review*, Vol. 118, n. 3 (2013), pp. 765–787.

——. *Caste, Conflict and Ideology: Mahatma Jotirao Phule and Low Caste Protest in Nineteenth-Century Western India*, CUP, Cambridge 2002 (first published 1985).

Omvedt, Gail. *Cultural Revolt in a Colonial Society: The Non Brahman Movement in Western India, 1873 to 1930*, Scientific Socialist Education Trust, Bombay 1976.

Orsini, Francesca. *The Hindi Public Sphere, 1920–40*, CUP, Cambridge 2002.

Owen, Nicholas. *The British Left and India: Metropolitan Anti-Imperialism 1885–1947*, OUP, New York 2007.

Palshikar, Sanjay. 'Virtue, Vice and the Origins of Militant Nationalist Thought in Western India', in V.R. Mehta and Thomas Pantham (eds.), *Political Ideas in Modern India: Thematic Explorations*, Sage, Thousand Oaks 2006.

Pande, Ishita. *Sex, Law and the Politics of Age. Child Marriage in India 1891-1937*, CUP, Cambridge 2020.

Paranjpye, R.P. *Gopal Krishna Gokhale*, Aryabhushan Press, Poona 1918.

Ranade, M.G. *Essays on Indian Economics: A Collection of Essays and Speeches*, Taraporevala Sons & Co, Bombay 1900.

——. *Ranade's Economic Writings*, in Bipan Chandra (ed.), Gyan Publishing House, New Delhi 1990.

——. *Rise of the Maratha Power*, Punalekar, Bombay 1900.

——. *The Wisdom of a Modern Rishi: Writings and Speeches of Mahadev Govind Ranade with an Address on Rishi Ranade by the Rt. Hon'ble V.S. Srinivas Sastri* (edited by T.N. Jagadisan), Rochouse and Sons Ltd., Madras 1942.

Ranade, Ramabai. *Ranade: His Wife's Reminiscences*, translated by Kusumavati Deshpande from Marathi, *Amchya Ayushatil Kahi Athavani (Memoirs of Our Life Together)*, Publications Division, Ministry of Information and Broadcasting, Gov. of India, September 1963.

Rao, Parimala V. 'Introduction', in Parimala V. Rao (ed.), *New Perspective on the History of Indian Education*, Orient Blackswan, New Delhi 2014, pp. 1–42.

——. "Women's Education and the Nationalist Response in Western India: Part I—Basic Education", *Indian Journal of Gender Studies*, Vol. 14, n. 2 (2007), pp. 307–316.

——. "Myth and Reality in the History of Indian Education", *Espacio, Tiempo y Educación*, Vol. 6, n. 2 (2019), pp. 217–234.

——. "New Insights into the Debates on Rural Indebtedness in 19th Century Deccan", *Economic and Political Weekly*, Vol. 44, n. 4 (2009), pp. 55–61.

——. *Foundations of Tilak's Nationalism. Discrimination, Education, and Hindutva*, Orient Blackswan, New Delhi 2007.

Roy, Anupama. *Gendered Citizenship. Historical and Conceptual Explorations*, Orient Blackswan, Hyderabad 2013.

Sarkar, Sumit. *Modern India 1885-1947*, Palgrave Macmillan, New York 1989.

Sarkar, Tanika. "A Prehistory of Rights: The Age of Consent Debate in Colonial Bengal", *Feminist Studies*, Vol. 26, n. 3 (2000), pp. 601–622.

Sartori, Andrew S. *Bengal in Global Concept History: Culturalism in the Age of Capital*, University of Chicago Press, London and Chicago 2008.

Seal, Anil. *Emergence of Indian Nationalism, Competition and Collaboration in the Later Nineteenth Century*, CUP, Cambridge 1968.

Sen, Amartya. *Poverty and Famines: An Essay on Entitlement and Deprivation*, OUP, Oxford 1983.

Seth, Sanjay. "Nationalism, Modernity, and the 'Woman Question' in India and China", *The Journal of Asian Studies*, Vol. 72, n. 2 (2013), pp. 273–297.

——. *Subject Lessons: The Western Education of Colonial India*, Duke University Press, Durham and London 2007.

Shahani, T.K. *Gopal Krishna Gokhale: A Historical Biography*, R.K Mody, Bombay 1929.

Shinde, Tarabai. *Stri Purusha Tulana* (translated and edited by Rosalind O'Hanlon as *A comparison Between Men and Women: Tarabai Shinde and the Critique of Gender Relations in Colonial India* with an Introduction), OUP, Madras 1994.

Siganporia, Harmony. *I Am the Widow: An Intellectual Biography of Behramji Malabari*, Orient Blackswan, Hyderabad 2018.

Simonow, Joanna. 'Famine Relief in Colonial South Asia, 1858-1947. Regional and Global Perspectives', in M. Framke and H. Fischer-Tiné (eds.), *Routledge Handbook of the History of Colonialism in South Asia*, Routledge, London and New York 2022, pp. 497–509.

Singleton, Mark. *Yoga Body: The Origins of Modern Posture Practice*, OUP, New York 2010.

Slate, Nico. *Gandhi's Search for the Perfect Diet: Eating with the World in Mind*, University of Washington Press, Seattle 2019.

Srinivasa Sastri, V.S. *Life of Gopal Krishna Gokhale*, Bangalore Printing and Publishing Co, Bangalore 1937.

——. *My Master Gokhale: A Selection from the Speeches and Writings of V. S. Srinivasa Sastri*, (edited by T.N. Jagadisan), Model Publications, Madras 1946.

Sturman, Rachel. *The Government of Social Life in Colonial India. Liberalism, Religious Law and Women's Rights*, CUP, Cambridge 2012.

Sweeney, Stuart. "Indian Railways and Famines, 1875–1914: Magic Wheels and Empty Stomachs", *Essays in Economic & Business History*, Vol. 26 (2008), pp. 147–158.

Tejani, Shabnum. *Indian Secularism: A Social and Intellectual History 1890-1950*, Permanent Black, New Delhi 2007.

Tirmizi, S.A.A. "The Cow Protection Movement and Mass Mobilization in Northern India 1882–93", *Proceedings of the Indian History Congress*, Vol. 40 (1979), pp. 575–580.

Tschurenev, Jana. *Empire, Civil Society, and the Beginnings of Colonial Education in India*, CUP, Cambridge 2019.

Vora, Rajendra M. '*Liberal Thought in Maharashtra from 1850 to 1920*', unpubl. Ph.D. Dissertation, University of Pune 1974.

——. 'Two Strands of Indian Liberalism: The Ideas of Ranade and Phule', in Thomas Pantham and Kenneth L. Deutsch (eds.), *Political Thought in Modern India*, Sage, New Delhi 1986, pp. 92–109.

Wacha, D.E. *Reminiscences of the Late Honourable Mr. G. K. Gokhale*, H. T. Anklesaria, Bombay 1915.

Watt, Carey A. "Cultural Exchange, Appropriation and Physical Culture: Strongman Eugen Sandow in Colonial India, 1904–1905", *The International Journal of the History of Sport*, Vol. 33, n. 6 (2016), pp. 1921–1942.

——. 'The Scouting Frontiers: The Boy Scouts and the Global Dimension of Physical Culture and Bodily Health in Britain and Colonial India', in Nelson R. Block and Tammy M. Proctor (eds.), *Scouting Frontiers: Youth and the Scout Movement's First Century*, Cambridge Scholars Publishing, Newcastle 1999, pp. 121–142.

——. *Serving the Nation. Cultures of Service, Association, and Citizenship in Colonial India*, OUP, New Delhi 2005.

Wolpert, Stanley A. *Tilak and Gokhale. Revolution and Reform in the Making of Modern India*, OUP, New Delhi 1989 (first published 1961).

2　Nationalism

I am by birth a Hindu, but for many years it has been the earnest aspiration
of my life to work for the advancement of this country only as an Indian.[*]

The approach in this chapter (and the next ones) departs from the previous one, where the discussions concerning Gokhale's intellectual and
political training were largely integrated into a chronological narrative of
his life. Leaving aside biographical facts and following only an approx-
imate chronological order, this chapter instead fleshes out the development of Gokhale's political vision, focusing on his idea of the nation. It
shows that for the Indian liberal, the consolidation of the nation-state –
although increasingly Indianised and realisable through the institutions
of the colonial government – was a bridgehead to 'modernity' that would
gradually de-emphasise forms of 'primordial' identities such as those associated with caste and religion. While exploring Gokhale's understanding
of Indianness and national belonging, the role he attributed to the (colonial) state as well as to the empire, and the educated classes, the chapter
demonstrates that the Indian liberal increasingly regarded nationalism as
a form of civic religion that entailed the sacralisation of the nation. Finally,
it examines Gokhale's unease towards the 'emergence' of the Muslim community as well as his increasing concern for the Depressed Classes.

Geographical entity or nation?

The 1901 election to the Imperial Legislative Council made Gokhale an
all-India leader and afforded him visibility well beyond the Indian public
sphere, both as an authoritative liberal voice against the injustice of the
colonial rule and in favour of the extension of political and civil rights
to Indians. It was in the decade following his election to the Supreme
Council – a period which corresponded approximately to the final phase

[*]　Gopal Krishna Gokhale, *Speeches of Gopal Krishna Gokhale*, edited by G.A. Natesan,
Natesan & Co, Madras 1920, p. 369.

DOI: 10.4324/9781003037422-3

of Gokhale's life and which saw important social and political developments in colonial India – that Gokhale developed and publicised a national vision, deeply rooted in the British political tradition and more generally in liberal ideas of human advancement and moral compassion.

The nation imagined by Gokhale was predicated on three main pillars, namely territorial unity as the foundation of the nation-state; the adoption of a constitutional system largely modelled on the British one and gradually freed from colonial control; and the endeavour led by the "educated classes" to realise a politically, socially and morally regenerated society. It was, therefore, a political vision of the nation, which was not rooted in the past, but which had to be built in the future. Indians would need to be educated and gradually qualify for it.[1]

The existence of the state was the overarching frame into which this 'modern' and secular national project was to be inserted. Gokhale implied that the basis of the Indian nation was the territorial unity achieved under the British administration from the 1870s onwards. From being a geographical unity well demarcated by the Indian Ocean and the Himalayan mountains, India had become for the first time a political unity, thanks to the administrative unification under British rule.[2] Unlike other contemporary thinkers, Gokhale's geographical conceptualisation of the Indian national space did not seem to depend on earlier imaginings of Hindustan or Bharatvarsha.[3] On the contrary, it depended on the colonial-bureaucratic 'production' of territory. The historical process that had allowed the overlapping of the Indian geographical and political unity was perceived as divinely predetermined to allow India to become *one* country.

Such territorial unification apart, Gokhale defined the state as the realisation of human reason, a sort of pedagogical category, which reveals a similarity with later ideas of Ambedkar.[4] As a matter of course, through government institutions, the state functioned as the legitimate unifier of a multifarious nation. This understanding of the state and its institutions is vital to grasp the reason the 'Moderate' leader never radically questioned the presence of the British Raj. The British "connection" was portrayed by Gokhale as "ordained, in the inscrutable dispensation of Providence, for India's good,"[5] to heal the manifold divisions that characterised India. Gokhale could not ignore the fact that India was a vast conglomerate of several ethnic and religious communities and feared that Indians would remain segmented by religion, caste and language; namely by those 'objective' elements of division which, in the colonial discourse, made India a geographical entity rather than a nation.[6] The unifying action of the colonial state was thus essential to avert the danger of a Balkanization process. Its continuance, although conditional on a steadily greater participation of Indians and combined with the political work of the educated classes, would contribute to holding together the nation; socio-religious divisions would become irrelevant under the wider emerging national consciousness.

Concepts of 'providence' and 'divine mission' are a recurring theme in Gokhale's speeches and writings. Such emphasis on providential intervention was appropriated from the colonial lexicon which stressed that British rule over India was part of a benevolent divine design. The adoption of those Christian theology concepts by the political sphere was fairly common in 19th-century Europe. For example, an 1854 despatch from the East India Company declared:

> It is one of our most sacred duties to be the means, as far as in us lies, of conferring upon natives of India those vast moral and material blessings which flow from the general diffusion of useful knowledge and which India may under Providence derive from her connection with England.[7]

Gokhale quoted the text to remind the rulers of the duties they were not complying with, be it compulsory education, the extension of citizenship rights, the end of racial discrimination, etc. Then, while adopting the colonial language of power masked behind the invocation of a sacred mission, he redefined it in ways that served 'national' interests.[8] If Gokhale never fully rejected the idea of a providential England-India connection, the meaning that he attributed to the divine mission, as will be seen later, was one which best suited the anticolonial nation-building agenda.

Gokhale theorised the Indian nation as a cultural (not only political) entity, too. This becomes visible in his interpretation of Indian history, which was shaped by colonial and orientalist themes.[9] As was common among his contemporaries, Gokhale endorsed the same periodisation as the one proposed by James Mill in his influential *History of British India*, dividing the history of the subcontinent in a flourishing ancient Hindu period, followed by a dark period under Muslim rule, and finally by the 'enlightening' period of British rule.[10] The stereotyped image of India as static and dormant for centuries recurs in the Indian politician's views: historically, Indian society had been over-religious, mulish to the love of free institutions and politically indifferent. 'Evil practices' and 'immoral customs' sanctioned by religion as well as a general absence among Indians of a sense of attachment beyond family or caste had contributed to India's decline as a civilisation. Such degeneration was situated vis-à-vis a romanticised view of a glorious Indian 'Hindu' past of tolerance that was mainly inspired by the works of the growing nationalist historiography.[11] The people of India were depicted as "an ancient race who had attained a high degree of civilisation long before the ancestors of European nations understood what civilisation was." India was not only the birthplace of great religions, but also the cradle of literature, philosophy, science and arts.[12] The "great destiny" of the Indian nation depended also on the capability to retain "many of those characteristics which once placed us in the van of the world's civilisation – the depth of our spirituality, our serene outlook on life, our conceptions of domestic and social duty."[13] This link between tradition and progress articulated by Gokhale reminds us of David Washbrook's argument that colonial discourses "did not – in the manner of Edward Said's 'Orientalism' paradigm – only foster a sense of Indian inferiority and Western superiority. It also flattered aspects of the Indian past, suggested that they made strong platforms for the future and encouraged their development through fusion with 'modern' instrumentalities."[14]

It is conspicuous that the concept of culture was intimately linked to Gokhale's liberal nationalism too, though in a different measure compared to the emerging forms of cultural and ethnic nationalism. While not envisioning the nation as rooted in the past, Gokhale had a residual sense of India's cultural uniqueness which existed *before* the unification of the subcontinent under British rule, and which could forge the special character of the nation-in-the-making. Like geographical unity, Indian cultural distinctiveness was a pre-political factor that provided the national project with a sense of destiny and continuity with a shared past, and therefore served as an 'objective' foundation on which the nation could stand. Establishing the distinctive character of India's culture and history was effective ammunition for questioning, on the one hand, the British discourse asserting that India lacked any common cultural traits and, on the other, for moderating the *vis polemica* of the more radical nationalists who saw liberal principles as being shallowly universal and therefore as jeopardising the national particularity.[15]

At the same time, according to Gokhale, despite all its material achievements, "India in the past was not known for that love of liberty and appreciation of free institutions which one finds to be so striking a characteristic of the West."[16] It had been its encounter with England and with Western knowledge that had brought it "under new influences," so that "a spirit of nationality had been aroused."[17] Therefore, even if Gokhale believed that India had historically been one of the greatest civilisations, he accepted the superiority of the West in terms of freedom, government and public life. A critical appraisal of India's history, thus, was crucial so as not to reproduce an idealised past in the present or to celebrate the purity of a pre-political 'nation,' as in the case of revivalist or fundamentalist cultural movements. Conversely, Gokhale held a utilitarian view of history as a means to understand the present and as guidance for the future. Thus, acknowledging the lack of a sense of freedom in India's past implied working towards its development, correcting the country's 'backwardness', and instilling a sense of unity and public spiritedness had to be firmly placed on the nation-building agenda.[18] In this manner, in a view that had much in common with the colonial epistemology, he considered the study of English history, closely associated with faith in the teleological idea of human progress and with the triumph of rationality, instrumental to making Indians "responsible and useful citizens."[19] However, if the colonial authorities' history teaching was mainly aimed at demonstrating the superiority of the Western system of thought in the course of history[20] and to justify the permanence of the colonial geopolitical order, Gokhale's progressive perspective of history saw a global movement towards liberty and democracy which had already begun to challenge the "traditional" East-West power ratio. The view of the "changeless and unresisting East" was no longer tenable:

> The aggression by Western nations in Eastern lands [...] could not go on for ever [...] as evidenced by the steady growth of a feeling of national self-respect in different Eastern lands [...]. The victories of Japan over Russia, the entry of Turkey among constitutionally-governed countries, the awakening of China, the spread of the national movement in India, Persia and Egypt, all point to the necessity of the West revising her conception of the East—revising also the standards by which she has sought in the past to regulate her relations with the East. East and West may now meet on more equal terms than was hitherto possible.[21]

The emergence of national feelings all over the world and the unfolding of a more peaceful global order were not, Gokhale argued, aporetic. The imagination of a peaceful future, informed by the same linear reading of history, was based on the conviction that if the 19th century in Europe had been a century of relative peace compared to the previous one, the 20th century was "bound to be even better."[22] Gokhale's hopeful predictions – which in light of the historical developments of the 20th century seem ingenuous to say the least – were based on his understanding of nationalism as a force of liberation rather than something inherently aggressive and dangerous for peace and democracy. Also, Gokhale overlooked those rivalries between European nations which had not disappeared but were being fought in the colonies rather than on the continental chequerboard.

On the basis of his view of history as a progressive development towards a more just world order, Gokhale also demanded that India be relieved of part of the Army expenditure that it had to sustain.[23] At the same time, interestingly, in what appears to be a contradiction, Gokhale seemed to be influenced by the social Darwinist beliefs – on the rise at the global level – in the virtues of war instilling manliness, courage and discipline.[24] The valorisation of 'martiality' resonated in his words when he commented on the fact that all classes of the Indian community were indiscriminately and compulsorily prohibited from being armed; it was a wrong which was "slowly crushing all manhood out of a whole race."[25] He also added that "citizen soldiership" was a privilege from which the Indian people were debarred so that they were denied the possibility to participate in the "responsibilities of national defence."[26] On the one hand, for Gokhale, 're-martializing' Indians, then, meant claiming for them the symbols of power, violence and masculinity that the empire believed were its prerogative. On the other hand, as noted by Niraja Gopal Jayal, military service was seen not just as a duty but also as a citizen's right. It was instrumental in claiming the ability of Indians to defend their own country and as such it was a requisite to self-government.[27]

From India to Indians: A civil religion

In Gokhale's understanding of the nation, pre-political factors like territorial unity and distinctive cultural entity were framed within the ongoing pursuit of a shared consciousness unfolding in time. Nationalism – for which Gokhale alternatively used the terms 'patriotism' or 'national self-respect' – was conceived mainly as a proactive sentiment resting on voluntarism. In other words, national self-determination revolved around the subjective will to *become* members of the national community and contribute to its welfare. This apparently tautological claim was based on a programme of political education as well as social and economic maturation, led by the educated classes, namely those politically empowered and informed Indians who used the idea of nationality as a means of identification and in whose acts and discourse the imagined Indian community was created. It was the task of these 'enlightened' subjects to infuse the people with a "we-feeling" and to set in motion a virtuous circle of moral bonds. Whoever worked towards this was a "fellow-worker, a brother."[28]

The formation of the nation became thus an emotive object of political struggle that implied a radical change in the individual, and by extension in public ethics, namely what Gokhale called "public life." The nation-builders had to carry out their work on different levels:

> First, the promotion of a closer union among the different sections of the Indian community - between the Hindus and Mahomedans - and among the different sections of the Hindus themselves; secondly, the development of a stronger and higher type of character, firm of purpose, and disciplined in action; and thirdly, the cultivation of an intense feeling of nationality throughout the country rising superior to caste and creed and rejoicing in all sacrifice for the motherland, accompanied by a spread of political education among the masses.[29]

If the state embodied modernity and rationality, the nation called for the emotional commitment of its citizens, actively seeking their solidarity, loyalty and readiness for self-sacrifice.

Liberalism provided nationalism with an ideological text that gave a certain moral imprimatur to the mission of nation-building, presented to the people as a mission having a strong moral legitimacy.[30] Gokhale maintained that "liberalism was higher than nationalism." Yet, liberalism had not to be reduced to impractical speculation about an abstract humanity, because "without a growing sense of common nationality," there was the risk of incurring an "inefficient humanitarianism."[31] Gokhale seemed to suggest that liberalism was the political aspect of universalism, which man-ifested itself in the realisation of the nation. Each individual's principal duties were towards humanity, but it was only through the more concrete cooperation in favour of the national common aim that a person could pursue that duty. The nation, in Gokhale's view, gave those individuals who wanted to be part of it a country to love as home and in which to work for the greater good of humanity: working for the country equated to working for humanity.[32]

This "call of duty" urged the country's educated men to take action in a variety of ways, like an "army of devoted missionaries." Their most pressing tasks were:

> The elevation of the depressed classes who have to be brought up to the level of the rest of our people, universal elementary education, co-operation, improvement of the economic condition of the peas-antry, higher education of women, spread of industrial and technical education, and building up the industrial strength of the country, pro-motion of closer relations between the different communities.[33]

This work, the same advocated by Gokhale through the Servants of India Society (SIS), was "the work of our country. It [wa]s also the work of Humanity."[34] National emancipation was in harmony with what Gokhale called "the liberal forces or tendencies of the age,"[35] along whose direc-tion the world and humanity were moving. Forming a nation then did not mean dividing humankind along exclusionary national lines but uniting it through the same values, ideas and practices of moral and material pro-gress, from technological advancement to human rights, across bounda-ries of cultures. Therefore, the nation was not to be built "in aggressive spirit" but had to "achieve equality with other nations in order that we may harmoniously proceed into the broad stream of the world."[36] It was not an exclusionary value, to be accomplished per se or to the detriment of other weaker nations. On the contrary, the emancipation from oppressive social and political structures was the highest duty of the nation and a contribution to the supreme end, namely the progress of Humanity. Thus, overcoming segmentations within a certain national community meant overcoming historical divisions that prevented the broader realisation of humanity. The national mission became a mission of divine origin, which did not clash with being part of the universal humankind. In this 'escha-tological' nationalism, Gokhale envisioned a hierarchy having humanity at the top where citizens exerted their duties as human beings, the nation made up of citizens exerting their rights and duties as social and political creatures and the self as a moral, rational and social being.

Nation-building then was for Gokhale a sort of civil religion that required the "spiritualisation of public life":[37] it called for the adoption of the same spirit with which religious work was carried out. This grammar of religious spirit and self-sacrifice undergirded the creation of the SIS, formed by Gokhale in 1905 with the explicit goal of building the nation through the dissemination of a sense of belonging to the country and commitment to the larger common good.[38] Its preamble to the constitution of the SIS, written by Gokhale himself, was a "confession of his political faith"[39] as well as an elucidation of what nation-building through active citizenship was.[40] Espousing sacrifice for the nation as a civic virtue, the constitution displayed the emotional tone of the mystic devotion to the nation:

> Public life must be spiritualised. Love of country must so fill the heart that all else shall appear as of little moment by its side. A fervent patriotism which rejoices at every opportunity of sacrifice for the motherland, a dauntless heart which refuses to be turned back from its object by difficulty or danger, a deep faith in the purpose of Providence that nothing can shake – equipped with these, the worker must start on his mission and reverently seek the joy which comes of spending oneself in the service of one's country.[41]

Here providence assumes a different meaning from that attributed by the colonial discourse and is clearly linked to the national mission of divine origin. It was central to the definition of nationality envisioned by Giuseppe Mazzini, for whom providence guided the course of history in the realisation of the collective good[42] and with whose thoughts Gokhale was certainly familiar. But moreover, providence was a common concept in the late 18th and 19th centuries of Western national discourses, assigning a divine mission to those peoples who were not politically unified yet.[43] Gokhale thus saw the men committed to sacrificing for, and serving, their country as instruments of such divine providence. That the constitution of the SIS echoed Mazzinian tones is clear if we read what Mazzini wrote, for instance, in *La Jenue Suisse*:

> Nationality is the role assigned by God to a people within the humanitarian travail. It is a people's mission, their task to accomplish on earth so that God's thought may be realised in the world. Nationality is the work that gives a people its right of citizenship within humanity. It is the baptism which gives character to a people and designates their rank among their brother peoples.[44]

Mazzini, largely considered one of the founding fathers of liberal nationalism, with his emancipatory imprimatur and internationalist views,[45] provided the language in which discourses of political and civil rights were framed by a variety of anticolonial nationalists in different colonial settings, especially in India and South America.[46] Most appealing about Mazzini's political ideas was the fact that he proposed a model that could serve as a message of hope for other national projects to overcome internal differences through faith in a common ideal.[47] Italy – an extremely diverse country with a poor peasant society and a great potential capitalist talent – shared many similarities with India and was seen as a fallen nation that had been able to rise up against imperialism, as could India.[48] Like Mazzini, Gokhale believed that, guided by the right political leadership, also the South Asian nation could be awakened to its common consciousness and liberate itself.

Articulating the awakening of the Indian nation in terms of a divine mission, however, contravened the fact that people should feel that their membership in the nation was based on their subjective will. In other words, the emphasis that Gokhale placed on divine providence together with the adoption of a religio-spiritual language detracted from the *choice* of national membership while making such membership appear as an almost inevitable, natural compulsion. Being unchosen, thus, the call of national duty had about it a halo of disinterestedness. For that reason, the nation, like the family, could ask for sacrifices[49] and raise deep passions.[50]

Emotional tones gained further momentum during the Swadeshi (of one's own country) movement, from 1903 to 1908, which called for the boycott of British goods and the promotion of India-made ones.[51] Despite being 'a practice of consumption' whose real objective was national productivity,[52] Swadeshi, with its moralising tones, embodied Hindu ideas of simplicity, purity and poverty, all in the name of the service of the nation.[53] The Swadeshi provoked mixed feelings among the political class that India was at an important historical juncture. Feelings of hope were spurred by the spread of political activism in Bengal and Western India, whereas riots between Muslims and Hindus[54] – to which the Hinduised discourses of Swadeshi contributed – and the emergence of a few extremist leaders at the national level were sources of anxiety for the moderate leadership of the Indian National Congress (INC). Like other intellectuals and political actors at the beginning of the century,[55] Gokhale too felt that Indian nationalism was entering a new international phase with new global "mysterious forces" at play.[56] He was also influenced by the intellectual campaign that increasingly challenged the image of the 'passive' East following Japan's victory over Russia in the 1904–1905 Russo-Japanese war. The defeat of the Russian juggernaut by a small Asian country had, in fact, generated great expectations about possible changes in the power relations between East and West.[57] It had engendered the hope that a resolute and vast programme of modernisation, like the one pursued by Japanese power, could put an end to Western hegemony and make India eligible for self-government. In the words of Gokhale, the "air" was "charged with new thoughts-currents and "a new consciousness of power was stirring [Indians] within,"[58] making them dispute Western unchallenged power.[59]

Gokhale believed that devotion to motherland was embodied by the Swadeshi: the idea of "one's own country [wa]s one of the noblest conception that ha[d] ever stirred humanity," whose influence was "so profound and so passionate that its very thought thrills and its actual touch lifts one out of oneself." The gospel of devotion had to be preached "to high and low, to prince and to peasant, in town and in hamlet, till the service of motherland becomes with us as overmastering a passion as it is in Japan." Swadeshi, being a patriotic and economic movement, presented national devotion to the mass of the people in a form "within their comprehension," investing them with the practical purpose of a highly patriotic mission. The masses could become accustomed to turning their thoughts to the country's welfare and to making voluntary sacrifices for its well-being, enabling them to take a keen interest in the national economic development while teaching the "important lesson of co-operating with one another for a national end."[60] Even if it was presented as a sacred action for the sake of the transcending nation, the sacrifice advocated by Gokhale was a 'material' one, as it sanctified individuals with a 'political' status that could be fulfilled outside the formal state structures but within the 'profanity' of the market, that is through the consumption of Swadeshi goods.

The Japanese case was exemplary for Gokhale not only for the tremendous economic and scientific achievements that had made the Far Eastern country one of the most advanced nations in a relatively short span of time, but also – and maybe more importantly for his ideology – for what he saw as a hierarchical and well-functioning society in which the people followed their leaders:

> [W]hat strikes me most in the history of Japan is the marvellous manner in which the lead of the leaders has been accepted by the bulk of the people of the land. Therein to my mind lies the great secret of Japan's success. Leaders of thought in that country laid down lines of work and the bulk of the people willingly accepted them, and patiently and quietly proceeded to do their part. The result was that there was a great concentration of effort which enabled Japan to cast off, so to say, its ancient dress and to put on new habiliments.[61]

Japan, then, had shown that the building of a 'modern' nation was successful only when the masses were directed from above and the popular will restrained for the sake of the greater national well-being. The Indian masses as well as the educated classes should learn the Japanese lesson and prove themselves to be a disciplined, self-restrained and dedicated citizenry that abided by the advice of 'earnest and patriotic' men – namely politicians of moderate views like Pherozeshah Mehta – and subordinate their judgement to those whom they were expected to follow.[62] Such appeals to unity, co-operation and subjugation – a recurring theme in Gokhale's speeches – to the views of leading public workers derived from political organicism according to which societies were organic wholes whose monolithic body could be weakened by partisan views. Conversely, they were also the consequence of the awareness of a decreasing influence being exerted by Congress as a credible political formation whose activities did not produce a concrete devolution of power.

The sacrifice of one's own views and interests, as posited by Gokhale, was not a passive sentiment, but involved the willingness to suffer for the sacred collective polity. This shows that, even among liberals like Gokhale,[63] renunciation and sacrifice, transferred from the religious domain, which entailed political indifference and abandonment of material pursuits, became politically relevant *topoi*, useful to define desireless and unattached ways of being modern and worldly.[64] Renouncing worldly well-being and personal desires for the common good was presented as an opportunity to demonstrate Indian moral and cultural superiority over the colonial rulers as well as the capability – denied by the colonial critique of Indian society – to generate a social ethic that enabled public action. Renunciation and sacrifice were also strategically used to counter those self-serving imperial narratives that claimed, on the one hand, that love of country and patriotism were unknown phenomena in India and, on the other, that Indians had to be unconditionally loyal and grateful towards British rule because of the material benefits it had generated.[65]

As we have seen, like many other members of the INC, Gokhale's knowledge was formed in a society characterised by a high level of acculturation that responded to the socio-political problems of the time, employing intellectual resources that were often the outcome of a process of multidirectional citations and whose origin is not always easy to trace. The emphasis on sacrifice and renunciation, which Gokhale deemed necessary for the class of educated Indians from which he came and to which he mostly spoke in order to retain a certain amount of control and respectability in the colonial social structure, seems to derive from the same exposition of different influences. Gokhale acknowledged the impact that Vivekananda's ideas and practices had on him: [66] the Swami was a vehicle of ideas of selfless action and social service that clearly resonated in the SIS's raison d'être. At the same time, it is difficult to deny the effect that Christian moralising values had on Gokhale's views and on the purpose of the SIS. Christian ideals and practices, underlying in many ways the colonial 'civilising' mission, shaped considerably Gokhale's encounter with Western epistemes. Compared to Ranade, who had considered the missionary activities in Maharashtra useful to "draw out [India's] faults" by engendering a reactive process of self-critique,[67] Gokhale's stance on Christian missions was more positive.[68] Also, during his visits to England, Gokhale met influential Christian figures, like the Anglican priest W. S. Caine (1942–1903), founder of the Anglo-Indian Temperance Association,[69] with whom he cooperated on the temperance front for several years.[70] What is important is that notions of sacrifice and self-abnegation, whether coming from Hindu or Christian traditions, became sources of public morality as well as instruments of social control, able to keep at bay radical tendencies of self-assertion.

The civil religion espoused by Gokhale was presented as a factor of national cohesion and tool of civic and moral improvement. Nevertheless, while promoting the sacralisation of politics, such civil religion did not identify in an exclusive and dogmatic manner with a particular political ideology. Therefore, it was different from what scholars have defined 'political religion' *stricto sensu* – even though historically such analytical distinction is never clear-cut and does not preclude the existence of common elements between the two.[71] It accepted the democratic system in-the-making, coexisted with traditional religions without fully or explicitly associating with any of them, and appealed for consensus in the observance of the injunction of public ethics. This is apparent, for instance, when Gokhale asked Indians to preach Swadeshi "not in a narrow, exclusive, intolerant spirit which says 'whoever is not with us is against us,'"[72] but "leaving each one free to select his own corner."[73] Gokhale did not fail to see that mystic devotion to the nation could rouse passions and turn a political subject into an instrument of violence, someone who might be called upon to coerce or kill in the name of the national cause. It could provide "the frontier of possibilities for the more militant, violent actions of the revolutionary groups"[74] in the post-Surat split tense climate, with the so-called Extremist wing of the INC, led by Aurobindo Ghose and Bipin Chandra Pal, calling for militant action. Also, Gokhale's call for moderation was motivated by the will to dissociate himself from the armed groups, especially considering the fact that colonial officials often tried to demonstrate the existence of links between the Congress anticolonial movement and radical organisations and individuals. That the British authorities were very keen to track those connections is expounded by the fact that during house-searching operations that took place in Dacca in late 1908 in connection with the activities of the Swadesh Bandhab Samiti, an association founded by the Bengali social reformer Ashwini Kumar Dutta (1856–1923) and aimed at promoting the consumption of Swadeshi products, the police took away Gokhale's speeches as evidence of sedition.[75]

Building the nation beyond the nation

As seen above, in Gokhale's view, and other liberals', British rule had been in many ways 'providential' for the subcontinent. The colonial state, having some of the characteristics of a modern state, could give India time and opportunity to renovate its social structure and consolidate itself into a single nation.

The *Raj* had brought material benefits[76] such as the extension, if limited to a very small minority, of political rights in representative bodies; the introduction of a Western type of administrative machinery, the diffusion of the press, and the creation of infrastructures which physically united the country; Western education; uninterrupted peace and order, after centuries of overwhelming chaos; the fair dispensation of justice between Indian and Indian, while "when it [came] to be a matter between Indian and Englishman, it [was] quite another story."[77] Western education, in particular, with its strong emphasis on representative principles and on the values of bourgeois liberal-democracy, was a "beneficent agency" that had had far-reaching consequences, making inevitable that "the people of India, having been brought up on Western knowledge, would in course of time demand European institutions in the government of the country."[78]

These advantages, however, were truly meaningful only as a means to a greater end, namely the moral and material interests of the people of India,[79] something which was realisable only through the achievement of the full rights of British citizenship.[80] Nevertheless, that end seemed distant, because British imperialism had become "narrow," looking "upon the world as though it was made for one race only" and nourishing itself on its own self-image of grandeur.[81] Moreover, it had become apparent that the main objective of the colonial rule was the systematic extortion of the subcontinent's resources to the advantage of Great Britain, and the creation in India of a market for British industrial products. As well known, this 'drain of wealth' theory, developed through a variety of accurate scientific studies, had become central in Indian nationalists' critique of colonial rule.[82] The people of India, therefore, could question their allegiance to a rule that did not behave responsibly towards them. Gokhale stressed this when he explained that "when Indians talk of loyalty to British connections it is not similar to that of feudal Europe or Rajput India but based on Enlightened self-interest."[83] Accepting the colonial order, then, was conditional and shifting. All this considered, according to Gokhale, it was high time to reflect on the meaning attached to the word 'empire.' If it meant inclusion under the British flag, then India was part of it. Conversely, if 'empire' designated, as everything suggested, the ascendancy of the British race, "then India was only a possession of the British Empire, and not part and parcel of it."[84] This points to a significant aspect of Gokhale's political vision, which has already been touched upon, namely that the Indian liberal understood modernity as a process that involved tecno-scientific modernisation as much as the realisation of a 'modern' emancipated society. More concretely, modernity consisted of the technocratic project engendering the improvement of infrastructures, the transformation of the environment, and the creation of industries *as well as* the societal and political liberation of the Indian population.[85] The former, relatively more tangible in the British Raj, was meaningless without the parallel advancement of the latter, which was instead highly problematic under colonial domination, clashing with the ideology of the empire despite British pronouncements in favour of liberty.[86] Gokhale's efforts towards the 'amelioration' of Indian citizenry through political education were defined largely by what the colonial rulers identified as the main weaknesses of Indian society – that is an alleged lack of 'character' and political indifference – and were aimed at proving that Indians could qualify for political legitimacy and freedom. So, Gokhale subscribed, at least in part, to the colonial argument that Indians – in his view specifically Indian masses – were not ready for self-rule and needed a period of political apprenticeship. At the same time, Gokhale looked up to Japan as a successful alternative to the 'colonial' brand of modernity.[87]

That the colonial discourse and policy were increasingly dominated by the language of realpolitik, rather than the moralising tones of the liberal civilising mission, was made clear by officials such as James Fitzjames Stephen who asserted that the rule over India was justifiable per se, on the basis of British superiority.[88] The Viceroy Lord Curzon (1899–1905) openly shared the same view: while attacking the Indian intellectual elite for aspiring to equality in vain, he maintained that "as you cannot acquire race, you really cannot have equality with Englishmen in India as long as British rule lasts."[89]

A similar situation required that Indians engaged in political work be of the highest character. Against the argument that Indians, being a colonised people, could not be political subjects, Gokhale said that:

> A subject race has as much right and as much reason as, and perhaps more right and more reason, to have politics of its own than the races which are self-governing and dominant. You have to fight against the ascendancy of a dominant class, you have to fight to get admittance into those ranks of power which are at present closed to you.[90]

Gokhale understood politics as a liberating practice, suggesting that its purpose was, on the one hand, to challenge racially exclusive forms of domination and, on the other, to open up political opportunities within the institutions of the colonial system. He fluctuated between the delusion that *some* Indians, namely the enfranchised, the property-holders, and the educated – including himself – were 'citizens,' if not yet fully, of British India, and the realisation that *all* Indians were equally racialised subjects of the British Empire. Gokhale then found himself in the double position of advantage and disadvantage, being at the same time a member of the small minority of 'protocitizens' enjoying some, albeit limited, political rights, and a member of the multitude of victims of racism. This implied that he was less sensitive to class than race hierarchies. It was an attitude which revealed the paradox of Indian liberals who, largely belonging to those groups which more directly benefitted from the 'moral and material' advantages of British rule, were split between the optimism of the positive impact that the colonial state could have on Indian society, and the frustration of not being able to transcend that which prevented them from becoming full citizens of the Empire; 'race.'[91] However, it became more and more clear that the disadvantages of racial discrimination greatly outnumbered any other advantage that colonial rule might have generated in

India. This awareness made plain the true intentions of the British in India, so that Indians' shared suffering as victims of racism was implicitly turned by Gokhale into a factor of common national identity and unity. Thus, from being a direct cause of national degeneration, racial discrimination could indirectly produce, through a reaction to it, national regeneration.[92] Gokhale's national vision, then, also presented reactive elements, which, if not chauvinistically anti-British, defined Indian nationality as formed by those who suffered from colonial racism, misrule and inefficiency, that is, an oppressed, colonised 'race.'

Similar denunciations did not exclude pronouncements of loyalty to British rule, however. It is hardly surprising that, for this, Gokhale was accused by his more radical contemporaries of being politically inconsistent. For Aurobindo Ghosh, Gokhale belonged to "a hybrid species, emotionally Nationalist, intellectually Loyalist."[93] For the *Mahratta,* which represented the Extremists' views in the Bombay Presidency that were increasingly impatient with the niceties of parliamentary institutions and with "universal patriotisms," Gokhale's position did not qualify as nationalism: this had to be based on "national rights above all other rights" and on "the hatred of the foreigner."[94] Thus, not unlike the arguments that emerged in the historiographical debate much later, liberal nationalism, lacking the 'anti-element,' was considered too universalist to be truly and effectively 'nationalist.'[95]

Overall, what was imputed to Gokhale was that he did not condemn imperialism *per se,* but its forms of discrimination. Indeed, he differentiated between good and bad imperialism. Initially, British imperialism had been – and could be again – "noble," its aim being "the elevation of all who are included within the Empire"[96] – a clear reference to the Queen's Proclamation Act. The INC leader then imagined India's future as part of the British Empire as a possibility which had a legal basis. He considered the Empire as the space where Indians could become free and enjoy the rights of imperial citizens as per the 1858 Queen Victoria's proclamation, depicted as India's 'Magna Carta' – its bill of rights. As argued by Sukanya Banerjee, the proclamation, from being an instrument of colonial power, was strategically transformed by anticolonial activists into a cornerstone to claim inclusion and political rights.[97] It gave concreteness to the otherwise vague idea of imperial citizenship, even though there was no such legally recognised category in the British Empire.[98] It was not the legitimacy of the empire itself which had to be challenged, but its terms. As a matter of fact, the ultimate goal for the moderate leader and more generally for the INC until the 1930s remained that:

> India should be governed in the interests of the Indians themselves, and that, in the course of time, a form of Government should be attained in this country similar to what exists in Self-Governing Colonies of the British Empire.[99]

The cases of the French in Canada and the Boers in South Africa were presented as evidence that there was room in the Empire for diversity and then for a "self-respecting India" too.[100] Gokhale believed that the Empire could provide Indians with the means to fight for better treatment in India and in other British colonies. In other words, the enjoyment of political and civil rights as citizens of the British Empire entailed, in his view, that Indians be no longer perceived as the 'Other' and should therefore transcend their inferior racial status. Alternatively, acquiring a political subjectivity that put great emphasis on secularity and individual freedom vis-à-vis community duties meant that caste and creed allegiances were destined to lose importance and to be subsumed in a broader national identity within the empire. The imperial power then could train the colony through the gradual application of the universal normative ideal of representative government and liberal formal 'equality' of individuals.[101]

Self-government within the Empire was a difficult task, but one that "built national character." Hinting at the Hindu concept of non-attachment to the results of an action,[102] Gokhale maintained that the moral interest of that struggle "would be entirely missed if [...] the value of our efforts [were judged] by tangible immediate results only."[103] It was not a question of dreams but "of muscles and character," namely it involved using what according to the British rulers Indians did not have, and, according to the Extremists, the Moderate leadership completely lacked. Gokhale, thus, implied that suffering in the struggle against the oppression of the colonial rulers was a regenerating and uplifting effort.

Besides affording Indians the opportunity to show that they were not effeminate and weak, the work towards self-government presupposed gradual change without putting in jeopardy the entire established order through any sudden or violent cataclysm. It involved "a minimum disturbance of present ideas, and it meant proceeding along lines" which were already known and understood, while at the same time incorporating values like political freedom and constitutional liberty into India's political life. Although self-government in India could be modelled on the British example, the political advance had to proceed "from experiment to experiment" and "by cautious and tentative steps," namely it had to be selectively adapted to the different social and historical characteristics of the "Oriental country."[104] Even if Gokhale's discourse did not entail an essentialist and uncritical picture of indigenous traditions, often understood as irrational and producing racial degeneration, his gradualism and his view of society as slowly moving undoubtedly included conservative elements that likened it to the colonial project of postponing the actual devolution of power to Indians. Evoking Burke,[105] Gokhale saw the nation-in-the-making as based on an ordered hierarchy, with leadership and political judgement limited to the few.[106] It is in this light that we should understand his acceptance of relatively high property qualifications, also at the level of panchayats, which he wanted to revive.[107]

Imagining that the liberal colonised elites could work with the imperial authority to build a more benign empire was not – Gokhale acknowledged – "theoretically perfect," since it clashed with the colonial realist policy that had emerged in the late 19th century. Yet it was "practically attainable." It was a proposal that could prove advantageous for the British too, as it could ensure greater stability for the *Raj* vis-à-vis the rise of more 'radical' political demands for full independence.[108] Gokhale knew that the emergence of radical leaders had brought about the enhancement of the moderates in the British eyes and wanted to use the colonial concerns as a political lever. After all, what the INC wanted for India was "a voice in the government of the country, not for the whole population, but for such portion of it as has been qualified by education to discharge properly the responsibilities of such association."[109] Was it so difficult for the Englishmen, Gokhale wondered, "to realise that you cannot have institutions like universities working for more than a half a century in India and then expect to be able to govern the people as though they were full strangers to ideas of constitutional freedom or to the dignity of national aspirations?" Or – Gokhale asked, suggesting the arbitrariness and backward-looking implementing methods of bureaucrats – was it that "bureaucracies, like the Bourbons, never learn[t]?"[110]

It is all very well to see Gokhale's ideology as politically weak and it is easy, in hindsight, to consider it as bound to fail given how it fostered the illusion that the nation could be built by reliance on imperialism. Undoubtedly, his reasoning ignored that colonialism depended on the rule of difference "without which British India would not have been 'British' for very long."[111] However, even when considered functional to nation-building and political 'modernisation,' the quest for equal Indian citizenship within the Empire demonstrates not only that, using Sugata Bose's words, the objectives, dreams, programmes and ideals of Indian patriots could not always be inscribed in the 'container nation.'[112] Although easily dismissible *ex post* as naïve and impracticable diversions from the main road to full independence,[113] these aspirations show that, whether the transition from imperial possessions to nation-states was a necessary and logical political evolution or not, they represented a political choice that Indians had to initially experience before elaborating more effective strategies.[114] Their failure was not inevitable, but depended on the response of the colonial rulers that finally chose not to abandon the categorical imperatives of race that justified their domination. This perspective is beneficial to keep us aware of the diversity of political visions of "self-determination, sovereignty and self-rule which in their historical emergence were compatible with and premised upon intensified connections and greater integration with imperial political structures."[115]

The main concrete means to achieve self-government was, in Gokhale's view, constitutional agitation, whose spectrum of possibilities ranged from prayers and appeals to passive resistance,[116] "including even its extreme

form of non-payment of taxes till redress was obtained at the other end."
Only physical force in the form of rebellion, aiding a foreign invasion or
resort to crime were excluded.[117] Therefore, Gokhale agreed with one of
the most radical techniques of passive resistance promoted by Aurobindo
Ghose and other Extremist nationalists, but unlike them, condemned, the
use of violence and, in the specific context of Swadeshi protests, boycott
too.[118] This is an interesting point, as tax-refusal was a form of law-break-
ing, whereas boycott was not – even though actions of boycott were often
turned into offences by the several instruments that colonial bureaucracy
had at its disposal, besides legislation.[119] Non-payment of taxes was, according to Gokhale, the "most effective form of passive resistance," useful also
to teach "each man the responsibility of his own action" and their commitment to the national cause.[120] In addition to political representation,
then, Gokhale had begun contemplating other methods and techniques to
limit colonial power: such new possibilities were suggested by Swadeshi politics as well as by Gandhi's coterminous struggle in South Africa. Passive
resistance was, for Gokhale, "the prerogative of the degraded," advocated
even by Jesus Christ himself.[121] Passive resistance arose from the distrust
of the state spurred by the Partition of Bengal as well as by the colonial
repression of the protests.[122] However, the delegitimation of the state was
not enough to justify the idea of a generalised boycott. The creation of
'national' schools and colleges would take years and a system of national
education, resources being limited as they were, could only supplement
and not replace government institutions.

While Gokhale was not opposed to the boycott of government service –
more workers in that case could be devoted to the service of the country through societies like the SIS – boycotting local and municipal boards
and legislative councils was disgraceful, its main implication being to waste
what little powers of administration and control Indians possessed to serve
their people.[123] As seen, the state, through its institutions, was perceived
as a founding element of modernity, the realisation of human reason, and
therefore as a strategic factor of qualitative changes in a Balkanised society
of proliferating identities.[124] The political therefore played an important
role in transforming the social. In other words, the state had the pedagogical role to help individuals realise their political national identities.[125]

The foundations of a 'modern' public life rested especially on the work
done at local level, namely smaller contexts where people could develop
a higher degree of common interests and internal cohesion through
working side by side. Mill's ideas of local representation and political and
moral progress through individual improvement were attractive because
they suited Indian needs of gradual participation[126] while embodying a
system of tutelage through which the higher orders of society could teach,
train and control the lower orders.[127] Explicitly citing Mill's *Considerations
on Representative Government*,[128] where it was argued that the objective of
municipal institution was not only about efficiency but also and more

importantly about instilling public spirit and raising the general level of intelligence of the people,[129] Gokhale understood local bodies as "real nurseries of self-government" that transmitted a sense of participation and citizenship.[130] Significantly enough, at the local level, political representation and participatory rights were closely linked to class privilege in terms of high property qualification, something which stood in the way of the democratization process.[131]

In Gokhale's view, local self-government had to be limited to an area that did not go beyond the administrative division of the *taluka* (township), with the *panchayat* (village council) being the smaller unit and the *taluka* the larger one. The *taluka* boards and the municipalities had to be made wholly popular assemblies, fully elected, and freed from the petty and harassing interferences of the officials. Instead, drawing upon themes of ancient constitutionalism and orientalism, Gokhale believed that the *panchayat* was "the natural constituency of the country," which had to be only partly elected and on the basis of pecuniary qualifications. Only the villagers that paid a minimum land revenue of 10 rupees were entitled to be elected and not, contrary to what the colonial rulers proposed, on the basis of an "abstract social influence" among the people: electability had to be based on 'civic duties,' the payment of taxes being a mark of responsible citizenship.[132] The village community, according to Gokhale, should be given extensive judicial and administrative powers, managing, among other affairs, forests, famine and plague relief, and primary education.[133] This idea, coming largely from orientalist interpretations of Indian history, that the *panchayat* was an essential and timeless component of India's ancient constitution, was adopted and constantly reinvented by the colonial state and by Indian nationalists. Under the influence of liberalism, the *panchayat* came to be increasingly seen as instrumental for the growth of civil society. In the midst of discussions about local bodies and village communities especially in Britain and Germany, Western intellectuals were fascinated by the role of the Indian village council which they interpreted through the lenses of their political views.[134]

In the context of the Indian anticolonial movement, the role envisioned for the *panchayat* was flexible and adaptable to the needs of the time. In fact, during the 1911 Allahabad Congress, in the wake of communal tensions, Gopal Krishna Devadhar (1871–1935), one of the first three members of the SIS and as such under the strong influence of Gokhale, proposed the *panchayat* as "conciliation boards" to solve caste and communal disputes so that the people could be trained to work together in harmony and for the common good.[135]

Gokhale wanted the participation of leading men elected by the people – at first merely advisory, but gradually entrusted with increasing powers of control – to be enlarged in district administration too, which needed to be decentralised and made less dependent on the control of the secretariat of the central government and to be more concerned "with human beings."[136] These reforms could prevent the alienation of the educated classes and the recreation in India of the situation in Ireland.[137] This argument, at the time of the discussions preceding the 1909 Indian Councils Act and in the heated political context of the Swadeshi movement, were used by John Morley, Secretary of State for India (1905–1914) to restrain criticism from India while implicitly warning that unrest would imply the loss of the reforms altogether.[138]

The importance attributed by Gokhale to local government can be also appreciated by the fact that, while he was a member of the Imperial Legislative Council, he was invited to preside over the Poona City municipality, made vacant by the death of the previous president Dorabji Padumji. Gokhale retained that post for four years, during which period, despite his commitment in the Supreme Council and in the INC, he worked towards expanding educational facilities. He also introduced a system that allowed members of the municipality to interrogate the executive officers regarding issues of administration – the same system that was enacted in the Imperial Council by the Morley-Minto reforms.[139] It was a useful experience that brought Gokhale in touch with the need to reform local bodies and make their revenues elastic and consistent with their expenditures – crucial issues in view of the importance the Indian liberal attributed to local bodies in carrying out local building activities.[140]

Accommodating difference: The Muslim question

It is useful at this point to consider the main differences of Indian society that, according to Gokhale, had to be domesticated through political work as well as the forms of identification which he saw as a hindrance to modernity and that, as such, had to be subsumed into national identity. We have seen that, since the people were not ready to fulfil the 'providential destiny' of the Indian nation, they had to be educated and informed of the advantages of belonging to the nation.

Gokhale had initially denied the Muslim contribution to Indian history, depicting the coming of the "Mahomedan invaders" in the 11th century as the beginning of the "seven centuries of darkness" and "intellectual gloom" – obscurity which was visible, among other things, in the degraded female condition.[141] Such stance gives the impression that, in line with a *leitmotiv* in British and Indian literary works as well as in the historical scholarship of the time, Gokhale perceived Hindus and Muslims as belonging to two different and conflicting civilisations. Nevertheless, later on – and, significantly, especially after the creation of the Muslim League – the Indian politician changed his mind and promoted the view that India was inhabited by three great ancient races, namely Hindus, Muslims and Parsees[142] who "[came] to make their home here [and] brought their own treasure into the common stock."[143] The fact that Gokhale expressed his opinion on Muslims both privately and publicly suggests a sincere change of mind, beyond merely political ends.

Religion, for Gokhale, was a most powerful factor in people's lived experience, so much that "it modified and sometimes profoundly modified race characteristics."[144] That was true also for Hindus and Muslims, who, despite the fact that they did not differ "in race," had inherited "over the greater part of India two different traditions." Hindus "were greatly hampered by castes, and by temperament they were mild and passive." Conversely, Muslims "were burdened with fewer divisions, their social structure rested on a more democratic basis, they had more cohesion among them, and they were more easily roused to action." While recognising the presence of cultural differences, very often based on colonial clichés, Gokhale believed that the "spread of education, a wide and efficient performance of civic duties, growth of national aspirations and a quickening of national self-respect in both communities were among the forces which would ultimately overcome the tradition."[145] Tradition, then, was given a pejorative connotation: it represented an obstacle to rational and ethical collective and individual decisions. It was political education that would create a common platform of thought and contribute to the cultivation of a sentiment of nationality "rising superior to caste and creed,"[146] because nationalism had deeper significance than religious belonging. Being himself a man of religious sensitivity, Gokhale did not expect that faith in the modern nation-state should replace religion. On the contrary, religion had to be relegated to the private sphere and made susceptible to rational criticism and to the pedagogical intervention of the 'ethical' state whenever it denied liberty and equality or promoted practices of exclusion and discrimination, as in the case of the depressed classes or women being barred from studying. The assumption was that liberal nationalism represented the antidote to the ills of 'sectarianism.'[147]

Gokhale was preoccupied because the 'emergence' of the Muslim minority, with its political claims, could pose a real threat to national unity. He was deeply concerned by the widening rift between Hindus and Muslims to which the Swadeshi movement – and the colonial political calculations – had contributed, "put[ting] back the clock of progress by several years."[148] Whereas in the past, differences in religious sensitivities had caused tensions between the two communities in matters of cultural rights such as the slaughter of cows and street music, the emergence of the Muslim League which aimed to win political rights for Muslims could jeopardise "the India of the future" by creating a pan-Indian Muslim political community.[149] The nation-in-the-making "could not be only a Hindu India, or a Mahomedan India but compounded of all the elements which existed at present in India – Hindu, Mahomedan, Parsee, Christian and the Englishman who adopted India as his country."[150] Embracing a view that was increasingly common by the beginning of the 20th century, Gokhale argued that in Indian history there was a long-standing tendency towards 'unity in diversity' that had made all communities equally legitimate and rooted in the country. In order to safeguard that long-term tradition of cultural pluralism, it was necessary to recognise the nation-in-the-making as a whole greater than the sum of its parts. In other words, knitting together India's diversity into a single political fabric entailed each inhabitant of the sub-continent giving priority to their identity as Indian first: the attribute of citizenship intended, though not exclusively, to be the individual's link to the nation-state, was, in Gokhale's view, the most important *political* iden-tity-mark. Only by subsuming sectarian identities into the larger Indian identity, could majoritarian prevarications and minoritarian separatist impulses be averted so that unity and, by extension, diversity could be pre-served. Paradoxically, then, it was the integrationist drive of the modern state, through its role of arbiter, that was able to guarantee the balanced co-existence of mutually respectful 'sections' of Indian society by mediat-ing hierarchies of power, access to political/economic resources, the iden-tity of the nation-state, etc.[151]

In order to tackle the growing alienation of the Muslim community, Gokhale toured Northern India in the early months of 1907: he visited Lucknow, Aligarh, Allahabad and Lahore where he addressed the Muslim League appealing to the need to serve the Motherland as "human beings." The campaign, according to Tilak's newspaper, *The Mahratta*, was suc-cessful, with Muslims, including members of the Muslim League, chant-ing 'Bande Mataram' (Hail to the Motherland) to express solidarity with Gokhale.[152] Describing Gokhale's three-day visit to Punjab, Lala Lajpat Rai wrote that he received a "splendid reception" and the crowd on the streets was "innumerable."[153]

However, Gokhale realised that, besides more or less vague declarations of unity, the situation required that the Hindu majority took concrete steps in the form of enforceable safeguards to ensure the protection of the Muslim minority. As a matter of course, during the negotiations for what came to be known as the Morley-Minto Reforms in which he played a considerable role, Gokhale, while asking for Indian majorities in the legislatures, accepted and promoted the allocation of separate electorates for Muslims[154] to free the community from dependence upon government nomination.[155] Against the background of the 'Moderate'/'Extremist' rivalry, the 'Extremists' launched bitter attacks against the "mild Hindu" Gokhale in their press, generally accusing him of having "forgotten to perform [his] duty to the Hindu Community" in the anxiety "to please the Muslims."[156]

Gokhale eventually condemned the regulations and rules which provided details of the 1909 Indian Council Act for granting Muslims excessive rep-resentation commensurate with a fair numerical share of that community. This, in particular, had "caused very great dissatisfaction throughout the country except in Mahomedans" and rekindled "fierce antagonism" between Hindu and Muslim, complicating the already difficult situation of the nation-alist movement after the Congress split of Surat.[157] Such antagonism had

> Already led in Upper India to a movement for the formation of a Hindu League, and the Punjab, where the relations between the two creeds

[were] the worst, [was] taking the lead in the matter. The movement [was] frankly anti-Mahomedan, as the Moslem League [was] frankly anti-Hindu, and both [were] anti-national.[158]

Gokhale thus seemed less optimistic about the Muslim party than a few years earlier: in 1906, in fact, he had declared that in the long run, the Muslim League "must inevitably merge itself sooner or later into the larger and older organisation of the National Congress."[159] In 1909, instead, albeit only in his private correspondence, he defined the Muslim League as 'anti-national,' by which he meant 'anti-Congress.' In both cases, the underlying allusion, which to a certain extent reminds us of Nehru and Gandhi's attitude in the following decades was that the INC was the only political organisation that could truly represent the nation.[160]

What was particularly deprecated by Gokhale was the fact that some Muslim leaders had demanded separate electorates on the basis of their historical importance and higher loyalty to British rule. In a passage worth quoting at length, it is not difficult to detect a certain emotional tone in Gokhale's protest which, while criticising the use of historical justification for political requests, seemed to yield to the rhetoric of the 'glorious' Hindu past:

> When any one urged that his community was specially [sic] important and should therefore receive the representation in excess of its fair share, the undoubted and irresistible implication was that the other communities were comparatively inferior and should receive less than their fair share. That was a position to which naturally the other communities could not assent. [...]. It was urged that the Mahomedans had ruled in India for five centuries. It must not however be forgotten that the Hindus had ruled for countless centuries before them and even afterwards, before the British came on the scene, the Mahomedan power had been broken and displaced over nearly the whole country by a revival of Hindu rule.[161]

Gokhale protested also against arguments according to which, since there were large Muslim communities in other countries, the Muslims of India were invested with special importance. Gokhale could not see how that mattered in terms of political representation, unless it was based on the assumption that in the administration of this country, "*those whose whole heart was not with India* were to have preference over those whose was."[162] It is not clear from the speech to whom Gokhale was specifically referring. It was, however, common among Muslim leaders, including Sayyid Ahmad Khan, to appeal to the universal ideal of the worldwide community of believers, the Ummah.[163] Similar appeals by Muslim leaders were also motivated by the will to depict their own community as numerically bigger by identifying it with their coreligionists outside India.[164] Although the sense of belonging to the Ummah was not necessarily incompatible with the affiliation to the Indian nation, Gokhale instead seemed to hint at the fact that the universality of the Muslim community made their loyalty to India dubious. As is known, the tension between the territoriality of the nation and the universal Ummah – and the threat that Muslims' other allegiances could present to the idea of a united India – is a question that has continued to characterise the Indian political debate for decades and be further complicated by the Partition of colonial India into the two independent nation-states of India and Pakistan.[165] These dynamics are the outcome of the emphasis on religion as the primary marker of identity in the demographic definition of minorities in colonial India during the 20th century.[166]

Even though disapproving of the colonial partiality in favour of the Muslim community, Gokhale continued to adhere to his national vision, according to which Hindu and Muslim political interests were generally identical, and tried to stem the tide of anti-Muslim feelings by appealing to the larger interests of the national cause.[167] In his views, demanding that the Government of India withdrew the measures by which Muslims[168] were overrepresented meant confirming the Muslims' fear of the "sectional narrowness" of the INC.[169] What really mattered in the light of the new reforms was the possibility conferred on elected members to raise discussion on administrative matters in the Legislative Councils. Such power required:

> The capacity, the public spirit and the sense of responsibility of the members. How many members were returned by any particular community was not of much consequence [...]. When once [sic] the new councils commenced to work it would be realized that there was no demand or scope there for work on sectarian lines and the man who worked for all would find his service appreciated by all communities.[170]

After all, if the increase in the proportion of elected members was without doubt a vital matter for the advance of the Indian political cause, they were "not so important as to afford to any community the shadow of an opportunity to obtain a monopoly of political power in the country"[171] as Indian politics under British rule was still such that Indian representatives had to count more on their moral influence than on the weight of their numbers.[172] Gokhale thus suggested that the colonial state and its institutions could serve as a common platform for the two communities to find union in political objectives: one more reason for the end of the *Raj* not to be hastened.

Notwithstanding the genuine intentions to work towards the unity of the two main Indian communities, both paternalistic tones and derogatory stereotypical images are detectable in Gokhale's analysis of the Hindu-Muslim question. In several public speeches, Gokhale appealed to the goodwill and generosity of Hindus – politically, socially, and educationally more advanced – to educate their fellow Muslim countrymen and rescue them from the political games of the British officials, thus denying Muslims the capability of making their own independent decisions. Although not lacking the ability of class analysis when trying to understand the reason behind the communal riots between Hindus and Muslims in East Bengal during the Swadeshi agitations, and despite blaming all three parties, namely Hindus, Muslims and British officials for the degeneration of the situation, Gokhale considered "Muslim rowdyism" a product of the profound ignorance and fanaticism of the Muslim masses.[173] On another occasion, while arguing that the whole country would benefit from the 'progress' of the Muslim community, Gokhale spoke of "Mahomedans" *and* "the people of Bengal"[174] (i.e., the Hindus, who were the minority of the population of Bengal). In doing so, Gokhale betrayed not only a certain emotional solidarity towards the Bengali Hindus but also an unselfconscious conception of Muslims as a category distinct from, and in contrast with, the population of Bengal. Even without speculating on the obliviousness of such differentiation, this incident is a telling example of the pervasiveness of Islamophobic sentiments, especially after the 1905 Partition of Bengal. Also, while in Allahabad for a public meeting in the same year, Gokhale made reference to the "holy Ganges and the noble Jumna," evoking Hindu mythology and adopting 'romantic' tones: "the two great rivers which [had] for ages meant so much to every Hindu" reminiscent of "the chequered past of the ancient land, her glories and misfortunes, the faiths, the hopes, the achievements, the trials of their race."[175] Given that the meeting took place in the United Provinces, where the Muslim minority had historically played a significant role, it might have been more appropriate, for the purpose of advocating Hindu-Muslim unity, to refer to the Ganges and Yamuna as symbolically suggestive in terms of communal harmony and exemplifying the shared culture between the two communities. Equally, Gokhale's comparison of Lord Curzon and Aurangzeb during his well-known Congress Presidential address in Banaras in 1905 attracted disproval from some sections of Indian Muslims.[176] Even if Gokhale's object was to attack the Viceroy's 'despotic' rule and not to vilify Aurangzeb, or much less to hurt Muslim sensitivities,[177] the unwanted effect was that, to some Muslims, the President of the INC censured Muslim rule and validated the narrative of it being tyrannical and highly oppressive towards Hindus. In contrast with many positive appraisals, the Urdu weekly *Riyaz-ul-Akhbar* from Gorakhpur, for example, commenting upon the address wrote that Gokhale was animated by religious prejudices.[178]

All this points to the fact that, while conceding that Muslims were a minority within the nation who needed to be granted special representation in the political body, Gokhale subconsciously demonstrated a certain awareness of dominance and self-asserted authority as a member of the Hindu majority. It is not difficult to detect in Gokhale the anxieties of separatism that the political claims of the Muslim minority could bring about:

however, such anxieties were allayed by the belief in the nation as progress, as an ongoing process of 'becoming,' finally resulting in national homogeneity embodied by the secular state. But it is important to note that, unlike the benevolent majoritarianism shown by several of his contemporaries who considered the inherent tolerance, accommodation and inclusiveness of the Hindu majority to be sufficient guarantee for acknowledging the difference of the Muslim community,[179] Gokhale was convinced that the peaceful coexistence of the two major Indian religious communities could be safeguarded only through the political representation of difference. Even though separate electorates had to be considered a temporary measure, the recognition and representation of the Muslim minority gave a clear connotation of the nation-state he envisioned.[180]

National pedagogies: The 'depressed classes'

In the previous chapter, we have seen that Gokhale perceived caste discrimination as a social 'evil' as well as a major impediment to the creation of a 'modern' nation. From the late 1890s in particular, in their critique of the caste system, several liberal Hindu social reformers and public men – Gokhale's *guru* Ranade had a prominent role among them – increasingly advocated for the social 'improvement' of the so-called 'depressed classes' (the term with which Dalits were categorised by the colonial ethnographic state) through a set of different initiatives.[181]

Gokhale conceded that in the past, castes had been useful for the preservation and the functioning of society but rejected culturalist explanations describing them as the Indian equivalent of 'Western' classes. Social classes in the West were, in Gokhale's overoptimistic reading, "perfectly elastic institutions" – so much as to allow Joseph Chamberlain, a shoemaker's son, to become a leading politician in the British empire – whereas castes were "rigid and cast-iron" and therefore residuals of an immutable order that was bound to change under the influence of "the larger humanity of these days." Caste, in other words, denied any prospect of success in life, relegating individuals to their initial place in the social system regardless of their talent.[182]

Notwithstanding this, Gokhale did nothing to espouse the end of the caste system as such. Presiding over a students' meeting held at the Wilson College in Bombay in 1910, he admonished a student who had argued in his paper that the caste system would soon disappear. In a rather paternalistic way, Gokhale dismissed the student's impassioned assertion as the fruit of his young age, thus inferring that such radical views would abate with the coming of age. The Congress leader also said that he disliked the idea of "attacking the higher classes."[183] This reminds us of Sarojini Naidu's comment about Gokhale, depicting him as not immune from "the conservative pride of his Brahminical descent which instinctively resented the least question of its ancient monopoly of power." Naidu referred to the All-India

Social Conference held in Calcutta in 1911, during which, talking about the 'depressed classes,' she said that their inhuman condition was mostly due to "the tyranny of arrogant Brahmins in the past." Gokhale, resentful, told her in private that "it was no doubt a brave and beautiful speech, but you sometimes use harsh, bold phrases."[184]

On the occasion of the 1910 Indian National Social Conference, Gokhale mentioned the virtuous example of Japan as a country that had been able to legally abolish its own form of 'untouchability,' a residual of the feudal era: the Japanese innate predisposition to discipline and obedience towards authority contributed to the success of the law so that the lower and upper orders could interact "in terms of absolute equality." However, given its social and cultural sensitivities and weaknesses, India needed a more moderate solution, one "of such a character as [wa]s likely to be adopted in practice." Gokhale went on to point out that the elevation of the 'depressed classes' did not mean that "you have all at once to mix with them and on terms of perfect equality"[185] – a comment that is telling not only of the deeply ingrained prejudices among the upper castes but also of Gokhale's own bias. He instead suggested a gradual but profound modification of the discriminating everyday practices prescribed by casteism. According to him, there were two paths, to be taken simultaneously: educating the upper elite to correct their "rigid adherence to caste," while at the same time uplifting morally, intellectually and socially the 'depressed classes.'[186]

The SIS took a keen interest in carrying out both courses of action. Since the inception of its activities, the Society had organised several country-wide conferences to make the public aware of the condition of the 'depressed classes' while advocating the "removal of the barrier of untouchableness that separated them from the rest of the Hindu world."[187] In practical terms, the SIS was active in the effort to spread literacy among members of the 'depressed classes'; it aimed to provide them with medical relief, public sanitation and life insurance at an affordable price, and teach "enlightened" values such as "thrift and self-help" so that they could free themselves from the burden of debt.[188] In doing so, the Society cooperated with other civil society organisations, such as V. R. Shinde's Bombay-based Depressed Classes Mission[189] and Ramabai Ranade's Seva Sadan in Poona.[190]

Emanating from the purposes and initiatives of the SIS is the perception of caste as a form of *social* difference that had to be elided in order to forge a homogenous Hindu community as an essential requirement to form a homogenous nation. The Gait circular, which proposed to enumerate the members of the 'depressed classes' separately from Hindus, had the effect to further galvanise the Hindu leaders' anxiety about the amelioration of the conditions of Untouchables so as to create "the appearance of a united Hindu community that unequivocally encompassed the lowest castes."[191] As research has shown, very often similar schemes to 'uplift' the 'depressed classes' were animated by a paternalistic rhetoric and by a discriminatory approach that could hardly create a sense of liberation among Dalits.[192]

The vague language of abstract equality, as well as the modernist rhetoric of nation building and public duty, were imbued with Brahmanical notions of social harmony and caste hierarchy; they were underpinned by the will to cleanse the 'depressed classes' from those practices which the members of the upper castes considered incompatible with their idea of Hinduism and their vision of the nation.[193] This desire to 'elevate' the lower orders of society through the transformation of cultural habits seen as backward and irrational, which in many ways resembled the colonial 'civilising mission,' had become a common trope from the beginning of the 20th century at global level: it was underpinned by the need to 'discipline' difference and conform to ideals of a rational, autonomous and industrious nation-in-the-making. It was a project which deployed liberal arguments of improvement and work ethic that could be combined with coercion, if necessary, for the greater cause of collective well-being.[194]

Also, fairly typical of the intellectual classes the world over, in India, too, the solution to the problems of the 'depressed classes,' and more generally of the rural and urban poor, was seen in essentially educational terms. Gokhale considered education a crucial social ladder for the lower strata of society, since, in his vision, the intention was to "having respectable careers thrown open to [the members of the depressed classes]."[195] However – and not surprisingly given the general opposition that mass education proposals aroused in conservative classes the world over – that was precisely the fear of those who wanted to preserve class and caste hierarchies and who found appalling "the children of higher classes w[ould] have to sit with those of the depressed classes." Commenting on whom raised similar objections, Gokhale observed that they were "born too late" and that such a view, when seriously expressed by representatives of the people in public bodies, showed "how much need there really [wa]s in the country, for the education not merely of the masses but also of the [educated] classes."[196]

The urgency to teach educated and putatively 'respectable' men and women that caste inequality was incompatible with the ideals of justice and humanity, which increasingly characterised modern civilisation and on which the nation had to be built, resembled, at least at the discursive level, Ambedkar's views. Ambedkar, however, was not only persuaded of the need to educate the Congress elite about the inherent incompatibility between democracy and caste discrimination. The Dalits' leader also demanded that the 'depressed classes' were recognised as a liberal, constitutional minority that needed special representation in the political body. Ambedkar held that the empowerment of Dalits was possible only through the acknowledgment of their historical specificity and different political interests from other communities, especially caste Hindus – something which the Congress upper ranks opposed because of their view of the nation and of the Hindu community as one and indivisible.[197]

Gokhale did not go so far as to advocate the recognition of *political* difference for the 'depressed classes.' Instead, he considered them part and parcel of the Hindu community, whose dominance could be threatened by accepting Hinduism's fragmentation along caste lines. Gokhale appealed to contemporary ideas of 'national efficiency' and to sentiments of national awakening to bring forth disciplined and self-sacrificing educated young citizens who could "dedicate their lives to this sacred work of the elevation of the low castes" and to enhance the country's public life. It was a question of "national self-interest" and future productivity:

> How can we possibly realize our national aspirations, how can our country ever hope to take her place among the nations of the world, if we allow large numbers of our countrymen to remain sunk in igno-rance, barbarism, and degradation? Unless these men are gradu-ally raised to a higher level, morally and intellectually, how can they possibly understand our thoughts or share our hopes or co-operate with us in our efforts? Can you not realize that so far as the work of national elevation is concerned, the energy, which these classes might be expected to represent, is simply unavailable to us? [...] I think that there is not much hope for us as a nation unless the help of all classes, including those that are known as low castes, is forthcoming for the work that lies before us.[198]

Therefore, humanitarian principles *and* pragmatic calculations of nation-building animated Gokhale's concerns.[199] The members of the 'depressed classes' were human beings to be treated with respect and dignity, but they were also human resources that could contribute to the well-being of the nation-in-the-making. In addition, Gokhale hinted at the fact that the removal of caste discrimination was crucial for the preserva-tion of Hinduism against conversions to Christianity. Was it, Gokhale asked:

> [C]onsistent with our own self-respect that these men should be kept out of our houses and shut out from all social intercourse as long as they remain within the pale of Hinduism, whereas the moment they put on a coat and a hat and a pair of trousers and call themselves Christians, we are prepared to shake hands with them and look upon them as quite respectable?[200]

Keeping low-caste and untouchable Hindus within the fold of Hinduism was, in other words, instrumental for protecting the Hindu commu-nity against the interferences and proselytisation from other religions, Christianity above all.[201]

It is also interesting to note that, contrary to what would be Ambedkar's position on the need of a vigorous state action for the elevation of 'untouchables,' Gokhale declared that had the government presented a ready-made plan to tackle the 'depressed classes' problem, he would have rejected it. The condition of these classes, in fact, could present an opportunity to arouse a sense of social duty and discipline among the members of the upper castes: in this way, the latter might be redeemed from the undue privilege obtained from the subservience of the former. This bold statement was criticised even by a weekly publication generally favourable to Gokhale, the *Indian Social Reformer*, for its high-caste-centric perspective: "The depressed classes have to be raised for the sake of themselves and not because the interests of the higher classes require them to be raised."[202]

This instrumental view of the elevation of the 'depressed classes' as beneficial to spreading values of civic virtues is very revealing of an issue that has already surfaced in this chapter: Gokhale implicitly drew a distinct line between active citizens, that is to say those who could take part in the building of the nation, participate in the public life of the country and enjoy some, if limited, political rights, and those people, the 'depressed classes,' the 'ignorant' masses, who were the object of the national pedagogical mission with which the 'brain of the country,' the educated elite, were invested.[203] The fact that the masses had to be politically educated meant that they were unprepared to become members of the nation.[204] These masses were mainly "inert and apathetic, except when under the sway of a religious impulse [...] deplorably divided and sub-divided, with hardly any true sense of discipline, plunged in abject poverty and ignorance, wedded to usages and institutions" which were not meant to promote progress.[205] They were unable to govern themselves and in constant need of an enlightened guidance from above.

Such conservative notions revealed a deep-seated fear of mass 'mediocrity,' so common among liberal thinkers such as John Stuart Mill, as well as more conservative thinkers by the beginning of the 20th century. Such unease was deepened by the extension of the vote through the Reform Acts in England which opened up possibilities of mass democracy.

For Gokhale, though, that fear could not justify a political self-determination that was undemocratic – notwithstanding all caveats implied by the previous discussion on the meaning of democracy and suffrage. The emphasis on national awakening led from above and requiring a hierarchical order was not so strong as to advocate national freedom that was detached from liberal ideas: the national polity, through its representative institutions, had to provide the political and social conditions conducive to the development and freedom of individual citizens. However, the very fact that it was a long-term goal meant that democratisation remained on hold.

Conclusion

Overall, the foregoing chapter has made a critical and nuanced analysis of Gokhale's national vision, arguing that even those ideas of the nation that claim to be inclusive and universal produce uncertainties and involve a measure of exclusion and discontent.

The chapter has demonstrated that the nation envisaged by Gokhale was based on a liberal political project, which attributed a pedagogical role to the state – perceived as the embodiment of the human reason – and considered national identity as something to be built in the future and not rooted in an idealised past. In his conceptualisation of the nation, Gokhale was also animated by majoritarian anxieties about the 'emergence' of minorities whose allegiances beyond and/or within the nation could undermine the central idea of a liberal political nationality, in which the politically most relevant relationship was the one between the state and the individual. Thus, the liberal ideological underpinnings were particularly instrumental for envisioning a nation committed to the agenda of 'modernity' and creating a freedom-enabling context for citizens *qua* individuals empowering their identification with the national polity over those of 'sub-national' communities.

The chapter has also argued that Gokhale's national vision included pre-political factors: it acknowledged a pre-existing sense of Indianness, which drew on colonial imaginings of India, giving unity to the envisaged nation. This grammar of cultural distinctiveness, however, even when assuming religious undertones, never escalated into ethnic revivalism. Also, the chapter has shown that Gokhale's nationalist discourse, although given an explicit rational thrust and ethical dimension by liberalism, was not immune to emotive tones that sacralised public life, conferring a transcending meaning to the national mission and an aura of sacredness to the nation.

It has also been argued here that, despite its adherence to the goal of expanding representative institutions, Gokhale's liberal nationalism had its own inherent ideological limits, being suspicious as it was of the political participation of the uneducated masses. While qualifying as Indians qua inhabitants of India, the masses could qualify as citizens only after being inculcated by the educated elite with a sense of civic duty, an ethic of discipline and ideals of social service. Furthermore, through the empirical case studies on Gokhale's perception of Muslims and members of the so-called 'Depressed Classes,' the chapter has demonstrated that the Indian 'Moderate' was not free from Hindu/upper caste prejudices. All in all, then, Gokhale oscillated between a language of universalism and the view that some sections of Indian society were still unprepared to become members of the national community and were relegated to the 'waiting room of history.'[206]

If it is thus undeniable that conservative elements in Gokhale's views were palpable, it is also important to keep in mind that his idea of national identity was tolerant and inclusive on the basis of the same liberal political values that made it conservative. Even if it is tempting to judge Gokhale's ideas *ex post* in the face of Gandhi's successful mass mobilisation or based on today's principles of democracy, Gokhale can be credited with having created, thanks to his visibility, a valid political space in which the language of cultural diversity, tolerance and peaceful coexistence between communities became largely accepted and adopted at the ideological and political level.

Notes

1. For an early discussion on this, see the dated but still useful Dietmar Rothermund, 'Emancipation or Re-Integration: The Politics of Gopal Krishna Gokhale and Herbert Risley', in D.A. Low (ed.), *Soundings in Modern South Asian History*, Weindenfeld and Nicolson, London 1968, pp. 131–157.
2. David Ludden, "Spatial Inequity and National Territory: Remapping 1905 in Bengal and Assam", *Modern Asian Studies*, Vol. 46, n. 3 (2012), p. 486.
3. On this, see for instance, Goswami, *Producing India* and Sumathi Ramaswamy, *The Goddess and the Nation: Mapping Mother India*, Duke University Press, Durham and London 2010. For a succinct yet valuable discussion on the need to historicise national geography, see Dilip M. Menon, "The Many Spaces and Times of Swadeshi", *Economic and Political Weekly*, Vol. 47, n. 42 (2012), pp. 47–48.
4. Partha Chatterjee, 'B.R. Ambedkar and the Troubled Times of Citizenship', in V.R. Mehta and Thomas Pantham, *Political Ideas in Modern India: Thematic Explorations*, p. 83.
5. Servants of India Society, Constitution, 12 June 1905, *GSW*, Vol. II, p. 181.
6. Thomas R. Metcalf, *Ideologies of the Raj*, CUP, Cambridge, 1997, p. 188.
7. Quoted by Gokhale in "Elementary Education", speech at the Imperial Legislative Council, March 1910, *GSW*, Vol. III, p. 75, quoted from *Despatch from the Court of Directors of the East India Company to the Governor-General of India in Council*, dated July 19, 1854, No. 49.
8. The Extremists preferred the invocation of Hindu dharma to Providence: they called 'the new Nationalist movement as a movement of the hand of Dharma presaging the disruption of the chains of evil Karma' ('An Open Letter to the Hon'ble Mr. Gokhale', *The Mahratta*, 7 November 1909, p. 535).
9. For the role of orientalism in representations of India, see David Ludden, 'Orientalist Empiricism: Transformations of Colonial Knowledge', in C.A. Breckenridge and P. Van Der Veer (eds.), *Orientalism and the Postcolonial Predicament: Perspectives from South Asia*, University of Pennsylvania Press, Philadelphia 1993, pp. 250–278.
10. For a discussion on how this periodisation is still in place, see Michelguglielmo Torri, 'For a New Periodisation of Indian History', in D.N. Jha (ed.), *The Evolution of a Nation: Pre-Colonial to Post-Colonial, Essays in Memory of R. S. Sharma*, Manohar, Delhi 2014, pp. 39–60, here p. 40.
11. On the 19th-century flourishing of Indian historical works as a battlefield where Indians could demonstrate their interest in history vis-à-vis the colonial discourse, see Georg G. Iggers, Q. Edward Wang and Supriya Mukherjee, *A Global History of Modern Historiography*, pp. 229–232. See also Vinay Lal, *The History of History: Politics and Scholarship in Modern India*, OUP, New Delhi 2003, pp. 27–78.
12. "England's Duty to India", National Liberal Club, London, 15 November 1905, *GSW*, Vol. II, p. 340.
13. "East and West in India", paper presented at the Universal Races Congress in July 1911 in London, *GSW*, Vol. II, p. 388.
14. David Washbrook, "Intimations of Modernity in South India", *South Asian History and Culture*, Vol. 1, n. 1 (2009), pp. 125–148, here 132.
15. For a discussion on the Indian effort to strike a balance between adopting western modes of 'progress' and emphasising India's cultural distinctiveness, see Partha Chatterjee, *Nationalist Thought and the Colonial World: A Derivative Discourse*, Zed Books, London 1986, pp. 54–81.
16. "England's Duty to India", p. 340.

17. "Indian View of Indian Affairs", Address to the Fabian Society, London, 9 October 1905, *GSW*, Vol. II, p. 327.
18. Gokhale attributed this view of history as a lesson for the present to his master Ranade too ("Mahadev Govind Ranade", speech in Madras, 1904, *GSW*, Vol. III, p. 295–296).
19. "History Teaching in Bombay", *GSW*, Vol. III, p. 203.
20. As argued by Gauri Viswanathan, history teaching in Indian schools and colleges, in the colonial view, was an instrument of colonial domination, aimed at disseminating principles of order, discipline and loyalty among the subjects (Gauri Viswanathan, *Masks of Conquests: Literary Study and British Rule in India*, Columbia University Press, New York 1989, pp. 100–101).
21. "East and West", p. 380.
22. "Budget Speech, 1907", *GSW*, Vol. I, p. 119.
23. "Budget Speech, 1907", pp. 117–120.
24. Paul Crook, *Darwinism, War and History: The Debate Over the Biology of War from the 'Origin of Species' to the First World War*, CUP, Cambridge 1994. On the advocacy of military enlistment by political and intellectual elites during the Great War, see Robert E. Upton, "'It Gives Us a Power and Strength Which We Do Not Possess': Martiality, Manliness, and India's Great War Enlistment Drive", *Modern Asian Studies*, Vol. 52, n. 6 (2018), pp. 1977–2012, esp. 2010–2012 for the influence of social Darwinist thought in Western India.
25. "Budget Speech, 1907", p. 119. Gokhale used the term 'demartialisation,' a term widely used from the 1880s in Western India. See Srinath Raghavan, 'Liberal Thought and Colonial Military Institutions', in Kanti P. Bajpai et al. (eds), *India's Grand Strategy: History, Theory, Cases*, Routledge, New Delhi 2014, p. 95.
26. "Budget Speech, 1903", *GSW*, Vol. I, p. 36.
27. Jayal, *Citizenship and its Discontents*, p. 35.
28. "The Work before Us", 4 February 1907, *GSW*, Vol. II, p. 222.
29. "The Work before Us", pp. 219–220.
30. Partha Chatterjee, "Empires, Nations, Peoples: The Imperial Prerogative and Colonial Exceptions", *Thesis Eleven*, Vol. 139, n. 1 (2017), p. 86.
31. "Nationalism and Liberalism", *The Indian Social Reformer*, 27 June 1909, p. 507.
32. According to Sudipta Kaviraj, "it is the emergence of the ideal of modern nationalism that produces the strange love of the land that marks modern political discourse, and creates an entirely unprecedented connection between fixed political space and a powerful emotion of inhabitance;" Sudipta Kaviraj, "A Strange Love of the Land: Identity, Poetry and Politics in the (Un)Making of South Asia", *South Asia Multidisciplinary Academic Journal*, n. 10 (2014), p. 4.
33. "Students and Politics", *GSW*, Vol. III, p. 198. See also "Advice to Students", Pachaiyappa College, Madras, 28 July 1904, *GSW*, Vol. III, p. 187.
34. "Students and Politics", p. 198.
35. "Servants of India Society Fifth Anniversary Day (12 June 1910): The first member's inaugural Address" (Gadgil Library, Rare Section, file n. 212940), p. 6.
36. "Fifth Anniversary Day", p. 6.
37. This is a phrase that recurs in Gokhale's speeches.
38. "The Servants of India Society", pp. 181–185.
39. Nanda, *Gokhale*, p. 171.
40. Watt, *Serving the Nation*, p. 171.
41. "The Servants of India Society", p. 182.
42. See Massimo Scioscioli, *Giuseppe Mazzini: i princìpi e la politica*, Alfredo Guida Editori, Napoli 1995, pp. 51–54.

43. Federico Chabod, *L'Idea di Nazione*, Laterza, Bari 2011 (first published 1961), pp. 70–75.

44. "'Nationalité': quelques idée sur une constitution nationale", *La Jeune Suisse*, 23 September 1831, in *Scritti Editi e Inediti di Giuseppe Mazzini*, Cooperativa Tipografico-Editrice Paolo Galeati, Imola 1909, Vol. 6, p. 127, quoted in Simon Levis Sullam, 'Mazzini and Nationalism as Political Religion', in Christopher A. Bayly and Eugenio F. Biagini (eds.), *Giuseppe Mazzini and the Globalization of Democratic Nationalism (1830-1920)*, OUP, Oxford 2008, p. 112.

45. Giuseppe Mazzini, *A Cosmopolitanism of Nations: Giuseppe Mazzini's Writings on Democracy, Nation Building, and International Relations* (edited by Stefano Recchia and Nadia Urbinati), Princeton University Press, Princeton 2009. See also David Ragazzoni, 'Giuseppe Mazzini's Democratic Theory of Nations', in A. Campi, S. De Luca and F. Tuccari (eds.), *Nazione e nazionalismi. Teorie, interpretazioni, sfide attuali*, Historica Edizioni, Roma 2018, Vol. I, pp. 279–305.

46. The volume edited by Bayly and Biagini, *Mazzini and the Globalization of Democratic Nationalism*, tracks the global influence exerted by Mazzini's ideals while at the same time shows that his thought could be easily adapted to different political ideologies. For Mazzini's influence on Indian nationalists, see also Enrico Fasana, "Deshabhakta: The Leaders of the Italian Independence Movement in the Eyes of Marathi Nationalists", *Asian and African Studies*, Vol. 3, n. 2 (1994), pp. 152–175 and Gita Srivastava, *Mazzini and His Impact on the Indian National Movement*, Chugh Publications, Allahabad 1982.

47. In Bayly and Biagini's edited volume, see C.A. Bayly, 'Liberalism at Large: Mazzini and Nineteenth-century Indian Thought', pp. 355–374; in Giorgio Borsa and Paolo Beonio Brocchieri (eds.), *Garibaldi, Mazzini e il Risorgimento nel risveglio dell'Asia e dell'Africa*, Università di Pavia/Franco Angeli, Milano 1984, see especially the contributions by Kenneth Ballhatchet, Giorgio Borsa, Giuseppe Flora and Enrico Fasana.

48. Bayly, 'Liberalism at Large', pp. 355, 359. It is significant that the most popular and translated work by Giuseppe Mazzini was *On the Duties of Men* (*Manushyon ke kartave* in Hindi). It sold thousands of copies in India. The work of the Risorgimento thinker dealt with a modernising religion which empowered the individual and the race in a march towards the Divine Spirit, very similarly to what the Brahmo Samajists advocated. The essence of divinity was the unity and wisdom of the human race (Bayly, 'Liberalism at Large', p. 362). See also Surendranath Banerjea, *A Nation in Making*, OUP, Bombay 1963 (1st edition 1925), p. 40.

49. Ben Anderson has stressed the link between the 'natural' membership in the nation, disinterestedness, and sacrifice. See Benedict Anderson, *Imagined Communities: Reflections on the Origin and Spread of Nationalism*, Verso, London 1991, p. 143.

50. On the emotional components of nationalism see, for instance, Stuart J. Kaufman, *Nationalist Passions*, Cornell University Press, Ithaca 2015 and the slightly dated, yet still helpful, Gavin Kitching, 'Nationalism: The Instrumental Passion', *Capital & Class*, Vol. 1 (1985), pp. 98–116.

51. The most complete work on the Swadeshi movement is Sumit Sarkar, *The Swadeshi Movement in Bengal, 1903–1908*, Permanent Black, New Delhi 2010.

52. Manu Goswami, *Producing India*, pp. 243–234, 257–258; Andrew Sartori, *Bengal in Global Concept History: Culturalism in the Age of Capital*, University of Chicago Press, London and Chicago 2008, p. 168.

53. Dipesh Chakrabarty, "Clothing the Political Man: A Reading of the Use of *Khadi*/White in Indian Public Life", *Journal of Human Values*, Vol. 5, n. 1 (1999), pp. 3–13. While seeking to assert cultural autonomy from the

British Empire, the Swadeshists aimed also at establishing international affiliations in terms of knowledge production beyond the epistemic boundaries of the empire in order to advance the Indian nationalist cause: Kris Manjapra, "Knowledgeable Internationalism and the Swadeshi Movement, 1903–1921", *EPW*, Vol. 47, n. 42 (2012), pp. 53–62.

54. Sarkar, *The Swadeshi Movement*, pp. 344–394.

55. Harald Fischer-Tiné, "Indian Nationalism and the 'World Forces': Transnational and Diasporic Dimensions of the Indian Freedom Movement on the Eve of the First World War", *Journal of Global History*, Vol. 2, n. 3 (2007), pp. 325–344.

56. "East and West", p. 383.

57. The critique of the Eurocentric world to which Gokhale contributed was part of a wider phenomenon. The defeat of Russia by a small Asian power engendered "a global anti-Western moment" as well as the emergence of a global public sphere in which the image of the decadent East was questioned. The Japanese model, however, did not represent an alternative modernity: on the contrary, Japan was seen as a successful example of a modernised nation along Western lines. Modernity was still seen as singular and universal. [Cemil Aydin, 'A Global Anti-Western Moment? The Russo-Japanese War, Decolonization, and Asian Modernity', in S. Conrad and D. Sachsenmaier (eds.), *Competing Visions of World Order: Global Moments and Movements 1880s–1930s*, Palgrave Macmillan, New York 2007, p. 215, 226].

58. "The Work before Us", p. 215.

59. Harald Fischer-Tiné, among others, has shown that the India Houses opened by diaspora Indians during the Swadeshi in the cities of London, New York and Tokyo became transnational foci of intellectuals committed to undermining the ideological hegemony of the West by creating connections with movements like Pan-Islamism, Pan-Asianism and Irish nationalism (see Harald Fischer-Tiné, "Indian Nationalism and the 'World Forces'").

60. All quotes are culled from the 1905 "Congress Presidential Address", Benares, December 1905, *GSW*, Vol. II, pp. 195–197.

61. "Our Political Situation", speech delivered by Gokhale in Madras, 25 July 1904, *GSW*, Vol. II, p. 178. It is indicative that Gokhale gave such a speech in Madras, where the Congress session had taken place the previous year, with low attendance of delegates and visible tensions and discontent against Pherozeshah Mehta.

62. "Our Political Situation", p. 179.

63. Sartori maintains that "in the moderate version of national political economy, the language of culture and self-sacrifice was being invoked as a supplement to salvage the salience of liberal political, economic, and social categories". Sartori, *Bengal in Global Concept History*, p. 165.

64. This phenomenon started around the end of the 19th century and Swami Vivekananda (1863–1902) played a prominent role in it. The idiom of renunciation, sacrifice and disciplined action came to represent an important factor of Indian distinctiveness vis-à-vis the Western culture of acquisitiveness. It was also valid to challenge the coloniser's argument that "Western knowledge was superior not just qua knowledge, but because it generated the most valid forms of practice." See Prathama Banerjee, "Between the Political and the Non-Political: The Vivekananda Moment and a Critique of the Social in Colonial Bengal, 1890s–1910s", *Social History*, Vol. 39, n. 3 (2014), pp. 324–325, 327.

65. For a discussion on this, see Jayal, *Citizenship and Its Discontents*, pp. 116–118.

66. Writing to the editor of the *Indian Social Reformer*, a few years later, Gokhale said that, while in Calcutta, he could understand better the aims and aspirations

of Vivekananda, suggesting that he had already approached the teachings of the Swami (Gokhale to K. Natarajan, 26 July 1902, GP). In a famous speech against untouchability held during the Social Conference in Dharvar in 1903, Gokhale mentioned Vivekananda's vision of national elevation to give more authoritativeness to the need to uplift the 'depressed classes.' While in Calcutta, he became very close to a disciple of the Swami Sister Nivedita, that is, the Irish Margaret E. Noble, with whom he had talks 'on spiritual-religious matters' (see Diaries of Gokhale, file 604, 1, GP) as well as on political issues. Some letters from Sister Nivedita to Gokhale have been published and show their level of intimate friendship (*Letters of Sister Nivedita*, collected and edited by Sankari Prasad Basu, 2 Vols., Advaita Ashrama, Kolkata 2017). For the intellectual synthesis at the basis of Vivekananda's ideas, with a special focus on his concept of *seva*, see Gwilym Beckerlegge, 'Swami Vivekananda and Seva: Taking "social service" seriously', in W. Radice (ed.), *Swami Vivekananda and the Modernisation of Hinduism*, OUP, New Delhi 1998, pp. 158–193.

67. Ranade to Gokhale, 24 June 1899, GP.
68. See chapter 3 for a discussion on this.
69. See Lucy Carroll, "The Temperance Movement in India: Politics and Social Reform", *Modern Asian Studies*, Vol. 10, n. 3 (1976), pp. 417–447.
70. See chapter 4 for this cooperation.
71. Political religion as posited, for instance, by scholars like Emilio Gentile and Christel Lane sacralises politics dogmatically, imposing on communities its political imperatives and participation in political cults; it sanctifies violence as a legitimate weapon against constructed enemies; it's hostile to traditional religions or attempts to incorporate them in their system of beliefs and myths, making them functional to the political cult (see Christel Lane, *The Rites of Rulers*, CUP, Cambridge and New York 1981; Emilio Gentile, *Le religioni della politica. Fra democrazie e totalitarismi*, Laterza, Roma and Bari 2001). The cult of the *Hindu Rashtra* promoted by the Rashtriya Swayamsevak Sangh arguably corresponds to this description of political religion.
72. "The Swadeshi Movement", Lucknow, 9 February 1907, *GSW*, Vol. II, p. 234.
73. "Congress Presidential Address", p. 197.
74. Chatterjee, *The Black Hole of Empire*, p. 279. The idiom of sacrifice was commonly adopted by the Extremist leadership too. See in the same work pp. 276–291.
75. *Dacca Prakash*, 13 December 1908, in Report of Native Press of Assam and Eastern Bengal, Jan-Jun 1909 (this volume also contains articles of the previous December). In all likelihood, it was the first edition of Gokhale's speeches, published in 1908 by Natesan's publishing house.
76. This recurs in Gokhale's speeches. See, for example, the already cited "England's Duty to India" and "Our Political Situation."
77. "New Reform Club Banquet", speech at the New Reform Club, London, 14 November 1905, *GSW*, Vol. II, p. 339.
78. "England's Duty to England", p. 342.
79. "England's Duty to England", p. 344. The recurring emphasis on the "moral and material progress" of India was based on the "Moral and Material Progress and Condition of India" reports that colonial officials, driven by emerging ideas of colonial governance, produced from the late 1850s onwards. See Michael Mann, '"Torchbearers Upon the Path of Progress": Britain's Ideology of a "Moral and Material Progress" in India. An Introductory Essay', in Harald Fischer-Tiné and Michael Mann (eds.), *Colonialism as Civilizing Mission: Cultural Ideology in British India*, Anthem Press, London and New York 2004 pp. 1–26.

80. "Our Political Situation", p. 174.
81. "Our Political Situation", p. 177.
82. See, among many others, Ratan Khasnabis, 'Evolution of Economic Thinking in Modern India' in S. Bhattacharya (ed.), *Development of Modern Indian Thought and the Social Sciences*, OUP, Delhi 2007, p. 7; Goswami, *Producing India*, pp. 224–232; Jayati Ghosh, 'Dissenting Economists. The Late Nineteenth-century Indian Tradition', in Claudio Sardoni and Peter Kriesler (eds.), *Keynes, Post-Keynesianism and Political Economy, Essays in Honour of Geoff Harcourt, Vol. 3*, Routledge, London 1999, pp. 94–109; Ajit K. Dasgupta, *A History of Indian Economic Thought*, Routledge, London and New York 1993, pp. 72–86; Bipan Chandra, "Indian Nationalists and the Drain, 1880-1905", *Indian Economic and Social History Review*, Vol. 2, n. 2 (1965), pp. 103–144.
83. "Seditious Meetings Bill", Imperial Legislative Council, 1 November 1907, *GSW*, Vol. II, p. 24.
84. "An Indian View of Indian Affairs", speech at the Fabian Society, London, 9 October 1905, *GSW*, Vol. II, p. 328.
85. There is no consensus among scholars on the meaning of modernity, given its being so ideologically laden. Useful interventions into the historiographical and sociological debates are, among others, Peter Wagner, 'Introduction', in P. Wagner (ed.), *African, American and European Trajectories of Modernity: Past Oppression, Future Justice?*, Edinburgh University Press, Edinburgh 2015, pp. 1–18; Dipesh Chakrabarty, "The Muddle of Modernity", *American Historical Review*, Vol. 116, n. 3 (2011), pp. 663–675; Sasheej Hegde, "Reassembling Modernity: Thinking at the Limit", *Social Scientist*, Vol. 37, n. 9/10 (2009), pp. 66–88; Björn Wittrock, "Modernity: One, None, or Many? European Origins and Modernity as a Global Condition", *Daedalus*, Vol. 129, n. 1 (2000), pp. 31–60. See also the concise but helpful discussion in Harald Fischer-Tiné, *Muscling in on South Asia: Colonial Difference, American Soft Power, and the Indian YMCA (c.1890-1950)*, Bloomsbury, London forthcoming 2022, chapter 2.
86. For an insightful historiographical discussion on this topic, see Washbrook, "Intimations of Modernity". For the search of alternative forms of modernity that looked back to 'authentic' Indian traditions, see by the same author, "Forms of Citizenship in Pre-Modern South India".
87. On the strong impact that Japan exerted on Indian imagination, see Carolien Stolte and Harald Fischer-Tiné, "Imagining Asia in India: Nationalism and Internationalism (ca. 1905-1940)", *Comparative Studies in Society and History*, Vol. 54, n. 1 (2012), pp. 65–92, here pp. 69–71.
88. See Homi Bhabha, *The Location of Culture*, Routledge, New York 1994, pp. 123–138; Uday Singh Mehta, *Liberalism and Empire*, pp. 29, 195–196.
89. "New Reform Club Banquet", p. 334.
90. "Our Political Situation", p. 177.
91. See Jayal, *Citizenship and its Discontents*, chapter 1, "The Subject-Citizen", pp. 27–50.
92. Michelguglielmo Torri, 'Nazionalismo indiano e nazionalismo musulmano in India nell'era coloniale', in Mario Mannini (ed.), *Dietro la bandiera. Emancipazioni coloniali, identità nazionali, nazionalismi nell'età contemporanea*, Pacini editore, Ospedaletto (Pisa) 1996, p. 154.
93. Quoted from *Nationalism, Religion, and Beyond: Writings on Politics, Society, and Culture* (edited by Peter Heehs), Permanent Black, Delhi and Ranikhet 2005, p. 138.
94. "Liberalism and Nationalism. Part III", *The Mahratta*, 1 August 1909, pp. 366–367.
95. See the Introduction of this book for a discussion on this.
96. "Our political situation", p. 177.

97. Sukanya Banerjee, *Becoming Imperial Citizens: Indians in the Late-Victorian Empire*, Duke University Press, Durham and London 2010, p. 23.
98. On citizenship and empire, see Daniel Gorman, *Imperial Citizenship: Empire and the Question of Belonging*, Manchester University Press, Manchester 2006, pp. 9–13; Charles V. Reed, 'Imperial Citizenship in a British World', in E.F. Isin and P. Nyers (eds.), *Routledge Handbook of Global Citizenship Studies*, Routledge, London 2014; Reiko Karatani, *Defining British Citizenship: Empire, Commonwealth and Modern Britain*, Frank Cass Publishers, London 2003; Keith McClelland and Sonya O. Rose, 'Citizenship and Empire, 1867–1928', in C. Hall and S.O. Rose (eds.), *At Home with the Empire*, CUP, Cambridge 2006, pp. 275–297. Not only the legal category of imperial citizenship, but also British citizenship was not instituted by legislation by the British government until 1981 (Karatani, *Defining British Citizenship*, p. 2.)
99. "Congress Presidential Address", p. 201.
100. "The Work before Us", pp. 216–217.
101. Srinivasa Sastri (1869–1946), one of the earliest members of the SIS, of which he became president in 1915, and founder of the Indian Liberal Federation (1922), continued Gokhale's campaign pressing for imperial citizenship until the hopes for the recognition of political rights within the empire were frustrated by the Paris Peace Conference and by the neglect of Wilson's Fourteen Points [on this, see Durba Ghosh, "Whither India? 1919 and the Aftermath of the First World War", *The Journal of Asian Studies*, Vol. 78, n. 2 (2019), pp. 389–397] as well as by the ongoing racial prejudices of the Dominions against non-whites.
102. This concept was elaborated in the Bhagavad Gita, which acquired very different meanings in the interpretations of Indian thinkers and politicians. Also, through multiple translations, the Gita had been circulated internationally from 1880s onwards. See *Political Thought in Action: The Bhagavad Gita and Modern India* (edited by Shruti Kapila and Faisal Devji), CUP, Cambridge 2013. For Tilak and his anti-liberal interpretation of the Gita, see in the same book chapter 9 by Shruti Kapila, 'A History of Violence', pp. 177–199.
103. "The Work before Us", p. 219.
104. "Self-Government for India", paper read at the East India Association, London, 11 July 1906, GSW, Vol. II, pp. 354–355.
105. On Burke and India as a hierarchically ordered society, see for instance Daniel O'Neill, *Edmund Burke and the Conservative Logic of Empire*, University of California Press, Berkeley 2016, chapter 3 'India'.
106. Gokhale was reported saying that he was conscious of the fact that his work was popular only among the educated classes, whereas he had no sympathisers or supporters among the 'ignorant' masses, who had no idea of who he was and what kind of work he was doing (quoted in Gordon Johnson, *Provincial Politics and Indian Nationalism: Bombay and the Indian National Congress 1880 to 1915*, CUP, Cambridge 1973, p. 117, from Weekly Report DCI, 20 February 1909, in *Home Political B*, June 1909, 104, NAI).
107. D.B. Mathur, *Gokhale, A Political Biography: A Study of His Services and Political Ideas*, Manaktalas, Bombay 1966, p. 62. Gokhale maintained that "all property, in its largest sense, must certainly have a large share of representation in this country" ("Council Regulations", p. 77). Gokhale agreed to separate representation for Muslims, landlords, and Anglo-Indian-dominated chambers of commerce too. That each section had to be represented proportionally was a Whig notion, strongly promoted for example by John Stuart Mill. In the Indian context, it was adapted to different notions of secular and religious hierarchies (Bayly, *Recovering Liberties*, p. 274).
108. "The Work before Us", p. 217. He referred mainly to Aurobindo and Bipin Chandra Pal who were asking for *purna swaraj*.

109. "Congress Presidential Address", p. 205.
110. "Self-Government for India", p. 354.
111. Washbrook, "Intimations of Modernity", p. 143.
112. Sugata Bose, *A Hundred Horizons: The Indian Ocean in the Age of Global Empire*, Harvard University Press, Cambridge, MA 2006, pp. 148–192. For an illuminating discussion on the shift from the inclusive ideal of imperial citizenship to the exclusive national citizenship, see Mrinalini Sinha, 'The Strange Death of an Imperial Ideal: The Case of *Civis Britannicus*', in S. Dube (ed.), *Handbook of Modernity in South Asia: Modern Makeovers*, OUP, New Delhi 2011.
113. Richard Drayton, "Federal Utopias and the Realities of Imperial Power", *Comparative Studies in South Asia, Africa and the Middle East*, Vol. 37, n. 2 (2017), pp. 401–406.
114. Mark R. Frost, "Imperial Citizenship or Else: Liberal Ideals and the India Unmaking of Empire, 1890–1919", *The Journal of Imperial and Commonwealth History*, Vol. 46, n. 5 (2018), pp. 845–873.
115. Karuna Mantena, 'Popular Sovereignty and Anti-colonialism', in R. Bourke and Q. Skinner (eds.), *Popular Sovereignty in Historical Perspective*, CUP, Cambridge 2016, p. 300.
116. Nonviolent forms of resistance were theorised and adopted for the first time in a considerable way under the name of 'passive resistance' by Aurobindo Ghose, Bal Gangadhar Tilak, Lala Lajpat Rai and Bipin Chandra Pal during the Swadeshi movement in 1905–1908. In 1907, in a completely different context from the Indian one, Gandhi launched his first passive resistance campaign in South Africa. See David Hardiman, *The Nonviolent Struggle for Indian Freedom, 1905-19*, OUP, New York 2018, esp. chapter 1 'Passive Resistance in India', 1905–1909.
117. "The Work before Us", p. 218. For Tilak's criticism of the use of the word 'constitutional' by Gokhale and the 'Moderates', see A. Appadorai (ed.), *Documents on Political Thought in Modern India*, OUP, London and New York 1973, Vol. I, pp. 186–188.
118. In the same speech, "The Work before Us", Gokhale advised that the weapon of boycott had to be reserved for extreme occasions. He argued that it would be impractical and suicidal to spread the movement all over the country. He gave the details of overall capacity of India's spinning mills and showed how they would not be able to satisfy the demand for cloth in the country. He, therefore, advised that the movement should be confined to Bengal where the grievance was genuine and the attitude of the government reprehensible. As known, the all-India extension of the boycott would be the bone of contention for the following Congress.
119. Hardiman, *The Nonviolent Struggle*, p. 41.
120. "The Work before Us", p. 222.
121. Gokhale, "On the Present Situation", *Bengalee*, 8 July 1909, quoted in Bayly, *Recovering Liberties*, p. 269.
122. Although considering passive resistance by itself a legitimate method, Gokhale, referring to the so-called Extremists, maintained that "those who advocate winning independence by passive resistance are either incapable of forming sound judgement or are hypocrites. I should not advocate repression towards these men, but I should ask Government to grant reform, take us in confidence, and reduce them to insignificance" ("Hon. Mr. Gokhale's Defamation Case", *The Mahratta*, 21 November 1909, p. 348).
123. "The Work before Us", p. 221.
124. Sugata Bose and Ayesha Jalal, *Modern South Asia: History, Culture, Political Economy*, University Press, Delhi 1998, p. 99. See also Bayly, *Origins of*

Nationality, pp. 293–295. Indian intellectuals and political activists did not ignore the fact that the colonial state was not created *ex nihilo* but derived a great deal from the Mughal empire in terms of legal and bureaucratic culture and institutions.

125. Elena Valdameri, 'Gopal Krishna Gokhale: Nazione e Impero tra "Oriente" e "Occidente"', in M. Casolari and C. Tresso (eds.), *Sguardi sull'Asia. Scritti in onore di Michelguglielmo Torri*, I Libri di Emil, Bologna 2017, pp. 106–111.

126. Bayly, *Recovering Liberties*, pp. 12–13.

127. John Stuart Mill, *Considerations on Representative Government*, Parker, Son, and Bourn, London 1861, 2nd edition, pp. 281–282.

128. See Jan Palmowski, "Liberalism and Local Government in Late Nine-teenth-Century Germany and England," *The Historical Journal*, Vol. 45, n. 2 (2002), p. 389.

129. "Mofussil Municipalities Bill", Bombay Legislative Council, 12 February 1901, *GSW*, Vol. II, p. 121.

130. "Responsibilities of Public Life", a lecture delivered by Mr Gokhale in Madras, published by Sons of India, Madras n.d., Reprints for Home Rulers, p. 14. We can argue that Gokhale replicated the tension that we can find in Mill's political thought between participation and competence. [On this aspect in Mill, see, for example, Dennis Thompson, *John Stuart Mill and Representative Government*, Princeton University Press, Princeton 1976, p. 11 and more recently Nadia Urbinati, *Mill on Democracy*, University of Chicago Press, Chicago 2002, p. 44 and Brandon P. Turner, "John Stuart Mill and the Antagonistic Foundation of Liberal Politics", *Review of Politics*, Vol. 72, n. 1 (Winter 2010), pp. 25–53].

131. See Sandip Hazareesingh, "The Quest for Urban Citizenship: Civic Rights, Public Opinion, and Colonial Resistance in Early Twentieth-Century Bombay", *Modern Asian Studies*, Vol. 34, n. 4 (2000), pp. 797–829, here 803. These views were very similar to those of Ranade: see Rajendra Vora, 'Two Strands of Indian Liberalism', p. 105.

132. On local self-government, see Gokhale's written and oral evidence in front of the 1907–08 Royal Commission upon Decentralisation in *GSW*, Vol. II, pp. 253–286, here p. 269.

133. For the measures taken by the British rulers to decentralise administration and promote local self-government, see James Jaffe, *Ironies of Colonial Governance: Law, Custom and Justice in Colonial India*, CUP, Cambridge 2015, esp. chapters 9 and 10. Chapter 10 also presents an insightful discussion on how the panchayat ideal emerged among the intelligentsia in Western India and was promoted by the Poona Sarvajanik Sabha as a court of arbitration in rural areas (pp. 260–267).

134. See Jaffe, *Ironies of Colonial Governance*. See also Bayly, "Rammohan Roy".

135. *The Mahratta*, 5 February 1911, p. 71.

136. Gokhale proposed the introduction of advisory councils at the district level in 1912 at the Imperial Legislative Council. The resolution was rejected. See "District Advisory Councils", *GSW*, Vol. II, pp. 88–108.

137. "Self-Government for India", p. 356.

138. Owen, *The British Left*, pp. 50–51.

139. Nanda, *Gokhale*, pp. 131–132; T.R. Deogirikar, *Makers of Modern India: Gopal Krishna Gokhale*, Publications Division, New Delhi 1992 (1964), p. 228.

140. On this, see chapter 4.

141. See, for example, the 1897 speech "Female Education in India", *GSW*, Vol. III, p. 180.

142. Gokhale to Krishnaswamy, 29 September 1906, GP.

143. "East and West", p. 388.

144. "The Hindu-Mohamedan Question", Poona Deccan Sabha, 11 July 1909, *GSW*, Vol. II, p. 308.

145. "The Hindu-Mohamedan Question", p. 308.

146. "The Work before Us", pp. 219–220.

147. The dichotomisation between 'positive' nationalism and religion, for long assumed in scholarly circles too, is being increasingly challenged in general debates. See, for example, Catarina Kinnvall, "Globalization and Religious Nationalism: Self, Identity, and the Search for Ontological Security", *Political Psychology*, Vol. 25, n. 5 (2004), pp. 741–767 and Saba Mahmood, *Religious Difference in a Secular Age: A Minority Report*, Princeton University Press, Princeton and Oxford 2016.

148. See letter from Gokhale to Wedderburn, 24 May 1907, GP (this letter is fully reproduced in H.D. Sharma, *100 Best letters: 1847–1947*, HarperCollins Publishers India, New Delhi 2000, pp. 100–104) and letter from Gokhale to Krishnaswami, 18 May 1909, GP.

149. "The Hindu-Mohamedan Question", p. 309.

150. "Indian Reception to Gokhale", 19 July 1912, *GSW*, Vol. II, pp. 393–394.

151. As noted by Sudipta Kaviraj, this contradiction between the sociology of diversity and the homogenising demands of the modern state continued to exist in post-independent India when 'unity in diversity' became the state ideology (Kaviraj, "A Strange Love", p. 10 and ff.). Although not dealing specifically with modern South Asia, the discussion in Fanar Haddad, 'Reconsidering the Relation Between "Secularism" and Nationalism in the Middle East', in G. Shani and T. Kibe (eds.), *Religion and Nationalism in Asia*, Routledge, London 2019 is an interesting survey of the complex relation between nationalism and 'sectarian' identities.

152. "Mr. Gokhale and the Hindu-Mahomedan Problem", *The Mahratta*, 3 March 1907, pp. 103–105.

153. *Lajpat Rai. Autobiographical Writings* (edited by Vijaya Chandra Joshi), University Publishers, Delhi and Jullundur 1965, pp. 116–117.

154. Sastri, *Life of Gokhale*, pp. 107–108; Nanda, *Gokhale*, pp. 337–353; Bayly, *Recovering Liberties*, pp. 266, 274.

155. For a discussion on the Morley-Minto Reforms and the different reactions in exponents of the Hindu and Muslim communities, see Shabnum Tejani, *Indian Secularism: A Social and Intellectual History 1980-1950*, Permanent Black, New Delhi 2007, p. 116 ff.

156. "Mr. Gokhale and the Hindu-Mahomedan Problem", *The Mahratta*, 3 March 1907, pp. 103–105.

157. Writing to Wedderburn (see Letter from Gokhale to Wedderburn, 3 December 1909, GP), Gokhale complained that "the Mahomedan representation in the Viceroy's council [was] so excessive as to be not only unjust but monstrously unjust" so much so that even a moderate like Pherozeshah Mehta felt disgusted. "The Hindus will probably have sometimes no representative and sometimes only one! And this when they are about half the polutation (sic) of the Province and in point of education, wealth and public spirit by far the more advanced. In East Bengal too, things will be equally bad [...]. What I, however, particularly dislike is the matter in which representation has been so arranged as to neutralize in practice the non-official majorities that have been created in the Provincial councils." Everywhere in the next few years, they would become a "hopeless minority."

158. Letter from Gokhale to Wedderburn, 24 September 1909, GP. The Hindu League mentioned by Gokhale was the original nucleus of the All-India Hindu Mahasabha, namely the Punjab Hindu Sabha founded in 1909 by some leaders of the Arya Samaj, including Lala Lajpat Rai. The first session

of the Sabha took place in Lahore in 1909 and was presided by Madan Mohan Malaviya (1862–1946).

159. "Self-Government for India", pp. 351–352.
160. Torri, *Storia dell'India*, pp. 564–565.
161. "The Hindu-Mahomedan Question", report of a speech originally delivered in Marathi at the Deccan Sabha, Poona, 4 July 1909, *GSW*, Vol. II, p. 310.
162. "The Hindu-Mahomedan Question", pp. 310–311 (italics mine).
163. See for instance, Faisal Devji, 'Qawm', in G. Dharampal, M. Kirloskar-Steinbach, R. Dwyer and J. Phalkey (eds.), *Key Concepts in Modern Indian Studies*, OUP, New Delhi 2015, pp. 217–219. Who a Muslim was and how particular or universal their affiliations were was a debated question among the Muslim political elite in colonial India. See, for example, David Lelyveld, "Next Year, If Grain is Dear, I Shall be a Sayyid: Sayyid Ahmad Khan, Colonial Constructions, and Muslim Self-Definitions", *JRAS*, Series 3, Vol. 30, n. 3 (2020), pp. 433–448; Faisal Devji, 'A Shadow Nation: The Making of Muslim India', in K. Grant, P. Levine and F. Trentmann (eds.), *Beyond Sovereignty: Britain, Empire and Transnationalism, c. 1880–1950*, Palgrave Macmillan, Basingstoke 2007, pp. 126–145.
164. Faisal Devji, "Changing Places: Religion and Minority in Pakistan", *South Asia: Journal of South Asian Studies*, Vol. 43, n. 1 (2020), pp. 169–176, here 175.
165. On Muslim 'separatism' and the expansion of nominally representative political institutions in 'British' India, influential works are Francis Robinson, *Separatism among Indian Muslims: The Politics of the United Provinces' Muslims, 1860–1923*, CUP, Cambridge 1974; Francis Robinson, *Islam and Muslim History in South Asia*, OUP, New Delhi 2001, pp. 156–209; David Lelyveld, *Aligarh's First Generation: Muslim Solidarity in British India*, Princeton University Press, Princeton 1978; Farzana Shaikh, *Community and Consensus in Islam: Muslim Representation in Colonial India*, CUP, Cambridge 1989; Barbara D. Metcalf, *Islamic Contestations: Essays on Muslims in India and Pakistan*, OUP, New Delhi 2004; Ian Talbot, *Freedoms Cry: The Popular Dimension in the Pakistan Movement and Partition Experiences in North India*, OUP, Karachi 1996; Ayesha Jalal, *Self and Sovereignty: Individual and Community in South Asian Islam since 1850*, OUP, New Delhi 2001.
166. See, to name just a few, Christophe Jaffrelot, *Religion, Caste and Politics in India*, Primus, Delhi 2010; Christopher Harding, *Religious Transformation in South Asia: The Meanings of Conversion in Colonial Punjab*, OUP, Oxford 2008; Laura Dudley Jenkins, *Identity and Identification in India*, Routledge, London and New York 2003; Harjot Oberoi, *The Construction of Religious Boundaries: Culture Identity and Diversity in the Sikh Tradition*, University of Chicago Press, Chicago 1994. On religious minorities in Pakistan, see the excellent discussion in Maria-Magdalena Fuchs and Simon Wolfgang Fuchs, "Religious Minorities in Pakistan: Identities, Citizenship and Social Belonging", *South Asia: Journal of South Asian Studies*, Vol. 43, n. 1 (2020), 52–67 and the contributions to the same special section.
167. Letter from Gokhale to Sir Lawrence Jenkins, 29 January 1909, GP.
168. In January 1911, Malaviya had moved a resolution in the Imperial Legislative Council, of which he had been a member since 1910, to ask for the appointment of a Committee to consider, among other aspects, what changes were to be made in the regulations of the Morley-Minto reforms in order to establish greater equality among the Hindu and Muslim and Hindu community. Gokhale appealed to Malaviya to withdraw the resolution. See Nanda, *Gokhale*, p. 379.
169. The expression was used by the young Muslim nationalist and future leader of the Khilafat movement Mohammed Ali Jauhar (1878–1931) in a letter to

Gokhale (Mohammed Ali to Gokhale, 8 February 1908, GP). Several members of the Muslim League wrote letters to Gokhale asking his support towards separate electorates.

170. "The Hindu-Mahomedan Question", pp. 311–312.

171. "The Hindu-Mahomedan Question", p. 311.

172. "Council Regulations", p. 79.

173. Letter from Gokhale to Wedderburn, 24 May 1907, GP. Gokhale had sent Srinivasa Sastri, member of the recently founded SIS, to the areas of communal unrest in early 1907 and given the alarming reports that he received from his disciple, he had decided to go in person to examine the situation. The letter to Wedderburn recalls his impressions after the visit. For Srinivasa Sastri's letter to Gokhale, see V.S. Srinivasa Sastri, *Letters of Right Honourable V.S. Srinivasa Sastri* (edited by T.N. Jagadisan), Rochouse and Sons, Madras 1944, pp. 5–15.

174. "The Seditious Meetings Bill", pp. 35–36.

175. "The Work before Us", p. 215.

176. "Congress Presidential Address", pp. 187–209.

177. Gokhale actually did not make any reference to religion in his speech. ("Congress Presidential Address", p. 190). He elsewhere argued, "[w]e could put up with it [despotism] under the Mughals and in the Native states, because it was their form of government. They did not rule us in one way and themselves in another. But it is not your [the British rulers'] method and you cannot apply it to us without despising us" (in Gordon Milburn, *England and India*, George Allen and Unwin Ltd, London 1918, p. 18).

178. *Ryaz-ul-Akhbar*, 24 February 1906, in *Selections from Native Newspapers published in the United Provinces 1906*.

179. Gurpreet Mahajan, 'From Community to Nation: The Making of the Majority-Minority Framework', in V.R. Mehta and Thomas Pantham (eds.), *Political Ideas*, pp. 167–185. For this construction of Hinduism as a tolerant cultural system, see also Tejani, *Indian Secularism*, p. 176.

180. According to Mahajan ("From Community to Nation", p. 183), it was benevolent majoritarianism that prevailed after independence: because of the fears of Partition and communal violence, granting political rights on the basis of religious belonging was considered inappropriate, so that alternative strategies of multiculturalism were deliberated by the constituent assembly.

181. The official designation today is 'Scheduled Castes.' For a discussion on the terms used to define this social group and their different connotations, see Oliver Mendelsohn and Marika Vicziany, *The Untouchables: Subordination, Poverty and the State in Modern India*, CUP, Cambridge 1998, pp. 2–5.

182. "Elevation of Depressed Classes", Dharwar Social Conference, 27 April 1903, *GSW*, Vol. III, pp. 260–261.

183. "Mr Gokhale on the Depressed Classes", *The Indian Social Reformer*, 28 February 1910, p. 306.

184. See GP, file 34, which contains a booklet "Gokhale the Man," written by Sarojini Naidu and published in Hyderabad by A.V. Pillai and Sons in 1915.

185. "The Indian Social Conference. A Full Report", *The Indian Social Reformer*, 7 February 1910, p. 269.

186. "Elevation of Depressed Classes", pp. 262–263.

187. *Lecture delivered by Mr. G K Devadhar, Member of the Servants of India Society, in the John Small Memorial Hall, Poona on Saturday, the 30th of August 1913*, Aryabhushan Press, Poona 1914, p. 6.

188. *A Brief Account of the Work of the Servants of India Society, Poona (From June 1905 to December 1916)*, Aryabhushan Press, Poona 1917, pp. 18–19.

189. Shinde was a member of the Prarthana Samaj who founded the Depressed Classes Mission in 1906. See Prashant Kidambi, 'From Social Reform to Social Service: Civic Activism and the Urban Poor in Colonial Bombay, c. 1900-1920', in Carey A. Watt and Michael Mann (eds.), *Civilizing Missions in Colonial and Postcolonial South Asia: From Improvement to Development*, Anthem Press, London 2011, pp. 220–221 and G.P. Deshpande, 'The World and Ideas: The Case of Colonial and Ex-Colonial Maharashtra', in V.R. Mehta and Thomas Pantham (eds.), *Political Ideas*, pp. 113–114. In GP Deshpande there are several letters from V.R. Shinde (1873–1944) showing Gokhale's interest for the cause of the 'depressed classes' as well as his financial support to Shinde's Mission in Bombay and his willingness to help extend its work in other areas of Maharashtra (see GP, file 510). It is possible that it was Gokhale's financial help that allowed the mission to expand after 1910.

190. *A Brief Account of the Work of the Servants of India Society, Poona (From 1st January 1917 to 30th June 1923)*, Aryabhushan Press, Poona 1924, pp. 31–32.

191. C.S. Adcock, "Debating Conversion, Silencing Caste: The Limited Scope of Religious Freedom", *Journal of Law and Religion*, Vol. 29, n. 3 (2014), p. 371. The Gait circular, issued in 1910 by the census commissioner E.A. Gait and sent to the provinces, was leaked to the press. Although dropped in 1911, the memo made likely the possibility that the Hindu constituency could be drastically reduced at the discretion of colonial authorities, thus increasing the political clout of the Muslim community (*ibidem*).

192. On the social activities aimed at 'improving' the 'depressed classes' and their broader implications, see Rupa Viswanath, *The Pariah Problem: Caste, Religion, and the Social in Modern India*, Columbia University Press, New York 2014, *passim*; Kidambi, "From Social Reform to Social Service"; Susan Bayly, *Caste, Society and Politics in India from the Eighteenth Century to the Modern Age*, CUP, Cambridge 1999, pp. 144–186; Carey A. Watt, "Education for National Efficiency: Constructive Nationalism in North India, 1909–16", *Modern Asian Studies*, Vol. 31, n. 2 (1997), pp. 340–341; Dilip M. Menon, *Caste, Nationalism and Communism in South India: Malabar, 1900–1948*, CUP, Cambridge 1994; R. Srivatsan, *Seva, Saviour and State: Caste Politics, Tribal Welfare and Capitalist Development*, Routledge, Abingdon and New York 2015, pp. 163–181; Chandra Lekha Singh, "Annie Besant's Defence of Indian Caste System: A Critique", *History and Sociology of South Asia*, Vol. 13 (2018), pp. 1–18.

193. Bayly, *Caste, Society and Politics in India*, pp. 183–185.

194. See Barbara Arneil, "Liberal Colonialism, Domestic Colonies and Citizenship", *History of Political Thought*, Vol. 33, n. 3 (2012), pp. 491–523.

195. "The Indian Social Conference. A Full Report", p. 269.

196. "Bengal Support to Bill", Calcutta Town Hall, 2 September 1911, *GSW*, Vol. III, p. 243.

197. See Gail Omvedt, *Dalits and the Democratic Revolution: Dr Ambedkar and the Dalit Movement in Colonial India*, Sage Publications, London 1994; Aishwary Kumar, *Radical Equality: Ambedkar, Gandhi, and the Risk of Democracy*, Stanford University Press, Palo Alto, CA 2015, pp. 219–275; Partha Chatterjee, 'B. R. Ambedkar and the Troubled Times of Citizenship', in V.R. Mehta and Thomas Pantham (eds.), *Political Ideas*, pp. 73–90.

198. "Elevation of Depressed Classes", p. 262. It is interesting to note that in the same well-known speech, Gokhale mentioned Swami Vivekananda to validate his views about the need to review traditional caste practices and to resort to *seva* to uplift the 'depressed classes.' For a discussion on Vivekananda and the discourse of caste discrimination as being in conflict with modernising trends in Indian society, see Beckerlegge, "Swami Vivekananda and Seva."

199. It should not be forgotten that whether the depressed classes were to be considered Hindus or not would have had an impact on the Hindu-Muslim majority and minority ratio and by extension to their communal representation. On this, see Tejani, *Indian Secularism*, pp. 202–203. The same considerations have been constantly made by the forces of Hindu nationalism in independent India too when these have tried, often successfully, to co-opt Dalits into the Hindutva fold [see, among many others, Gopal Guru, "Understanding Communal Riots in Maharashtra", *Economic and Political Weekly*, Vol. 28, n. 19 (1993), pp. 903–907]. See also Bhanwar Meghwanshi, *I Could Not Be Hindu: The Story of a Dalit in the RSS* (translated by N. Menon), Navayana, New Delhi 2020.
200. "Elevation of Depressed Classes", p. 262.
201. See Bayly, *Caste, Society and Politics in India*, p. 182; Adcock, 'Debating Conversion, Silencing Caste', p. 371. The fear of Christian conversions was caused by the activism of the Salvation Army and other Christian missionary bodies in favour of the 'depressed classes.' On the Salvation Army, see Peter van der Veer, *Imperial Encounters: Religion and Modernity in India and Britain*, Princeton University Press, Princeton 2001, pp. 151–157 and Harald Fischer-Tiné, 'Global Civil Society and the Forces of Empire: The Salvation Army, British Imperialism, and the "prehistory" of NGOs (ca. 1880-1920)', in Carey A. Watt and Michael Mann (eds.), *Civilizing Missions*, pp. 29–67. Islam and, to a lesser extent, Sikhism also claimed converts among Dalits, a fact that acquired significance in the framework of the communal rivalries especially from the 1920s onwards (see Yoginder Singh Sikand, *Islam, Caste and Dalit-Muslim Relations in India*, Global Media Publication, Delhi 2004). To reclaim the converted back to the Hindu fold, associations like the Arya Samaj developed practices of (re)conversion (*shuddhi*, literally 'purification') that were new to Brahmanical Hinduism (see Harald Fischer-Tiné, '"Kindly Elders of the Hindu Biradri": The Arya Samaj's Struggle for Influence and its Effect on Hindu-Muslim Relations', in A. Copley (ed.), *Gurus and their Followers: Studies in New Religious Movements in Late Colonial India*, OUP, New Delhi 2000, pp. 107–127). However, the 'depressed classes' were not passive recipients of *shuddhi* practices. Conversely, they actively pursued *shuddhi* and made it instrumental in their politics of low-caste assertion against discrimination. For a discussion on this, see Adcock, 'Debating Conversion, Silencing Caste', pp. 363–377.
202. *The Indian Social Reformer*, 21 February 1910, p. 290.
203. For a discussion on the Moderates' perception of the people, see Seth, "Rewriting Histories of Nationalism." See also Susan Bayly, 'Hindu "Modernisers" and the "Public" Arena: Indigenous Critiques of Caste in Colonial India', in William Radice (ed.), *Swami Vivekananda*, pp. 93–137.
204. To use Chatterjee's words, for men like Gokhale, "democracy was a good form of government only when it could be adequately controlled by men of status and wisdom" (Partha Chatterjee, *The Politics of the Governed: Reflections of Popular Politics in Most of the World*, Columbia University Press, New York 2004, p. 48).
205. "The Work before Us", p. 216.
206. Dipesh Chakrabarty, *Provincializing Europe: Postcolonial Thought and Historical Difference*, Princeton University Press, Princeton 2000, p. 9.

References

A Brief Account of the Work of the Servants of India Society, Poona (From June 1905 to December 1916), Aryabhushan Press, Poona 1917.

A Brief Account of the Work of the Servants of India Society, Poona (From 1st January 1917 to 30th June 1923), Aryabhushan Press, Poona 1924.

Adcock, C.S. "Debating Conversion, Silencing Caste: The Limited Scope of Religious Freedom", *Journal of Law and Religion*, Vol. 29, n. 3 (2014), pp. 363–77.

Anderson, Benedict. *Imagined Communities: Reflections on the Origin and Spread of Nationalism*, Verso, London 1991 (revised edition).

Appadorai, A. (ed.). *Documents on Political Thought in Modern India*, Vol. I, OUP, London and New York 1973.

Arneil, Barbara. "Liberal Colonialism, Domestic Colonies and Citizenship", *History of Political Thought*, Vol. 33, n. 3 (2012), pp. 491–523.

Aydin, Cemil. 'A Global Anti-Western Moment? The Russo-Japanese War, Decolonization, and Asian Modernity', in S. Conrad and D. Sachsenmaier (eds.), *Competing Visions of World Order: Global Moments and Movements 1880s–1930s*, Palgrave Macmillan, New York 2007, pp. 213–236.

Banerjea, Surendranath. *A Nation in Making*, OUP, Bombay 1963 (1st edition 1925).

Banerjee, Prathama. "Between the Political and the Non-Political: The Vivekananda Moment and a Critique of the Social in Colonial Bengal, 1890s–1910s", *Social History*, Vol. 39, n. 3 (2014), pp. 323–339.

Banerjee, Sukanya. *Becoming Imperial Citizens: Indians in the Late-Victorian Empire*, Duke University Press, Durham and London 2010.

Bayly, C.A. *Recovering Liberties, Indian Thought in the Age of Liberalism and Empire*, CUP, Delhi 2012 (first published 2011).

——. 'Liberalism at Large: Mazzini and Nineteenth-Century Indian Thought', in C.A. Bayly and Eugenio F. Biagini (eds.), *Giuseppe Mazzini and the Globalization of Democratic Nationalism (1830-1920)*, OUP, Oxford 2008, pp. 355–374.

——. "Rammohan Roy and the Advent of Constitutional Liberalism in India, 1800-1830", *Modern Intellectual History*, Vol. 4, n. 1 (2007), pp. 25–41.

——. *Origins of Nationality in South Asia. Patriotism and Ethical Government in the Making of Modern India*, OUP, Delhi 1998.

——. and Biagini, Eugenio (eds.). *Mazzini and the Globalization of Democratic Nationalism (1830-1920)*, OUP, Oxford 2008.

Bayly, Susan. *Caste, Society and Politics in India from the Eighteenth Century to the Modern Age*, CUP, Cambridge 1999.

——. 'Hindu "Modernisers" and the "Public" Arena: Indigenous Critiques of Caste in Colonial India', in William Radice (ed.), *Swami Vivekananda and the Modernisation of Hinduism*, OUP, New Delhi 1998, pp. 93–137.

Beckerlegge, Gwilym. 'Swami Vivekananda and Seva: Taking 'Social Service' Seriously', in W. Radice (ed.), *Swami Vivekananda and the Modernisation of Hinduism*, OUP, New Delhi 1998, pp. 158–193.

Bhabha, Homi. *The Location of Culture*, Routledge, New York 1994.

Borsa, Giorgio and Paolo Beonio Brocchieri (eds.). *Garibaldi, Mazzini e Il Risorgimento Nel Risveglio dell'Asia e dell'Africa*, Università di Pavia/Franco Angeli, Milano 1984.

Bose, Sugata. *A Hundred Horizons: The Indian Ocean in the Age of Global Empire*, Harvard University Press, Cambridge, MA 2006.

—— and Jalal, Ayesha. *Modern South Asia. History, Culture, Political Economy*, University Press, Delhi 1998.

Carroll, Lucy. "The Temperance Movement in India: Politics and Social Reform", *Modern Asian Studies*, Vol. 10, n. 3 (1976), pp. 417–447.

Chabod, Federico. *L'Idea di Nazione*, Laterza, Bari 2011 (first published 1961).

Chakrabarty, Dipesh. "The Muddle of Modernity", *American Historical Review*, Vol. 116, n. 3 (2011), pp. 663–675.

——. "Clothing the Political Man: A Reading of the Use of *khadi*/White in Indian Public Life", *Journal of Human Values*, Vol. 5, n. 1 (1999), pp. 3–13.

——. *Provincializing Europe: Postcolonial Thought and Historical Difference*, Princeton University Press, Princeton 2000.

Chandra, Bipan. "Indian Nationalists and the Drain, 1880-1905", *Indian Economic and Social History Review*, Vol. 2, n. 2 (1965), pp. 103–144.

Chatterjee, Partha. 'B. R. Ambedkar and the Troubled Times of Citizenship', in V.R. Mehta and Thomas Pantham (eds.), *Political Ideas in Modern India: Thematic Explorations*, Sage, Thousand Oaks 2006, pp. 73–90.

——. "Empires, Nations, Peoples: The Imperial Prerogative and Colonial Exceptions", *Thesis Eleven*, Vol. 139, n. 1 (2017), pp. 84–96.

——. *Nationalist Thought and the Colonial World: A Derivative Discourse*, Zed Books, London 1986.

——. *The Black Hole of Empire: History of a Global Practice of Power*, Princeton University Press, Princeton and Oxford 2012.

——. *The Politics of the Governed: Reflections of Popular Politics in Most of the World*, Columbia University Press, New York 2004.

Crook, Paul. *Darwinism, War and History: The Debate Over the Biology of War from the 'Origin of Species' to the First World War*, CUP, Cambridge 1994.

Dasgupta, Ajit K. *A History of Indian Economic Thought*, Routledge, London and New York 1993.

Deogirikar, T.R. *Gopal Krishna Gokhale*, Publications Division, New Delhi 1992 (1964).

Deshpande, G.P. 'The World and Ideas: The Case of Colonial and Ex-Colonial Maharashtra', in V.R. Mehta and Thomas Pantham (eds.), *Political Ideas in Modern India: Thematic Explorations*, Sage, Thousand Oaks 2006, pp. 110–120.

Devadhar, G.K. *Lecture Delivered by Mr. G K Devadhar, Member of the Servants of India Society, in the John Small Memorial Hall, Poona on Saturday, the 30th of August 1913*, Aryabhushan Press, Poona 1914.

Devji, Faisal. 'Qawm', in G. Dharampal, M. Kirloskar-Steinbach, R. Dwyer and J. Phalkey (eds.), *Key Concepts in Modern Indian Studies*, OUP, New Delhi 2015, pp. 217–219.

——. 'A Shadow Nation: The Making of Muslim India', in K. Grant, P. Levine and F. Trentmann (eds.), *Beyond Sovereignty: Britain, Empire and Transnationalism, c. 1880–1950*, Palgrave Macmillan, Basingstoke 2007, pp. 126–145.

——. "Changing Places: Religion and Minority in Pakistan", *South Asia: Journal of South Asian Studies*, Vol. 43, n. 1 (2020), pp. 169–176.

Drayton, Richard. "Federal Utopias and the Realities of Imperial Power", *Comparative Studies in South Asia, Africa and the Middle East*, Vol. 37, n. 2 (2017), pp. 401–406.

Fasana, Enrico. "Deshabhakta: The Leaders of the Italian Independence Movement in the Eyes of Marathi Nationalists", *Asian and African Studies*, Vol. 3, n. 2 (1994), pp. 152–175.

Fischer-Tiné, Harald. 'Global Civil Society and the Forces of Empire: The Salvation Army, British Imperialism, and the 'prehistory' of NGOs (Ca. 1880-1920)', in Carey A. Watt and Michael Mann (eds.), *Civilizing Missions in Colonial and Postcolonial South Asia: From Improvement to Development*, Anthem Press, London 2011, pp. 29–67.

——. "Kindly Elders of the Hindu Biradri': The Arya Samaj's Struggle for Influence and Its Effect on Hindu-Muslim Relations', in A. Copley (ed.), *Gurus and Their Followers. Studies in New Religious Movements in Late Colonial India*, OUP, New Delhi 2000, pp. 107–127.

——. "Indian Nationalism and the 'World Forces': Transnational and Diasporic Dimensions of the Indian Freedom Movement on the Eve of the First World War", *Journal of Global History*, Vol. 2, n. 3 (2007), pp. 325–344.

——. *Muscling in on South Asia: Colonial Difference, American Soft Power, and the Indian YMCA (c.1890-1950)*, Bloomsbury, London forthcoming 2022.

Frost, Mark R. "Imperial Citizenship or Else: Liberal Ideals and the India Unmaking of Empire, 1890–1919", *The Journal of Imperial and Commonwealth History*, Vol. 46, n. 5 (2018), pp. 845–873.

Fuchs, Maria-Magdalena and Simon Wolfgang Fuchs. "Religious Minorities in Pakistan: Identities, Citizenship and Social Belonging", *South Asia: Journal of South Asian Studies*, Vol. 43, n. 1 (2020), pp. 52–67.

Gentile, Emilio. *Le Religioni della Politica. Fra Democrazie e Totalitarismi*, Laterza, Roma and Bari 2001.

Ghosh, Durba. "Whither India? 1919 and the Aftermath of the First World War", *The Journal of Asian Studies*, Vol. 78, n. 2 (2019), pp. 389–397.

Ghosh, Jayati. 'Dissenting Economists. The Late Nineteenth-Century Indian Tradition', in Claudio Sardoni and Peter Kriesler (eds.), *Keynes, Post-Keynesianism and Political Economy, Essays in Honour of Geoff Harcourt*, Vol. 3, Routledge, London 1999, pp. 94–109.

Gokhale, Gopal Krishna. *Gokhale Speeches and Writings (GSW), Vol. I Economic*, in R.P. Patwardhan and D.V. Ambekar (eds.), Asia Publishing House, Poona 1962.

——. *Gokhale Speeches and Writings (GSW), Vol. II Political*, in R.P. Patwardhan and D.V. Ambekar (eds.), Asia Publishing House, Poona 1966.

——. *Gokhale Speeches and Writings (GSW), Vol. III Educational*, in D.G. Karve and D.V Ambekar (eds.), Asia Publishing House, Poona 1967.

——. *Speeches of Gopal Krishna Gokhale*, in G.A. Natesan (ed.), Natesan & Co, Madras 1920.

Gorman, Daniel. *Imperial Citizenship: Empire and the Question of Belonging*, Manchester University Press, Manchester 2006.

Gosh, Aurobindo. *Nationalism, Religion, and Beyond: Writings on Politics, Society, and Culture* (edited by Peter Heehs), Permanent Black, Delhi and Ranikhet 2005.

Goswami, Manu. *Producing India: From Colonial Economy to National Space*, University of Chicago Press, Chicago 2004.

Guru, Gopal. "Understanding Communal Riots in Maharashtra", *Economic and Political Weekly*, Vol. 28, n. 19 (1993), pp. 903–907.

Haddad, Fanar. 'Reconsidering the Relation Between 'Secularism' and Nationalism in the Middle East', in G. Shani and T. Kibe (eds.), *Religion and Nationalism in Asia*, Routledge, London 2019.

Hardiman, David. *The Nonviolent Struggle for Indian Freedom, 1905-19*, OUP, New York 2018.

Harding, Christopher. *Religious Transformation in South Asia: The Meanings of Conversion in Colonial Punjab*, OUP, Oxford 2008.

Hazareesingh, Sandip. "The Quest for Urban Citizenship: Civic Rights, Public Opinion, and Colonial Resistance in Early Twentieth-Century Bombay", *Modern Asian Studies*, Vol. 34, n. 4 (2000), pp. 797–829.

Hegde, Sasheej. "Reassembling Modernity: Thinking at the Limit", *Social Scientist*, Vol. 37, n. 9/10 (2009), pp. 66–88.

Iggers, Georg G., Q. Edward Wang and Supriya Mukherjee. *A Global History of Modern Historiography*, Pearson Education Limited, Edinburgh 2008.

Jaffe, James. *Ironies of Colonial Governance. Law, Custom and Justice in Colonial India*, CUP, Cambridge 2015.

Jaffrelot, Christophe. *Religion, Caste and Politics in India*, Primus, Delhi 2010.

Jalal, Ayesha. *Self and Sovereignty. Individual and Community in South Asian Islam Since 1850*, OUP, New Delhi 2001.

Jayal, Niraja Gopal. *Citizenship and Its Discontents, An Indian History*, Harvard University Press, Cambridge, MA 2013.

Jenkins, Laura Dudley. *Identity and Identification in India*, Routledge, London and New York 2003.

Johnson, Gordon. *Provincial Politics and Indian Nationalism: Bombay and the Indian National Congress 1880 to 1915*, CUP, Cambridge 1973.

Kapila, Shruti and Faisal Devji (eds.). *Political Thought in Action: The Bhagavad Gita and Modern India*, CUP, Cambridge 2013.

Kapila, Shruti. 'A History of Violence', in Shruti Kapila and Faisal Devji (eds.), *Political Thought in Action: The Bhagavad Gita and Modern India*, CUP, Cambridge 2013, pp. 177-199.

Karatani, Reiko. *Defining British Citizenship: Empire, Commonwealth and Modern Britain*, Frank Cass Publishers, London 2003.

Kaufman, Stuart J. *Nationalist Passions*, Cornell University Press, Ithaca 2015.

Kaviraj, Sudipta. "A Strange Love of the Land: Identity, Poetry and Politics in the (Un)Making of South Asia", *South Asia Multidisciplinary Academic Journal*, n. 10 (2014), pp. 1–16.

Khasnabis, Ratan. 'Evolution of Economic Thinking in Modern India', in S. Bhattacharya (ed.), *Development of Modern Indian Thought and the Social Sciences*, OUP, Delhi, 2007.

Kidambi, Prashant. 'From "social Reform" to "social Service"', in Carey A. Watt and Michael Mann (eds.), *Civilizing Missions in Colonial and Postcolonial South Asia: From Improvement to Development*, Anthem Press, London 2011, pp. 217–240.

Kinnvall, Catarina. "Globalization and Religious Nationalism: Self, Identity, and the Search for Ontological Security", *Political Psychology*, Vol. 25, n. 5 (2004), pp. 741–767.

Kitching, Gavin. 'Nationalism: The Instrumental Passion', *Capital & Class*, Vol. 1 (1985), pp. 98–116.

Kumar, Aishwary. *Radical Equality: Ambedkar, Gandhi, and the Risk of Democracy*, Stanford University Press, Palo Alto, CA 2015.

Lal, Vinay. *The History of History: Politics and Scholarship in Modern India*, OUP, New Delhi 2003.

Lane, Christel. *The Rites of Rulers*, CUP, Cambridge and New York 1981.

Lelyveld, David. "Next Year, If Grain is Dear, I Shall be a Sayyid: Sayyid Ahmad Khan, Colonial Constructions, and Muslim Self-Definitions", *JRAS*, Series 3, Vol. 30, n. 3 (2020), pp. 433–448.

Lelyveld, David. *Aligarh's First Generation: Muslim Solidarity in British India*, Princeton University Press, Princeton 1978.

Levis Sullam, Simon. 'Mazzini and Nationalism as Political Religion', in C.A. Bayly and Eugenio F. Biagini (eds.), *Giuseppe Mazzini and the Globalization of Democratic Nationalism (1830-1920)*, OUP, Oxford 2008, pp. 107–124.

Ludden, David. 'Orientalist Empiricism: Transformations of Colonial Knowledge', in C.A. Breckenridge and P. Van Der Veer (eds.), *Orientalism and the Postcolonial Predicament: Perspectives from South Asia*, University of Pennsylvania Press, Philadelphia 1993, pp. 250–278.

Ludden, David. "Spatial Inequity and National Territory: Remapping 1905 in Bengal and Assam", *Modern Asian Studies*, Vol. 46, n. 3 (2012), pp. 483–525.

Mahajan, Gurpreet. 'From Community to Nation: The Making of the Majority-Minority Framework', in V.R. Mehta and Thomas Pantham (eds.), *Political Ideas in Modern India: Thematic Explorations*, Sage, Thousand Oaks 2006, pp. 167–185.

Mahmood, Saba. *Religious Difference in a Secular Age: A Minority Report.* Princeton University Press, Princeton and Oxford 2016.

Manjapra, Kris. "Knowledgeable Internationalism and the Swadeshi Movement, 1903– 1921", *EPW*, Vol. 47, n. 42 (2012), pp. 53–62.

Mann, Michael. '"Torchbearers Upon the Path of Progress": Britain's Ideology of a "Moral and Material Progress" in India. An Introductory Essay', in Harald Fischer-Tiné and Michael Mann (eds.), *Colonialism as Civilizing Mission: Cultural Ideology in British India*, Anthem Press, London and New York 2004, pp. 1–26.

Mantena, Karuna. 'Popular Sovereignty and Anti-Colonialism', in R. Bourke and Q. Skinner (eds.), *Popular Sovereignty in Historical Perspective*, CUP, Cambridge 2016, pp. 297–319.

Mathur, D.B. *Gokhale, A Political Biography: A Study of His Services and Political Ideas,* Manaktalas, Bombay 1966.

Mazzini, Giuseppe. *A Cosmopolitanism of Nations: Giuseppe Mazzini's Writings on Democracy, Nation Building, and International Relations* (edited by Stefano Recchia and Nadia Urbinati), Princeton University Press, Princeton 2009.

McClelland, Keith and Sonya O. Rose. 'Citizenship and Empire, 1867–1928', in C. Hall and S. O. Rose (eds.), *At Home with the Empire*, CUP, Cambridge 2006, pp. 275–297.

Meghwanshi, Bhanwar. *I Could Not Be Hindu: The Story of a Dalit in the RSS* (translated by N. Menon), Navayana, New Delhi 2020.

Mehta, Uday Singh. *Liberalism, and Empire. A Study in Nineteenth-Century British Liberal Thought*, University of Chicago Press, London 1999.

Mendelsohn, Oliver and Marika Vicziany. *The Untouchables: Subordination, Poverty and the State in Modern India*, CUP, Cambridge 1998.

Menon, Dilip M. "The Many Spaces and Times of Swadeshi", *Economic and Political Weekly*, Vol. 47, n. 42 (2012), pp. 44–52.

——. *Caste, Nationalism and Communism in South India: Malabar, 1900–1948.* CUP, Cambridge 1994.

Metcalf, Barbara D. *Islamic Contestations. Essays on Muslims in India and Pakistan*, OUP, New Delhi 2004.

Metcalf, Thomas R. *Ideologies of the Raj*, CUP, Cambridge, 1997.

Torri, Michelguglielmo. 'For a New Periodisation of Indian History', in D.N. Jha (ed.), *The Evolution of a Nation: Pre-Colonial to Post-Colonial, Essays in Memory of R. S. Sharma*, Manohar, Delhi 2014, pp. 39–60.

Milburn, Gordon. *England and India*, George Allen and Unwin Ltd, London 1918.

Mill, John Stuart. *Considerations on Representative Government* (2nd edition), Parker, Son, and Bourn, London 1861.

Naidu, Sarojini. *Gokhale the Man*, A.V. Pillai and Sons, Hyderabad 1915.

Nanda, B.R. *Three Statesmen: Gokhale, Gandhi and Nehru*, OUP, New Delhi 2004.

O'Neill, Daniel I. *Edmund Burke and the Conservative Logic of Empire*, University of California Press, Berkeley 2016.

Oberoi, Harjot. *The Construction of Religious Boundaries: Culture Identity and Diversity in the Sikh Tradition*, University of Chicago Press, Chicago 1994.

Omvedt, Gail. *Dalits and the Democratic Revolution: Dr Ambedkar and the Dalit Movement in Colonial India*, Sage Publications, London 1994.

Owen, Nicholas. *The British Left and India: Metropolitan Anti-Imperialism 1885–1947*, OUP, New York 2007.

Palmowski, Jan. "Liberalism and Local Government in Late Nineteenth-Century Germany and England", *The Historical Journal*, Vol. 45, n. 2 (2002), pp. 381–409.

Ragazzoni, David. 'Giuseppe Mazzini's Democratic Theory of Nations', in A. Campi, S. De Luca and F. Tuccari (eds.), *Nazione e Nazionalismi: Teorie, Interpretazioni, Sfide Attuali*, Historica Edizioni, Roma 2018, Vol. I, pp. 279–305.

Raghavan, Srinath. 'Liberal Thought and Colonial Military institutions', in Kanti P. Bajpai et al. (eds.), *India's Grand Strategy: History, Theory, Cases*, Routledge, New Delhi 2014, pp. 86–110.

Rai, Lala Lajpat. *Autobiographical Writings* (edited by Vijaya Chandra Joshi), University Publishers, Delhi and Jullundur 1965.

Ramaswamy, Sumathi. *The Goddess and the Nation: Mapping Mother India*, Duke University Press, Durham and London, 2010.

Reed, Charles V. 'Imperial Citizenship in a British World', in E.F. Isin and P. Nyers (eds.), *Routledge Handbook of Global Citizenship Studies*, Routledge, London 2014.

Robinson, Francis. *Islam and Muslim History in South Asia*, OUP, New Delhi 2001.

——. *Separatism Among Indian Muslims: The Politics of the United Provinces' Muslims, 1860–1923*, CUP, Cambridge 1974.

Rothermund, Dietmar. 'Emancipation or Re-Integration: The Politics of Gopal Krishna Gokhale and Herbert Risley', in D.A. Low (ed.), *Soundings in Modern South Asian History*, Weindenfeld and Nicolson, London 1968, pp. 131–157.

Sarkar, Sumit. *The Swadeshi Movement in Bengal, 1903–1908*, Permanent Black, New Delhi 2010.

Sartori, Andrew S. *Bengal in Global Concept History: Culturalism in the Age of Capital*, University of Chicago Press, London and Chicago 2008.

Scioscioli, Massimo. *Giuseppe Mazzini: i Principi e La Politica*, Alfredo Guida Editori, Napoli 1995.

Shaikh, Farzana. *Community and Consensus in Islam: Muslim Representation in Colonial India*, CUP, Cambridge 1989.

Sharma, H.D. *100 Best Letters: 1847–1947*, HarperCollins Publishers India, New Delhi 2000.

Sikand, Yoginder Singh. *Islam, Caste and Dalit-Muslim Relations in India*, Global Media Publication, Delhi 2004.

Singh, Chandra Lekha. "Annie Besant's Defence of Indian Caste System: A Critique", *History and Sociology of South Asia*, Vol. 13 (2018), pp. 1–18.

Sinha, Mrinalini. 'The Strange Death of an Imperial Ideal: The Case of *Civis Britannicus*', in S. Dube (ed.), *Handbook of Modernity in South Asia: Modern Makeovers*, OUP, New Delhi 2011.

Nivedita, Sister. *Letters of Sister Nivedita*, collected and edited by Sankari Prasad Basu, 2 Vols, Advaita Ashrama, Kolkata 2017.

Srinivasa Sastri, V.S. *Letters of Right Honourable V.S. Srinivasa Sastri* (edited by T.N. Jagadisan), Rochouse and Sons, Madras 1944.

——. *Life of Gopal Krishna Gokhale*, Bangalore Printing and Publishing Co, Bangalore 1937.

Srivastava, Gita. *Mazzini and His Impact on the Indian National Movement*, Chugh Publications, Allahabad 1982.

Srivatsan, R. *Seva, Saviour and State: Caste Politics, Tribal Welfare and Capitalist Development*, Routledge, Abingdon and New York 2015.

Stolte, Carolien and Harald Fischer-Tiné, "Imagining Asia in India: Nationalism and Internationalism (Ca. 1905-1940)", *Comparative Studies in Society and History*, Vol. 54, n. 1 (2012), pp. 65–92.

Talbot, Ian. *Freedoms Cry: The Popular Dimension in the Pakistan Movement and Partition Experiences in North India*, OUP, Karachi 1996.

Tejani, Shabnum. *Indian Secularism. A Social and Intellectual History 1980-1950*, Permanent Black, New Delhi 2007.

Thompson, Dennis. *John Stuart Mill and Representative Government*, Princeton University Press, Princeton 1976.

Torri, Michelguglielmo. *Storia dell'India*, Laterza, Roma e Bari 2000.

——. 'Nazionalismo Indiano e Nazionalismo Musulmano in India nell'era Coloniale', in Mario Mannini (ed.), *Dietro La Bandiera. Emancipazioni Coloniali, Identità Nazionali, Nazionalismi nell'età Contemporanea*, Pacini editore, Ospedaletto (Pisa) 1996, pp. 139–199.

Turner, Brandon P. "John Stuart Mill and the Antagonistic Foundation of Liberal Politics", *Review of Politics*, Vol. 72, n. 1 (2010), pp. 25–53.

Upton, Robert E. "'It Gives Us a Power and Strength Which We Do Not Possess': Martiality, Manliness, and India's Great War Enlistment Drive", *Modern Asian Studies*, Vol. 52, n. 6 (2018), pp. 1977–2012.

Urbinati, Nadia. *Mill on Democracy*, University of Chicago Press, Chicago 2002.

Valdameri, Elena. 'Gopal Krishna Gokhale: Nazione e Impero Tra "Oriente" e "Occidente"', in M. Casolari and C. Tresso (eds.), *Sguardi sull'Asia. Scritti in Onore Di Michelguglielmo Torri*, I Libri di Emil, Bologna 2017, pp. 101–127.

van der Veer, Peter. *Imperial Encounters: Religion and Modernity in India and Britain*, Princeton University Press, Princeton 2001.

Viswanathan, Gauri. *Masks of Conquests: Literary Study and British Rule in India*, Columbia University Press, New York 1989.

Vora, Rajendra. 'Two Strands of Indian Liberalism: The Ideas of Ranade and Phule', in Thomas Pantham and Kenneth L. Deutsch (eds.), *Political Thought in Modern India*, Sage, New Delhi 1986, pp. 92–109.

Wagner, Peter. 'Introduction', in P. Wagner (ed.), *African, American and European Trajectories of Modernity: Past Oppression, Future Justice?*, Edinburgh University Press, Edinburgh 2015, pp. 1–18.

Washbrook, David. "Forms of Citizenship in Pre-Modern South India", *Citizenship Studies*, Vol. 23, n. 3 (2019), pp. 224–329.

——. "Intimations of Modernity in South India", *South Asian History and Culture*, Vol. 1, n. 1 (2009), pp. 125–148.

Watt, Carey A. *Serving the Nation: Cultures of Service, Association, and Citizenship in Colonial India*, OUP, New Delhi 2005.

——. "Education for National Efficiency: Constructive Nationalism in North India, 1909-16", *Modern Asian Studies*, Vol. 31, n. 2 (1997), pp. 340–341.

Wittrock, Björn. "Modernity: One, None, or Many? European Origins and Modernity as a Global Condition", *Daedalus*, Vol. 129, n. 1 (2000), pp. 31–60.

3   Cosmopolitanism

> The movement of the world in the East and West is towards representative
> Government on a democratic basis. The East and the West have come to
> stand [...] on the same platform.[*]

This chapter analyses Gokhale's political and cultural activism beyond the
bounds of the nation, demonstrating his increasing capability to exploit
different border-crossing networks and platforms in the promotion of
his political vision. It does so by considering some exemplary case studies
which shed light on the importance that both transnational mobility and
cross-cultural borrowings had for the Indian politician. In particular, the
chapter explores the impact that the encounter with Britishness had on
Gokhale at the personal and political level, as well as his engagement with
circles which were more or less critical of the world order, especially those
that revolved around the Liberal Party. It then scrutinises Gokhale's contribution to the Universal Races Congress and his involvement in the activities of the Moral Education League. Finally, the last part of the chapter
provides an account and in-depth analysis of Gokhale's active participation
in the South Africa Indian question, bringing into sharper focus his views
on the relationship between empire and nation and the often-ambivalent
relationship which existed between imperial affiliations and anticolonial
endeavours. The conclusion generates some insights into Gokhale's cosmopolitanism, arguing that it never translated in a specific political project,
but remained largely a discursive mode.[1]

A Hindu in the heart of empire: A passage to England

During his political career, Gokhale described himself as a patriot, a
nationalist and a liberal, but never proclaimed himself a cosmopolitan.
Nevertheless, this does not necessarily mean that he did not have a cosmo-
plitan outlook or lived a cosmopolitan life. What is certain is that, when he

---

[*]   Gopal Krishna Gokhale, *Public Life in India: Its needs and responsibilities*, National
   Literature Publishing Company, Bombay 1922, pp. 15–16.

DOI: 10.4324/9781003037422-4

travelled to England for the first time in 1897 to give evidence in front of the Welby Commission as a representative of the Deccan Sabha, Gokhale hardly fit the stereotypical ideal of the 'gentlemanly' cosmopolitan who feels at home everywhere.[2] His first journey abroad and across the *kala pani*[3] was made financially affordable thanks to a fund-raising campaign organised by Ranade and Wedderburn.[4] Although Gokhale did not bequeath a first-hand account of his three-month stay in Great Britain, it is possible to partially reconstruct it thanks to the somewhat amusing recollections left by Wacha, Gokhale's travel companion and representative of the Bombay Presidency before the same Commission.

Like any other personal memory commemorating somebody, Wacha's *Reminiscences* ought to be taken with a pinch of salt. They do though remain an interesting source and remind us that the colonial fixation with civilising the colonised had been internalised by Indians, like Gokhale, to such an extent that it engendered the desire to assimilate bourgeois and liberal habits to prove oneself 'respectable.'[5] At the same time, Wacha's recollections are fascinating also inasmuch as they shed light on Gokhale's cultural sensitivities, his deep intellectual curiosity as well as his spontaneous reactions and changes of behaviour in light of new encounters and influences.

In London, Wacha and Gokhale stayed in East Putney, with Dadabhai Naoroji. The description that Wacha gives of Gokhale's initial behaviour is that of a person overwhelmed by cultural shock. The young politician from Poona showed a general and profound shyness, if not diffidence, about finding himself in an unfamiliar domestic environment in an English suburb and in 'the strange company' of English ladies and gentlemen. Eating with non-Hindus (both Wacha and Naoroji were Parsis) and non-Indians did not seem to be a problem – after all, the Poona Sarvajanik Sabha had publicly promoted commensality across castes and religion communities as a way to defy caste-based and communal discriminations. Yet, Gokhale, suspicious about the food he was served, was extremely punctilious about not breaking taboos, like touching eggs or other ingredients polluting for a Brahman: everybody, in Wacha's reconstruction at least, found it hilarious the way in which Gokhale suddenly dropped his knife and fork as soon as he realised that a certain dish contained something prohibited by his rigorous Chitpavan Brahman diet.

Not without some sarcasm, Wacha gave cultural explanations to Gokhale's initial mistrust and 'awkwardness,' namely he attributed his colleague's 'provincial' behaviour to his being Hindu. The Parsi seemed to suggest that Hindus were much less cosmopolitan and exposed to 'modern civilisation' than his own community. The awe Gokhale felt for Naoroji was equally, in Wacha's view, a consequence of the domestic reverence into which young Hindus were trained and disciplined.

Dietary habits and putative cultural idiosyncrasies apart, Gokhale soon began to appear more confident. According to Wacha, the catalyst of this change was his friendship with an English lady, Mrs Congreve, who lived in the same house in East Putney. We know very little about Mrs Congreve[6] except that she was one of the several English women to defy imperial orthodoxy by blurring rigid cultural boundaries between coloniser and colonised; she had volunteered to nurse Gokhale who had been prescribed by a doctor a period of full rest following an injury caused by a train door in Calais that struck against his chest and produced a severe cardiac concussion.[7] Wacha held that the sisterly care showed by "a highly polished lady, [...] sympathetic and full of humanity"[8] reflected positively on Gokhale's attitude towards his British experience. Not only did he become more talkative during new encounters and seemed at ease even in the company of the much-revered Naoroji, but he also began to take advantage of his social and intellectual competences and was more at ease in the circles of British intelligentsia and politics.

It is difficult to say whether Wacha was right in reading the friendly relationship between Gokhale and Mrs Congreve as the main factor that cleared away the former's mistrust. It seems safe to argue, however, that the gesture of solidarity by an English woman made Gokhale aware of the interdependency with others. In other words, this micro-form of cross-cultural communication might have had an impact on Gokhale's outlook, showing that it was possible to challenge imperial fantasies of clear-cut binarisation between ruler and ruled at the individual level and not only in more formal anticolonial political relations. Nonetheless, a caveat is in order here; these innocent practices of intercultural encounter were not free from the hierarchies of race and dynamics of infantilisation of the colonised either. In this specific case, it was humour that re-established colonial normativity. In fact, as Wacha recounted, Gokhale was dubbed as "Mrs Congreve's brown baby"[9] by a witty English lady that used to frequent the house where they stayed. While there was perhaps no intent to offend the affective sympathy that linked Gokhale and his 'nurse,' this humorous comment betrayed a patronising, if benevolent, maternalism that in all likelihood would not have been socially acceptable if addressed to a white middle-class man of the same age as Gokhale.

Gokhale was increasingly eager to use the time spent in Britain to meet personalities committed to several causes that he too considered relevant for India. William Wedderburn and W. S. Caine, Liberal Members of Parliament, who became Gokhale's close friends for years to come, were instrumental in introducing him in the milieux that sympathised with the work of the Indian National Congress (INC), such as the National Liberal Club. The young political activist from Poona would also meet the Liberal Charles Dilke as well as exponents of the Irish nationalist movement, such as T. P. O'Connor and John Redmond,[10] and visited several educational institutions, those for female students in particular. He even managed, thanks to Wedderburn's mediation, to have a meeting arranged with Lord Morley, with whom he discussed the "Irish question" and Burke's political ideas but whom he found "unaccountably cold" towards Indian aspirations.[11]

That these encounters took place indicates that Gokhale had overcome his initial insecurity and felt confident enough to exchange thoughts and opinions with people whom he looked up to and who possessed political power. The openness towards social interaction in the imperial metropolis[12] suggested that Gokhale acted as somebody who thought of himself as belonging to the cosmopolitan community of liberal intellectuals and politicians who were generally loyal to the empire yet criticised some of its aspects. From a personal and political point of view, this was a significant confirmation of his 'status.'

According to Wacha, Gokhale had a strong desire "to leave behind him among those with whom he mixed the impression that he acted as a courteous, polished citizen of London would act."[13] In fact, exhibiting one's 'respectability' was imagined as a mark of belonging to the community of empire and as a requirement for imperial citizenship that could transcend boundaries of race or ethnicity.[14] Adopting a 'civilised' behaviour and a gentlemanly habitus (including European style of dress) was seen as a means of promoting social acceptability and empowerment, which, however, could have ambivalent results.[15] As Wacha tells us, his junior colleague adopted "conventional manners and courtesies" which, while being worthy of the "most polished Oriental at the court of the Great Moghul," at times, carried him "on the verge of the ridiculous," such as, for instance, the obsession with removing his tall silk hat even on occasions when it was not required by etiquette.[16] It was apparently in this period that Gokhale abandoned his Brahman orthodox dress and started wearing English clothes, so that some years later a member of the Viceroy's Executive Council on leave in England wrote about Gokhale, after meeting him in London, that:

> He dresses in the smartest of English clothes, frock-coat, high hat, patent-leather boots and all the rest of it. He has turned very white in this country, and he looks more like a Portuguese financier than anything else... I am quite sure he is full of mischief.[17]

This rather scornful comment is self-explanatory of the fact that a 'respectable' look as a claim of Britishness and imperial citizenship often reinforced colonial prejudices, so that Indians were perceived as laughable aberrations.

But Gokhale's quest for assimilation and British approval through apparel and etiquette was not so all-encompassing as to push him to fully abandon his traditional attire.[18] At important social and political events, Gokhale proudly wore his golden orange 'Mahratta turban,' arousing the enthusiastic and soft-orientalist admiration of the participants.[19] By showing off in places of great political significance such as the Houses of Parliament, the National Liberal Club and the Imperial Institute, this item of apparel that had long been a metonymy by which the irrational and tradition-bound 'Orient' was represented, Gokhale at the same time evoked and defied the colonial imagination. In fact, through what we could describe as an act of self-determination and – to use Leela Gandhi's phrase – "a flight from imperial similitude,"[20] Gokhale seemed to suggest that his cultural identity, depicted by the colonisers as inherently incompatible with freedom, political representation and liberal ideas, was fully compatible with the British political universe. Thus, while seemingly embodying the stereotypical image of the turban-wearing oriental, Gokhale was actually questioning it through a rebellious act: ostentatiously embracing 'Western' values of liberty, ideas of progress and 'modern' social norms did not require an abnegation or depreciation of one's own history and cultural experience.[21]

Campaigning for the Indian cause in the metropole

The evidence he gave to the Welby commission was undoubtedly Gokhale's greatest accomplishment during his first visit to England – one that elicited acknowledgement from several British and Indian quarters. Besides elucidating the material damages that the irresponsible colonial regime was causing to India,[22] Gokhale did not mince his words in denouncing the widespread 'moral evil' of racial discrimination that led to the 'dwarfing or stunting of the Indian race.' Being continuously denied a greater share of the Indian Civil Service, Indians were forced to live all the days of their life 'in an atmosphere of inferiority,' without any 'upward impulse,' without 'the moral elevation which every self-governing people feel.'[23] Gokhale also expressed the view that education – and primary education in particular – needed to receive higher budgetary provisions.[24] This was particularly urgent in rural areas, where primary education was entrusted to local boards, which had at their disposal only a very small proportion of land revenue, fixed for 30 years, and therefore inflexible and stationary. The government would add a grant in aid for one third of the total expenditure of the local board. Gokhale therefore asked that local boards be allowed to levy special educational taxes as the government was not willing to devote more money to the cause.[25]

It should not be forgotten that, for Gokhale, the performance in front of the Royal Commission was a test of his future career as a politician, as the anxious preparation of his evidence demonstrates.[26] More generally being in England and in the capital of the British Empire was a unique opportunity to expand his networks and give his views resonance outside the Deccan and India. Frequenting bourgeois salons to discuss politics, then, was not only an exercise of sociability but a way to educate the British public about the costs of their rule over India. In the few months spent on the island, Gokhale kept himself very active promoting the Indian cause. He toured Great Britain giving lectures on the political situation in the subcontinent, creating some uneasiness among British authorities.[27] Moreover, his friendship with Caine made Gokhale increasingly interested in the temperance question in India.[28] Caine was, in fact, a leader of the temperance movement and co-founder of the Anglo-Indian Temperance Association, formed in 1888.[29] Through Caine, Gokhale made contact with other temperance reformers, such as Lord Kinnaird – football player and president of the Young Men's Christian Association (YMCA) – and Frederick Grubb. Overall, as will be seen in Chapter 4, Caine encouraged Gokhale to take active part in temperance reform in Poona, including organising meetings in that city, as well as suggesting he raise temperance-related topics in the Bombay Legislative Council and in the Imperial Council, when Gokhale became a member. They would remain in touch until Caine's death in 1903.

The understanding he exhibited in giving a voice to India in the imperial capital made Gokhale a worthy delegate of the INC in England on several occasions after his first visit.[30] On the advice of the British Committee, the 1904 Congress session, held in Bombay, decided that Gokhale join a deputation to Great Britain the following year. The Tories were losing ground and it was expected that the Liberals would win if new elections took place. That presented an opportunity for furthering the Indian cause among the British public opinion. In particular, Wedderburn wanted Gokhale to infuse new vitality in the British Committee of the INC and to persuade leading members of the Liberal Party that India was fit for self-government within the empire. On Gokhale's suggestion, Lala Lajpat Rai decided to join the delegation too and left India weeks before Gokhale.[31]

In the seven weeks of his stay, from the beginning of October 1905, Gokhale addressed an impressive number of public and private meetings promoting 'England's duty to India.'[32] Whereas Lajpat Rai spoke at mass meetings of working men all over the country, Gokhale appeared mainly before Liberal parliamentarians and members of the aristocracy. This is somewhat telling of the opposing styles of the two Indian politicians and maybe explains Gokhale's choice to be accompanied by the Punjabi leader during the campaign.[33] Sometimes, though, the two Indian politicians addressed the same audiences, especially when meetings were arranged by the Labour Party.[34] In Lajpat Rai's opinion, the speeches made by Gokhale in this tour were "very vigorous."[35]

Gokhale, however, did not limit his indefatigable work[36] of political sensitisation to the circles of high politics. He participated more broadly in the public sphere, engaging with diverse groups in clubs and societies – even though these were mostly friendly – and contributed to interviews and debates in newspapers. In his own words, his mission was to "bring the claims of India before the electors, before the Parliamentary candidates and before the political leaders."[37] Among Gokhale's audiences was the Cambridge Union Society, where he proposed a resolution for the introduction in the British colony of a government on more popular lines. His speech was praised as worthy not merely of a politician, but of a statesman, and the resolution was supported even by John Maynard Keynes, ex-president of the Society.[38] In Manchester, where discontent was mounting among textile producers due to the Indian boycott against British goods in protest against the partition of Bengal, Gokhale explained that they were victims, like many more on the subcontinent, of "a wave of imperialism" that had "swept over the whole of the Empire,"[39] thus suggesting once again that the British empire could exist without imperialism. The Congress delegate from Poona also gave speeches at the Fabian Society, whose leading lights were Sidney and Beatrice Webb, and at the Political Committee of the National Liberal Club, where he strongly criticised the British bureaucracy in India as unaccountable because it was made up of "birds of passage."[40]

It is also noteworthy that Henry Hyndman,[41] the so-called father of British Socialism, commented in a letter to Naoroji that Gokhale had been 'plucky [...] to appear on the same platform with myself and I told him so.'[42] While seemingly paying a compliment, Hyndman, who had recently inaugurated Shyamji Krishnavarma's India House in London,[43] was hinting at Gokhale's excessive political moderation. Significantly, the *Indian Sociologist*, edited by the radical Shyamji Krishnavarma in London, quoted an excerpt from Hyndman's *Justice*: "Mr. Gokhale owes his position to the Indian Government and except when speaking at the East End of London is essentially the most moderate of moderate men. Butter will not melt in his mouth, so to say, and he enjoys the intimate personal friendship of Sir Henry Cotton, Sir William Wedderburn and other Anglo-Indian pensioners who are even more moderate than Mr. Gokhale himself."[44]

That Gokhale was moderate in his ambitions for India was not only the opinion of the radical voices within the nationalist movement. The Liberal Lord Coleridge, who presided over the meeting at the National Liberal Club, defined Gokhale's moderation 'extraordinary,' admitting that he would not be so moderate if he had been in his place.[45] While asserting that 'the only solution' was 'the steady introduction of self-government in India,' thus 'substituting the Indian for the English agency,'[46] Gokhale suggested practical measures for the short term as 'small steps' towards such a goal. These were the election of half of the members of the Imperial Legislative Council (namely 12 instead of four) and the formal approval of the budget with the right to move amendments to it; in the Provincial Councils, Indians should be given more opportunities to influence the finance administration; in the Council of the Secretary of State, three out of ten members should be Indians and at least six members of the House of Commons should be representatives from India.[47] Of course, that a prominent Liberal praised Gokhale as a moderate was encouraging and raised hopes that the new government would be more sensitive towards Indian grievances.

On his return to India, Gokhale was welcomed by a huge procession in Poona, joined also by Tilak's followers. Gokhale even visited Tilak, in what seemed a momentary rapprochement of the two clashing personalities and political rivals.[48] In Benares, too, where he presided over the Congress session, Gokhale was given a splendid reception, so much so that,

Lajpat Rai wrote, "one thought the evil days of the nation would soon be over."[49] In his presidential speech,[50] while harshly criticising the colonial economic policy, Gokhale called for the attainment, in time, of a form of Government similar to that which existed in self-governing colonies of the British Empire, so that India could be governed in the interests of the Indians themselves.[51] Gokhale's address, which the Anglo-Indian press unsurprisingly found alarming, was commented upon by Khaparde, Tilak's associate, as "not quite in the ultra-moderate style" and "cheered in its stronger parts."[52] Tilak's *Mahratta* also praised it, especially its criticism of Curzon.[53] Naoroji, addressing the 1906 Calcutta session of the Congress as its President – a desperate and vain attempt at reconciling the increasing divergences that had emerged within the party as a result of the post-partition political situation in Bengal – reiterated Gokhale's call for self-government.[54] The fact that the Grand Old Man adopted 'the magic word *swaraj*'[55] that had earlier been popularised by Tilak was greeted as a propitious sign by the latter,[56] who pretended to ignore that the Calcutta presidential speech was perfectly in line with moderate views. Events, however, were quickly moving towards the 1907 split of the Congress.

A liberal empire?

The Liberal Party won the 1906 elections and Gokhale left again for England in April that same year to request further reforms. With the Liberals in power in England and the rise of the Extremist party in India, demonstrating moderation and pragmatism seemed even more urgent. The work carried out in England, moreover, was influenced by the very nature of the British Committee which, relying on British sponsors to validate Congress grievances, made deference to British liberalism in general, and to Liberals in particular, inevitable.[57]

Gokhale, for his part, counted extensively on the new Secretary of State Lord Morley's good intentions to bring about reforms, and became victim of his own moderation.[58] Despite the fact that Morley had made no secret that 'for many a day to come' self-government for India was 'a mere dream,'[59] the Congress leader was unwilling to break away from his conviction, seen in the previous chapter of this book, that reforms, albeit modest, were vital for the expression and education of Indian public opinion. Aware of this, and although disliking the Congress and the many "rascals' connections with it," Morley took advantage of Gokhale and used him "to get help in guiding the stray currents of democratic feeling that are running breast-high in the House of Commons."[60] At the same time, the Secretary of State persuaded Gokhale that political unrest in India would entail the certain loss of reforms.[61] This threat, along with the fear that the Congress could be taken by the radical wing and 'communalise' the nationalist movement, made Gokhale's negotiations difficult. Overall, Gokhale's mission to England bore no fruit: despite his efforts, in fact, the Government delayed

the hoped-for reforms and Morley declared the Partition of Bengal a settled fact. Cooperation with the Labour Party, which was part of the government led by the Liberal Campbell-Bannerman, proved difficult, too: not
only was the boycott of British cotton in India a problem for Lancashire
workers and industries, but also the Congress social compositions raised
doubts among Labour leaders that Indians' aspirations could be compatible with their own ideals.[62] British public opinion, in addition, was very
lukewarm towards the Indian cause.[63]

Gokhale was attacked for his alleged submissiveness by the more radical exponents of the nationalist movement, both in India and abroad.
In London, it was mainly Shyamji Krishnavarma through the columns of
the *Indian Sociologist* that ridiculed Gokhale and the moderates, giving
voice to their critics. For instance, among the several pieces against the
moderate leadership, the monthly journal reported an extract of the New
York-published Irish nationalist journal *Gaelic American* which implicitly
referred to Gokhale and the British Committee as "afraid of liberty."[64] It
published part of a letter to Shyamji Krishnavarma "from a thoughtful
Indian now residing in the United States," which argued that Gokhale had
shown "the deepest ignorance of the aspirations and activities of the coming generation of India by saying that India wants representation in the
British Parliament" instead of "complete freedom and a parliament of her
own in the historic city of Delhi."[65] In addition, Gokhale, Krishnavarma
wrote, was an illustration of the "relation between mendacity and fear and
of the truth of the remark made by Livingstone who, while speaking of the
falsehood of East Africans, says: *One can scarcely induce a slave to translate
anything truly. He is so intent on thinking of what will please.*"[66]

For Gokhale, Shyamji's views were "altogether crude" and based on political inexperience. He was "such an impractical man, based at a distance of
six thousand miles from his country, where all work of regeneration has to
be done."[67] While it was important to put pressure on the ruling government in London, the real political education had to take place in India
itself. Gokhale, in fact, believed that the work to be carried out in Great
Britain was mainly aimed at attaining political reforms, crucial for the
national awakening in India. When the reforms were finally announced,
he decided to focus mostly on the activities in India, mostly through the
Servants of India Society (SIS) and in South Africa.

While moderates were losing ground in India and doubts were raised
among both extremist and moderate fronts about the representativeness
of the post-Surat Congress, Gokhale was perceived in Great Britain as a
'native' opinion-maker that could provide guidance to British political
activists and intellectuals who needed instructions about Indian politics,
history and economics. When, between 1907 and 1912, the Labour MPs
Keir Hardie and Ramsay MacDonald, the *Manchester Guardian* journalist
Henry Nevinson, and Beatrice and Sidney Webb visited India, Gokhale was
a reference point and a source of views on socio-political developments.[68]

At the same time, Gokhale showed the capacity to strategically use his contacts to further his political and social reform purposes. In 1906, he was invited to speak at the annual meeting of the Gloucestershire Band of Hope Union, a temperance organisation.[69] The temperance movement had been galvanised by the Liberal victory and by the new government's promise that legislation would be introduced to discourage the vice of drinking. Gokhale said, to general applause, that the cause of temperance was "the cause of humanity without distinction of race and creed." He went on to say that the evil of alcohol was not felt so much in India as in England, but still Indians "must look out for themselves." It was a fact that "the people in India regarded drink there as due directly to the support given by the government;" the excise duty imposed on alcohol provided the colonial government with an incentive to encourage the habit. The pressure from Great Britain was necessary to persuade the Government of India to bring the trade to an end. The Labour MP present at the gathering, Will Crooks, praising Gokhale's speech, said that he wished it could be published in every newspaper in the kingdom.[70] Thanking Gokhale for his presence at the meeting, the Labour representative wrote to Gokhale that "he would be glad to be of use to India as far as it lay in his power."[71] The following year, Gokhale became the president of a newly-founded Temperance Association in Poona.[72]

Although not particularly enjoying the company of British politicians – he could appreciate the value of Liberal, Radical or Labour representatives only when compared with Tories[73] – Gokhale increasingly learnt to move confidently in the corridors of British power "to strengthen [the moderates'] position in the India Council" and to get "at the brain of the Liberal Party in London."[74] During his fourth visit to England in 1908, once again in connection with constitutional reforms, Gokhale visited the India Office, addressed a meeting of the Indian Parliamentary Committee, interviewed several members of the House of Lords and was invited as a chief guest to a party thrown by Nevinson where he met other influential journalists like Alfred G. Gardiner, editor of the *Daily News*, the leading liberal journal, and Henry W. Massingham, editor of the radical weekly *The Nation*.[75]

Gokhale's visibility went even beyond the centre of imperial power. He was aware of the importance of global connections to give momentum to the Indian cause in "the civilised world."[76] Later that year, Ghokale was invited to visit the United States and speak on 'The National Movement" in front of the Civic Forum of New York City in early 1909.[77] The platform, which had the Republican President of the United States William H. Taft (1909–1913) as its Vice-President,[78] was far from being 'non-political,' as Nanda claims.[79] It supported, instead, liberal and moderate political views as shown by the fact that among those who addressed it in 1908 were Charles W. Eliot, the well-known American academic, philanthropist and opponent of American imperialism, and Pavel Milyukov, founder of the Russian Constitutional Democratic party, a Duma representative and historian, and later the Minister of Foreign Affairs in the 1917 Russian Provisional Government.[80] It was for health reasons and, more importantly, for the priority given to political work in India in view of the forthcoming reforms that Gokhale eventually decided not to go to the United States.

The US-based Scottish missionary and Marathi scholar Justin E. Abbott, who had spent 40 years in India but who had never met Gokhale in person, wrote a letter to the editor of the New York newspaper *The Tribune* to praise Gokhale's political action and dissipate the misleading idea spread by Indian students in America that India was "on the verge of revolt." Gokhale was presented as a representative of "the major part of the educated class [who was] sober and loyal to the British government," whereas "unrest in India [was] like a boil on a man's face – serious and painful, but localised."[81]

The Universal Races Congress

It was in view of his prominence as spokesperson of the largely more 'acceptable' moderate wing of the Indian national movement that Gokhale was invited to present a paper at the Universal Races Congress at the University of London in 1911, as a representative of India – "a big and important country."[82] The invitation came from Gustav Spiller (1864–1940), the lead organiser of the Congress. Spiller, a London-based Hungarian émigré, was a psychologist and author of several educational and psychological works. With Felix Adler (1851–1933), a professor of Political and Social Ethics at Columbia University and founder of the so-called Ethical movement, he promoted non-sectarian moral instruction for children and was active in the Moral Instruction League, a leading secularist lobbying group.[83] While the origins of the congress related to the intensification of international peace movements after the 1899 and 1907 Hague Conferences, the more immediate idea emerged in the context of the Moral Education Congress of 1908 held in London, another international event linked to the above-mentioned League and whose masterminds were Adler and Spiller.[84]

The Universal Races Congress has already been dealt with by a number of scholars,[85] who have highlighted its ambivalences and paradoxes.[86] Suffice it to say here that the internationalist convention aimed at fostering inter-racial amity, as well as global cooperation in health and medicine. In particular, its object was:

> To discuss, in the light of science and the modern conscience, the general relations subsisting between the peoples of the West and those of the East, between so-called white and so-called coloured peoples, with a view to encouraging between them a fuller understanding, the most friendly feelings, and a heartier co-operation.[87]

Writing to Gokhale, Spiller stressed the organisers' wish that "every paper referring to a non-European country or race [wa]s to be written by persons belonging to those races or countries. In this way justice [wa]s most likely to be done." In other words, Spiller suggested breaking away from hegemonic Western perspectives and narratives on non-Western experiences and culture, to let the 'other' speak.[88]

The congress was eventually attended by about 2,100 participants from more than 50 countries and collected together the growingly familiar faces of international and pacificist organisations.[89] It was not only a critique of Western imperialism 'from within,' but also the fruit of the impact of a rising cosmopolitan consciousness among non-European thinkers and activists, marking a global turn in discussions on race, science, imperial domination, cultural differences and inequality. On the one hand, the event was a significant intercultural encounter, which drew attention to the fact that "empire can be seen in a more metaphorical way, as a means by which wider connections with humanity could be imagined by colonised peoples."[90] On the other hand, Western alleged epistemic superiority and racial assumptions were not entirely dethroned, while cultural diversity was not always taken seriously, if not ridiculed as bizarre.[91]

Gokhale was asked to consider two main points in his paper; a very general sketch of Indian civilisation, touching on "the conditions for national self-government and common tendencies towards parliamentary rule," and the political history, contemporary condition and outlook.[92] Unable to travel to England due to work connected with the presentation of the Elementary Education Bill in March 1911, Gokhale agreed to contribute anyhow to the Congress with a paper, significantly titled "East and West in India" – as already seen in the course of the previous chapters. He could not miss the opportunity to give visibility to the Indian cause on such a global stage. His paper was inserted in the third session 'Conditions of Progress: Special Problems,' to which among others, delegates from China (the diplomat Wu Tingfang), Japan, Turkey, Egypt, Russia and Persia also participated.

In his paper,[93] Gokhale celebrated the rise of Asia, freshly united by the (re-)discovered feeling of "national self-respect" against "Western aggression and domination." He linked the realisation of "the dignity of nationhood" with the "new pride in the special culture and civilisation of the East," significantly pointing to the ontological rootedness of nationalism in the particular. Gokhale did not explain what Asian specificity was, but we should be on firm ground to say that he was influenced by the running trope of Western Orientalism depicting Asia as spiritual and contemplative; a discourse that had been later on appropriated by several Indian intellectuals – Swami Vivekananda and Rabindranath Tagore (1861–1941), and Japanese ones too – the art historian Okakura Kazuko, who had visited India and met both the Swami and the would-be Nobel Laureate.[94] But, against romantic visions of the 'Orient,' Gokhale was also claiming that, when 'intimated' by the needs of modernity and contrary to what defenders of racial hierarchies and cultural essentialism asserted, Asia was able to change and resist, as political developments in the region demonstrated, calling for a more equal relationship with the West. Asian (and Indian) specificities, thus, were not incompatible with political advancement. The rise of India was inserted in the frame of these larger global events.

Gokhale did not even make explicit how precisely he defined Asia.[95] But since he mentioned those nations that had started raising their heads against Western aggressions, namely India, Japan, China, Turkey and Egypt, it is clear that he saw Asia as a potential alternative to the Western powers' global hegemony. This attention to Asia as a counterbalance to the West had been spurred, as seen in the previous chapter, by the victory of Japan over Russia in 1905, an event of great significance in India as well as at the global level that had engendered a sort of 'cult of Asianism' and several, often divergent, theories and political projects on Asia. Nor had Gokhale remained unaffected by the wave of enthusiasm generated by the Japanese experience; he referred to it on more than one occasion. For instance, at the prestigious New Reform Club in London in 1908, he said that:

> Asia has been affected by a new movement – a movement towards nationalities and for constitutions. It is the same movement as that which affected the greater part of Europe about the middle of the 19th century. We, in the East, have been about 50 years behind Europe in the matter; *that is all*. One has only to look at what is taking place in Turkey, in Egypt, in Persia, in China – not to speak of Japan – to understand the new thought that has been working in India. Then the victories of Japan over Russia have lent a new dignity to the East. Lastly, the treatment to which we have been subjected in England's colonies has brought home most emphatically to our minds what a mockery was all the talk that is sometimes indulged in of our being citizens of this empire. And we have begun to feel and realise keenly that unless our status in our own country is improved, we are not likely to receive better treatment elsewhere.[96]

It is interesting to observe how Gokhale dismissed cultural explanations that denied the existence of national feelings and claims of political rights in Asia. Conversely, the Asian awakening was used as a discursive strategy to push the British to acknowledge India's important status. While emphasising the need of substantial and immediate political reforms vis-à-vis the British fence-sitting attitude, Gokhale warned the colonial rulers that, without a definite improvement in terms of civic and political rights for Indians, Asia stood as an alternative supranational political framework to that of the British empire.

In the paper presented at the Universal Races Congress, Asia was defined in similar terms. Gokhale's conception of Asia was vague and largely emotional and it was never developed into a proper form of Asianism:[97] the empire and the nation remained the cornerstones of his political vision. Therefore, although dividing the world into East and West according to a commonplace cliché bound to last for a long time, Gokhale did not perceive them as watertight compartments in a dialectic of struggle. India, being an eastern country, rejoiced at Asia's political developments, but at the same time it aspired to remain an integral part of the empire if Indians were enabled to enjoy the political rights 'prescribed' by the British tradition.

The tone was rational when Gokhale shifted the focus on the Indian situation, despite an excessively romanticised image of the association between England and India. He was very mild in his denunciation of state violence, considering it a matter of individual episodes rather than systematic – something curious given the recent extension of, and Gokhale's opposition to, the Prevention of Seditious Meetings Act. Racial discrimination was acknowledged, given that even "the proudest and most distinguished Indian cannot shake off from himself a certain sense that he belongs to a subject race." Nevertheless, Gokhale preferred to present political, rather than racial inequality, as being at the heart of India's problems. This was a choice probably dictated by the will to highlight constructive ways to establish future Indo-British relations and partnership in the settings of an international congress that intended to foster mutual understanding among peoples.

The analysis of the Indian political situation was predicated on the assessment of the promises of British liberalism, only partially kept, and on the consideration that the newly introduced Morley-Minto constitutional reforms made sense only as a starting point towards representative government on a democratic basis. The social intercourse between rulers and ruled, still too limited, could only partially improve relations between the two sides if the conditions of political inequality persisted. Only the achievement of self-government could substantially contribute to a redistribution of global justice and would constitute an important international precedent for humanity. The "axiom that Oriental people ha[d] no desire, at any rate, no capacity for representative institutions" was a "cool and convenient assumption" that was "not standing the test of experience" and which could not support for long the vast building of the empire. So, even if he did not refer to specific contemporary theories of race, Gokhale did not fail to see that racism could be more subtly elaborated in terms of culture through the idiom of essentialised cultural difference.

Also, it is worth noting that, in the same paper, Gokhale lamented that, while Indian students had been introduced to English – or more generally Western – literature, philosophy, history, sciences and religion in universities and through missionary bodies, a similar effort to understand Indian culture and civilisation was neither detectable in England nor among the Englishmen on the subcontinent. Gokhale undoubtedly considered

Western education as emancipating and formative for the Indian mind: he afforded primacy to Western knowledge as normalised and 'valid knowledge' based on its perceived superior scientific rigor, and on its intimate link to modernity. Therefore, he did not question the colonial epistemic structures entrenching Western knowledge as universally applicable, implicitly entitling Western scholars to interpret India to the West often in most unflattering terms. He believed that the nation-in-the-making could be empowered by adapting and using Western-based knowledge rather than by rejecting it, as other Indian nationalists advocated against the supposed risk of 'de-nationalisation.'[98] In other words, it would be implausible to argue that Gokhale was decidedly challenging West-centric knowledge or suggesting epistemic distance from it in favour of indigenous forms of knowledge. Nevertheless, it is true that he was trying to rectify the marginalisation of Indian narratives and, in so doing, was coyly hinting at the need to pluralise knowledge. He called for a deeper and less asymmetric mutual understanding to foster intercultural dialogue and tolerance as well as facilitate greater cooperation and respective cultural enrichment. A greater attention to the Indian experience meant a higher recognition of difference and diversity at large.

Overall, two main aspects emerged in Gokhale's contribution to the London-based convention. First, and in line with what we have seen before, Gokhale tried to combine the political realism of nationalism and internationalism: not only did he consider the wider geography of the empire, but he also placed the Indian nation among other emerging Asian nations undergoing a similar process of forging their own political identity within the framework of colonial social and political developments.

Second, whereas he regarded culture as a factor of differentiation between human beings, Gokhale did not see difference as an absolute humanity-defining trait locating human beings in a boundaried world as bearers of *a* self-contained culture.[99] Far less could difference be used as a justification for the continuation of an unjust global order. Differences between cultures were bridgeable thanks to reciprocal knowledge and continuing communication and 'hybridisation' – of which Gokhale must have perceived himself as an agent – as well as, at least in the colonial setting, through the recognition of political equality. Political rights, in fact, reflecting the liberal belief, made cultural membership less significant than universal political individuals, able to settle their misapprehensions and disputes through political dialogue.[100]

A moral education for the Indian youth

In all likelihood, it is through Gustav Spiller that Gokhale was contacted by the Vice-President of the Moral Education League,[101] St George Lane Fox Pitt (1856–1932), an electrical engineer who took an interest in, and wrote on, questions of secular education and social problems. The League – its name was Moral Instruction League until 1909 – had been formed in London in 1897 with the aim of propagating values of secular humanism through non-religious moral education. Until the First World War it remained a leading lobby group in Britain, but later it lost importance.[102] It was based on the idea that "the highest educational necessity of the children [wa]s not theology but a complete and rational conception of human life and conduct as we seek to make it out of regard to our human brothers."[103] School education had to instil knowledge, virtues, behaviour and practices that were drawn from fundamental moral principles, to which all religious sects agreed, and that would prepare pupils to become good adult citizens. While resolving the problem of religious differences and creating a common humanistic morality, the League intended to foster international goodwill and understanding through a sort of moral world-citizenship. In order to do so, its members attempted to create a global network.[104] India, with many faiths within its borders, was the perfect training ground for the universality of the instruction promoted. The League's members were at pains to show that theirs was not a colonial enterprise but one in which India could participate actively as a peer. However, perceiving their activities as bringing moral unity to the subcontinent,[105] they betrayed their 'civilising' convictions: the imperial centre was enlightening the East with its ethics.

Fox Pitt had been advised by Ratan Tata to get in touch with Gokhale given 'his splendid work.'[106] Gokhale's SIS, being ostensibly non-denominational and revolving around the idea of moral discipline and intellectual development, certainly resonated with the ideals of the League. Also, the practical work of the SIS included activities against the much-feared moral degradation of Indians, for example through teaching bourgeois values of temperance and thrift. Moreover, Gokhale had acquired worldwide fame as a liberal and secular leader who had given a voice to a progressive ideology of the nation which belonged to all its inhabitants, regardless of religious community and caste. For these reasons, Gokhale was asked to give his opinion regarding a chapter of *Youth's Noble Path*.[107] The book was a collection of moral tales gathered from Hindu, Buddhist, Sikh, Jain and Muslim sources for use in schools and families in India, written by the educator and secular humanist Frederick James Gould (1855–1938).[108] It had already been "widely circulated in India among several persons engaged in education and could gather good feedback."[109] Gokhale objected to some of the stories dealing with exploits of certain Indian gods; Fox Pitt suggested changes to the publishing house.[110]

Fox Pitt also provided Gokhale with a sample lesson that was given by Frederick Gould at Tata's residence in Twickenham with the Gaekwar of Baroda present. Boys and girls (more or less a dozen from a nearby school) were invited and told anecdotes from different religious traditions showing that "the losses of our ordinary life, when suffered for the sake of helping others, brought compensating gains; self-denial in the matter of food, comfort, of time, of money and even of life itself, were according to the judgement of the children entirely worthwhile." In India, moral education would consist of "a system of moral and character forming education,[111] based upon and in the main illustrated by Indian classical literature and the scriptures of the East." The project had already gained the enthusiastic approval of leaders like Ameer Ali and Romesh Chandra Dutt. However, Fox Pitt believed that "in order to give the movement real strength in India," it was necessary to "form a group of sympathetic supporters in India preferably in Bombay who would recommend the plan to the Indian people and who would help to organise the training of teachers for the purpose." He noticed that the official attitude, while thoroughly sympathetic, was against taking the initiative in the matter "but they would not object and hav[e] their hands forced if they found that there was a real Indian demand for that kind of instruction."[112]

Since Gokhale's replies to Fox Pitt are missing, we cannot reconstruct exactly his views on the Moral Education League and its project in India. Nevertheless, the number of letters from Fox Pitt and their content suggests that Gokhale took an interest in the question. It appears that, when Fox Pitt travelled to India to sensitise Indian opinion before Gould's book was published, he benefitted from Gokhale's support and advice. He spent most of his time in the Bombay Presidency, where he founded an Indian Moral Education Society, but not before having obtained Gokhale's permission.[113] Gokhale apparently wanted some reassurances that among the supporters of the initiative, there were Muslims too, as Fox Pitt confirmed.[114]

The leading purpose of the Indian Society was stated as the formation of high character, to be recognised as the

> Supreme aim of all educational efforts. It is not, of course, suggested thereby that education as a means to practical self-advancement, or as means of gaining livelihood, should be neglected or ignored; but only that all such purposes should be carefully subordinated to the higher aim of endeavouring to develop in each individual pupil those qualities of heart and mind as will conduce to his leading a blameless and noble life. Thus, while advocating the introduction of systematic moral instruction into all schools, the Society will at the same time urge that the whole curriculum should be coordinated with the higher aim always in view. It is hoped that the Society will help to find, and give practical expression to, a common moral basis of character-training acceptable to all schools of religious and philosophic thought that are to be with in India.[115]

R. G. Bhandarkar (1837–1925), the social reformer, supporter of female education and scholar of religions, agreed to be President of the society, whereas the Chairman of the Committee was N. G. Chandarvarkar (1855–1923), Vice-Chancellor of Bombay University.[116] Both men had cooperated with Ranade and the Prarthana Samaj and were close to Gokhale.

Thus, it is probable that it was the latter who introduced them to Fox Pitt. Among the committee members, including Ghokale, were R. P. Paranjpe, Gokhale's former student at Fergusson College, and Natesan, editor of the *Indian Review* and publisher of several editions of Gokhale's *Speeches*, and many other works of national-political interest.[117] Overall, Gokhale's influential network had proved vital for the formation of the Indian Moral Education Society.

Fox Pitt's visit to India was generally fruitful. Besides the establishment of an Indian branch of the League, the Bombay Government had decided to use the material of Gould's book. *Youth's Noble Path* would be prescribed for the 1913 matriculation exams by Calcutta University.[118] William H. Sharp, the Director of Public Instruction for Bombay, suggested that Gokhale "should train some of [his] enthusiastic young 'Servants of India' to go about giving model lessons in Moral Education in various parts of the Presidency and the Government would after a time take over their services if they were willing to be taken over."[119]

While the records of the SIS do not show that Sharp's suggestion was put into practice, we know that Gokhale publicly shared some of the beliefs of the Moral Education League, whose programme, after all, fitted with discourses, already existing in colonial India, of a much-needed moral education to compensate the 'godless' colonial education.[120] Gokhale found religious instruction divisive and "that nothing worthy the name could be imparted in secular schools." Moral instruction, instead, could usefully be taught through moral lessons and be a healthier alternative. To this end, even the *Bhagavad Gita* could be "used both as a religious and as a moral text-book though in reality it is only the latter."[121] At the same time, though, Gokhale appreciated the humanistic philosophy and values that mission schools, if "remolded into a more morally holistic light," could help propagate. Their "cosmopolitan morality and humanism could serve India as a nation."[122] Gokhale, then, did not seem to make a clear-cut distinction between 'moral education' and missionary education. And these, in fact, presented some commonalities. Although they differentiated themselves from the promotors of religious education and from mission schools, the members of the League shared with their 'rivals' the globally widespread fear of moral decadence brought about by urbanisation, industrial capitalism and rampant individualism, all of which could be tackled with projects of character-building education and the cultivation of 'good' habits. Also, the theory of fulfilment that had emerged within protestant theology and that was the basis of the more humanistic approach of missionary activities was due to the influence of social Darwinism, positivism and secular ideas.[123] According to these theories and ideas, all religions derived from a common original source and therefore all contained a certain degree of fundamental truth – a belief that obviously formed the core of the League's views.

Even if we do not have enough archival evidence to track his relationship with the League and its members, in India and abroad, the very fact that

Gokhale decided to contribute to the cause of moral instruction is telling of the fact that the League's message struck a sympathetic chord with him. What proved attractive to Gokhale, as seen above, was the moral-spiritual orientation of the League, which could provide a sort of 'principled distance' in secular education while being a much-needed antidote to the divisive influence of traditional religious teachings. Advocating an education which was moral and simultaneously "secular, not prejudiced and not religion-biased"[124] acquired particular significance in light of the debate around the Elementary Education Bill: in fact, among the many objections to it, several referred to the risk of an education which could be prejudicial towards a certain religious community. Furthermore, the moral education advocated by the members of the League, largely reflecting liberal assumptions about morality, individual freedom and self-development, and social duty, served as a factor of nation-building that tallied with Gokhale's idea of the nation. On the one hand, showing no animosity towards organised religions, it could function as a platform of interfaith dialogue and mutual understanding in favour of a plural society, and against emerging forms of cultural nationalisms.[125] On the other hand, by training "the child's feeling, imagination, reasoning, and will, so as to fit him for a useful and honourable life as a man, a member of the family, a worker, a citizen, and a servant of the common weal,"[126] moral instruction was compatible with the ideas that underpinned the SIS, and more generally Gokhale's national project: it educated children in ideals of social service, self-help, and community-based activities, promoting ties between the individual and the collectivity, training them in responsibilities and obligations. Ultimately, we can speculate that the League's programme functioned as a bridge of cooperation and understanding between West and East, promoting at the same time cultural diversity as well as the common basis of humanity, both of which resonated with Gokhale's worldview.

The South African question: A means to other ends?

In the last years of his life, Gokhale achieved popularity beyond the spectrum of the British political and cultural elite, becoming a patron of Indians abroad. The main factor of his visibility overseas was the support he provided to Gandhi in South Africa against the racial discrimination afflicting the emigrated Indian population in Natal and Transvaal. These provinces were crucial locales where anti-Indian laws were introduced by the administrators and contested by the non-white population.

The majority of Indians in Natal were indentured labourers who, from the 1860s onwards, had been employed in sugar plantations, mines and railways constructions. By the 1870s, nonindentured Indian migrants, mainly but not exclusively traders from Gujarat, had started settling down in Natal and Transvaal.[127] At the turn of the 20th century, like those Indians in other white settler colonies of the British Empire, they became the target of rising anti-Asian prejudices that resulted in laws restricting immigration. Sophisticated methods of exclusions had already been introduced in 1895 in Natal with the Indian Immigration Amendment Act, which imposed a tax of £3 on all ex-indentured labourers in order to push them to return to India or to enter once more in contracts of indenture. The following year, the government of Natal attempted to ban the immigration into the country of coloured people. While the Colonial Office prohibited the introduction of that law, it required the Government of India to impose limitations on Indian emigration to South Africa.[128] That same year, in order to disenfranchise Indians, Natal restricted the right to vote to those who already enjoyed it in their home country. In Transvaal too, between 1895 and 1910, domiciled Indians saw their rights to free mobility, property ownership and trade restricted by a set of discriminatory laws. They were also barred from franchise and compelled to conduct their business and to settle in segregated urban areas. The notorious 1906 Black Act required Indians to record their fingerprints with a special register of 'Asiatics' and to carry registration certificates: without these they could be jailed or deported.[129] The annexation of the Transvaal to the British Empire in 1902 after the Anglo-Boer Wars, then, did not improve, contrary to Indian expectations, the living and working conditions of Indians who had settled down in the region.

What made the number of exclusionary laws introduced in South Africa particularly disturbing for Indian public men was that it disregarded the fact that Indians were British subjects, a status that, in their view, should afford them equality with white settlers as well as the right of free migration within the empire. Also, it paid no attention to social class distinction while lumping Indians together with Africans.[130]

This was made clear by Gokhale when, as early as 1897, he wrote a piece for the INC organ, *India*,[131] condemning the fact that Gandhi, returning from India to Durban, had almost been lynched by a European mob because of the *Green Pamphlet* that he had circulated on the subcontinent denouncing the Indian plight in Natal.[132] Gokhale protested against the attack and humiliation involving a "highly-cultured and respected Indian gentlemen," a disgraceful event that brought to Indian minds the fact that they were "British slaves" and not British subjects. Like Gandhi, Gokhale believed in the opportunities of the British Empire. It was in the name of imperial citizenship and British constitutionalism that Indians could claim their right to equality and justice and should be afforded protection and mobility. Gandhi's efforts in South Africa, thus, resonated with Gokhale's vision of belonging to the empire while at the same time calling for the recognition of India as a nation-state.

Gokhale had met Gandhi in 1896 when the latter, visiting India to raise public awareness on the South African question, had stopped in Poona en route to Madras. It was the beginning of a relationship that Gandhi would often define in *chela/guru* terms.[133] Later, in January 1901, just after the Calcutta annual Congress session, during which Gokhale was instrumental in issuing a resolution on British Indians in South Africa, Gokhale and Gandhi spent a month together. That was a critical period in which they consolidated their friendship as well as exchanged their political views.[134] Despite his reservations about the Westernised middle-class, whom he perceived as detached from the masses and their real problems, Gandhi was strongly attracted to Gokhale by what Sastri defined as an 'inner magnetism.'[135] But apart from 'elective affinities,' Gandhi, being the shrewd politician he was, could not ignore Gokhale's network in the upper echelons of the empire, as well as the credibility he enjoyed in several British political circles which would prove helpful in giving proper visibility to the Indian cause in South Africa.

After meeting Gandhi in Calcutta, Gokhale kept a close watch on his activities[136] and endorsed his battle for Indian civil rights on several occasions. For instance, when in London in 1905, Gokhale chose the Indian South African problem as the topic of a lecture he gave in front of the Lambeth Radical Club. The Natal Indian Congress and the British-Indian Association of the Transvaal, in 1894 and 1903 respectively, in whose foundation Gandhi was instrumental, acknowledged "the great and good work" Gokhale was carrying out for them in England.[137] It was, however, only after the Morley-Minto reforms had taken shape that Gokhale was able to make more concrete efforts to support "the indomitable Gandhi"[138] in his cause.

Over the years, the INC had passed resolutions that condemned the treatment of Indians in South Africa. But such condemnations were no more than lip service to stopping the degrading exclusionary practices affecting Indians. Indian politicians shared the belief that their political activities had to focus on India and that South Africa was a minor issue.[139] As late as 1906, Naoroji was still persuaded that "the real issue for Indians was India."[140] If it is true that the Indian political scene was monopolised by the turbulent events that followed the partition of Bengal, it should be remembered that the lack of interest in what was happening in the South African context was also in part the consequence of class prejudices against indentured labour and the effect of the conviction that emigration was a vital social safety valve of which India should take advantage, thanks to its belonging to the empire.[141]

From 1909 onwards, Gokhale began to mobilise sentiment for the South African question and contributed to make the improvement of conditions of the Indian diaspora a legitimate field of nationalist activity against the initial scepticism of many Indian political leaders. The fact that he presented the struggle as part of a wider national one, a question which was tightly intertwined with "the honour and the future interests of our motherland,"[142] gave it increasing credibility in front of a lukewarm Indian public opinion. While the immediate motive of passive resisters was to fight unjust laws discriminating against them, there were higher and long-term motives for continung the battle, that is "the interests of those who m[ight] want to go there and not for those who [we]re there." It was therefore India's struggle more than the struggle of a small Indian diaspora in South Africa.[143]

Gokhale claimed Indians' right to mobility in the space of what he perceived as a non-racial empire as subjects of the King. At the same time and rather paradoxically, he played a major role in pressuring the Government of India in limiting such mobility by banning the recruitment of indentured labour as a retaliatory measure against those colonies which discriminated against Indians. The ban was implemented for Natal in 1911, but only in 1917, that is after Gokhale's death, for the rest of the colonies.[144] Also, in return for the abolition of the £3 tax fixed by the Union Government in South Africa, Gokhale, while on a political tour in the dominion, agreed with Gandhi that restrictions should be imposed upon the emigration of Indians to Transvaal. Since the ill-treatment of Indians was due to the fear of South African whites being 'swamped' numerically and being deprived of their cultural standards and government methods by the South Asian minority, appeasing that fear was seen as the best practical solution to reach a compromise, even though it entailed accepting the exclusionary racial values which underpinned self-governing colonies.[145] In other words, in order to secure a better treatment for those Indians already residing in South Africa, it was decided to drastically limit what many Indians perceived as an inherent right of imperial citizenship, that is emigrating to and settling in any part of the empire. It is hardly surprising that several influential Indian public men, such as Pherozeshah Mehta,[146] came down heavily on Gokhale and Gandhi because they were convinced that that was too high a price to pay for the welfare of a hundred thousand Indians.[147]

Gokhale did not deny the fundamental idea that all the territories of the Empire should equally be open to Indians, but he also knew that free mobility was an 'imaginative' right, fully subjected to the discretion of the executive governments of white colonies. He defended his and Gandhi's strategy by saying that the establishment of a fixed number of Indians able to enter the country every year – a number that equated to the annual average of migrants from India to South Africa – was a limitation at the discretion of the executive, including the freedom to decide not to admit anyone at all.[148] After all, Gokhale argued, it was not a huge loss, particularly for "educated men" as there were no career opportunities for them there.[149]

While Gokhale's speeches against indenture suggested a humanitarian and well-documented interest in the workers' conditions as victims of an unjust system of exploitation, they also betrayed his concern that the contempt and stigma attached to indenture labourers could extend to free Indians in South Africa and affect their respectability.[150] However, it is difficult to say whether this view truly reflected Gokhale's opinion, or whether it was a strategic way in which to win over unconvinced members of the political elite into banning the system with arguments that would more easily resonate with their class prejudices. Perhaps it was a mixture of both.

Issues of respectability and national honour were explicitly made reference to when, in March 1912, Gokhale moved another resolution in the Imperial Legislative Council for the abolition of the indenture system altogether, because it was "wrong in itself."[151] He said that the system was degrading to the people of India "from a national point of view" as wherever it existed, "Indians [we]re only known as coolies, no matter what their position [might] be," adding to the "disabilities" already attached to their status of colonised people.[152] Questions of "frightful immorality," too, urged the end of indenture. In fact, "very few respectable women" could be persuaded to go such long distances. The risk of depravity was increased by the skewed sex ratio established by the law, according to which every hundred male indentured labourers must be accompanied by 40 females.[153] The anxieties that indentured women of "admittedly loose morality" would put the entire nation to shame abroad was tightly tied to the specific notion of womanhood being involved in the construction of Indian nationhood[154] – a phenomenon that is historically common in national projects and processes.[155] Since female bodies were increasingly represented as signifiers, metaphors or allegorical emblems of the national community, they had to be vessels of respectability, morality, and virtue or, otherwise, kept under strict patriarchal control. Gokhale, then, pitted the ideal Indian woman – mostly imagined by the nationalist elite as defender of the home, religiously devoted, and traditionally dressed – against the stereotypical classist image of the indentured female labourer contaminated by the "profane activities of the material world."[156]

Besides this combination of female reputation, morality and national respectability,[157] from Gokhale's arguments against the indenture system there emerged a patronising view of 'the adorable peasant' forced into such "slave trade." He perceived indentured labourers as hopeless victims of their own simplicity, ignorance and misery. If this was certainly true in many cases, it should be remembered that, by the time Gokhale advocated the end of indenture, that system had provided opportunities to those who had left the Indian subcontinent. For instance, in South Africa, two major organisations, the Natal Indian Patriotic Union (NIPU) and the Colonial Born Indian Association (CBIA) founded in 1908 and 1911 respectively, and formed by ex-indentured labourers and their descendants, appeared to be more interested in enhancing their economic status than in abolishing the system.[158] This was also the case in the West Indies.[159] Overall, then, Gokhale too was bound by the same class bias that influenced other contemporary political leaders: indentured workers belonged to the anonymous mass of people incapable of overseeing their own welfare and needed the educated class to voice their complaints.

It is noteworthy that Gokhale could understand, and condemn, the indenture question not only through the lenses of the values and virtues which Indians were supposed to embody as reputable citizens of the empire and members of the Indian community. Quoting the Sanderson Committee, which had been appointed in 1909 by the Government of India to review laws regarding indentured emigration to other colonies of the empire, Gokhale pointed to the consequences that the indentured system had beyond the Indian diaspora. As regards the West Indies, he saw the system as a major reason why 'emancipated negroes' in Jamaica had to emigrate elsewhere for want of employment. In order to maximise their profits, planters preferred recruiting the cheaper indentured labour. The fact that 'emancipated negroes' thought that the indenture system was "not good enough for them" was per se sufficient to condemn it as "a system unworthy of free or even emancipated men."[160] Gokhale went on to say that "if the people of India and of the colonies belong[ed] to the Empire, so d[id] the emancipated negroes." It was a "heart-rendering tale," albeit one relegated to the appendices of the Sanderson Committee, that those people had to leave their home country due to the unfair competition of indentureship.[161] In Gokhale's view, thus, the indenture system was *a fortiori* wrong because it pitted emigrated Indians and emancipated slaves against one another, according to imperial and colonial patterns of labour exploitation that affected the subject 'races' of the British empire.

Diaspora, empire and nation

After several requests from Gandhi, Gokhale eventually visited South Africa in 1912 for three weeks between October and November, en route to India from England, where he had spent some months in the summer that year in connection with his membership in the Royal Commission on Decentralisation. In 1909, Gandhi wrote to Gokhale that if he had "cross[ed] the Transvaal border as a citizen of the Empire, [he] would give it a worldwide significance."[162] However, it was only when he was given approval from both the British and Indian Government that Gokhale made up his mind.

Both the British Colonial Office and the South African government, worried that any racially discriminating act against Gokhale could radicalise the movement led by Gandhi, took measures to ensure that the Indian politician was looked after all the time and had a train compartment and a carriage at his disposal.[163] Despite these precautions, Gokhale was not spared the humiliation of racial prejudice. The Union Castle Company, with which Gokhale had booked his ticket for Cape Town, wanted him to pay for the entire two-berth cabin, as it was unlikely that any European would have agreed to share it with an Indian. After Whitehall intervened in the matter, the company cancelled the condition and tried to compensate Gokhale for the mistreatment. The latter protested emphatically writing that he wanted no favour but only "bare justice."[164]

Apart from this initial incident, Gokhale's eagerly anticipated three-week tour through Natal, Transvaal and the Cape proceeded without further problems. The cordiality shown by European dignitaries was such that several newspapers – e.g., *Pretoria News* through the pen of its editor Vere Stent – carried vitriolic comment on the humbug orchestrated by Downing Street to protect Gokhale from ill-treatment and create the impression that there was no uneasy relationship between the dominant white community and Indians in South Africa.[165]

From Cape Town, Gokhale visited Beaconsfield, Kimberly, Johannesburg, New Castle, Ladysmith, Pietermaritzburg, Durban, Phoenix and Pretoria as well as other small municipalities.[166] Wherever he went, he addressed large meetings and was welcomed with receptions described in the local press as being of typical oriental magnificence and grand royal style. His visit ignited such boisterous enthusiasm in the local Indian community that it "served inadvertently as a significant step towards mass Indian mobilisation."[167] It was also fundamental in reviving Gandhi's political fortunes,[168] – at a low ebb due to the difficult negotiations with the Union and British Governments – as well as contributing to creating conditions of cooperation among local civil society organisations. Gandhi, acting as Gokhale's secretary, was always behind his 'political guru' and planned a very tight schedule during his stay. This created discontent about the "regrettable haste" imposed upon Gokhale's movement among some Indian associations which felt neglected.[169]

Gokhale spoke in front of many different audiences and showed his usual ability in tailoring his message in order to suit the circumstances. At a European reception committee in Johannesburg, for example, while claiming Indians' right to civic equality, he raised the risk of losing India to the Empire if the British Government backed South Africa in the continued persecution of local Indians. A similar occurrence, he hinted, would damage not only British interests but the welfare of the whole empire. As long as it remained within the empire – something which depended on the treatment of Indians in the self-governing colonies – India was open to the white South African community and their commerce. Inversely, a self-governing India could implement retaliatory measures against anti-Asian discrimination by introducing exclusionary laws against Europeans.[170] This insinuation immediately provoked alarmed reaction in the press.[171]

In the same town, Gokhale was received by the Transvaal Indian Women's Association (TIWA). Addressing the meeting, Gokhale said that even though Indian women's domestic ties were very strong, the women of Transvaal had courageously come forward to take part in the passive resistance movement in what was "an object lesson to their sisters in India." Although the satyagraha campaign between 1907 and 1911 had been male-dominated, according to notions of Indian masculinity and to segregated gender roles whose aim was the exclusion of women from the domain of politics, the struggle galvanised women into collective action. They formed women's organisations which became platforms for denouncing the racial policies enacted by the government and for mobilising support among women for the struggle. The TIWA, created in 1909 with the patronage of white women like Millie Polak, Henry's wife, and Sonja Schlesin, who assisted Gandhi as a clerical servant, was one of these.[172] Gokhale went on to say that the women's sacrifice in South Africa, when known in India, had struck an emotional chord so that "hardly an eye was dry or a heart untouched." He regarded the Indian woman as "one of the finest types of womanhood to be seen anywhere," never "lacking in a spirit of self-denial." Gokhale, thus, while lauding the 'essentially' feminine and Indian virtue of self-sacrifice, celebrated the exercise of that virtue beyond the domestic sphere in the Transvaal and hoped that it would be an example for women in India. For him, the struggle of Indian women in South Africa was an experiment in anticipation of "the great destiny that awaited India."[173]

While declarations of imperial allegiance prevailed in Gokhale's addresses before European audiences, references to a self-governing India, to national solidarity and the sense of belonging were recurring themes in his speeches before the Indian masses. Where ostensible values of imperial inclusion became more and more feeble and the possibility of becoming reputable members of the empire were frustrated by everyday racial discrimination, the integration into the much more 'tangible' national community appeared to be the more promising alternative.

In Johannesburg, the Transvaal Chinese Association, which had allied with the Transvaal British Indian Association during the passive resistance movement, hosted a breakfast in honour of Gokhale.[174] Its chairman, Mr. Gonzalez, the Acting Chinese Consul-General in South Africa, said that the interests of Indians and Chinese, so far as the attitude of the Government and the European population towards them was concerned, were very similar, if not identical. The President of the Cantonese Club, Mr. Quinn, declared that in Gokhale "they had one who ha[d] championed not only the Indian cause, but the cause of the Chinese." Pleading for the removal of the disadvantages of his own countrymen, Gokhale did so "in the interests of righteousness and justice" which "had universal application."[175] In replying, however, Gokhale lowered the Chinese expectations. He said that he was in South Africa to seek redress of the grievances of *his own* countrymen, even if no one would rejoice more than himself if their Chinese brothers also found that their disabilities were removed together with those of Indians'. He made a point that a function of that character should suggest "serious reflections in all thoughtful Europeans" inhabiting the empire. How was it possible that the Chinese community, "owing allegiance to their own Government – a foreign power" – and the Indians, "living under the flag of England" found themselves in the same boat? Not that Gokhale "objected to Indians being bracketed with the Chinese in itself": they were both an ancient people, "having much of their civilisation in common." But Indians, being supposedly imperial citizens, had a right to precedence over the Chinese minority; the latter, with their own independent government behind them, were in a position of advantage. Thus, Gokhale implied, disenfranchising the Chinese was more acceptable than disenfranchising Indians.[176] It did not matter that the white ruling class oppressed both equally.

It is also notable that indigenous Africans' perspectives are absent in Gokhale's perception of the South African problem. In November, Gokhale, accompanied by Gandhi, met Natal-born John Dube (1871–1946), the founder and first president (1912–1917) of the South African Native National Congress (which later would become the African National Congress). The meeting took place at the Ohlange Institute, a stone's throw from Gandhi's Phoenix settlement. The Institute was a Zulu Christian industrial school that Dube had established along the lines of the Tuskegee Institute, funded by the African-American educator Booker T. Washington (1856–1915). According to the *Indian Opinion*, Gokhale and Dube "spent some time together discussing the native question" while "the students sang a couple of Zulu songs and the band played popular music."[177] In his newspaper, *Ilanga*, Dube wrote: "We have seen and heard a great man whose knowledge is equal to that of the foremost statesmen of our day, and he is a black man."[178] The meeting, however, is not mentioned in the succinct, yet detailed, diary that Gokhale kept of his tour,[179] nor in the special edition of the *Indian Opinion* dedicated to his visit. This omission can be read as an indication in itself of the little consideration that the Indian political elite afforded to black Africans. Lacking any real political clout, they were kept at the margins even by Gokhale, who in his political imaginings preferred to identify with the 'whiteness' of imperial citizenship rather than with the blackness that, Dube implied, made Indians and Africans natural allies against the dominant white minority.[180] Notwithstanding the fact that for them, unlike the Chinese minority, "there was no country other than South Africa and to deprive them of their rights over land was like banning them from their home,"[181] no sympathy for Africans is detectable in any of Gokhale's speeches. He made reference to the indigenous population only as a cause of anxiety for the white colonists. The 'natives' were "at a totally different grade of civilisation" and the contact between blacks and whites had created "grave problems – social, political, economic and moral – which were already filling the European mind with uneasiness, misgivings, and even dread."[182]

Gokhale founded his argument on Indians' loyalty and belonging to the empire. While calling for the recognition of India as a dominion, he indirectly agreed to exclusionary imperial logic that ordered the inhabitants of the empire along racial lines. The anti-colonial language he used when condemning the discriminating policies and practices against Indians became an imperial one when he justified Indians' greater rights to imperial citizenship. The limits of this approach become even more conspicuous if contrasted with the attitude that other contemporary nationalists had towards the possibilities of forging alliances beyond the national and imperial boundaries. Shyamji Krishnavarma's global network[183] and Virendranath Chattopadhyaya's Berlin Committee[184] stand as clear examples, among many others, that viewpoints alternative to the 'liberal' empire existed both in rhetoric and in practice.[185]

Gokhale's posture to the grievances of Indian labourers was no more radical than his views of the conditions of other racial communities in South Africa. During the mass rallies that were organised to greet him in Durban and in some of the townships around Natal's capital, Gokhale did not urge political mobilisation nor did he explicitly raise any issue of labour conditions. In Isipingo, where around 10,000 petty cultivators and agricultural labourers had gathered, he thanked the European planters for the "humane and tolerant" treatment of their servants. In Mount Edgecombe, during a brief speech before thousands of indentured labourers, he vaguely promised to do all in his power "to make their condition happy and comfortable."[186] In Durban, "in a *durbar*-like setting,"[187] he heard the complaints of some £3 taxpayers chosen from the 5,000 labourers present.

Gokhale himself gives us some explanation of the somewhat ambiguous attitude he had to adopt during his tour. Once back in India, speaking at a public meeting in Bombay, he admitted that when he was in South Africa, he felt like he was walking "on a difficult and delicate ground," pressed between the "special courtesy and consideration" of the Union Government and the "rather excessive jubilation" of the Indian community. He went on to say that in such circumstances, "a single thoughtless act or even an unguarded expression might have resulted in serious unpleasantness and embarrassment all round inflicting an injury on the cause, difficult soon to remedy."[188] This might seem nothing more than confirmation of Gokhale's conservative views, or at best, a 'strategic conservatism' aimed at receiving more guarantees from the South African and Imperial governments. Nevertheless, a letter written to *The Times of India* regarding the Indian workers' strikes, begun in Natal in October 1913,[189] shows that Gokhale could overcome his conservatism. While in South Africa, he had obtained private assurances from members of the Union Government that the £3 tax would soon be repealed, so that he could leave the country with the conviction that Indian demands would be met. In reality, it took 14 months and another satyagraha campaign. When it became clear that the government had no intention of yielding on any of India's requests, passive resistance resumed in September 1913 and the strikes erupted amid this campaign.[190] In his letter to *The Times of India*, Gokhale went as far as to justify the strikers' violent actions against private property:

> I agree with you in deploring the burning of 150 acres of sugar cane [...]. But supposing that the cruelties, such as are complained of, have been perpetrated – and we have the emphatic statement of Mr. Ritch, an English Barrister now practising at Johannesburg, that he had conclusive evidence of brutal floggings by employers – can you wonder that starving men, deprived of most of their leaders, should be driven to a point of despair where they might commit such acts?[191]

Overall, Gokhale's visit, in what was supposed to be a tour of study, infused new life into Indian politics in South Africa across the social spectrum,[192] even becoming unwittingly the banner of resistance under which the strikers marched.[193] His work against the indenture system and against anti-Indian racial discrimination made him a symbol of the fight for Indian rights in the empire; several organisations and individuals contacted him regarding issues such as the conditions of Indian 'coolies' in British Malaya,[194] Hindus' emigrating rights to Canada and the USA,[195] the suspension of recruitment of indentured labour for Fiji Islands,[196] etc. Even Anagarika Dharmapala (1864–1933), the promotor of Sinhalese Buddhist nationalism, asked Gokhale to go to Ceylon to fight for the Sinhalese cause against British capitalism.[197] But Gokhale was physically exhausted. He preferred concentrating his remaining energies on the last phase of the South African struggle and on the work of the Public Services Commission.[198]

It has been written that for Gokhale, "negotiations with similarly qualified whites over tea was the way to conduct political life."[199] This is only partially true, though. After observing Gandhi's methods, Gokhale was not unconditionally against mass agitation, provided that it was led from above. Firstly, passive resistance was a moral duty more than a right, one that could temper irrational patriotic passions with a mature sense of responsibility, placing "conscience and self-respect above [one's] material and immediate interests."[200] It was a fight with "moral and spiritual weapons" through which a passive resister "deliberately and openly violate[d] an unjust law because he c[ould] not conscientiously submit to it but at the same time d[id] not seek to evade the consequences of breaking the law" but he "invite[d] them and he glorie[d] in them." It was a spiritual struggle essentially in line with the highest traditions of Indian spirituality.[201] As Henry Polak[202] wrote to Gandhi from Madras, Gokhale was "the one man who ha[d] deeply understood passive resistance."[203] Secondly, and perhaps more importantly, the passive resistance movement was managed in such a way that members of different religious communities *became* Indians in the struggle, forgetting "their usual differences and suffering with wonderful self-restraint."[204] In Gokhale's view, Gandhi's work in South Africa provided the perfect blueprint for 'making' Indians.[205] Gandhi was a charismatic leader: his spirit had the power to transform the minds of "poor humble individuals, hawkers, working men and so forth, men without education, men not accustomed in their life to think or talk of their country," who agreed to brave the horrors of jail rather than submit to the degrading legislation against their nation.[206] That is why Gokhale wanted Gandhi in India: he anticipated that the methods adopted among the diaspora could work in India too.

That diplomacy was not the only method of which Gokhale could avail himself is explained also by the active support he gave to the South African struggle through a relief fund which he inaugurated in Bombay in October 1913.[207] Against the advice of his doctors and at the expense of his fragile health, Gokhale, assisted by the members of the SIS, toured India to sensitise the people and to fundraise, so that by mid-November the initiative had made "excellent progress."[208] Contributing to the fund was a matter of a citizen's duties, as Gokhale himself made clear while reproaching Natesan, his friend and enterprising publisher, for donating a very paltry sum:

> Other nations have from time to time to go to war, when they find themselves compelled to make enormous sacrifices in men and money. We in this country have no occasion to go to war [...]. Our patriotism invariably goes with soft and easy living, brave words, and the feeblest possible action. Can we not once at least vire [sic] above all this and make a money sacrifice for this cause which we may afterwards recall with pride?[209]

It was, in sum, a sacrifice that provided a 'mollified' political and cultural elite with the opportunity to overcome their comforting patriotism and show that they were worthy citizens. The struggle in favour of the Indian diaspora was a means through which the development of nationalism in India could gain momentum.

Conclusion

The preceding account and analysis of Gopal Krishna Gokhale's 'global' career has shed light on under-studied aspects of his political thought and practice, whose relevancy places him among debates on cultural and political cosmopolitanism.

If we understand cosmopolitanism along the lines proposed by Pratap Bhanu Mehta,[210] that is, as the capability to engage with alterity and critically reflect upon one's own belonging to a certain cultural community,[211] there is little doubt that Gokhale could be called a cosmopolitan. As we have seen, Gokhale did not envision human beings as rigidly determined products of culture, but rather as agents that, by choice, capacity or chance, could converse and connect across cultures, mediating actions, norms, ideals and politics oriented both to the universal and the particular, the global and the local. That Gokhale's personal habitus, cultural references and political convictions were affected by his exposure to Britishness and by the several contacts with non-Indians demonstrate that he was culturally anti-essentialist and open to cultural transactions beyond the merely theoretical level. Of course, we should keep in mind that, as seen above, appropriating the cultural, political and social values of the English elite was not entirely a free choice for the colonised, but a necessity linked to the pursuit of respectability and of acceptance by the coloniser.[212] At the same time, it would be simplistic to judge Gokhale's attitude as exclusively driven by strategic or pragmatic reasons. As a matter of fact, Gokhale approached India's cultural traditions not as non-negotiable aspects of its identity – worth practising qua essentially *Indian* – but as practices and norms based on reason and, as such, questionable and subjected to change and interchange among different cultures. Gokhale's rational attitude towards his own cultural beliefs implied accepting the innumerable sets of cultural connections and borrowings brought about by imperialism and globalisation. Education, in his view, could be a useful means to make individuals open to otherness and able to tolerate cultural difference and to understand that a universal moral existed.[213]

Whether Gokhale was a political cosmopolitan and believed in cosmopolitan justice requires a more nuanced answer. It is beyond doubt that Gokhale demonstrated, through his activism, that he was able to feel and think beyond the bounds of the nation. Although he never promoted concrete transnational alliances nor, much less, a well-structured political programme of world-state or global federation of states – and cannot be defined a political cosmopolitan in the normative sense – Gokhale believed that politics represented a fundamental commitment to the interests of humanity. The making of the Indian nation was meaningful only as *tessera* of a global mosaic of free nations, ruled through norms of justice and political equality and made up of right-bearing individuals. This entailed not only recognition of the interdependency with others, but also acknowledging the co-existence of different forms of allegiance and identity, which could not be limited to the national one – something which, as seen in the current and the previous chapter, could result in the apparently volatile combination of transnational visions and national commitment, imperial affiliations and anti-colonial efforts. The fact that Gokhale considered himself a citizen of the empire did not mean that he was detached from national political obligations or disengaged with local political contexts, as illustrated by his lifelong connection with Poona, which continued to be an important basis for his political activities and networks. Therefore, in Gokhale's outlook, nationalism and cosmopolitanism were far from being antithetical projects, as national freedom could survive only in a just global order. All this suggests that cosmopolitanism, as understood by Kwame Anthony Appiah, was part of Gokhale's world view.[214]

A tension in Gokhale's ideology comes to the surface, however. The experience in South Africa made it clear that his political cosmopolitanism was largely a rhetorical rather than a practical imperative that could translate in transversal acts of solidarity. As seen above, Gokhale did not stand up against the discrimination of the Chinese minority nor the black South African population and their civil rights. He did not take advantage of the political crisis in South Africa to engage in – or at least suggest – anti-imperial alliances in the name of a cosmopolitan justice. In other words, Gokhale was not ready to question his imperial political imagination even when the putative 'inclusive' values of the empire had lost their credibility. His faith in British constitutionalism and imperial citizenship, thus, made him blind to political possibilities that looked beyond the empire.[215] His indifference towards the black population is symptomatic of the fact that inclusive and universalist claims were vitiated by the same prejudices and hierarchies that undergirded British imperial principles. Therefore, the empire, which along with the Indian nation-state was an important corner-stone upon which Gokhale had built his ideology, both fostered and challenged his cosmopolitan views. While it offered the opportunity to think and belong beyond the nation, it imposed its exclusionary norms to those who invoked allegiance to it.

Notes

1. It will be seen that while being the leitmotiv of the chapter, cosmopolitanism is more relevant to some sections than to others: this is mainly due to the fact that it is not always easy to consistently combine historical events and chosen thematic foci. However, even at the cost of the uniformity of the chapters, cosmopolitanism remains a helpful lens through which we critically judge some important, and generally overlooked, aspects of Gokhale's life while casting them in a different light from what has been done so far in existing literature.
2. Michael Ignatieff, 'Benign Nationalism? The Possibilities of the Civic Ideal', in E. Mortimer and R. Fine (eds.), *People, Nation and State*, I. B. Tauris, London 1999, p. 142.
3. There still was a strong, if slowly diminishing, Hindu prejudice against travelling across the oceans, known as *kala pani* (black waters). According to Ranade, Gokhale faced some opposition from the orthodox faction of his community and was only informally admitted by some members upon his return (Ranade, 'Revival or Reform', in *Wisdom of a Modern Rishi*, p. 40). On the broader debate around the *kala pani* taboo in colonial India, see Susmita Arp, *Kalapani: Zum Streit über die Zulässigkeit von Seereisen im kolonialzeitlichen Indien*, Franz Steiner Verlag, Stuttgart 2002.
4. Shahani, *Gokhale*, p. 88.
5. See for instance Utsa Ray, 'Cosmopolitan Consumption: Domesticity, Cooking, and the Middle Class in Colonial India', in C. Dejung, D. Motadel and J. Osterhammel (eds.), *The Global Bourgeoisie: The Rise of the Middle Classes in the Age of Empire*, Princeton University Press, Princeton 2019, pp. 123–142.
6. It is not known whether she was a relative of the positivist and proto-anti-imperialist Richard Congreve (Priyamvada Gopal, *Insurgent Empire*, pp. 72–80). Had that been so, Wacha would have probably been aware and mentioned it in his book.
7. Nanda, *Gokhale*, p. 94. The heart troubles that followed the collision persisted throughout Gokhale's life and were ultimately the main cause of his death.
8. Wacha, *Reminiscences of Gokhale*, p. 27.
9. Wacha, *Reminiscences of Gokhale*, p. 36.
10. On the interaction between Irish and Indian nationalists, see Kate O'Malley, 'Violent Resistance: The Irish Revolution and India', in D. Roberts and J. Wright (eds.), *Ireland's Imperial Connections, 1775–1947*, Palgrave, Cham 2019; Michael Silvestri, *Ireland and India: Nationalism, Empire and Memory*, Palgrave Macmillan, London 2009; Kate O'Malley, *Ireland, India and Empire: Indo-Irish Radical Connections, 1919–64*, Manchester University Press, Manchester 2008; C.A. Bayly, "Ireland, India and the Empire: 1780-1914", *Transactions of the Royal Historical Society*, Vol. 10 (2000), pp. 377–397.
11. Letter from Gokhale to G.V. Joshi, 14 May 1897, GP.
12. According to Sarojini Naidu, who was very close to Gokhale and met him in London in 1912, his participation in British social life included also attending parties, frequenting theatres, playing bridge and entertaining ladies at dinner on the terrace of the National Liberal Club (Deogirikar, *Gokhale*, p. 194).

13. Wacha, *Reminiscences of Gokhale*, p. 33.
14. On the question of respectability among people of colour in the British empire, see chapter 4 '"Positively Cosmopolitan": Britishness, Respectability, and Imperial Citizenship', in Charles V. Reed, *Royal Tourists, Colonial Subjects and the Making of a British World, 1860–1911*, Manchester University Press, Manchester 2016, pp. 124–161. For a definition of Victorian respectability, see also Vivian Bickford-Smith, *Ethnic Pride and Racial Prejudice in Victorian Cape Town*, CUP, Cambridge 1995, p. 39.
15. The rich literature on 'babudom' in Bengal provides us with useful insights on these dynamics. See, for example, Rosinka Chaudhuri, "Cutlets or Fish Curry?: Debating Indian Authenticity in Late Nineteenth-Century Bengal", *Modern Asian Studies*, Vol. 40, n. 2 (2006), pp. 257–272; Giuseppe Flora, 'Dandyism in Nineteenth Century Bengal – an Exploration', in *Le dandysme et ses representations, textes réunis par Marie-Noëlle Zender*, L'Harmattan, Paris 2014, pp. 107–137.
16. Wacha, *Reminiscences of Gokhale*, p. 32.
17. Quoted in Nanda, *Gokhale*, p. 406.
18. In several photographs taken in India and South Africa, Gokhale appears wearing Indian clothes. See, for example, the illustrations in Nanda's biography of Gokhale. Also, while in India, and even in the company of British guests, Gokhale did not give up eating with his fingers while sitting on the floor (E.M. Collingham, *Imperial Bodies: The Physical Experience of the Raj, c. 1800-1947*, Polity, Cambridge 2001, p. 188).
19. Wacha, *Reminiscences of Gokhale*, pp. 35–36.
20. Gandhi, *Affective Communities*, p. 7.
21. It is tempting to see Gokhale wearing his turban as an antecedent of Gandhi wearing a khadi dhoti and shawl at Buckingham Palace when he was invited for tea with Queen Mary and King George V in 1931. However, by choosing the traditional loincloth on that occasion, Gandhi was rejecting Western culture as well as the status and respectability obtained through dress and manners, while urging the return to the pre-colonial 'Indian' culture.
22. A point that Gokhale made strongly in Gloucester, in one of the lectures he gave throughout Great Britain in the months following the Royal Commission (see *India*, July 1897, pp. 214–215). A greater participation of Indians in the civil service and a higher number of them in high-ranked positions was for Gokhale complementary to the slow constitutional advancement. This remained part of his political agenda until the end of his career and life. Gokhale was a member of the Royal Commission of Public Services between 1912 and 1914. The Commission, which lost importance with the beginning of the war, was too conservative and unwilling to meet Gokhale's demand of at least 35% Indians in the ICS (see Nanda, *Gokhale*, pp. 435–450)
23. "Welby Commission. Written Evidence", 1897, *GSW*, Vol. I, p. 488.
24. "Welby Commission. Written Evidence", 1897, *GSW*, Vol. I, p. 501–502.
25. "Welby Commission. Oral Evidence", 1897, *GSW*, Vol. I, p. 633.
26. Shahani, *Gokhale*, pp. 85–86.
27. The Secretary of State for India, for example, criticised the inconsistency of commending British rule in India as providential while claiming representative government and jeopardising the internal and external peace and stability of that rule, a stand that would be reiterated in the years to come (*Standard*, 24 May 1897, quoted in Nanda, *Gokhale*, p. 99).
28. Letter from Caine to Gokhale, 27 May 1897, GP.
29. See next chapter.

30. On the activities of the British Committee and on the attempts by Indian nationalists – both moderates and extremists – in London to influence the 1906-elected Liberal government, see respectively chapters 1 and 2 of Owen, *The British Left*, pp. 22–48 and 48–77.

31. Lajpat Rai, *Autobiographical Writings* (edited by Vijaya Chandra Joshi), University Publishers, Delhi and Jullundur 1965, p. 100.

32. This is the title of Gokhale's address at the National Liberal Club in London in November 1905.

33. V.S. Srinivasa Sastri, *Life and Times of Sir Pherozeshah Mehta* (edited by S.R. Venkataraman), Bharatiya Vidya Bhavan, Bombay n.d. (first published 1945), p. 108. Gokhale was used to small meetings like the ones of the Bombay Legislative Council of the Supreme Council. He used official data and reports to support his arguments. If these methods were useful in front of well-educated audiences, they were understandably less effective in appealing to the emotions of the masses. Henry Nevinson, correspondent for the *Manchester Guardian*, wrote that Gokhale was "not a great speaker and [made] no attempt at emotional eloquence" (Henry Wood Nevinson, *The New Spirit in India*, Harper & Brothers, London and New York 1908, p. 35). It was only in South Africa that Gokhale became more accustomed to mass meetings.

34. The Labour support was due to a significant extent to Dadabhai Naoroji's activities in Great Britain, who could find sympathisers for Indian political reforms among the leaders of the recently founded party (Dinyar Patel, *Naoroji: Pioneer of Indian Nationalism*, Harvard University Press, Cambridge, MA 2020, p. 114). Cf. also *Manchester Evening News*, 13 October 1905, p. 6).

35. Lajpat Rai, *Autobiographical Writings*, p. 108.

36. Gokhale wrote to Dravid, one of the first three members of the SIS which was founded a few months earlier, that the pressure of work he had to endure was so terrible as to drive him almost mad. He had to work 17, 18 hours a day, addressing meetings and giving interviews, rushing from one place to the other, taking care of urgent correspondence and welcoming visitors (from Gokhale to Dravid, 17 November 1905, GP). These were impressive rhythms if we consider that Gokhale had a heart condition.

37. "Labour and India", *Manchester Evening News*, 13 October 1905, p. 6.

38. Letter from C.R. Reddy to S.S. Campion, 2 November 1905, GP.

39. "Discontent in India", 6 October 1905, *GSW*, Vol. II, p. 321.

40. *A Debate on the Awakening of India*, Political Committee of the National Liberal Club, London 1905, pp. 3 and ff.

41. On Hyndman, see, for instance, Marcus Morris, "From Anti-Colonialism to Anti-Imperialism: The Evolution of H.M. Hyndman's Critique of Empire, c.1875-1905", *Historical Research*, Vol. 87, n. 236 (May 2014), pp. 293–314; Prabha Ravi Shankar, "Henry Mayers Hyndman (1842-1921) and the Radicalization of the Indian National Congress", *Proceedings of the Indian History Congress*, Vol. 66 (2005), pp. 1041–1049.

42. From H.M. Hyndman to Naoroji, 9 October 1905, GP. It is not clear from the documents which platform Gokhale and Hyndman shared. Historian Dinyar Patel has uncovered Naoroji's long friendship with and influence over Henry Hyndman. Among the leading members of the British socialist movement, Hyndman drew heavily upon Naoroji's drain theory in his article titled '*The Bankruptcy of India*' (in Dinyar Patel, *Naoroji: Pioneer of Indian Nationalism*, p. 84 and ff.).

43. Fischer-Tiné, *Shyamji Krishnavarma*, pp. 74–75.

44. *Indian Sociologist*, Vol. II, n. 6, June 1906. Another extract from *Justice* reported in the *Indian Sociologist*, Vol. IV, n. 7, July 1908, p. 27, defined Gokhale's speech in East London "as vehement and as anti-British as any

article which has ever appeared in the much-denounced 'vernacular' press." I am grateful to Harald Fischer-Tiné for making the *Indian Sociologist* available to me.

45. *Awakening of India*, p. 5.
46. "New Reform Club Banquet", London, 14 November 1905, *GSW*, Vol. II, p. 339. The Reform Club was considered a sort of unofficial headquarters for the Liberals, although its membership was not limited to them.
47. "England's Duty to India", National Liberal Club, London, 15 November 1905, *GSW*, Vol. II, pp. 348–349. These were the same "modest beginnings" that Gokhale proposed a few weeks later at his presidential speech in Benares.
48. Nanda, *Gokhale*, p. 205. As Nanda notes, Tilak believed that the pressure from England was vital to "get any rights or privileges." For this reason, he and his supporters were happy about Gokhale's work in England. However, with the radicalisation of politics following the Bengal Partition, he started to ridicule the Congress strategy overseas as 'mendicancy' (Nanda, *Gokhale*, pp. 248–249).
49. Lajpat Rai, *Autobiographical Writings*, p. 110.
50. "Congress Presidential Address", *GSW*, Vol. II, pp. 187–209.
51. "Congress Presidential Address", p. 201. It is interesting to note that the *Irish Times* (2 January 1906, p. 4), a significant voice of British Unionism in Ireland, commented on Gokhale's speech as not being representative of the Indians' views but only a small minority of Hindu educated classes.
52. Khaparde Diaries, 27 December 1905, NAI, quoted in Nanda, *Gokhale*, p. 209.
53. *Mahratta*, 31 December 1905, p. 10.
54. For Naoroji's speech, see *The Indian National Congress Presidential Addresses*, G. A. Natesan & Co, Madras 1935, pp. 854–886.
55. Nanda, *Gokhale*, p. 259.
56. Patel, *Naoroji*, p. 253. See also Srinivasa Sastri, *Life and Times of Mehta*, p. 109.
57. Owen, *The British Left*, p. 62.
58. Gokhale's cautiousness to appease the Liberals' fear of political agitation in the colony did not prevent the Viceroy Lord Minto from seeing his presence in London as dangerous, poisoning Morley's mind against the 'malicious' Mahratta Brahman (see Nanda, *Gokhale*, pp. 223–240; Jayal, *Citizenship and its Discontents*, p. 112). Morley had consented to meet Gokhale again after their encounter the previous year.
59. At least according to what he wrote to the Viceroy (Morley to Minto, 2 August 1906, Morley Papers, BL/IOR Mss Eur D 573).
60. Morley to Minto, 11 May 1906
61. Morley to Minto, 2 August 1906.
62. For the development of the relationship between the INC and the Labour Party, see Owen, *The British Left*, pp. 80–83.
63. Nevinson, *New Spirit*, pp. 323–324, 327.
64. Quoted in *Indian Sociologist*, Vol. II, n. 6 (June 1906), p. 23. The *Indian Sociologist* and the *Gaelic American* mutually reprinted articles, declared reciprocal sympathy and exchanged political advice in the hope of building a united Indo-Irish front against British colonialism (see Fischer-Tiné, *Krishnavarma*, pp. 68–70).
65. *Indian Sociologist*, Vol. II, n. 6 (June 1906), p. 23.
66. *Indian Sociologist*, Vol. II, n. 9 (September 1906), p. 35. Italics in the original. See also Fischer-Tiné, *Krishnavarma*, pp. 129–131 for the consistent critique of the moderates.

67. This was a note written by Gokhale as a response to a letter in GP, file 404, 1. The file contains also a letter from the Paris Indian Society, whose members were very close to Shyamji and wanted Gokhale's opinion about India's attainment of "an absolutely free and independent form of National Government", in line with the article "A Momentous Problem" published by the *Indian Sociologist* in August 1906 (Vol. II, n. 8, pp. 45–46) and attached to the letter. On the Paris Indian Society, see Fischer-Tiné, *Krishnavarma*, pp. 113–116.

68. For the journey of these representatives of the British left, see Owen, *The British Left*, pp. 84–105.

69. On the Band of Hope, see Stephanie Olsen, *Juvenile Nation: Youth, Emotions and the Making of the Modern British Citizen, 1880-1914*, Bloomsbury, London 2014, chapter 1, pp. 21–49.

70. *Gloucester Citizen*, 12 May 1906, p. 3. The quotes above are from the same article.

71. Gokhale to Dravid, 6 July 1906, GP.

72. Frederick Grubb (ed.), "Cuttings from the Press", *Abkari: The Quarterly Organ of the Anglo-Indian Temperance Association*, Vol. I, n. 71 (1908) quoted in Colvard, 'A World Without Drink: Temperance in Modern India, 1880–1940', unpubl. Ph.D. dissertation, University of Iowa 2013, p. 90.

73. From Gokhale to Patwardhan, 17 July 1908, GP.

74. From Gokhale to Patwardhan, 19 June 1908, GP.

75. From Gokhale to Patwardhan, 19 June 1908, GP.

76. From Gokhale to Patwardhan, 10 July 1908, GP.

77. From Gokhale to Patwardhan, 10 July 1908, GP.

78. See "Reply by John Bigelow in answer to an invitation by the Civic Forum of New York City to attend its annual municipal dinner", 20 December 1909, Document 201, in *Senate Documents. 61st Congress, 2nd Session. 1909-1910*, US Government Printing Office, Washington 1910.

79. Nanda, *Gokhale*, p. 310.

80. Both addresses were published (see Charles W. Eliot, *Lawlessness; An Address Delivered Before the Civic Forum*, New York City, December 12, 1908 and Pavel N. Milyukov, *Constitutional Government for Russia; An Address Delivered Before the Civic Forum*, New York City, January 14, 1908).

81. The letter to the editor of *The Tribune* was forwarded to Gokhale by Abbott himself (see letter from Justin E. Abbott to Gokhale, 6 November 1910, GP). In New York, there was a significant presence of Indian students that were receptive to the propaganda work instigated from London by the leaders of the Indian House (Harald Fischer-Tiné, "Indian Nationalism and the 'World Forces': Transnational and Diasporic Dimensions of the Indian Freedom Movement on the Eve of the First World War", *Journal of Global History*, Vol. 2, n. 3 (2007), pp. 333–335). The political work in the United States was then accelerated by the arrival of Har Dayal (1884–1939), a charismatic disciple of Krishnavarma (Maia Ramnath, *Haj to Utopia: How the Ghadar Movement Charted Global Radicalism and Attempted to Overthrow the British Empire*, University of California Press, Berkeley, Los Angeles and London 2011).

82. Gustav Spiller to Gokhale, 5 April 1910, GP.

83. For the League, see ahead.

84. Michael D. Biddiss, "The Universal Races Congress of 1911", *Race & Class*, Vol. 13, n. 1 (1971), p. 37.

85. Christian Geulen, 'The Common Grounds of Conflict: Racial Visions of World Order 1880-1940', in Sebastian Conrad and Dominic Sachsenmaier (eds.), *Competing Visions of World Order: Global Moments and Movements, 1880-1930s*, Palgrave, New York 2007, pp. 69–96.

86. Helen Tilley, "Racial Science, Geopolitics, and Empires: Paradoxes of Power", *Isis*, Vol. 105, n. 4 (2014), pp. 773–781; Vanderlei De Souza and Ricardo Santos, "O Congresso Universal de Raças, Londres, 1911: contextos, temas e debates", *Boletim do Museu Paraense Emílio Goeldi. Ciências Humanas*, Vol. 7 (December 2012), pp. 745–760; Marilyn Lake and Henry Reynolds, *Drawing the Global Colour Line: White Men's Countries and the Question of Racial Equality*, Melbourne Univ. Publishing, Carlton 2008, pp. 249–262; Tracie Matysik, 'Internationalist Activism and Global Civil Society at the High Point of Nationalism: The Paradox of the Universal Races Congress, 1911', in A.G. Hopkins (ed.), *Global History: Interactions Between the Universal and the Local*, Palgrave, New York 2006, pp. 131–159; Susan Pennybaker, "The Universal Races Congress, London Political Culture, and Imperial Dissent, 1900–1939", *Radical History Review*, Vol. 92, n. 2 (2005), pp. 103–117; Robert John Holton, "Cosmopolitanism or Cosmopolitanisms? The Universal Races Congress of 1911", *Global Networks*, Vol. 2, n. 2 (2002); Biddiss, "The Universal Races Congress of 1911."

87. *Papers on Inter Racial Problems Communicated to the First Universal Races Congress Held at the University of London, July 26-29, 1911* (edited by Gustav Spiller), P. S. King and Son, London 1911, p. v.

88. Spiller to Gokhale, 5 April 1910.

89. Glenda Sluga, *Internationalism in the Age of Nationalism*, University of Pennsylvania Press, Philadelphia 2013, pp. 27–32. For a contemporary account, see Saint Nihal Singh, "Trying to Solve the World's Problems of Race", *Review of Reviews*, Vol. 44 (1911), pp. 339–343.

90. Holton, "Cosmopolitanism or Cosmopolitanisms?", p. 167.

91. Tilley, "Racial Science, Geopolitics, and Empires", p. 776. An anonymous member of the congress wrote in rather uncomplimentary terms that the congress lacked "unity of purpose." The effort to make fit the "scientific" foundation of anthropological theories and the "immense superstructure of idealism" had bafflingly incoherent results ("The Universal Races Congress: Science and the Millennium", *Evening Mail*, 28 July 1911, p. 8). The same piece was scornful about "smile-wreathed" delegates in turban or fez "bowing from the platform, breathing peace and brotherhood in broken English or very slightly chipped French" (*Ibidem*).

92. Spiller to Gokhale, 5 April 1910.

93. "East and West", *GSW*, Vol. II, pp. 381–388. Unless otherwise stated, the quotes in this subchapter are taken from this paper.

94. See Mark Frost, "'The Great Ocean of Idealism': Calcutta, the Tagore Circle and the Idea of Asia, 1900–1920', in S. Moorty and A. Jamal (eds.), *Indian Ocean Studies: Cultural, Social and Political Perspectives*, Routledge, New York and London 2010, pp. 251–279; Rustom Barucha, *Another Asia: Rabindranath Tagore and Okakura Tensin*, OUP, New York 2006.

95. On the diverging definitions of Asia, see Carolien Stolte, 'Orienting India: Interwar Internationalism in an Asian Inflection, 1917-1937', unpubl. Ph.D. Dissertation, Leiden University 2013, pp. 13–38. This is an issue that even after several decades from Gokhale's time has remained open to debate. See Martin W. Lewis and Kären Wigen, *The Myth of Continents: A Critique of Metageography*, University of California Press, Berkeley 1997; John Steadman, *The Myth of Asia*, Simon and Schuster, New York 1969.

96. "The Indian Problem", New Reform Club, 30 November 1908, *GSW*, Vol. II, p. 371. Italics are mine.

97. Later on, in the 1920s, members of the INC had more concrete discussions about the possibility to establish an Asian federation. However, for a variety of reasons, the plans were never realised. See Carolien Stolte and Harald Fischer-Tiné, "Imagining Asia in India", pp. 73–74.

98. See, for example, Harald Fischer-Tiné, *Der Gurukul Kangri oder die Erziehung der Arya Nation: Kolonialismus, Hindureform und 'nationale Bildung' in Britisch-Indien (1897-1922)*, Ergon-Verlag, Würzburg 2003. The promotors of vernacular/national education did not refuse modernity in favour of Indianness. On the contrary, they wanted to combine Indian national difference with a global modernity. On this, see, for example, Michael Brunner, *Education and Modernity in Colonial Punjab: Khalsa College, the Sikh Tradition and the Webs of Knowledge, 1880-1947*, Palgrave, Cham 2020 and Sanjay Seth, *Subject Lessons: The Western Education of Colonial India*, Duke University Press, Durham and London 2007, pp. 159–182. For more recent critiques of West-dominated epistemic structures see, among many others, Edward Said, *Orientalism: Western Conceptions of the Orient*, Penguin, New York 1978; Walter D. Mignolo, "Epistemic Disobedience, Independent Thought and Decolonial Freedom", *Theory, Culture & Society*, Vol. 26, n. 7–8 (2009), pp. 159–181; Boaventura de Sousa Santos, "Public Sphere and Epistemologies of the South", *Africa Development*, Vol. 37, n. 1 (2012), pp. 43–67. For the effort made by Indian intellectuals and political activists to understand and confront 'the West,' see Dipesh Chakrabarty, "From Civilization to Globalization: The 'West' as a Shifting Signifier in Indian Modernity", *Inter-Asia Cultural Studies*, Vol. 13, n. 1 (2012), pp. 138–152; and Harald Fischer-Tiné, "'Deep Occidentalism'? — Europa und der Westen in der Wahrnehmung hinduistischer Intellektueller und Reformer (ca. 1890-1930)", *Journal of Modern European History*, Vol. 4, n. 2 (2006), pp. 171–203.

99. A useful and comprehensive survey on debates of cultural essentialism within the political discourse is R.D. Grillo, "Cultural Essentialism and Cultural Anxiety", *Anthropological Theory*, Vol. 3, n. 2 (2003), pp. 157–173.

100. The anxiety to combine nationalist and internationalist aspirations undergirded the very idea of the congress, as demonstrated by several papers. A "universal humanity" that would "regulate the conflict of Nations and National Ideals and Values on the immutable foundation of Justice" was also the topic of Brajendranath Seal's paper at the Races Congress. Seal (1864–1938), Bengali philosopher and at the time of the Congress principal of the Maharajah College in Cooch-Behar, considered that "nationalism, imperialism, and federationism" were "world-building forces, working often unconsciously, and in apparent strife, towards the one far-off divine event, a realised Universal Humanity with an organic and organised constitution superintending as a primum mobile the movements of subordinate members of the World system" (quoted in "The First Universal Races Congress", *The Modern Review*, Vol. X, n. 8, August 1911, pp. 222–223).

101. On the origins and development of the Moral Instruction League, see Susannah Wright, *Morality and Citizenship in English Schools: Secular Approaches, 1897–1944*, Palgrave Macmillan, London 2017, pp. 51–114 and Robert Bérard, "The Movement for Moral Instruction in Great Britain: The Moral Instruction League and its Successors", *Fides et Historia*, Vol. 16, n. 2 (Spring-Summer, 1984), pp. 55–73.

102. In the first years of its existence, the League had started giving moral lessons in several schools all over England in addition to Scripture lessons ("Moral Instruction in Schools", letter to the editor of the Pall Mall Gazette, *Pall Mall Gazette*, 2 January 1905, p. 4).

103. This is an extract of an appeal which appeared in Hyndman's *Justice* (15 January 1898, p. 8) asking its readers to join the League. The Social Democratic Federation was already represented in the meeting.

104. See Wright, *Morality and Citizenship*, esp. chapters 5 and 6, pp. 115–176.

105. Wright, *Morality and Citizenship*, p. 132.

106. From George Lane Fox Pitt to Gokhale, 6 December 1910, GP.
107. Frederick James Gould, *Youth's Noble Path. A Volume on Moral Instruction Mainly Based on Eastern Tradition, Poetry and History*, Longmans, Green & Co, London, New York, Bombay and Calcutta 1911. The *Modern Review* published a very positive review of the book, recommending it heartily to Indian teachers and schools for having shown the universality of moral principles ("Moral Education for Indian Youth", *Modern Review*, Vol. X, n. 7, July 1911, pp. 97–99).
108. Robert Bérard, "Frederick James Gould and the Transformation of Moral Education", *British Journal of Educational Studies*, Vol. 35, n. 3 (1987), 233–247. On Gould's activities in India, see Wright, *Morality and Citizenship*, pp. 130–143.
109. Fox Pitt to Gokhale, 6 December 1910, GP.
110. Fox Pitt to Gokhale, 9 October 1911, GP. It seems that original copies of the book had been published as an experiment by a publisher from Madras (Wright, *Morality and Citizenship*, p. 131). In all likelihood, this was Natesan. The definitive version was published in 1911 by Longmans.
111. Character-building was a ubiquitous pedagogical goal in Victorian and Edwardian Britain. It was lauded as the "hallmark of the moral and manly individual" and was prized as an essentially English quality inexorably lacking among Oriental 'races.' See Nathan Roberts, "Character in the Mind: Citizenship, Education and Psychology in Britain, 1880–1914", *History of Education*, Vol. 33, n. 2 (2004), 177–197 and Stefan Collini, "The Idea of 'Character' in Victorian Political Thought", *Transactions of the Royal Historical Society*, Vol. 35 (1985), pp. 29–50.
112. Fox Pitt to Gokhale, 9 December 1910, GP.
113. Fox Pitt to Gokhale, 11 April 1911, GP.
114. Fox Pitt to Gokhale, 14 March 1911, GP.
115. File 426, file 8, 13 June 1911, GP. This was a printed file circulated in India inviting "cooperation in the formation of propagandist society to promote the cause of Moral Education in India on the basis of the International Congress which held its first meeting at the University of London in the year 1908."
116. Fox Pitt to Gokhale, 27 May 1911, GP.
117. File 426, file 8, 13 June 1911, GP.
118. Fox Pitt to Gokhale, 9 October 1911, GP.
119. Fox Pitt to Gokhale, 14 April 1911, GP. See also J.A.M. Aikins, *Report on the Second International Moral Education Congress at The Hague, August 1912: And as Related Thereto Moral Instruction in the Canadian Public Schools*, King's Printer, Ottawa 1913, p. 28. Apparently, Gould's material had a global circulation (Bérard, 'Frederick James Gould', p. 245, f. 29).
120. Hayden J.A. Bellenoit, *Missionary Education and Empire in Late Colonial India, 1860–1920*, Pickering & Chatto, London and Brookfield 2007, p. 39. That some form or another of moral education against moral decline and lack of character was required is revealed by the abundance of moral texts circulating in late colonial India, both in English and in the vernaculars. Anxiety of a moral crisis was largely shared by rulers and ruled who saw moral education as a necessary means to develop a moral character. On these pervasive debates see, among others, Seth, *Subject Lessons*, esp. chapter 2, pp. 47–78. The question of moral education vis-à-vis religious education kindled some interest in post-independent India until relatively recently (see C. Seshadri, "The Concept of Moral Education: Indian and Western-A Comparative Study", *Comparative Education*, Vol. 17, n. 3 (1981), pp. 293–310).
121. *Papers regarding the Educational Conference, Allahabad, February 1911*, Superintendent Government Printing India, Calcutta 1911, p. 16. This document is telling of how moral and religious instructions were debated issues (esp. pp. 77–106)

122. Bellenoit, *Missionary Education and Empire*, p. 85.

123. Charles D. Cashdollar, *The Transformation in Theology, 1830-1890: Positivism and Protestant Thought in Britain and America*, Princeton University Press, Princeton 1989; Bellenoit, *Missionary Education and Empire*, passim; Harald Fischer-Tiné, "Third-Stream Orientalism: J. N. Farquhar, the Indian YMCA's Literature Department, and the Representation of South Asian Cultures and Religions (ca. 1910–1940)", *The Journal of Asian Studies*, Vol. 79, n. 3 (2020), pp. 659–683.

124. "Elementary Education", Imperial Legislative Council, 18 March 1910, *GSW*, Vol. III, p. 88.

125. Paranjpe expressed this view in 1910 at a Conference on Moral and Religious Instruction held in Bombay: "Let boys be taught to see that there are some principles which they can all believe irrespective of the fact that they belong to one religion or several. It is only in this way that our various races can be brought closer together" (quoted in "Note on Moral Instruction, by the Hon'ble Mr. W.H. Sharp, Director of Public Instruction, Bombay", *Papers regarding the Educational Conference, Allahabad, February 1911*, p. 84).

126. Gould, *Noble Path*, pp. xiii–xiv.

127. See Goolam Vahed, "Passengers, Partnerships, and Promissory Notes: Gujarati Traders in Colonial Natal, 1870-1920", *International Journal of African Historical Studies*, Vol. 38, n. 3 (2005), pp. 449–479; Maureen Swan, *Gandhi: The South African Experience*, Raven Press, Johannesburg 2017 (first published 1985), esp. the first chapter; Surendra Bhana and Joy B. Brain, *Setting Down Roots: Indian Migrants in South Africa, 1860-1911*, Witwatersrand University Press, Johannesburg 1990; Thomas R. Metcalf, *Imperial Connections: India in the Indian Ocean Arena, 1860-1920*, University of California Press, Berkeley, Los Angeles and London 2007, chapter 5, pp. 136–164.

128. Lake and Reynolds, *Drawing the Global Colour Line*, pp. 125–129.

129. B. Pachai, *The International Aspects of the South African Indian Question 1860-1971*, C. Struik, Cape Town 1971, pp. 10–14.

130. See Ashwin Desai and Goolam Vahed, *The South African Gandhi: Stretcher-Bearer of Empire*, Stanford University Press, Stanford 2016, pp. 30–48.

131. Gopal Krishna Gokhale, "British Indians in South Africa", *India*, June 1897, reproduced in *GSW*, Vol. II, pp. 399–408.

132. Desai and Vahed, *The South African Gandhi*, pp. 36–42.

133. Mohandas Karamchand Gandhi, *Gokhale, My Political Guru*, Navajivan Publishing House, Ahmedabad 1955.

134. Nanda, *Gokhale*, pp. 407–410.

135. Sastri, *My Master Gokhale*, p. 220. On the time spent together in that year, Gandhi wrote, revealing the somewhat paternalistic attitude of Gokhale, that "he simply 'took me in hand' and began to fashion me. He was concerned about how I spoke, dressed, walked and ate. My mother was not more solicitous about me than Gokhale. There was, so far as I am aware, no reserve between us. It was really a case of love at first sight and it stood the severest strain in 1913 (when rather than cooperating with a government commission of inquiry, as Gokhale advised, Gandhi initiated another mass campaign which Gokhale strongly opposed). He seemed to me all I wanted as a political worker – pure as crystal, gentle as a lamb, brave as a lion and chivalrous to a fault… Not therefore that we had no difference. We differed even in 1901 in our views on social customs, e.g. widow remarriage. We discovered differences in our estimate of Western civilization. He frankly differed from me in my extreme views on non-violence. But these differences mattered neither to him nor to me. Nothing could put us asunder. It were blasphemous to conjecture what would have happened if he were alive today. I know that I would have been working under him" (quoted in Thomas Weber, *Gandhi as Disciple and Mentor*, CUP, Cambridge 2004, p. 47).

136. On Gandhi's emergence, see Jonathan Hyslop, 'Gandhi 1869-1915: The Transnational Emergence of a Public Figure', in Anthony Parel and Judith Brown (eds.), *The Cambridge Companion to Gandhi*, CUP, Cambridge 2011, pp. 30–50.

137. George Godfrey to Gokhale, 3 November 1905, GP.

138. "Indians in the Transvaal", Town Hall Bombay, September 1909, *GSW*, Vol. II, p. 409.

139. Swan, *Gandhi*, p. 91.

140. Swan, *Gandhi*, p. 102.

141. Nanda, *Gokhale*, p. 47; Tejaswini Niranjana, "'Left to the Imagination': Indian Nationalisms and Female Sexuality in Trinidad", *Public Culture*, Vol. 11, n. 1 (1999), pp. 223–243; Isabel Hofmeyr, 'Seeking Empire, Finding Nation. Gandhi and Indianness in South Africa', in Joya Chatterji and David Washbrook (eds.), *Routledge Handbook of the South Asian Diaspora*, Routledge, London 2013, p. 160.

142. "Indians in the Transvaal", p. 413.

143. "Passive Resistance in South Africa", Resolution before the 1909 Lahore INC, *GSW*, Vol. II, p. 423.

144. For Gokhale's speech in the Imperial Legislative Council, see *Proceedings of Legislative Department*, Delhi, 3 March 1910, pp. 239–285.

145. This thesis was strongly supported, and given voice to, by the newspaper *Pretoria News*, edited by the English Vere Stent. His opinion, which was the opinion of a part of the white population, was effectively summarised in an open letter to Gokhale, while he was touring South Africa, published in the same newspaper, whose bottom line was the following: "No more Indians to come into the country, but those who are legitimately here to be treated justly [...]. Most of the Indians who come here, now that the indentured system of labour in Natal is done away with, belong to the parasitic classes. Now we have got all the traders we can do with in South Africa. We have a cosmopolitan community of aliens who produce nothing, who brought no capital into the country, who merely deal with the produce and the money of the country, and who insert themselves between producer and consumer, to their own advantage, but to the detriment of both the others ["Open Letter to the Honourable Gopal Krishna Gokhale", *Pretoria News*, 2 November 1912, reported in *Indian Opinion, Special Edition. Souvenir of the Hon. Gopal Krishna Gokhale's Tour in South Africa, October 22nd – November 18th, (1912)* p. 58].

146. Sastri, *Life and Times of Mehta*, pp. 176–178.

147. Sastri, *Life of Gokhale*, pp. 98–99; Kathryn Tidrick, *Gandhi. A Political and Spiritual Life*, I. B. Tauris, London and New York 2006, p. 98.

148. See "South African Report", Annual INC, Bankipore 1912, *GSW*, Vol. II, pp. 457–459. The agreement was that only six Indians out of the 40 that on average emigrated yearly to South Africa could be allowed in the Transvaal.

149. "South African Report", p. 460.

150. Proceedings of Legislative Department, Delhi, 3 March 1910, p. 240.

151. "Indentured Labour", Imperial Legislative Council, 4 March 1912, *Speeches of Gopal Krishna Gokhale* (edited by G.A. Natesan), Natesan & Co, Madras 1920, p. 519. This resolution was rejected and, as already said, only in 1917 was the system fully abolished.

152. "Indentured Labour", p. 529.

153. "Indentured Labour", p. 528. This view was shared by several women's associations too. See, among others, "Transvaal Indian Women's Address" (in *Indian Opinion, Special Edition*, p. 23) in which Gokhale was thanked for his "work in connection with the abolition of the indentured labour system with its incidents which so nearly touches the honour of our womanhood".

154. Literature on this topic is vast and sophisticated. Among many others, see Mrinalini Sinha, 'Gendered Nationalism: From Women to Gender and Back Again?', in *Routledge Handbook of Gender in South Asia* (edited by L. Fernandes), Routledge, Oxon and New York 2018, pp. 13–27; Sanjay Seth, "Nationalism, Modernity, and the 'Woman Question' in India and China", *The Journal of Asian Studies*, Vol. 72, n. 2 (2013), pp. 273–297; Anupama Roy, *Gendered Citizenship: Historical and Conceptual Explorations*, Orient Blackswan, Hyderabad 2013; Geraldine Forbes, *Women in Modern India*, CUP, Cambridge 1996; Tanika Sarkar, *Hindu Wife, Hindu Nation: Community, Religion, and Cultural Nationalism*, Indiana University Press, Bloomington 1992.
155. A classic reading is Nira Yuval-Davis, *Gender and Nation*, Sage Publication, London 1997.
156. Partha Chatterjee, "Colonialism, Nationalism, and Colonialized Women: The Contest in India", *American Ethnologist*, Vol. 16, n. 4 (1989), p. 624. For a discussion on the physical body of the emigrant woman as "evocative site on which stereotypes of morality, sexuality, national honour, citizenship, sister-hood, deceit and exploitation" were inscribed, see Charu Gupta, *The Gender of Caste: Representing Dalits in Print*, University of Washington Press, Seattle 2016, pp. 240–241.
157. For Gokhale's view on indentured women and the need to put an end to the system, see Madhavi Kale, *Fragments of Empire; Capital, Slavery, and Indian Indentured Labour Migration in the British Caribbean*, University of Pennsylvania Press, Philadelphia 1998, pp. 167–171.
158. Ashutosh Kumar, *Coolies of the Empire*, CUP, Cambridge and New Delhi 2017, pp. 210–212. For the new life the indenture labourers built in South Africa, see Ashwin Desai and Goolam Vahed, *Inside Indian Indenture: A South African Story 1860–1914*, HSRC Press, Cape Town 2010, *passim*.
159. Gokhale was attacked for his position by ex-indentured workers in the West Indies, who saw indentureship as a social ladder for escaping from the "perpetual servitude" of bonded labour in India and become instead "self-respecting citizens of the empire" (quoted in Kale, *Fragments of Empire*, p. 170).
160. "Indentured Labour", p. 539.
161. "Indentured Labour", p. 541.
162. Gandhi to Gokhale, 11 November 1909, in *CWMG*, Vol. IX, pp. 532.
163. Nanda, *Gokhale*, p. 418 and Yogesh Chadha, *Rediscovering Gandhi*, Century, London 1997, p. 175.
164. Gokhale to the Union Castle Company, 29 July 1912, GP.
165. See the already cited open letter to Gokhale from Stent and the article "Gokhale", *Pretoria News*, 15 November 1912, reported in *Indian Opinion, Special Edition*, p. 64.
166. The details of Gokhale's visit to South Africa appeared in the special edition of the *Indian Opinion*, already referred to above; see also Desai and Vahed, *Inside Indian Indenture*, pp. 372–378.
167. Tidrick, *Gandhi*, p. 235.
168. Tidrick, *Gandhi*, p. 98.
169. *Indian Opinion, Special Edition*, p. 24.
170. "Interview with Mr. Gokhale. Feeling in India. Growing Demands for Retali-ation. The Imperial Aspect", *Transvaal Leader*, 2 November 1912; see also the already cited "A Powerful Speech", p. 33.
171. For example, *The Voice of Labour*, a weekly journal that dealt with socialism, industrial unionism and politics, wrote that "if ever India step[ped] outside the British Empire it w[ould] be the beginning of the end of the white man's dominance on this earth. Let India join, China Japan and other coloured

peoples and nothing but a return from the nebula from which our earth came, will save the white races of the world" ("Mr. Gokhale", *Voice of Labour*, 1 November 1912).

172. See E.S. Reddy and Kalpana Hiralal, *Pioneers of Satyagraha: Indian South Africans Defy Racist Laws, 1907-1914*, Navajivan, Ahmedabad 2017, pp. 142–160 and Kalpana Hiralal, 'Gender, Labour and Resistance: Mapping the Lives of Indentured Women in Natal, South Africa 1860–1914', in Farzana Gounder, Kalpana Hiralal, Amba Pande and Maurits S. Hassankhan (eds.), *Women, Gender and the Legacy of Slavery and Indenture*, Routledge, London 2021.

173. All the quotes from this paragraph are taken from "Reception from the Transvaal Indian Women's Association", *Indian Opinion, Special Edition*, p. 23.

174. In 1904, the British Government authorised the import of more than 60,000 Chinese indentured labourers to work in the goldmines of the Transvaal. The decision was made in spite of the fact that Transvaal, conquered by Britain in the recent South African war, was expected to remain a 'white' colony. See Karen L. Harris, "Sugar and Gold: Indentured Indian and Chinese Labour in South Africa", *Journal of Social Sciences*, Vol. 25, n. 1–3 (2010), pp. 147–158 and, for the imperial repercussions of Chinese labour's immigration into Transvaal, see Rachel K. Bright, *Chinese Labour in South Africa, 1902–10: Race, Violence, and Global Spectacle*, Palgrave Macmillan, Basingstoke 2013.

175. "Chinese and Indian. Bond of Brotherhood", *Indian Opinion, Special Edition*, p. 21.

176. The quotes from this paragraph are culled from "Imperial Intervention", *Indian Opinion, Special Edition*, p. 22. Italics mine.

177. *Indian Opinion*, 23 November 1912.

178. Quoted in Nico Slate, *Gandhi's Search for the Perfect Diet: Eating with the World in Mind*, University of Washington Press, Seattle 2019, p. 129.

179. "Diary of Gokhale's Tour", *GSW*, Vol. II, pp. 472–474.

180. For John Dube's own considerations on Gokhale and the attention he was paid by the South African ruling elite, see Desai and Vahed, *The South African Gandhi*, pp. 169–170.

181. This is part of a speech by Dube reported in *Indian Opinion*, 2 September 1905.

182. "Indian Reception at Pretoria", 14 November 1912, *GSW*, Vol. II, p. 449.

183. Fischer-Tiné, *Krishnavarma*.

184. On 'Chatto' (1880–1937), see Niroda K. Baruwā, *Chatto: The Life and Times of an Indian Anti-Imperialist in Europe*, OUP, London 2004.

185. As shown by Priyamvada Gopal, anti-imperialist resistance and transnational cooperation can be traced back to the 1860s (Gopal, *Insurgent Empire*). On revolutionary networks see also Tim Harper, *Underground Asia: Global Revolutionaries and the Assault on Empire*, Harvard University Press, Cambridge: MA, 2021; Ali Raza, *Revolutionary Pasts: Communist Internationalism in Colonial India*, CUP, Cambridge 2020; Michael Silvestri, *Policing 'Bengali Terrorism' in India and the World: Imperial Intelligence and Revolutionary Nationalism, 1905-1939*, Palgrave Macmillan, Cham 2019.

186. *Indian Opinion*, 23 November 1912.

187. Swan, *Gandhi*, p. 235.

188. "South African Impressions", pp. 443–444.

189. On the strikes and Gandhi's role in them, see Swan, *Gandhi*, pp. 246–256 and Desai and Vahed, *Inside Indian Indenture*, pp. 381–395.

190. For the last phase of the South African struggle, see Nanda, *Gokhale*, pp. 422–434.

191. Gokhale to the *Times of India*, file 242/412 GP (no date).

192. Sugata Bose, *A Hundred Horizons: The Indian Ocean in the Age of Global Empire*, Harvard University Press, Cambridge, MA 2006, pp. 163–164.

193. See Desai and Vahed, *The South African Gandhi*, pp. 224, 231; Swan, *Gandhi*, p. 252.

194. See file 293 in GP containing five letters sent to Gokhale by a group of residents of Kuala Lumpur from February to March 1913.

195. Letter to Gokhale, dated 10 May 1912 (file 242/56, GP), from a certain Sunder, who was connected with the *Aryan*, described as "a monthly organ devoted to the spread of the eastern views of the truth, the interests of the Hindus in the British dominions and the causes of the present unrest in India."

196. Appeal from the Acting Secretary of the Interior in Fiji to Gokhale, 11 November 1911 (file 242/75, GP).

197. Anagarika Dharmapala to Gokhale, 16 January 1912, GP.

198. See Nanda, *Gokhale*, pp. 435–450.

199. Desai and Vahed, *Inside Indian Indenture*, p. 377.

200. "The Indians in the Transvaal", 9 September 1909, Bombay, *GSW*, Vol. II, p. 414. A few years later, Gokhale went so far as to justify violence when commenting on the burning of 150 acres of sugar cane by Indian coolies in Natal in November 1913 [Newspaper clipping in GP (242, n. 412, no date)].

201. "Passive Resistance in South Africa", p. 424.

202. Polak was an English Jew and barrister who had been working alongside Gandhi in Transvaal for a long time. Gandhi decided to send him to India in 1909 to mobilise public opinion on the subcontinent about the South African problem (Desai and Vahed, *The South African Gandhi*, pp. 145–147). To silence false insinuations circulating among official circles that Gandhi's movement was funded by Indian Extremists, Polak was instructed to limit his contacts to Moderates and to consider Gokhale as his main reference point (Nanda, *Gokhale*, p. 415). On the collaboration between Gokhale and Polak towards the end of indentureship, see Goolam Vahed, 'Gokhale, Polak, and the End of Indian Indenture in South Africa, 1909–1911', in Neilesh Bose (ed.), *South Asian Migrations in Global History*, Bloomsbury, London 2021, pp. 37–62.

203. Quoted in S.R. Mehrotra, "Gandhi and the Servants of India Society, 1915–16", *Gandhi Marg: The Journal of the Gandhi Peace Foundation*, Vol. 34, n. 4 (2013), p. 497.

204. "Indians in Transvaal", p. 414.

205. Gokhale's view on the discovery of Indianness away from the subcontinent reminds us of Peter Van der Veer's words, according to which "those who do not think of themselves as Indians before migration become Indians in the diaspora." See 'Introduction', in Peter van der Veer (ed.), *Nation and Migration: The Politics of Space in the South Asian Diaspora*, University of Pennsylvania Press, Philadelphia 1995, p. 7.

206. "South African Impressions", Bombay Town Hall, 13 December 1912, *GSW*, Vol. II, pp. 444–445.

207. *A Brief Account of the Work of the Servants of India Society (1905-1916)*, pp. 10–11.

208. *Indian Social Reformer*, 13 November 1913, p. 121.

209. Gokhale to Natesan, 9 November 1913, GP. In the same letter, Gokhale wrote that he had donated 1000 rupees out of his meagre 7000 rupees of savings and was ready to donate 1000 more.

210. In order to better situate these conclusions, see the introduction of the present book.

211. Mehta, 'Cosmopolitanism and the Circle of Reason'.

212. See Homi Bhabha, "Of Mimicry and Man: The Ambivalence of Colonial Discourse", *October*, Vol. 28 (1984), pp. 125–133.

213. This idea of a 'liberal' education that could get rid of the bondage of tradition and custom resonates with what Martha Nussbaum argues in *Cultivating*

Humanity: A Classical Defense of Reform in Liberal Education, Harvard University Press, Cambridge, MA 1997, pp. 9–11, and *passim.*
214. Appiah, "Cosmopolitan Patriots".
215. On this topic, see also the insights provided by Peter Van der Veer in 'Cosmopolitan Options', in J. Friedman and S. Randeria (eds.), *Worlds on the Move: Globalization, Migration and Cultural Security,* Palgrave Macmillan, New York 2004, pp. 167–178.

References

A Brief Account of the Work of the Servants of India Society, Poona (From June 1905 to December 1916), Aryabhushan Press, Poona 1917.

Aikins, J.A.M. *Report on the Second International Moral Education Congress at The Hague, August 1912: And as Related Thereto Moral Instruction in the Canadian Public Schools,* King's Printer, Ottawa 1913.

Appiah, Kwame Anthony. "Cosmopolitan Patriots", *Critical Inquiry,* Vol. 23, n. 3 (1997), pp. 617–639.

Arp, Susmita. *Kalapani: Zum Streit über Die Zulässigkeit Von Seereisen Im Kolonialzeitlichen Indien,* Franz Steiner Verlag, Stuttgart 2002.

Barucha, Rustom. *Another Asia: Rabindranath Tagore and Okakura Tensin,* OUP, New York 2006.

Baruwā, Niroda K. *Chatto: The Life and Times of an Indian Anti-Imperialist in Europe,* OUP, London 2004.

Bayly, C.A. "Ireland, India and the Empire: 1780-1914", *Transactions of the Royal Historical Society,* Vol. 10 (2000), pp. 377–397.

Bellenoit, Hayden J. *Missionary Education and Empire in Late Colonial India, 1860–1920,* Pickering & Chatto, London and Brookfield 2007.

Bérard, Robert. "The Movement for Moral Instruction in Great Britain: The Moral Instruction League and Its Successors", *Fides et Historia,* Vol. 16, n. 2 (Spring-Summer, 1984), pp. 55–73.

——. "Frederick James Gould and the Transformation of Moral Education", *British Journal of Educational Studies,* Vol. 35, n. 3 (1987), pp. 233–247.

Bhabha, Homi. 'Of Mimicry and Man: The Ambivalence of Colonial Discourse', *October,* Vol. 28 (Spring 1984), pp. 125–133.

Bhana, Surendra and Joy B. Brain. *Setting Down Roots: Indian Migrants in South Africa, 1860-1911,* Witwatersrand University Press, Johannesburg 1990.

Bickford-Smith, Vivian. *Ethnic Pride and Racial Prejudice in Victorian Cape Town,* CUP, Cambridge 1995.

Biddiss, Michael D. "The Universal Races Congress of 1911", *Race & Class,* Vol. 13, n. 1 (1971), pp. 37–46.

Bose, Sugata. *A Hundred Horizons: The Indian Ocean in the Age of Global Empire,* Harvard University Press, Cambridge, MA 2006.

Bright, Rachel K. *Chinese Labour in South Africa, 1902–10: Race, Violence, and Global Spectacle,* Palgrave Macmillan, Basingstoke 2013.

Brunner, Michael. *Education and Modernity in Colonial Punjab: Khalsa College, the Sikh Tradition and the Webs of Knowledge, 1880-1947,* Palgrave, Cham 2020.

Cashdollar, Charles D. *The Transformation in Theology, 1830-1890: Positivism and Protestant Thought in Britain and America,* Princeton University Press, Princeton 1989.

Chadha, Yogesh. *Rediscovering Gandhi*, Century, London 1997.

Chakrabarty, Dipesh. "From Civilization to Globalization: The 'West' as a Shifting Signifier in Indian Modernity", *Inter-Asia Cultural Studies*, Vol. 13, n. 1 (2012), pp. 138–152.

Chatterjee, Partha. "Colonialism, Nationalism, and Colonialized Women: The Contest in India", *American Ethnologist*, Vol. 16, n. 4 (1989), pp. 622–633.

Chaudhuri, Rosinka. "Cutlets or Fish Curry?: Debating Indian Authenticity in Late Nineteenth-Century Bengal", *Modern Asian Studies*, Vol. 40, n. 2 (2006), pp. 257–272.

Collingham, E.M. *Imperial Bodies: The Physical Experience of the Raj, C.1800-1947*, Polity, Cambridge 2001.

Collini, Stefan. "The Idea of 'Character' in Victorian Political Thought", *Transactions of the Royal Historical Society*, 35 (1985), pp. 29–50.

Colvard, Robert Eric. "*A World Without Drink: Temperance in Modern India, 1880–1940*". Unpubl. Ph.D. diss., University of Iowa, 2013.

de Sousa Santos, Boaventura. "Public Sphere and Epistemologies of the South", *Africa Development*, Vol. 37, n. 1 (2012), pp. 43–67.

de Souza, Vanderlei and Ricardo Santos. "O Congresso Universal De Raças, Londres, 1911: Contextos, Temas e Debates", *Boletim do Museu Paraense Emílio Goeldi. Ciências Humanas*, Vol. 7 (December 2012), pp. 745–760.

Deogirikar, T.R. *Gopal Krishna Gokhale*, Publications Division, Gov. of India, Delhi 1992 (1964).

Desai, Ashwin and Goolam Vahed. *Inside Indian Indenture. A South African Story 1860–1914*, HSRC Press, Cape Town 2010.

——. *The South African Gandhi: Stretcher-Bearer of Empire*, Stanford University Press, Stanford 2016.

Eliot, Charles W. *Lawlessness; An Address Delivered Before the Civic Forum*, New York City, December 12, 1908.

Fischer-Tiné, Harald. "Third-Stream Orientalism: J. N. Farquhar, the Indian YMCA's Literature Department, and the Representation of South Asian Cultures and Religions (Ca. 1910–1940)", *The Journal of Asian Studies*, Vol. 79, n. 3 (2020), pp. 659–683.

——. *Shyamji Krishnavarma: Sanskrit, Sociology, and Anti-Imperialism*, Routledge India, New Delhi 2014.

——. "Indian Nationalism and the 'World Forces': Transnational and Diasporic Dimensions of the Indian Freedom Movement on the Eve of the First World War", *Journal of Global History*, Vol. 2, n. 3 (2007), pp. 325–344.

——. "'Deep Occidentalism'? — Europa Und Der Westen in Der Wahrnehmung Hinduistischer Intellektueller Und Reformer (ca. 1890-1930)", *Journal of Modern European History*, Vol. 4, n. 2 (2006), pp. 171–203.

——. *Der Gurukul Kangri Oder Die Erziehung Der Arya Nation: Kolonialismus, Hindureform Und 'nationale Bildung' in Britisch-Indien (1897-1922)*, Ergon-Verlag, Würzburg 2003.

Flora, Giuseppe. 'Dandyism in Nineteenth Century Bengal – an Exploration', in *Le Dandysme Et Ses Representations, Textes Réunis Par Marie-Noëlle Zender*, L'Harmattan, Paris 2014, pp. 107–137.

Forbes, Geraldine. *Women in Modern India*, Cambridge, CUP 1996.

Frost, Mark R. '"The Great Ocean of Idealism": Calcutta, the Tagore Circle and the Idea of Asia, 1900–1920', in S. Moorty and A. Jamal (eds.), *Indian Ocean Studies: Cultural, Social and Political Perspectives*, Routledge, New York and London 2010, pp. 251–279.

Gandhi, Leela. *Affective Communities: Anticolonial Thought, Fin-De-Siècle Radicalism, and the Politics of Friendship*, Duke University Press, Durham 2006.

Gandhi, Mohandas Karamchand. *Gokhale, My Political Guru*, Navajivan Publishing House, Ahmedabad 1955.

Geulen, Christian. 'The Common Grounds of Conflict: Racial Visions of World Order 1880-1940', in Sebastian Conrad and Dominic Sachsenmaier (eds.), *Competing Visions of World Order: Global Moments and Movements, 1880-1930s*, Palgrave, New York 2007, pp. 69–96.

Gokhale, Gopal Krishna. *Gokhale Speeches and Writings (GSW), Vol. I Economic*, in R.P. Patwardhan and D.V. Ambekar (eds.), Asia Publishing House, Poona 1962.

——. *Gokhale Speeches and Writings (GSW), Vol. II Political*, in R.P. Patwardhan and D.V. Ambekar (eds.), Asia Publishing House, Poona 1966.

——. *Gokhale Speeches and Writings (GSW), Vol. III Educational*, in D.G. Karve and D.V. Ambekar (eds.), Asia Publishing House, Poona 1967.

——. *Public Life in India: Its Needs and Responsibilities*, National Literature Publishing Company, Bombay 1922.

——. *Speeches of Gopal Krishna Gokhale*, in G.A. Natesan (ed.), Natesan & Co, Madras 1920.

Gopal, Priyamvada. *Insurgent Empire: Anticolonial Resistance and British Dissent*, Verso, London 2019.

Gould, Frederick James. *Youth's Noble Path. A Volume on Moral Instruction Mainly Based on Eastern Tradition, Poetry and History*, Longmans, Green & Co, London, New York, Bombay and Calcutta 1911.

Grillo, R.D. "Cultural Essentialism and Cultural Anxiety", *Anthropological Theory*, Vol. 3, n. 2 (2003), pp. 157–173.

Gupta, Charu. *The Gender of Caste: Representing Dalits in Print*, University of Washington Press, Seattle 2016.

Harper, Tim. *Underground Asia: Global Revolutionaries and the Assault on Empire*, Harvard University Press, Cambridge: MA, 2021.

Harris, Karen L. "Sugar and Gold: Indentured Indian and Chinese Labour in South Africa", *Journal of Social Sciences*, Vol. 25, n. 1-3 (2010), pp. 147–158.

Hiralal, Kalpana. 'Gender, Labour and Resistance. Mapping the Lives of Indentured Women in Natal, South Africa 1860–1914', in Farzana Gounder, Kalpana Hiralal, Amba Pande and Maurits S. Hassankhan (eds.), *Women, Gender and the Legacy of Slavery and Indenture*, Routledge, London 2021.

Hofmeyr, Isabel. 'Seeking Empire, Finding Nation. Gandhi and Indianness in South Africa', in Joya Chatterji and David Washbrook (eds.), *Routledge Handbook of the South Asian Diaspora*, Routledge, London 2013, pp. 153–165.

Holton, Robert John. "Cosmopolitanism or Cosmopolitanisms? The Universal Races Congress of 1911", *Global Networks*, Vol. 2, n. 2 (2002), pp. 153–170.

Hyslop, Jonathan. 'Gandhi 1869-1915: The Transnational Emergence of a Public Figure', in Anthony Parel and Judith Brown (eds.), *The Cambridge Companion to Gandhi*, CUP, Cambridge 2011, pp. 30–50.

Ignatieff, Michael. 'Benign Nationalism? The Possibilities of the Civic Ideal', in E. Mortimer and R. Fine (eds.), *People, Nation and State*, I. B. Tauris, London 1999, pp. 141–147.

Jayal, Niraja Gopal. *Citizenship and Its Discontents, An Indian History*, Harvard University Press, Cambridge, MA 2013.

Kale, Madhavi. *Fragments of Empire; Capital, Slavery, and Indian Indentured Labour Migration in the British Caribbean*, University of Pennsylvania Press, Philadelphia 1998.

Kumar, Ashutosh. *Coolies of the Empire*, CUP, Cambridge and New Delhi 2017.

Lake, Marilyn and Henry Reynolds. *Drawing the Global Colour Line: White Men's Countries and the Question of Racial Equality*, Melbourne Univ. Publishing, Carlton 2008.

Lewis, Martin W. and Kāren Wigen. *The Myth of Continents: A Critique of Metageography*, University of California Press, Berkeley 1997.

Matysik, Tracie. 'Internationalist Activism and Global Civil Society at the High Point of Nationalism: The Paradox of the Universal Races Congress, 1911', in A.G. Hopkins (ed.), *Global History: Interactions Between the Universal and the Local*, Palgrave, New York 2006, pp. 131–159.

Mehrotra, S.R. "Gandhi and the Servants of India Society, 1915–16", *Gandhi Marg: The Journal of the Gandhi Peace Foundation*, Vol. 34, n. 4 (2013), pp. 495–516.

Mehta, Pranab Bhanu. "Cosmopolitanism and the Circle of Reason", *Political Theory*, Vol. 28, n. 5 (2000), pp. 619–639.

Metcalf, Thomas R. *Imperial Connections: India in the Indian Ocean Arena, 1860–1920*, University of California Press, Berkeley, Los Angeles and London 2007.

Mignolo, Walter D. "Epistemic Disobedience, Independent Thought and Decolonial Freedom", *Theory, Culture & Society*, Vol. 26, n. 7-8 (2009), pp. 159–181.

Milyukov, Pavel N. *Constitutional Government for Russia; An Address Delivered Before the Civic Forum*, New York City, January 14, 1908.

Morris, Marcus. "From Anti-Colonialism to Anti-Imperialism: The Evolution of H.M. Hyndman's Critique of Empire, c. 1875-1905", *Historical Research*, Vol. 87, n. 236 (2014), pp. 293–314.

Nanda, B.R. *Three Statesmen: Gokhale, Gandhi and Nehru*, OUP, New Delhi 2004.

Nevinson, Henry Wood. *The New Spirit in India*, Harper & Brothers, London and New York 1908.

Niranjana, Tejaswini. "Left to the Imagination": Indian Nationalisms and Female Sexuality in Trinidad", *Public Culture*, Vol. 11, n. 1 (1999), pp. 223–243.

Nussbaum, Martha. *Cultivating Humanity: A Classical Defense of Reform in Liberal Education*. Harvard University Press, Cambridge, MA 1997.

O'Malley, Kate. 'Violent Resistance: The Irish Revolution and India', in D. Roberts and J. Wright (eds.) *Ireland's Imperial Connections, 1775–1947*, Palgrave, Cham 2019.

——. *Ireland, India and Empire: Indo-Irish Radical Connections, 1919–64*, Manchester University Press, Manchester 2008.

Olsen, Stephanie. *Juvenile Nation: Youth, Emotions and the Making of the Modern British Citizen, 1880-1914*, Bloomsbury, London 2014.

Owen, Nicholas. *The British Left and India: Metropolitan Anti-Imperialism, 1885-1947*, OUP, New York 2007.

Pachai, B. *The International Aspects of the South African Indian Question 1860-1971*, C. Struik, Cape Town 1971.

Papers on Inter Racial Problems Communicated to the First Universal Races Congress Held at the University of London, July 26-29, 1911, edited by Gustav Spiller, P. S. King and Son, London 1911.

Papers regarding the Educational Conference, Allahabad, February 1911, Superintendent Government Printing India, Calcutta 1911.

Patel, Dinyar. *Naoroji: Pioneer of Indian Nationalism*, Harvard University Press, Cambridge, MA 2020.

Pennybaker, Susan. "The Universal Races Congress, London Political Culture, and Imperial Dissent, 1900—1939", *Radical History Review*, Vol. 92, n. 2 (2005), pp. 103–117.

Rai, Lala Lajpat. *Autobiographical Writings* (edited by Vijaya Chandra Joshi), University Publishers, Delhi and Jullundur 1965.

Ramnath, Maia. *Haj to Utopia: How the Ghadar Movement Charted Global Radicalism and Attempted to Overthrow the British Empire*, University of California Press, Berkeley, Los Angeles and London 2011.

Ranade, M.G. *The Wisdom of a Modern Rishi: Writings and Speeches of Mahadev Govind Ranade with an Address on Rishi Ranade by the Rt. Hon.ble V.S. Srinivas Sastri* (edited by T.N. Jagadisan), Rochouse and Sons Ltd., Madras 1942.

Ravi Shankar, Prabha. "Henry Mayers Hyndman (1842-1921) and the Radicalization of the Indian National Congress", *Proceedings of the Indian History Congress*, Vol. 66 (2005), pp. 1041–1049.

Ray, Utsa. 'Cosmopolitan Consumption: Domesticity, Cooking, and the Middle Class in Colonial India', in C. Dejung, D. Motadel and J. Osterhammel (eds.), *The Global Bourgeoisie: The Rise of the Middle Classes in the Age of Empire*, Princeton University Press, Princeton 2019, pp. 123–142.

Raza, Ali. *Revolutionary Pasts: Communist Internationalism in Colonial India*, CUP, Cambridge 2020.

Reddy, E.S. and Kalpana Hiralal. *Pioneers of Satyagraha: Indian South Africans Defy Racist Laws, 1907-1914*, Navajivan, Ahmedabad 2017.

Reed, Charles V. *Royal Tourists, Colonial Subjects and the Making of a British World, 1860–1911*, Manchester University Press, Manchester 2016.

Roberts, Nathan. "Character in the Mind: Citizenship, Education and Psychology in Britain, 1880–1914", *History of Education*, Vol. 33, n. 2 (2004), pp. 177–197.

Roy, Anupama. *Gendered Citizenship: Historical and Conceptual Explorations*, Orient Blackswan, Hyderabad 2013.

Said, Edward. *Orientalism: Western Conceptions of the Orient*, Penguin, New York 1978.

Sarkar, Tanika. *Hindu Wife, Hindu Nation: Community, Religion, and Cultural Nationalism*, Indiana University Press, Bloomington 1992.

Seshadri, C. "The Concept of Moral Education: Indian and Western-A Comparative Study", *Comparative Education*, Vol. 17, n. 3 (1981), pp. 293–310.

Seth, Sanjay. "Nationalism, Modernity, and the 'Woman Question' in India and China", *The Journal of Asian Studies*, Vol. 72, n. 2 (2013), pp. 273–297.

——. *Subject Lessons: The Western Education of Colonial India*, Duke University Press, Durham and London 2007.

Shahani, T.K. *Gopal Krishna Gokhale: A Historical Biography*, R.K Mody, Bombay 1929.

Silvestri, Michael. *Policing 'Bengali Terrorism' in India and the World: Imperial Intelligence and Revolutionary Nationalism, 1905-1939*, Palgrave Macmillan, Cham 2019.

——. *Ireland and India: Nationalism, Empire and Memory*, Palgrave Macmillan, London 2009.

Singh, Saint Nihal. "Trying to Solve the World's Problems of Race", *Review of Reviews*, Vol. 44 (1911), pp. 339–343.

Sinha, Mrinalini. 'Gendered Nationalism: From Women to Gender and Back Again?', in L. Fernandes (ed.), *Routledge Handbook of Gender in South Asia*, Routledge, Oxon and New York 2018, pp. 13–27.

Slate, Nico. *Gandhi's Search for the Perfect Diet: Eating With the World in Mind*, University of Washington Press, Seattle 2019.

Sluga, Glenda. *Internationalism in the Age of Nationalism*, University of Pennsylvania Press, Philadelphia 2013.

Srinivasa Sastri, V.S. *Life and Times of Sir Pherozeshah Mehta* (edited by S.R. Venkataraman), Bharatiya Vidya Bhavan, Bombay n.d. (first published 1945).

——. *My Master Gokhale: A Selection from the Speeches and Writings of V. S. Srinivasa Sastri* (edited by T.N. Jagadisan), Model Publications, Madras 1946.

Steadman, John. *The Myth of Asia*, Simon and Schuster, New York 1969.

Stolte, Carolien. "*Orienting India: Interwar Internationalism in an Asian Inflection, 1917-1937*", Unpublished Ph.D. Dissertation, Leiden University, 2013.

—— and Fischer-Tiné, Harald. "Imagining Asia in India: Nationalism and Internationalism (Ca. 1905-1940)", *Comparative Studies in Society and History*, Vol. 54, n. 1 (2012), pp. 65–92.

Swan, Maureen. *Gandhi: The South African Experience*, Raven Press, Johannesburg 2017 (first published 1985).

The Indian National Congress Presidential Addresses, G. A. Natesan & Co, Madras 1935.

Tidrick, Kathryn. *Gandhi. A Political and Spiritual Life*, I. B. Tauris, London and New York 2006.

Tilley, Helen. "Racial Science, Geopolitics, and Empires: Paradoxes of Power", *Isis*, Vol. 105, n. 4 (2014), pp. 773–781.

Vahed, Goolam. 'Gokhale, Polak, and the End of Indian Indenture in South Africa, 1860 – 1911', in Neilesh Bose (ed.), *South Asian Migrations in Global History*, Bloomsbury, London 2021, pp. 37–62.

——. "Passengers, Partnerships, and Promissory Notes: Gujarati Traders in Colonial Natal, 1870-1920", *International Journal of African Historical Studies*, Vol. 38, n. 3 (2005), pp. 449–479.

van der Veer, Peter. 'Cosmopolitan Options', in J. Friedman and S. Randeria (eds.), *Worlds on the Move: Globalization, Migration and Cultural Security*, Palgrave Macmillan, New York 2004, pp. 167–178.

——. 'Introduction', in Peter van der Veer (ed.), *Nation and Migration: The Politics of Space in the South Asian Diaspora*, University of Pennsylvania Press, Philadelphia 1995, pp. 1–16.

Wacha, D.E. *Reminiscences of the Late Honourable Mr. G. K. Gokhale*, H. T. Anklesaria, Bombay 1915.

Weber, Thomas. *Gandhi as Disciple and Mentor*, CUP, Cambridge 2004.

Wright, Susannah. *Morality and Citizenship in English Schools: Secular Approaches, 1897–1944*, Palgrave Macmillan, London 2017.

Yuval-Davis, Nira. *Gender and Nation*, Sage Publication, London 1997.

4 Citizenship

> In public life there can be no public spirit unless we learn to subordinate
> our judgement to the judgement of those above us, of leaders of public
> movements, who are entrusted with the responsibility of leading us.[*]

This final chapter focuses on Gokhale's definition of citizenship, highlighting its specificities and fleshing out its ambivalences and complexities. It demonstrates that while, for the Indian liberal, citizenship was a
legal/formal status regulating the citizen/polity relationship and including rights and duties, the attainment of this status involved a process of
'education into citizenship,' too. This was tied to issues of moral authority
and legitimacy, which gave it a conservative content and made it potentially exclusionary. In order to explicate these questions, the chapter first
analyses the political framework of citizenship envisioned by Gokhale
and the influence that liberalism had on this. It goes on by exploring the
double role of the Servants of India Society (SIS) in the citizen-making
process as well as in welfare schemes, both considered by Gokhale central
to nation building. The last section of the chapter looks at Gokhale's commitment to the cause of elementary education and how this was linked,
more or less directly, to what it meant, for the Indian 'moderate' to be a
citizen. Overall, the chapter strives to demonstrate that the civic construction articulated by Gokhale showed propensity to preserve social hierarchies while at the same time having the potential to open up possibilities
of change and even improvement for those at the margins of political,
economic and social power.

Envisioning citizenship, making citizens

The importance that Gokhale attributed to the question of citizenship has already figured quite prominently in the previous chapters.
The liberalism that emerged in the Indian colonial settings and that

---

[*] Gopal Krishna Gokhale, *Public Life in India: Its needs and responsibilities*, National
Literature Publishing Company, Bombay 1922, p. 9.

DOI: 10.4324/9781003037422-5

underpinned Gokhale's political vision provided a basis, if somewhat uncertain and ambiguous, for the emergence of a discourse of citizenship consisting of civil, political and social rights. While cast in the language of equality and belonging, the citizenship envisioned by Gokhale was embedded in, and influenced by, the inequalities and hierarchies that existed in Indian colonial society. Thus, it often fell short of being common and equal.

In line with the logic of nationalism, for Gokhale, citizenship meant being a member of the nation state and deriving both duties and rights from that status. But since that status was a fairly remote one for Indians, both the imperial and local level functioned as strategic frameworks of reference in order to articulate the discourse of citizenship. It has been seen that Gokhale was among those who adopted the language of imperial citizenship as an important category for claim-making and asked that Indians be recognised as citizens of the empire on a par with members of the White dominions. As shown by Sukanya Banerjee, similar pronunciations of an imperial citizenship predicated on the concept of abstract equality inherent in liberal values were functional to transcend the status of 'racialised' Indians: it was more convenient to claim political rights as subjects of the Crown than as colonised subjects of the *Raj*. Appealing to imperial citizenship also served the purpose of condemning colonialism without being anti-British.[1] While perhaps it is too much to dismiss the discourse of imperial citizenship as "little more than an unselfconsciously imitative impertinence" of the Western-educated elite,[2] it is true that it remained largely elusive and fettered, and had several shortcomings.[3] The Congress leader could not ignore that aspiring to be citizens of the empire was a thorny question, since it was becoming increasingly clear that imperial citizenship was "foundered on the shoals of white supremacy,"[4] as would become undisputable especially after the First World War.[5] A more tractable and palpable scale of citizenship was at the local level – municipalities and local boards – which Gokhale deemed optimal to organise political work, become aware of one's rights and responsibilities, and develop a sense of participation and belonging beyond one's family, caste and religious community.[6] As a site where participation was more 'real,' the local level was ideal to train individuals in the modern political relationship between state and citizen. Thus, the polyvalent and multilocal conceptualisation of citizenship for Gokhale need not be read as an inconsistency or in contradiction with his broader national project, for the state level remained significant as the framework within which citizenship was to be finally achieved. After all, both imperial citizenship and local citizenship – the former being more concerned with self-definition in relation to the coloniser and the latter with civic responsibilities and the common good – were ultimately instrumental in shaping a political community possessed with a common identity and a common purpose. This was part of the project of making the liberal and secular nation, which, as seen, Gokhale considered an evolutionary socio-political process that required time and training and could not be jump-started as the more radical nationalists wanted. Until then, the persistence of the British *Raj* was a necessary, if temporary, condition: working under "British democracy," it ensured the gradual development of political reform and provided the political spaces required for the performance of citizenship.[7]

At the same time, Gokhale stressed the importance of the civil society domain, too, as an arena where citizens could be 'made.' As fairly typical for his time, Gokhale believed that it was crucial to "build up the strength" of the Indian people: this was to be achieved through the uplift of public life, which was acquiring increasing importance due to the advancement of a "more democratic" form of government but was overall perceived as dormant as well as lacking character and capacity. Indian public life, encompassing several fields "from councils of the country down to the village unions, in the municipal councils and local bodies, in the press and the [political] platform, and in the various movements which we have inaugurated for the education of public opinion," was not as strong as it should have been: it was devoid of public spiritedness, that is the will to sacrifice personal gain, comfort, convenience and judgement for the common good. In order to counter such "defects," it was necessary to take up a sort of collective self-purification through voluntary selfless service "in the interests of [Indian] fellow beings," by which Gokhale largely meant the masses. In other words, Gokhale was calling for a greater engagement in active citizenship through social service and humanitarianism, which, by instilling values of obedience and discipline, were indispensable to fill the abyss existing between India's ancient, sophisticated civilisation and its 'inadequate' civic education and 'underdeveloped' political life. At the same time, he invoked self-sacrifice as a virtue against individualistic and materialistic pursuits. The emphasis given to the concept of sacrifice and work, irrespective of their outcome, was influenced by the reading of the Bhagavad Gita in the context of colonial modernity and by a new worldly interpretation of ascetic renunciation, popularised by Vivekananda, as selfless political action.[8] It is significant in this sense that Gokhale attempted to discredit government service, by arguing that public service should not equate any more with Indians serving as government officials. This kind of service had to be "dethroned from the place which it ha[d] held in [Indian] hearts all these years" as a means to achieve social respectability, and the *real* public service, now invested with a new moral superiority, had to be installed in its place.[9]

In line with customary liberal principles and with the limited colonial model of citizenship rights,[10] Gokhale considered 'modern' education and the respectability generally attached to it as factors that made some Indians worthier citizens and more able than others to carry out nation-building, and to participate in socially relevant initiatives. In fact, his appeals in favour of social service and civic activism were mostly directed to "educated young men," whose task was to:

> Teach [Indian people] the habits of co-operation and habits of discipline and spread among them the ideas of our rights, and then [...] bring this [newly acquired] strength [in public life] to bear upon the government, so that the bonds of freedom in this country may be widened, so that concessions might be followed by other concessions till at last we are able to hold our head high like other people in other lands.[11]

In this call to public duty, we see the paternalistic concern for the masses typical of liberalism spilling over into a discourse of civic activism in which the role of the agents pertains to the 'educated' few, whereas the 'passive' recipients of 'betterment' are those perceived as 'backward' sections of Indian society, never quite ready to be members of the nation and unprepared for citizenship and self-government. Such civic pedagogy, a recurring theme in Gokhale's political vision, was aimed at training Indians as citizens engaging politically with the state and bearing rights, duties and responsibilities, as well as participating in civil society activities. At the same time, this 'education into citizenship' reiterated the opposition between the 'brain of the country' and the 'ignorant masses,' namely between fitness of citizenship and lack of it, locating the issue of qualification to citizenship not in political terms, but in social and moral ones, largely shaped by the upper-caste bias. Especially moral notions such as sacrifice, discipline and austerity – belonging to the Brahmanical ethos and underpinning citizenship values – were problematic not only because they were depicted as 'normative' and therefore worthy to be extended to the masses, but also due to their vague and undefined nature, which made them ever-changing and possibly unattainable and easily exclusionary. As the following section shows, all these aspects also characterised Gokhale's SIS, whose members were selected for their being 'deserving' citizens who had the task to pursue the 'improvement' of the larger populace, seen as needy of moral and material 'uplift.'

Serving India?

Training educated men as national missionaries in the service of India[12] was chief among the declared objectives of the SIS. Its members, in Gokhale's words, "would go about, rouse people to a sense of duty, raise local money and energy, gradually building up small institutions and develop the public life of this country."[13]

The foundation of the SIS in 1905 represented what Carey Watt has called a real push towards a more systematic and this-worldly form of social service, underpinned by new global ideas, but inflected with indigenous (Hindu) traditions of giving and philanthropy.[14] It initiated a process of growth of similar associations and institutions that were run by urban elites of the upper and middle classes, and that contributed to shaping

India's public sphere and civil society, even after independence. The deriving associational culture played an important role in devolving to Indians greater control over the subcontinent public life and eroding the legitimacy of the colonial state, while at the same time showing collaboration with it.[15] In these settings, Hindu 'living traditions' and religious virtues such as *seva* (service), *dana* (charity), *brahmacharya* (celibacy) and *sannyas* (renunciation, asceticism) were transferred to the worldly domain and adopted new meanings and significance.[16] These religious notions became central in making prudent participatory citizenship and social service naturalised as 'Indian' while, in many cases, presenting them as essential to creating ethical alternatives to the materialistic individualism of the West.[17] Moreover, they had a strategic value to mobilise the (upper-caste Hindu male) citizen to engage in activities to serve the larger community drawing on the familiar. This was true also for the nominally secular SIS, whose members had to be political *sannyasi*s, living in poverty and dedicated to *jan seva* (public service), as per its constitution.[18] This shows not only that both religious indigenous traditions and social altruism had increasingly permeated Indian liberalism. More importantly, it reveals that even a 'modern' and secular idea of the nation had to be transmitted and put into practice through the adoption of concepts belonging to Indian (Hindu) culture, transformed into more intelligible and culturally distinct political instruments. Thus, the rationality of a liberal conceptualisation of the nation had to be compensated by invoking the religio-spiritual domain and everyday political understandings.[19]

The SIS had its headquarters in Poona; other branches were opened in Bombay, Madras, the Central Provinces and the United Provinces in the years immediately after the foundation of the Society.[20] Its goals, as listed in the constitution, were to create among the people a deep and passionate love of the motherland; organising the work of political education and agitation and strengthening the public life of the country; promoting relations of common good-will and cooperation among the different communities; assisting educational movements, especially those advocating education for women and 'backward' classes; spreading industrial and scientific education; elevating the so-called 'depressed classes.'[21] This project of nation-building through active citizenship, already in itself demanding, would be dented, Gokhale maintained, if India did not benefit, for the necessary span of time, from the political unity brought about by the British *Raj*. On the one hand, as seen in the course of the book, Gokhale was sincerely convinced that the stability ensured by the continuance of the colonial rule was an indispensable condition to "mastering the first lessons of the new polity" and fundamental requisites of progress[22] for a country as diversified as India. On the other hand, declarations of loyalty to the *Raj* were also intended not to raise suspicion in government towards the SIS. This, however, did not always work. Lord Curzon, just to cite a well-known example, found incompatible the fact that Gokhale's society aimed at "awaken[ing] and appeal[ing] to the spirit of nationality in India and, at the same time, profess[ing] loyal acceptance of British rule."[23] Despite some anxieties, generally, colonial administrators saw such self-help initiatives from 'lettered' Indians as consistent with their own imperial civilising mission.[24]

At the time of its foundation, the SIS had only three members, namely G. K. Devadhar (1871–1935), who would become a prominent social reformer in Western India, A. V. Patvardhan and N. A. Dravid. V. S. Srinivas Sastri (1869–1946) and Hriday Nath Kunzru (1887–1978), who would play leading political roles in the National Liberal Federation[25] and more generally in the political life of the country, joined the society in 1906 and 1909 respectively, soon after becoming foremost members.[26] N. M. Joshi (1879–1955), prominent social reformer and founder member of both the Social Service League and the Bombay Textile Labour Union, became SIS member in 1909.[27]

The SIS rules, drawn up by Gokhale himself, prescribed a life-long service on a very meagre salary. The admitted candidates, who had to be university graduates and undergraduates or individuals who had already distinguished themselves in social service and social reform, had to undergo five years "under a vow of absolute obedience to the First Member"[28] (i.e., Gokhale until his death). During that period, they were not allowed to deliver public addresses or write in newspapers and journals without the approval of their superior. The five-year training under the guidance of Gokhale was meant to build the members' character by instilling the spirit of obedience, selflessness and discipline that formed the basis of the Society. Members under training had to spend at least four months per year in the Servants of India Home in Pune where they were expected to conduct a "monastic" life. While there was no intention to "bind [members] together religiously" and there were no common prayers in the Home, Gokhale held that the aims of the Society as well as the serious renunciation and self-mastery imposed by membership were in themselves "deeply religious."[29] Despite the emphasis on upper-caste Hindu virtues of moral rectitude and self-mastery – virtues that combined well with the liberal teleological vision of progress through individual self-development – the education imparted to the trainees of the SIS was essentially political and based on 'modern' knowledge. Unlike those of his generation calling for an Indian 'national education,' 'Western knowledge' and English education were not seen by Gokhale as the cause of India's moral disruption and lack of national character.[30] The SIS library, as per Gokhale's words, had to have as its central idea "the growth of freedom all over the world. You will find in it an account of all nationalistic and humanitarian movements that have ever been started in any country. There will also be there [sic] standard histories of every country in the world. Books bearing on the ancient greatness of the three races inhabiting India at present – the Hindus, the Mahomedans and the Parsees – will also be there."[31] According to a later report of the SIS activities, the library was well provided with books on history, politics and economics and possessed a unique collection of reports, parliamentary blue books and other publications relating to India. Gokhale's own books formed the nucleus of the library which was subsequently enriched by donations from Mr. H. A. Wadya [very close associate of Pherozeshah Mehta], D. E. Wacha and Dr. Dadabhai Naoroji.[32]

The strictness of the Society's rules – especially the fact that the First Member was virtually the autocratic head – attracted severe criticism from Gokhale's friends. For instance, the Principal of the Deccan College, F. G. Selby, who was close to Gokhale, wrote to him that:

> It is rather an awful thing that you should ask men to surrender absolutely to you their conscience and the right of private judgment for five years. This is popularly supposed to be the first condition of admission to the Society of Jesus and is the main ground of Protestant condemnation of that Order. It reads to an Englishman rather like a rule of a Russian Secret Society.[33]

Although not ignoring the danger posed to individual liberty by the rules he drafted, Gokhale believed that it was necessary to take this risk, given "the want of self-restraint which characterises[d] most of [India's] young men."[34]

Unsurprisingly, from the exchange of letters between Gokhale and his juniors, it is not possible to discern any specific discontent with the presumed autocratic attitude of the First Member.[35] However, the correspondence shows simmering and ongoing discontent with the general lack of democracy, which allowed senior members to concentrate excessive powers in their hands. Abuses and indifference towards the wishes of the junior recruits were reported.[36] Gokhale was aware of the perfectible nature of his creation and was willing to accept changes in the constitution – "certainly [...] not to be regarded as sacrosanct" – but, at the same time, he was irritated that the servants of India kept busy with "all this talk of autocracy, inner and outer circles, and so forth" rather than with serving the country and the Society. He suggested as the best way forward to remedy the complaints that every member draft clear amendments to the rules and regulations, or even draft altogether new constitutions.[37]

All this seems to suggest that Gokhale maintained an open and democratic attitude towards the requests of his juniors and was ready to compromise for the sake of the society, a view inconsistent with that of an autocratic figure. Nevertheless, the strict rules that defined the association created a strong hierarchy within it, leaving scope for abuses and dissatisfaction as well as difficulties in combining the commitment to public work and one's own family life. For these reasons, too, the society remained a niche organisation: five years after its foundation, it counted only 25 members, even though Gokhale, evidently unconcerned by the exclusive nature of the SIS, considered it "a fairly good number."[38]

Furthermore, despite being a non-denominational organisation and notwithstanding Gokhale's keen desire to have non-Hindus among its members, the SIS encountered difficulties in attracting Muslims.[39] The society thus lacked credibility as an inter-communal association, one which acted as the kind of peace committee to contain communal polarisation that Gokhale wanted. This weakness became visible during the 1921 so-called Mappila rebellion in the Southern Indian region of Malabar. The Mapillas (or 'Moplahs' in colonial terminology) were low-class Muslim peasants that had been mobilised during the early phase of the Khilafat movement (1919–1924). After attacking colonial representatives and symbols, they assaulted the Hindu landlords and moneylenders that exploited them, with tens of people killed in the resulting riots and hundreds of Hindus forcibly converted to Islam. Thousands of Hindu families had to flee their villages and shift to refugee camps where the living conditions were often unbearable. The rebellion was eventually suppressed by the Indian Army in December 1921.[40] In its aftermath, the SIS began relief work in the refugee camps and cooperated not only with the YMCA, but also, and significantly enough, with the Arya Samaj, whose primary aim was not humanitarian relief but reconversion campaigns.[41] The SIS equally fell short of being a body that promoted caste equality. This became apparent during the relief operations that the SIS provided during the famine that hit the United Provinces in 1907/1908, namely when Gokhale was still alive and presumably had influence over the practices of the society. In famine-stricken Mirzapur, where they operated, the SIS members opened poorhouses so as to be able to offer relief to the weakest.[42] Here, meals and tasks were assigned according to caste norms and inter-caste dining was prohibited.[43]

That life on the austere lines that the SIS members were supposed to lead could equate with virtuous citizenship was something that not everybody in the largely elitist Indian political class liked. Pherozeshah Mehta, for example, disapproved of the values underpinning the SIS, because he insightfully feared that, with their self-abnegating life conduct, they would constitute "a sort of superior caste among those who did not do service to the country in the same way" and that "their bearing towards their colleagues and other patriots would be marked by a feeling of moral superiority," holding themselves worthy of "greater respect from their lay brethren."[44] Gandhi came to a similar conclusion, arguing that the renunciation and voluntary abnegation on which the SIS was supposedly predicated existed only on paper and was a mask to keep social hierarchies in place:

> You pride yourselves on being Servants of India. You don't go amongst the poor Harijans or labourers. I wonder what you do, you who live this sort of life here. You don't live amongst them. You don't know the language they speak. You don't eat their food. You don't suffer their sufferings. And what good is it?[45]

Srinivasa Sastri remembered Gandhi talking to the SIS members in the above terms, using "rasping tones" and condemning their comfortable lives shortly after Gokhale's death, in 1915. Now that his "political guru" was no more, Gandhi felt free to speak his mind.

Gokhale had hoped that the SIS could become Gandhi's power base in India, something from which it too could benefit, by attaining a spectacular outreach, given Gandhi's popularity after the struggle in South Africa. On Gandhi's return to India, Gokhale asked him to travel throughout the subcontinent for a year in order to temper his views and "prevent him making early blunders out of ignorance and enthusiasm which would lessen his potential for public work."[46] While accepting Gokhale's advice, Gandhi made publicly clear that he was not sure about joining the SIS.[47] The final decision came in January 1916, almost a year after Gokhale's death, when Gandhi wrote to Srinivasa Sastri that the methods of the SIS were "so totally different" from his own that he would become "a disturbing factor." The members, for their part, were deeply distrustful of Gandhi's stance on Western civilisation and modern education, and saw him more as a religious preacher and a social reformer than a political figure.[48] Thus, fearing that if the would-be Mahatma took the lead he would hijack the SIS and its creed, they diplomatically suggested that he should not seek formal admission.

Years earlier, the would-be Mahatma had already expressed his doubts about the SIS in a letter, worth quoting at length, to Maganlal Gandhi, one of his followers and a distant relative:

> It is simply an indifferent imitation of the West. Is it proper for the servants to have servants? [...]. Why do they have others to cook for them? What do these 'servants' think of religion? Why should there be large buildings in India? Why should not huts be enough? It is like digging up a mountain to kill a mouse. When will the mission undertaken by Prof. Gokhale end? How much money will it cost? What a superstition that only an M.A. or B.A. could become a 'servant'! [...] I do feel that the aims of Phoenix as well as the way of life there surpass those of the Society [...]. What we are doing here is the real thing, what goes on in Poona is, leaving aside the motive, unreal. The motive is good, but what is being done is bad [...]. The work of Mr. Gokhale's 'servants' cannot be regarded as proper. It is likely to add to our slavery. If I tried to turn East into West, I also would sigh like Gokhale and lose heart [...]. We do not aspire to improve India; we want to improve ourselves.[49]

In Gandhi's anti-modernist perspective, ideals of religious asceticism and poverty were invoked not only as citizenship virtues but also as a means of resistance and self-discipline, whereas the discipline pursued by the SIS was that of modern civilisation. Gandhi wanted poverty, a widespread condition in colonial India, to become a cultural practice, a factor of national identity, and an individual expression of self-realisation. In his view, these ideals had to replace the materialistic values spread by the decadent 'Western civilisation' whose failure to represent the highest aspirations of humanity would be once and for all exposed by the Great War.[50] The SIS, on the contrary, intended to provide Indian society with all the necessary means to make the citizenry fit for the imagined challenges of the future, namely a secular and democratic modern state, industrialisation and urbanisation. The concern for the underprivileged was combined with investment in the making of the new productive and efficient citizenry: making India, thus, entailed a painstaking work that would transform the colonial subjects into Indian citizens as 'performers' of the nation.[51] Based on the faith of political progress as centred on technology and the spirit of science, modern education, a secular approach to socio-political problems and the acceptance of the nation-state as the prime unit of the polity, Gokhale's SIS could not but be spurned by Gandhi as the epitome of the "fetish of literacy and mundane knowledge" of which India had to rid itself: the servants' attitude was "material not spiritual" and thus inferior.[52] However, despite his negative opinion of the SIS, Gandhi never broke with Gokhale. Conversely, also in the years to come, he continued to regard Gokhale as his "political guru,"[53] whose highest merit was to have taught Indians that political and social life had to be spiritualised and become a quasi-religious self-negating mission.[54] Besides the deep "currents of mental and moral identity"[55] that bound the guru and his disciple and abridged their differences while Gokhale was alive, on a broader level, Gandhi still had faith, if wavering, in the same liberal values and in the empire as Gokhale. When he was commenting negatively on Gokhale's society, the would-be Mahatma was in a transitional phase in which he was becoming progressively disillusioned with the idea of imperial citizenship and liberalism but had not yet disavowed them.[56]

And even after he rejected the empire as amoral and illegitimate (not for betraying those liberal principles of formal equality, as held by Gokhale, but as a by-product of the European nations' greediness which had to be supplanted by a simpler yet more sustainable pre-modern life),[57] Gandhi continued to collaborate with the SIS.[58] Indeed, for all the SIS's nation-building and 'uplifting' project, its attitudes and values were never completely alien to Gandhi's.[59]

Teaching temperance

Besides the more explicitly political work, efforts to spread education among different disadvantaged social groups, providing relief to victims of calamities, dispensing medical assistance and disseminating principles of sanitation were just some of the social welfare activities carried out by the SIS in the first years of its existence.[60] While these initiatives have been largely analysed by Carey Watt,[61] the SIS and Gokhale's commitment to the

campaign in favour of temperance by promoting education against intoxicating substances, alcohol in particular, deserves some new attention. It
is, in fact, a significant *pars pro toto* of projects of citizenship-making in
which civic virtue was constructed through a moral discourse differentiating between 'deserving' and 'non-deserving' members of the citizenry.

We have seen in the previous chapter that during his first visit to London
in 1888, Gokhale had met William S. Caine, MP, the staunch temperance
advocate, and founder of the Anglo-Indian Temperance Association
(AITA).[62] In the 1880s and 1890s, Caine and other AITA members travelled
the subcontinent to promote their cause and collaborated with Indians
to form temperance organisations in several cities.[63] The 1896 Indian
National Social Conference held in Calcutta had praised their activities
and called for greater "active co-operation between the temperance movements in India and those in England and America." The same resolution
added that "the vice of intemperance" was not of "ancient growth" in India
and was still confined to minorities, by which it meant the lower social
strata.[64] It was therefore necessary that the "majority of total abstainers
should exert themselves to popularise their views."[65] Some years later, commending the several temperance and purity associations that had emerged
in Punjab, Ranade, the social reformer and Gokhale's teacher, made a plea
to temperance workers all over the country "to reform the lower classes of
our population" which were "so much addicted to this vice [of drinking]."[66]

As shown by recent scholarship, by the late 19th century, temperance
activism had become a global phenomenon "that transcended religious
and cultural boundaries as well as the infamous divide separating the col-
onising imperial powers from the colonised world."[67] Although initially
organised and instructed by English temperance agitators and underpinned by the tenets of Christianity, the movement in India was neither
inherently Western nor the prerogative of Christian reformers. Anti-vice
campaigning was a modern trend that acquired a specific meaning in the
Indian colonial context. It became largely an expression of the upper- and
middle-caste and class activists who formed the aspiring elite and made the
issue of temperance part and parcel of their anticolonial political struggle,
by appealing to religious sentiments and cultural difference.[68]

The diffusion among the Indian population of habits such as drinking
was considered the evil import of Western civilisation: it was in fact a belief
shared by European, American and Indian reformers that drinking had
never been a problem of significant dimension in pre-British India.[69] The
trope of the "abstemious Indian," invented by both Western and Indian
temperance activists, was turned into a discursive resource, undergirded
by Brahminical values and social prejudices, aimed at legitimising the
critique of colonial rule as well as demonstrating the superior morality
of Indian culture.[70] That temperance and anticolonial politics merged
is easily explained, for example, by the fact that the annual meeting of
the AITA held in London would be addressed by political figures such as

Surendranath Banerjea, Gokhale and C. F. Andrews.[71] This combination did not leave indifferent the colonial rulers who looked with suspicion at the "methods and objects of temperance."[72]

The colonial policy in terms of intoxicants – liquor, opium, *mhowra* and cannabis – was guided by two contradictory objectives. On the one hand, it was inspired by the vested interests of an increased capacity to generate revenue and, on the other, by the Victorian imperative to control intemperance among Indian subjects in order to 'safeguard their morality.' The self-serving argument justifying such an ambivalent posture was that the intoxicants' higher costs would act as a significant deterrent. The official condemnation of intoxicant abuse was, therefore, combined with the refusal to enact total prohibition. Total prohibition was not only harmful from a fiscal policy point of view: it was also driven by an awareness that the lower classes habitually resorted to stimulants, which in many cases served as an antidote to the climactic [sic] influences to which they were exposed.[73]

Gokhale had taken an early interest in colonial policies that regulated the production and use of intoxicating substances. His initial concern regarded mostly the damaging economic consequences that the excise policy had on the lower social strata in India. During the discussion of the Mhowra Bill in 1892 in the Bombay Legislative Council, the Poona Sarvajanika Sabha (PSS), through its journal, whose editor at the time was Gokhale, took a pro-poor and anti-prohibition position. Passed in that same year, the Bill aimed at safeguarding government revenue interests by controlling the possession and sale of mahua (*mhowra*) flowers, which were used to make 'illicit' liquor. The PSS condemned the revenue-driven bias of the act which did not take into account the other uses of mahua flowers, "largely used by the wild tribes and the poorer classes of Thana and Kolaba as an important supplement to the food-grains when the stock of the latter fail[ed]," and also "as fodder for cattle."[74]

We can see that in the following years, Gokhale's concern regarding the effects that the colonial excise policy had on the poor persisted. However, his views were increasingly linked to moral considerations against revenues obtained at the cost of the 'demoralisation' of Indian people. This change of discourse was undoubtedly a consequence of his proximity to British temperance circles. From the letters sent by William Caine to him, it appears that Gokhale had become an important local interlocutor and ally in the British battle against intemperance. When the prominent temperance leader and secretary of the AITA Frederick Grubb visited India to promote the cause, it was Gokhale who, at Caine's request, made preparations to welcome him.[75] More importantly, Caine invited his Indian friend to "putting in a spoke for temperance" in the Bombay Legislative Council[76] and to "keep [his] eye [open] in the Excise administration" when working in the Viceroy's Council[77] – which Gokhale promptly did.

In 1901, the Bombay Abkari Act Amendment was introduced in the Bombay Legislative Council and eventually accepted by the Government.

The measure integrated the previous 1878 Abkari Act, which had imposed the centralisation and licensing of liquor production,[78] with the enforcement of control of both the cultivation of hemp and the sale and production of hemp-derivate drugs like ganja, charas and bhang. It encouraged the adoption of the Bengal model of raising taxes on the trade in cannabis. Gokhale as a non-official member of the assembly opposed the Bill.[79] His opposition was predicated on statistics data from 1885 and 1899 which indicated that there had been no increase in the cultivation of hemp and, by extension, in the consumption of hemp-derived drugs. Restriction of cultivation was therefore unnecessary. The regulation proposed by the government, moreover, of introducing a quantitative duty on drug use gave the Abkari Department a vested interest in increasing consumption. It also invested the lower subordinates of the Revenue with the power of harassing and blackmailing the cultivator. Gokhale maintained that he was, overall, in favour of "total prohibition" as "the most effective way of dealing with the problem, in spite of the fancied interests of what are called moderate consumers." However, his prohibitionist tendencies were tempered by the fear that the implementation of prohibition could drive some consumers to use liquor or other drugs like *dhatura*.[80] Thus, the "next best policy" was "not to make the intoxicants dearer, but to make them scarcer." He went on to say that:

> Any one [sic] who knows anything of the fearful hold which these intoxicants [liquor and drugs] come to acquire over their victims will see that these helpless creatures will make any sacrifice to satisfy their craving, and that increased taxation under such circumstances, without a reduction of the facilities for obtaining the intoxicants, only means, as I have already observed, the misery of less food added to the curse of drunkenness.[81]

Gokhale indiscriminately considered the use of hemp drugs a ruinous vice that pertained mainly to the lower social classes. He disregarded the cultural-religious value of cannabis preparations of which the Indian Hemp Drugs Commission (IHDC) had given plenty of evidence.[82] What mattered were issues of government responsibility rather than the safeguard of long-standing Indian customs. In this light, taxation was unfair – and not the expression of an ethical state that cared for the common good of its citizens, as the colonial rulers deceptively presented it: higher duties, instead of having a pedagogical function in acting as a deterrent against excessive consumption, led merely to increased poverty.

Gokhale held the same views in terms of the colonial liquor policy. He ridiculed the government for imagining that "its duty [in reducing drunkenness] [wa]s done by simply making liquor as costly as it c[ould] be made," whereas he proposed the reduction of liquor shops as an option to be tried with the view to test "if it [wa]s really impossible to wean the people from drink."[83] The "tender solicitude" that the Abkari Department showed for the interests of the "moderate" or "legitimate consumer" – a category that, according to Gokhale, had been created by the colonial state to serve its own stake in securing revenue from intoxicants – actually contributed to expanding consumption.[84] The "curse of drink" was "on the increase, especially among the lower classes and the wild aboriginal tribes, spreading ruin and misery among them."[85] Education was, once again, promoted as "an effective remedy."[86]

There is no acknowledgement by Gokhale of the symbolic, cultural and ritual value that intoxicating substances had in colonial India,[87] much less of the right of consumers to choose their leisure practices. While recognising that less-costly substances were less ruinous to the pockets of the poorer classes, Gokhale saw users of intoxicants as poor victims of the colonial state, unable to administer proper care and thus considered amoral. It was then the moral duty of the aspiring Indian political elite – distinguished for their higher moral stand from both the British rulers and the underclass – to reach out to their uneducated poor compatriots and guide them to the right path and, at the same time, reveal the inadequacy of colonial policies. Such views, along with civilising impulses, notions of cultural superiority and class anxieties, reflected a correlation that is still valid, namely that the way in which "vices" are perceived and regulated depends upon the social status of those identified as the primary consumers.[88]

Gokhale did not exploit Hindu religious symbolism to make his arguments against intoxicants. Rather, in supporting the temperance movement, he felt he was part of a cosmopolitan moral community comprised of liberals, Hindu conservatives and Christian missionaries, animated by reform principles largely seen as universal. As a matter of fact, Gokhale became a prominent figure in the crusade against vice well beyond the boundaries of colonial India. This is revealed by the fact that he received a letter by the American National Temperance Society, based in New York, which requested that the Indian politician sign a petition for the retention of the 1851 prohibitionist Maine Law, defined an "old social-hygienic landmark" that "the determined efforts of the alcohol capital" were trying to overthrow.[89] Also, in 1911, Gokhale represented the subcontinent at the International Prohibition Confederation, led by an American living in London, Edward Page Gaston (1868–1956), and organised by reformers from 13 countries.[90] The following year, he visited the India Office and, before Lord Crewe, the Secretary of State, he referred to the need to reduce licences and opening times for liquor shops as well as to remove the licensing function from the control of the Abkari Revenue Department.[91]

It might seem surprising that, when in 1907 the Poona Temperance Association (PTA) was formed, Gokhale became its president.[92] In fact, Gokhale's long-term rival had a leading role in the PTA. Both Tilak and Gokhale remained members of the association even after the Congress split. This fact signals that the temperance cause was increasingly seen as a 'national' one, cutting across 'extremist' and 'moderate' politics. That Bhandarkar, Gokhale, Tilak and British missionaries had joined hands was, according to several Indian newspapers, "evidence enough of the momentous issues involved and of the earnest self-denying work carried on by the Poona Temperance Association."[93] Gokhale's presidency of the PTA, retained until his death, was aimed at giving visibility to the association as well as to make it more credible in the eyes of Muslims, as Tilak and his acolytes' participation gave it a Hindu tilt.[94] Gokhale approved and encouraged the PTA's methods of picketing liquor shops, started by students in Poona in 1908,[95] and condemned the arrest of some picketers, while at the same time pointing out that repression would contribute to further politicise the issue of temperance.[96] As a matter of fact, the temperance movement was not only, as per the words of the *Indian Social Reformer,* "acquiring a position of predominant interest among administrative reforms":[97] it was also set to become a crucial part of the anticolonial battle for a 'different' (read: superior) Indian morality and justice. Gandhi, who had already promoted temperance in South Africa, would become a leading exponent of this battle in India from the 1920s onwards.[98]

Whereas Tilak's Marathi *Kesari* stated that the PTA volunteers of all castes took part in picketing activities,[99] another Marathi newspaper, the *Dinbandhu,* an outlet of the Satyashodhak Samaj, dismissed the campaigns of the PTA as expressions of high-caste members which the newspaper accused of focusing on reforming the morality of the masses while neglecting their education, and deriving benefits from their ignorance.[100] Such complaints – besides showing the class and caste conflict underlying temperance politics – remind us of Ambedkar's criticism of programmes of social reform targeting the 'Depressed Classes' and including "temperance, gymnasium, co-operation, libraries, schools" which were calculated to make better and virtuous individuals,[101] without fighting the social roots of caste oppression. It is significant that the Dalit leader referred to the social uplifting programmes of the Anti-Untouchability League (*Harijan Sevak Sangh*), founded by Gandhi after the Poona Pact with A.V. Thakkar (1869–1951), the famous social reformer and member of the SIS, as its secretary.[102] Ambedkar condemned the imposition of a moral code of 'good' citizenship based on a 'superior' morality depicted as 'Indian' but in reality corresponding with upper-caste social values.[103]

A similar moral code was already clearly visible in the early temperance work of the SIS among the "drinking classes." The Society was active in "purging" the Holi festival of the "abuses" associated with its celebrations which caused the economic hardships, social problems and "moral degradation" of the poor: it did so by offering alternative "healthy amusements," such as games, musical performances and *kirtans* [devotional singing]. Defined by the same society as a "splendid success" that was spreading to Gujarat and the Deccan, the movement was met with the praise of the "leading citizens": "the presence of men 'high in the social scale' ha[d] a stimulating effect on the poor people."[104] In the early 1920s, the same spirit animated the temperance campaigning among the aboriginal community of the Bhils of Panch Mahal in Gujarat, the industrial workers of Jamshedpur and the 'Depressed Classes' in Mangalore.[105] The common underlying aspect of these activities was that to be a member of the community was invested both with virtues generally associated with the upper castes, such as abstinence and restraint, as well as with liberal ideals of morality, decorum and thrift. Those who were seen as not embodying such values were considered morally inferior and in need of help to become part of the respectable citizenry. Such views, however, did not remain unchallenged. Not only for Ambedkar, but also – and perhaps more markedly – for Ramaswami Naicker 'Periyar' (1879–1973). In their construction of citizenship, civic virtues were the fight against Brahminism and caste discrimination, something still very visible today, especially in the Dravidian politics of the Indian state of Tamil Nadu.[106]

Social rights between welfare and charity

Sarojini Naidu, commemorating Gokhale's political work after his death, described the SIS as the "actual embodiment of his dreams and devotion for India" and the object of some of his greatest concerns.[107] The importance that Gokhale attributed to the SIS can be explained by the fact that he was convinced that it was instrumental for the conscious effort towards his vision of national 'progress' and modernity. An essential part of the purpose of the SIS was to create a new civic consciousness based on shared concerns for collective welfare and on greater awareness of social problems. In this sense, the work of Gokhale's association was not predicated on the separation between *samaj* (society) and *sarkar* (state), which another eminent liberal like Rabindranath Tagore deemed necessary for the regeneration of India. Tagore believed that historically Indian society had been completely autonomous from politics and resistant to its intervention: in India the driving force of civilisation rested on the social order, unlike in Europe, where it resided in the power of the state.[108] Thus, in the Nobel Laureate's view, the state-centric vision adopted by the vast majority of Indian politicians was an aberration that came from colonial domination, whereas the real political work had to be carried out from village to village through the improvement of industry, education, sanitation and religion.[109] It is clear that Gokhale shared Tagore's ideas that a change of sovereignty was by no means enough for India's awakening and that a radical social transformation against the perceived wrongs and weaknesses of Indian society was critical, and should be carried out on top-down social policies as well as bottom-up activities of non-state associations. Although it is very likely that the two public men exchanged their visions in Calcutta and that Gokhale, in creating the SIS, was influenced by the towering figure of Tagore – whom he had got to know through the scientist J. C. Bose[110] and with whom he remained in touch over the years – the main goal of the SIS was the *integration* of state and society and not their separation.[111] The objectives of Gokhale's association were essentially political, and in order to achieve them how could the Society insulate itself from the political sphere?[112]

As the Webbs wrote with reference to the SIS, the "self-education and the self-discipline of Indian people" through social service and "the persistent pressure" to attain self-government were two sides of the same coin.[113] The agenda of the SIS was, in fact, tied to the demand for a more inclusive and just government for India and, in order to be implemented, it necessitated engagement with the political actors, too. The SIS acted as an intermediate space between Indian individuals and the colonial state that could be used to control important areas of Indian public life providing social services to the people, reaching where the state did not offer solutions.[114] The society also sensitised "public opinion on the necessity of universal elementary education, on technical, industrial and agriculture education, improved sanitation,[115] the growth of the co-operative movement, the relief of agricultural indebtedness and the development of local self-government."[116] These activities, which Gokhale considered vital for nation-building,[117] embraced much of what were his liberal social battles in the Imperial Council to press the colonial government for state provisions. The social work carried out by the SIS, then, compensated for, and lobbied, a state that was largely irresponsible towards the Indian citizenry. In other words, Gokhale, both through the SIS and through his political work in the Council, promoted a greater role for government in society: the state could not be limited to the most basic responsibilities of providing law and order, but it had to act as provider of social solidarity through the dispensation of social rights by eradicating poverty and discrimination.[118] At the same time, though, the SIS, like the plethora of social service and voluntary associations that were emerging in this period, gave individuals scope for inclusion, membership and participation in the civil society domain beyond the state, a space for action that was claimed even after the end of colonial rule, when the Nehruvian state became the promoter of development, and that was considered important to balance the state power.[119]

We have noted, especially in the first and second chapters of this book, that the Congress leader contributed significantly to the debate on the welfare of Indian people as an important test for the perception of the colonial state as being legitimate or not. Until self-government would be attained, British rule, identified as the main cause of the pauperisation of Indian society through its policies of 'modernisation' and commercialisation, had to take rectifying measures "to secure for [India] those moral and material advantages which the Governments of more advanced countries [thought] it their paramount duty to bring within the easy reach of their subjects."[120] The colonial rule, Gokhale held, had to take increasing interest in such social policy issues and gradually "conform […] to those advanced notions of the functions of the State which ha[d] found such wide [...] acceptance throughout the Western world."[121]

The welfare schemes proposed by Gokhale to improve the living conditions of the masses were undoubtedly often modest in their scope and nature and were generally articulated as ad hoc measures to address specific needs rather than as rights based on citizenship or occupation. Also, according to Gokhale, public welfare could largely be funded through budget surpluses, namely an uncertain and ever-changing source that could undermine the delivery of services.[122] It should be remembered that Gokhale had to work under conditions that were altogether different from those under which his peer politicians worked in non-colonial contexts or in independent India. Compared to most European polities, the colonial state was much less exposed to democratic pressures and in less immediate need of having its authority legitimated by its action in the field of welfare. The British, who had been among the first nations to recognise the new role of the state in the well-being of its citizens, perceived the problems of the Indian poor as a direct result of their 'innate backwardness.' The colonial efforts to establish social security for the colonised remained very limited: generally, these were based on older forms of poor relief or they were meant to reach only a few segments of the populace, especially those whose dissatisfaction could undermine the stability of the colonial rule. Welfare was therefore either the consequence of a charitable action from a 'virtuous' state or, at best, it was conceived as a special right conferred on certain legally defined categories.[123] So, even though not proposing a radical project – something which would have been unfeasible under British rule and *a fortiori* in the 1910s – the rationale behind Gokhale's ideas was to ensure that the lower social strata, too, would see its hardship and misery lessened and have a share in the general increase of prosperity. This appears, for example, in Gokhale's numerous appeals to the colonial rulers and non-official members of the councils to take into consideration the amelioration of the lives of those most vulnerable elements of society – largely, but not exclusively, associated with the oft-idealised and romanticised rural poor – when utilising the available resources. Throughout his political career, in fact, Gokhale remained focused on the impact colonial policies had on the poor: even before starting his mandate as non-official member of the Imperial Council, he stated that the "poverty problem"[124] was one of his top priorities as a public worker.[125] This discourse promoted by individuals and associations such as Gokhale and the SIS, of having one's basic needs met, contributed, to an extent, to making impoverished and marginalised people in colonial India more aware of their right to demand greater rights by making claims on the state and hold it accountable for their well-being.[126] At the same time, despite undeniable noble intentions, the patronising tone towards the lower orders of society which Gokhale adopted, as well as more generally in philanthropic and charitable milieux, are telling of the fact that the providers of social service initiatives saw themselves as superior and of a more civilised nature than the recipients. The role of non-state actors committed to voluntary and philanthropic activities remained salient in the post-colonial period, too.[127] It appears that, also after independence, the realm of voluntary initiatives and social service was considered by many as morally superior to, and sometimes even at odds with, state action and, therefore, worthy of being extended in order to support its role in "the vital field of social welfare activities."[128] Civil society institutions represented therefore an arena where the divide between the higher and lower orders of society, between the educated Indians and the rest of the populace could be reaffirmed and crystallised.[129] Voluntary effort was also considered conducive to democracy and economically advantageous because it provided citizens with the opportunity to express their "social idealism" while offering "more effective and speedy and economical" undertakings.[130]

How such initiatives contributed to giving voice to the poorer classes and increase their access to the democratic state similarly needs further investigation. An in-depth study of these issues, especially if looked at from a historical perspective, can enrich existing larger debates which have shown how civil society associations can be either subversive or supportive of forms of social democracy.[131]

Mass education, national development, democracy

The fact that Gokhale saw welfare policies and social service as essential nation-building instruments is telling of the fact that he was aware of their national strategic value. Social work was not only beneficial for improving national efficiency and defusing impulses of social conflict that could escalate in unrest: providing and attaining social rights was a means that had the potential to produce among citizens a greater sense of belonging to the national political community, enhance their trust in the authority as well as foster greater compliance with state policies.[132] The concern that deep-seated inequality might weaken the meaning of citizenship for the poor as well as, more generally, endanger national cohesion – a concern that has continued to animate debates on citizenship and social rights throughout the 20th century[133] – explains, at least in part, the importance that Gokhale attributed to the universalisation of primary education.

The Elementary Education Bill that Gokhale introduced in the Imperial Legislative Council in 1911 was the culmination of his efforts to draw the attention of both the colonial government and his Indian fellows to the needs of mass education in the country, namely what the Indian liberal saw as a crucial social right.[134] Prior to the Bill's proposal, Gokhale had already stressed the urgency of mass elementary education on several occasions and made it a lively debated issue on the subcontinent, both at the political and cultural level. As early as 1896, Gokhale declared that the spread of primary education meant future salvation for India.[135] As a member of the Bombay and the Imperial Legislative Councils, he pushed for greater public expenditure on mass education, highlighting how laughable the contribution of the Indian government was compared to the British one. In 1910, taking advantage of the right given to non-official members by the reforms, Gokhale moved his first resolution which recommended that a start be made in the direction of making elementary education free and compulsory throughout the country.[136] Even though the resolution was voted down, the government created a Department of Education in charge of extending the reach of education.

While believing in the universality of education, Gokhale's reform of the education system was proposed in such a way as to meet the least opposition. To use the words of Harcourt Butler, the officer of the Indian Civil Service and first Member of the Viceroy's Executive Council in charge of the newly created Department of Education, the 1911 Elementary Education Bill was a "modest and unassuming measure [...] full of safeguards" – yet, unsurprisingly, too "premature" to be passed.[137] Gokhale's Bill provided that, since those countries that had achieved swift progress in schooling expansion had done so by relying on compulsion, in India, too, education should become compulsory, although gradually. The cases of the Indian princely state of Baroda,[138] Ceylon[139] and Japan were exemplars of the fact that even in polities that were still much poorer than the most advanced Western nations, expanding the reach of education was a concrete possibility. Whereas the (semi-)colonial settings of Baroda and Ceylon made a case against the British argument that India was not yet ready for compulsory and free education, Japan served, once again, as the role model for the subcontinent. In the East Asian country, when by 1910 the population was almost fully literate, the constructive role of the state – albeit authoritarian – towards the universalisation of schooling had shown with clarity the link between school education and modern economic development, as early as the Meiji era (1868–1912).[140] Moreover, Japan represented, once again, a successful example of a nation that had applied "Western methods to Eastern conditions of life,"[141] thus challenging culturalist explanations according to which universal education was essentially a Western concept and therefore unsuitable for non-Western contexts.[142]

Elementary education – previous experiences from all over the world had demonstrated – once made compulsory was also to be made free, because otherwise compulsion "would operate harshly on the poorer classes of the community."[143] However, given the opposition from Local Governments, which in Gokhale's proposal had to bear the costs of primary education with the state by a ratio of 1 to 2, the final version of the Bill provided for gratuitous instruction only for children from extremely poor backgrounds, whose parents did not earn more than a certain sum per month (Gokhale indicated that sum between 10 and 25 rupees monthly), leaving to the local bodies the choice of whether those with an income just above that line were required to pay or not.[144]

That the Elementary Education Bill was conceived with conservative impulses in mind – both colonial and Indian – which could determine its defeat is clear from the cautiousness with which it dealt with the question of compulsion, whose introduction had to be gradual, given the wave of unpopularity that it could cause. In the first place, the compulsion principle had to be introduced by the local bodies and not directly by the state, whose actions were immediately associated by many with colonial repression. Secondly, it concerned only boys from six to ten and not girls. Lastly, it applied to those areas where 33 per cent of the male population was already at school.[145] Given the little resources colonial rulers were willing to spend for elementary education, imparting rudiments of knowledge to as many children as possible for a few years was better than no knowledge at all, or than high-quality education for the few selected ones.

The exclusion of girls from compulsory education was based on the same compromising logic and was due to the many difficulties that surrounded the question of female education.[146] Gokhale was well aware of the opposition that the direct interference of the colonial authorities in such a sensitive social issue could raise, as well as of the belief shared by several sections of Indian society that the rightful place for women was the home and, consequently, school education was of no use to them. Thus, while admitting that female education was even more urgent than male education, Gokhale's Bill recommended only that it be pushed on vigorously but remained on a voluntary basis. Interestingly enough, clause 17, namely a measure of safeguard which allowed for the extension of the provisions of the Bill to girls between six and ten, was among the most disputed issues of the entire proposal, thus confirming Gokhale's concerns. However, it is worth mentioning that Gokhale also recognised different spheres for men and women. This was a "wellworn [sic] fact" requiring that "their preparation and equipment should be on distinct and different lines, to suit them in their different spheres." It was essential that Indian girls should be fully prepared "for the efficient discharge of their duties in after-life, within the home sphere especially, and in this view which *[could not] be questioned*, the training and instruction they are to receive must be of the best possible and most uptodate [sic] character."[147] It is therefore legitimate to think that, given the distinction between the public/private sphere and the disparate male/female occupancies of such spaces, Gokhale actually understood education for boys as being more immediately required: boys were to be educated and trained for political participation and for the responsibilities of citizenship. Girls could wait. While encouraging universal education, Gokhale assigned women to their 'proper' role, thus implying that education was potentially transformative and emancipatory only for boys.[148]

All this caution notwithstanding and even though the Department of Education and the Viceroy Lord Hardinge were in favour of it, in March 1912, the Bill was defeated by 38 votes to 13. While the provincial governors wielded the greatest clout in throwing out Gokhale's proposal, some non-official members, despite the large consensus within both the Congress and the Muslim League, also voted against it. The unfortunate destiny of his Bill had become clear to Gokhale by October 1911 when he wrote to Wedderburn that the entire Civil Service – few exceptions apart – was strongly opposed to the measure. His only consolation was that "the Indian public" was "solidly behind the idea of free and compulsory education and the enthusiasm which the [...] Bill ha[d] evoked in all parts of the country ha[d] exceeded any wildest anticipation."[149]

Arguing that "an ignorant and illiterate nation c[ould] never make any solid progress and must fall back in the race of life,"[150] Gokhale gave particular prominence to the link between mass education and national economic development. In the 1906 Budget speech, the Indian liberal included the spread of "technical and industrial education" among the measures that, in his view, the colonial government should take to improve conditions of the masses.[151] The linkage between mass education and the growth of the industrial sector – generally perceived as the benchmark of the hoped-for 'modernisation' – was a recurring and strong argument during the long 19th century.[152] Gokhale's suggestion, implying that the educated masses could contribute to the common welfare by developing skills which would help the country become economically competitive, challenged the conservative view according to which an unskilled and uneducated labour force was not a hindrance to the country's economic success. It also showed the gradual transformation of knowledge in hard currency in an increasingly competitive world. In order to sustain the argument that the key to economic advancement lay in an educated workforce, Gokhale not only perused a mass of statistical documents but relied also on theories by experts in the field. He often quoted, for instance, the essay *Popular Education and National Economic Development* by the German leftist reformer Johannes Tews.[153] Gokhale concurred with Tews that while being a crucial factor in national efficiency, general popular education was instrumental for the development of a less divisive and more inclusive society too. It enhanced all branches of national production and favoured the division of labour. Through a "more equal distribution of the proceeds of labour," it contributed to the general prosperity of the people and to the social peace of the nation. All this fostered the economic and social development of the citizenry.[154]

Gokhale's view of education, though, went beyond utilitarian questions of human capital investment and embraced broader ethical issues. Education was important on different levels: it meant "for the bulk of the community a higher level of intelligence, a greater aptitude for skilled labour, and a higher capacity for discriminating between right and wrong."[155] Its ultimate goal was to help people become decent human beings and develop a sense of respect for others and responsibility towards society. It could mitigate social differences by fostering cross-class ties and by giving greater recognition to human dignity.

Gokhale belonged to those growing sectors of the intellectual globe that believed in the power of education as a civilising and moral force. He was influenced by the pedagogical rhetoric that had long figured among liberals the world over that the school had a major role in promoting material and moral public welfare. This was a view that originated from Enlightenment ideas that saw human beings as perfectible and educable, and was grounded in the belief that the dissemination of rational knowledge would result in a better general conduct and in the elevation of the individual and collective character. Education had to provide the would-be citizens with those moral and intellectual qualities that were required in the modern world, with the consequent marginalisation of those forms of knowledge which were not seen as conducive to modernity.

Similar exclusionary impulses are noticeable in Gokhale's views, which sometimes infantilised the 'backward' and the 'ignorant.' For example, in supporting an amendment to the 1911 Indian Factories Bill[156] regulating the daily working hours, Gokhale maintained that Indian mill workers were "too ignorant to understand time quite accurately." They did not carry watches with them, "whereas in regard to sunrise and sunset those [we]re broad facts that everybody [could] understand."[157] His words echoed broader colonial and Indian elite prejudices from which derived an image of the factory worker as being deeply entrenched in an agricultural background, unable to adapt to factory work and its environment, and hardly efficient.[158] These constructions, based on the Orientalist knowledge depicting India and its population as rooted in a timeless past, pitted Eastern culture versus Western efficiency as well as the Indian agriculturalist versus 'modern' labour.[159] Conversely – and more germane to our theme – this example is just one among many that show Gokhale's perception of Indian society as irrational and, as such, requiring an education based on 'progress' through reason and science: an education which had to impart knowledge, skills and practices of the modern, that for Gokhale, was the one produced in the modern West.

Not only science, but also subjects associated with a British liberal education like history, literature, economics, philosophy and politics were considered essential to arrest India's "intellectual stunting"[160] as well as to "be qualified to become better citizens."[161] Those subjects, besides providing Indians with the *forma mentis* required by modernity, gave a real grounding in the political, economic and social life of society: the link between intellectual formation and 'better' citizenship revealed, although implicitly, who was seen to belong to the polity, while involving distinguished future roles as citizens for those few who had access to a higher level of education and the many with only the "rudiments of knowledge."[162] Such hierarchical differentiation, albeit transitional in Gokhale's view, was a significant reminder of the fact, already indicated by the exclusive nature of the SIS, that the proper citizen was the one equipped with the intellectual capacity to engage in responsible public activity.

It would be tempting to argue that Gokhale conceived a two-tier system of education for the haves and have-nots, that is, liberating for the elite and inculcating obedience for the masses. However, much to the dismay of the more cynical, he did not perceive education as a tool of cultural indoctrination and social control, nor did he want it to reinforce class structures by training citizens to submit to the authority within the existing hierarchies. Education, on the contrary, could be instrumental for social change and upward mobility, contributing to the 'liberation' of the oppressed and the amelioration of their living conditions. It seemed to him "a monstrous and cruel wrong" that millions and millions should be left without the rudiments of knowledge and that "the joy of that knowledge" should be absolutely unexperienced by them.[163]

At odds with deep-seated conservative beliefs, Gokhale did not agree that education should keep the masses in a subordinate position. Rather, he held that the "solid strength of a nation [...] really [lay] in the life, thoughts and actions of the average man and woman."[164] In his view, educating the mass of the people involved "something more than a mere capacity to read and write" such as "a keener enjoyment of life and a more refined standard of living [...], greater moral and economic efficiency of the individual, [...] and a higher level of intelligence for the whole community generally."[165] The value of education rested on its capability to create a more civil society, where 'good' and 'effective' citizenship was predicated not only on productivity and morals, but also on a shared understanding of the national common good. A fair meritocracy and a greater awareness of one's rights, too, could be achieved through equal educational opportunities: there would be "hope for better success for all efforts" and the mass of the people would be "better able to take care of themselves against the exactions of unscrupulous money-lenders or against the abuses of official authority by petty men in power."[166] The benefits of sanitation, the harmfulness of superstition,[167] the advantages of thrift[168] would be better understood by the worker and the peasant.

During the discussions of the Elementary Education Bill, Gokhale strongly attacked the position of Indian leaders who opposed mass education because they saw it as a threat to the permanence of the social order.[169] He condemned those who feared that the spread of education would cause scarcity of servants and other menial workers in the country: that class of people, Gokhale held, perceived "the poorer classes of the country as made solely to serve" them,[170] to "shampoo the legs of the rich, or to fill the "hukkas" of the *zemindars*.[171] Similar arguments made by non-official members of the Supreme Council that the children of poorer classes could become gentlemen if educated" were derided by Gokhale as anachronistic.[172] Poor people were not necessarily born to remain poor. Also, countering the colonial objection that the educated Indians that supported mass education did not represent the will of the people – an argument which the colonial rulers often made to discredit the majority of the reforms proposed by the anticolonial activists – Gokhale recounted that around 2,500 members of the Mahar community had gathered in Berar and passed a resolution in favour of his Bill. It was difficult to dispute, Gokhale argued, that they had "a fairly general idea that the Bill was intended to make education compulsory and that under it their children would be compelled to go to school so that they might derive the benefits of education"[173].

For Gokhale, expanding mass education among poor children was also an essential step towards the eradication of child labour. His concern for child welfare was part of a series of far-reaching discourses that, from the early 20th century onwards, gave prominence to childhood as an object of protection, both in the project of imperial 'rescue' as well as in Indian reform schemes.[174] On the one hand, the category of age was made 'natural' by the colonial census operations; on the other, the emergence of a transnational humanitarian discourse posited the treatment of the child as a new indicator of a nation's capacity and political legitimacy.[175] Despite the circulation of such new global notions of the child as a subject to be protected, opposition to mass education was connected to the broader question of child labour, from which both Anglo-Indian planters and Indian factory owners derived profits. Gokhale's Bill, in fact, prohibited the employment of child labour below the age of ten, raising the age limit by one year. In addition to this, Gokhale proposed an amendment to the abovementioned Factories Bill. Since the report on which the Bill was based excluded compulsory education for working children but recommended that measures be taken in that direction, Gokhale's proposal, which was eventually withdrawn, intended to make it mandatory that every factory which employed more than 20 children maintain an elementary school and give those children between nine and 12 free and compulsory instruction.[176] It was, Gokhale held, a question of justice and humanity to provide such a service to the most vulnerable section of the labour population. The responsibility, which the Education Department should supervise, had to fall mainly on the factory-owners as a form of redress for their exploitative activities. Since children had to work by split shifts and were often asked to remain on the factory premises between the first and the second, the presence of schools would prevent unscrupulous managers from getting them to work for longer hours than the law allowed.

The picture reconstructed so far suggests that Gokhale's focus on education was not driven by the will to repress the masses, nor was it restrained by anxieties of popular uprisings. Education as envisioned by Gokhale had different functions with significant, and apparently contradictory, political impacts. Expanding education was, first of all, a nation-building tool that fostered national integration and compliance as well as a socialisation into social norms, 'modern' attitudes, and citizenship duties. To this end, education was collective and horizontal: it meant learning to belong and to obey, thus including its own form of coercion. But, as a staunch liberal, Gokhale saw education also as individual and vertical intellectual development and, as such, promoting individual autonomy, empowerment and freedom of choice so that criticising the government and protesting against unjust measures would become a duty.[177] He did not perceive these facets of education as being inconsistent. Membership of a national community was a requirement of liberal modernity as much as being able to think critically and to challenge social and political injustice. Education in this sense contributed to the country's democratisation.[178] This view remained influential in the postcolonial period, too, when the government recognised that an educated citizenry was essential to ensure the success of India's democracy.[179] Furthermore, loyalty to the nation-state was not an absolute value and, since individual rights had primacy over collective self-determination, individuals had the right and duty to resist what they considered politically and morally unacceptable. Hence, Gokhale believed that it was morally illegitimate to embrace ideals of national self-determination and condemn injustice by foreigners, without simultaneously accepting that politics was not supposed to represent exclusively the interests and rights of the elite but to bring about a fairer democratic order:

> We all love to talk of the desirability of Self-Government [...]. But let us realise that Self-government implies the strength to bear responsibilities, as it implies the opportunities to enjoy privileges. Let us clearly bear in mind that any progress that we make as a people must now be on a democratic basis [...]. And for this purpose, it is not a few towering individuals that will suffice, but the average strength of the mass of the people must be raised.[180]

Being a 'good' nationalist and being a 'good' citizen would be aporetic, if building the nation was not driven by an earnest concern for the unprivileged section of society.

Unfortunately, Gokhale did not discuss at any meaningful length the specific epistemic and pedagogic content of education.[181] Gokhale had little doubt that education had to be 'on Western lines,' with only a secondary place assigned to Indian classics and vernacular forms of knowledge. In this, he did not see the risk of an educational system that was removed from the real needs of the community. While not going against the religious prejudices and cultural sensitivity of any community,[182] education had to become a means of imagining a common secular future. How all this was to be practically achieved was not stated by Gokhale, even though the question of moral education dealt with in the previous chapter provides us with some clues. It was implied, overall, that 'modern' education would weaken the 'traditional' ascriptive attachments based on 'narrow' identities such as class and religion, in favour of the benefits brought about by its diffusion.

Gokhale's contribution becomes more significant when we consider the emphasis he placed on school education as the ally of the poor and, more generally, on educational opportunities as critical in the welfare of (would-be) citizens. Even though his remark that education was the only salvation for India was extreme as it did not consider that illiteracy was just one of the many problems India faced, Gokhale's perception remains deeply insightful. The Indian liberal could see the link between education and the uplifting of people's quality of life in terms of social development, economic opportunities and health improvement. Education would also make a difference to the ability to understand and claim one's rights, thus enhancing the voice and power of the poorest classes. It would contribute to reducing class and caste inequalities, too. Gokhale's Elementary Education Bill was, in his own words, "a small and humble attempt to suggest the first steps of a journey, which [wa]s bound to be long and tedious" but which had to be performed if the mass of Indian people were to emerge from the current condition.[183] He stressed that the moral and economic duty of the state to promote the universal diffusion of education was a question of humanity and the "elementary right of every child"[184], thus suggesting that access to education was not only a right inherent in the citizen's status but also, and more importantly, a *human* right.

When his Bill was thrown out, Gokhale said that it would "come back again and again till on the stepping-stones of its dead selves, a measure ultimately rises which w[ould] spread the light of knowledge throughout the land."[185] The battle for free and compulsory education that he began proved longer and harder than Gokhale would ever have expected. In 1917, a measure largely based on Gokhale's Bill was passed by the Bombay Province under Vithalbhai Patel (1873–1933), enforcing compulsion for primary education. With the end of direct colonial responsibility for education enacted by the 1919 Government of India Act, the following decades saw similar laws approved by other provinces as well as by princely states. While the principle of compulsion met with increasing consensus, Compulsory Education Acts often remained a dead letter since Indian ministers had no control over crucial Government departments such as finance.

After independence, in spite of Indian policymakers' rousing rhetoric claiming the importance of education as essential to the welfare state and, more broadly, to the socialist project, both arguments of inadequate resources as well as of non-enforceability contributed to postponing the right of universal free and compulsory education.[186] As a matter of fact, in independent India, social and economic rights, unlike political and civil rights, were not included among the fundamental rights of the Indian Constitution.[187] Consequently, the welfare state was never institutionalised to any significant extent – a phenomenon that was justified by Indian politicians who argued that resources were scarce and hence social services unaffordable.[188] Accordingly, as during the colonial rule, the independent state remained relatively weak in terms of state provisions and social welfare regulation: it ended up relying largely on philanthropic benevolence and charity rather than bearing the legal obligation and moral responsibility for the economic and social well-being of all its members.[189] Further research is required to investigate the role that the social service and philanthropy, which emerged in the colonial period, played in perpetuating "the predominance of the language of relief, charity, and alleviation"[190] and which made it so intrinsic to the discourse on poverty and welfare in the post-colonial era. Furthermore, the extent to which the action of intermediary associations was responsible for deferring reforms of the social service system – thus potentially undermining the construction of public welfare capabilities in independent India – ought to be examined.

The perspective on socio-economic rights based on need and not on the citizens' right to welfare undercut the transformative scope of the 1950 Constitution; this defined freedom not only as political independence from colonial rule but also as the removal of social and economic inequality.[191] It also dented ambitious visions of a more socialistic pattern of society.[192] In spite of the thorough engagement of Indian legislators, reformers and union leaders with global debates on welfarism and social policy, welfare entitlements were not made a universal right inherent in the status of citizen, but were conditional on specific forms of employment or membership of vulnerable groups. Explaining underdeveloped welfare institutions in India with its "Third World" socio-economic backwardness does not explain the striking differences of welfare state between, for example, Mainland China and India from the late 1940s onwards.[193] Tellingly enough, it was only in 2002 that education in India was recognised as a justiciable fundamental right by the Constitution. In 2010, and nearly a century from Gokhale's Bill, the Right of Children to Free and Compulsory Education Act was enacted, making education free and compulsory for all Indian children from age six to 14.[194] Even though this breakthrough is undeniably a welcome one, decades of neglect of public education have widened the gap between the quality of education available to different classes of Indians, engendering forms of exclusion and inequality that have affected those very classes most dependent on state provision, precluding their access to avenues of social mobility. Despite the international visibility and success of a small elite of "first boys"[195] who enjoy high, if not excellent, educational resources – and the ensuing advantages of flexible citizenship[196] – India's education system for the bulk of the population remains, in several ways, poor and deficient.[197] It is a sad paradox that, despite the early acknowledgement of the central role of education for development and social progress, the expansion of school education in India (and generally in South Asia) has been so slow as to be more similar to sub-Saharan Africa than to the rest of Asia.[198]

Conclusion

This chapter has illustrated that Gokhale understood citizenship not only as a legal/formal status denoting the relationship between citizens and the political community, as defined through rights, obligations, distributed social and economic benefits, and political recognition, but also as the relationship between individuals within the same political community, defined by a set of norms and values often underpinned by a moral discourse, therefore dividing the populace into citizens and citizens in-the-making.

The chapter has focused on the rationale behind the foundation of the SIS and its general goals to improve Indians morally and materially as part of the greater good of the 'modern' nation. Engagement in civil society and in social service activities promoted by the SIS came to represent a significant realm of citizenship performance, where selected individuals could develop their full potential as responsible members of the polity. The strong emphasis on the progressive mission of the SIS in bringing about the moral and material advancement of India and its people served the purpose of showing that, contrary to what the British colonisers would say, Indians were able to provide for their own progress.[199] Its members had to be role models and embody values such as discipline, obedience, self-restraint and sacrifice that needed to be extended to the rest of the population so as to ready them to be part of the nation. So, while Gokhale's society was animated by the desire to raise Indian citizenry's standard of living and allow them to have their share in the hoped-for national progress and prosperity, the civic construction promoted by it included conservative aspects which emphasised the need to discipline, regenerate, purify and moralise the masses in order to overcome their lack of modernity, as well as to instill a sense of what Gokhale would call 'public spiritedness,' thus more or less unconsciously perpetuating the hierarchies between the 'educated classes' and the rest. The question of temperance, in particular, has demonstrated how the promoters of temperance initiatives perceived themselves as embodying a superior moral stand vis-à-vis those at the other end of the spectrum.

However, this chapter has also argued that Gokhale's and the SIS's focus on the moral and material 'progress' was not just an empty formula aimed at creating a realm for the aspiring political elite to claim their moral authority and political legitimacy before both the coloniser and the colonised. Conservative elements aside, Gokhale's understanding of citizenship entailed the possibility of change for those at the margins of Indian society through the attainment of social and economic rights, dispensed by a state that had to be increasingly responsible for the welfare of its citizens. The spread of universal education and the battle against poverty to which Gokhale was committed were undoubtedly indicators of a nation's stand in terms of modernity and political capacity which Gokhale could not ignore.[200] But they were also concrete instruments capable of making a positive change in the lives of the impoverished and the marginalized. So, if claiming that Gokhale was "the most important exponent of [...] liberalism as the basis of a modern democratic welfare state"[201] sounds an overstatement, it is not an exaggeration to argue that the Indian liberal contributed to the discourse which defines as more or less legitimised a government in accordance with its contribution to the well-being of the people it rules. The lack of such legitimacy makes the initiatives within civil society imperative to remind the state of its role.

Notes

1. Banerjee, *Becoming Imperial Citizenship*, p. 11. See also chapter 2 of the present book for a discussion on this.
2. Jayal, *Citizenship and its Discontents*, p. 27.
3. As argued in chapter 3 of this book, his South African experiences illustrated that Gokhale combined the condemnation of the racial logic that characterised the structure of the British empire with limited real interest in the grievances of other discriminated groups – be it 'coolies,' Chinese or Blacks – thus reproducing the imperial prejudices and hierarchies characteristic of the time.
4. Sunil Amrith, 'Empires, Diasporas and Cultural Circulation', in Andrew Thompson (ed.), *Writing Imperial Histories*, Manchester University Press, Manchester 2013, p. 232.
5. In fact, despite its ostensible universality, the claim to imperial citizenship became less and less appealing after the First World War and more decidedly so in the 1920s when the 'white' dominions increasingly excluded Indians from entering their territories, making racial discriminatory immigration legislation a norm. For a discussion on the shifts in citizenship debates from 1880 to 1950 see Elena Valdameri, "Debates on citizenship in colonial South Asia and global political thought (*c.*1880–1950)", in Harald Fischer-Tiné and Maria Framke (edited by), *Routledge Handbook of the History Colonialism in South Asia*, Routledge, Abingdon and New York 2022, pp. 450-462.
6. On this, see also chapter 2. For the variability of citizenship in relation to political territories in space and time, see Alexander C. Diener, 'Re-Scaling the Geography of Citizenship', in Ayelet Shachar et al. (eds.), *The Oxford Handbook of Citizenship*, OUP, Oxford 2017, pp. 36–52.
7. Gokhale, "Responsibilities of Public Life", p. 15.
8. See Prathama Banerjee, "Between the political and the non-political: the Vivekananda moment and a critique of the social in colonial Bengal, 1890s–1910s", *Social History*, Vol. 39, n. 3 (2014), pp. 323–339; Nagappa Gowda K., *The Bhagavadgita in the Nationalist Discourse*, Delhi 2011; Shruti Kapila and Faisal Devji (eds.), *Political Thought in Action: The Bhagavad Gita and Modern India*, CUP, Cambridge 2013. See also ch. 2 of this book.
9. Quotes from this paragraph are culled from Gokhale, "Responsibilities of Public Life", pp. 7–24.
10. In late 19th and early 20th century India, the colonial regime marked all the inhabitants of the British *Raj* as subjects but at the same time it recognised some sections of the population as proto-citizens entitled to differential rights, such as the right to vote, according to criteria such as modern education, property and wealth. The gradual political reforms confirmed the privileged nature of colonial citizenship and introduced group representation in the proto-democratic colonial politics (Jayal, *Citizenship and its Discontents*, pp. 36–48).
11. Gokhale, "Responsibilities of Public Life", p. 14. See also "Elevation of the Depressed Classes", *GSW*, Vol. III, p. 262.
12. *Account of the Servants of India Society (1905–1916)*, p. 4.

13. "Fifth Anniversary Day", p. 4.
14. Watt, *Serving the Nation*, pp. 87–88, 97–107. For a discussion on the place of *seva* (service) in historiography and political theory, see R. Srivatsan, *Seva, Saviour and State: Caste Politics, Tribal Welfare and Capitalist Development*, Routledge, Abingdon and New York 2015, pp. 7–20.
15. Watt, *Serving the Nation*, pp. 181–182.
16. Watt, *Serving the Nation*, p. 18 and passim. See also Bayly, *Origins of Nationality in South Asia*, on which Watt's book is built.
17. These religious notions in the precolonial period, too, had informed modes of moral and social protest. See Washbrook, "Forms of Citizenship in Pre-Modern South India", p. 235.
18. "The Servants of India Society", *GSW*, Vol. II, pp. 181–186.
19. Not only liberalism, but other ideologies too were refashioned and woven with Hindu ethical morality in what appears to be a creative blending of religious leanings and anticolonial issues. See, for instance, Charu Gupta, «'Hindu Communism': Satyabhakta, apocalypses and utopian Ram Rajya», *The Indian Economic and Social History Review*, Vol. 58, no 2 (2021), pp. 213-248.
20. The SIS is still in existence and Pune remains its headquarters. Its operational areas are described as "Children, Nutrition, Rural Development & Poverty Alleviation, Tribal Affairs, Vocational Training, Women's Development & Empowerment" (https://www.ngofoundation.in/ngo-directory/servants-of-india-society-pune-trust-in-pune-maharashtra_i8602).
21. Industrialist Ratan Tata (1871–1918), who was the main sponsor of the SIS, wrote to Gokhale that among the purposes mentioned in the pamphlet, there was no mention of future efforts to stimulate the industrial development of the country (Wolpert, *Tilak and Gokhale*, 164), something that was added later on. Several leading political figures like Motilal Nehru and Tej Bahadur Sapru helped raise funds in favour of the society.
22. Srinivasa Sastri, *My Master Gokhale*, p. 54.
23. Lord Curzon to Lamington, 24 July 1905. *Curzon Papers*, quoted in Nanda, *Gokhale*, p. 176.
24. Carey A. Watt, 'Philanthropy and Civilizing Missions in India c. 1820–1960: States, NGOs and Development', in C.A. Watt and M. Mann (eds.), *Civilizing Missions in Colonial and Post-Colonial South Asia: From Improvement to Development*, Anthem Press, London 2011, pp. 271–316. See also the excellent discussion in Fischer-Tiné, *Muscling in on South Asia, Colonial Difference, American Soft Power, and the Indian YMCA (c. 1890-1950)*, Bloomsbury, London 2022, chapter 2.
25. The National Liberal Federation was formed in 1918, after the Montagu-Chelmsford reforms were rejected by Congress. The moderates who, instead, supported these reforms formed the National Liberal Federation. Among them, besides Srinivas Sastri and Kunzru, were Surendranth Banerjea, R.P. Paranjape, Tej Bahadur Sapru and Satyendra Sinha.
26. See Nanda, *Gokhale*, pp. 173–174.
27. On N.M. Joshi, see Priyanka Srivastava, *The Well-Being of the Labor Force in Colonial Bombay: Discourses and Practices*, Palgrave Macmillan, Cham 2018, esp. chapters 4 and 5, pp. 109–195. See also Ravi Ahuja, "A Beveridge Plan for India: Social Insurance and the Making of the 'Formal Sector'", *International Review of Social History*, Vol. 64, n. 2 (2019), pp. 218–219 and 223.
28. "The Servants of India", p. 182.
29. The quotes are selected from J.N. Farquhar, *Modern Religious Movements in India*, MacMillan, London 1924 (first published 1915), p. 377 and are based on an interview that Gokhale gave to the author in London in June 1913. Farquhar had written to Gokhale (Letter dated 25 March 1913, GP) inform-

ing him that he had to deliver eight lectures on Modern Eclectic Movements in India, which would then be published in a book, and that he wanted to include the SIS too. Interestingly, the book was published with a different title. On Farquhar, see Harald Fischer-Tiné, "Third-Stream Orientalism: J. N. Farquhar, the Indian YMCA's Literature Department, and the Representation of South Asian Cultures and Religions (Ca. 1910–1940)", *The Journal of Asian Studies*, Vol. 79, n. 3 (2020), pp. 659–683.

30. The question of 'national' education was diversely answered by Indian nationalists, all trying to preserve Indian difference while at the same time achieving modernity. On this, see Seth, *Subject Lessons*, pp. 159–182; S. Bhattacharya, J. Bara and C.R. Yagati (eds.), *Educating the Nation: Documents on the Discourse of National Education in India 1880–1920*, Kanishka Publishers and Distributors and Jawaharlal Nehru University, New Delhi 2003; see also Harald Fischer-Tiné, *Der Gurukul Kangri oder die Erziehung der Arya Nation: Kolonialismus, Hindureform und 'nationale Bildung' in Britisch-Indien (1897-1922)*, Ergon-Verlag, Würzburg 2003; Sabyasachi Bhattacharya (ed.), *The Contested Terrain: Perspectives on Education in India*, Orient Longman Limited, Hyderabad, India 1998. For a survey of the historiographical debates on education in India, see Catriona Ellis, "Education for All: Reassessing the Historiography of Education in Colonial India", *History Compass*, Vol. 7, n. 2 (2009), pp. 363–375; Tim Allender, "Understanding Education and India: New Turns in Postcolonial Scholarship", *History of Education*, Vol. 39, n. 2 (2010), pp. 281–288; Barnita Bagchi, "Connected and Entangled Histories: Writing Histories of Education in the Indian Context", *Paedagogica Historica*, Vol. 50, n. 6 (2014), pp. 813–821.

31. Gokhale to Krishnaswami Iyer, 29 September 1906, GP. The original collection of the SIS library has been incorporated by what is today the Gadgil Library of the Gokhale Institute of Politics and Economics (GIPE), in Pune. However, it is impossible to identify the books that constituted it. In fact, in the Gadgil Library's access registry, we have the books' date of publication but not their date of entry up to December 1924. Until that date, the library of the SIS collected more than 4200 books. So, we do not know when the books before that date were acquired and we cannot reconstruct the order of acquisition of those items of the library. I am grateful to Dr Nanaji Shewale, librarian at GIPE, for pointing this out to me.

32. *Account of the Servants of India Society (1905–1916)*, p. 4.

33. Srinivas Sastri, *Life of Gokhale*, p. 53. According to John S. Hoyland, a Quaker and a missionary in India, Gokhale "loved to show its [of the SIS] affinity to the religious orders of medieval Christianity" (Hoyland, *Gopal Krishna Gokhale: His Life and Speeches*, YMCA Publishing House, Calcutta 1933, p. 106).

34. Gokhale to Krishnaswamy Iyer, 31 July 1905, GP.

35. We have some glimpses from Srinivasa Sastri's diary (*Srinivasa Sastri Papers*, NMML). See Nanda, *Gokhale*, pp. 462–463.

36. Letter from Deva to Gokhale, 19 July 1914, *Servants of India Society Papers* (SISP), NMML. Deva was the Chief Medical Officer in the princely state of Sangli until he decided to give up his post and join the Servants of India. He was a close friend of Gokhale and his medical doctor too. From the SISP, it appears that he had the ear of Gokhale in the society's affairs.

37. Gokhale to Deva, 10 July 1914, SISP. The discussions led to the introduction of bye-laws under rule 30 of the constitution which made alterations possible if agreed by the majority of the members ("Servants of India", pp. 185–186 and *A Brief Account of the Work of the Servants of India Society, Poona, From 1st January 1917 to 30th June 1923*, Aryabhushan Press, Poona 1924, pp. 55–57).

38. "Fifth Anniversary Day", p. 3. In a 1905 letter to Sarla Ray (3 June 1903, GP), however, he had expressed great expectations for the society. He had written: "If I live ten years more, I feel confident that my Society will by the end of that time have become a great power for good in the land."

39. On this issue, see Watt, *Serving the Nation*, pp. 12, 184–185. From later correspondence, it emerges that there was resistance towards admitting Dalits to the Servants of India. Gandhi wrote to the President of the Society, Devadhar (12 October 1933, SISP) that the behaviour held by certain members towards "Harijans" was no different than the British behaviour towards Indian subjects.

40. On the Mappila rebellion, the most comprehensive work is K.N. Panikkar, *Against Lord and State: Religion and Peasant Uprisings in Malabar, 1836–1921*, OUP, New Delhi 1989.

41. Muhammedali T., "In Service of the Nation: Relief and Reconstruction in Malabar in the Wake of the Rebellion of 1921", *Proceedings of the Indian History Congress*, Vol. 68 (2007), pp. 789–805, here 800. While it is certainly a gross exaggeration to state that "the SIS cherished an imagined homogenous pan-Indian Hindu religion to be the religion of the nation" (ibidem), the Malabar facts give us a clear idea of the Hindu bias, that, more or less consciously, permeated the society. On the cooperation between SIS and YMCA as well as the aftermath of the Mappila rebellion as a stage for the activities of different social service organisations, see Harald Fischer-Tiné, *Muscling in on South Asia*, chapter 2.

42. The establishment of poorhouses was a practice that had been initially adopted by colonial officials during famine relief in India. As argued by Joanna Simonow, the fact that the SIS copied and adapted colonial practices "demonstrates that colonial anti-famine policies left an imprint on non-governmental famine relief in India" [Joanna Simonow, *From Famine to Famine: Hunger Relief, Nutritional Reform and Political Mobilisation in South Asia (c. 1890-1955)*, chapter 2, Leiden University Press, forthcoming].

43. Gopal Krishna Devadhar, "The Famine of 1908 in India and the Work Done by Non-Official Agencies", *Modern Review*, September 1909, p. 260.

44. Srinivasa Sastri, *Life of Mehta*, p. 71.

45. Srinivasa Sastri, *Life of Mehta*, p. 203.

46. Judith Brown, *Gandhi: Prisoner of Hope*, Yale University Press, New Haven 1989, p. 71.

47. *Indian Opinion*, 10 March 1915 in *The Collected Works of Mahatma Gandhi* (CWMG), Vol. 13, p. 8.

48. *The Letters of the Right Honourable V.S. Srinivasa Sastri* (edited by Jagadisan), pp. 40–41. According to Srinivasa Sastri, Gandhi had "Anarch views."

49. Gandhi to Maganlal Gandhi, 27 January 1910, M.K. Gandhi, *The Collected Works of Mahatma Gandhi* (CWMG), Vol. 10, Ministry of Information and Broadcasting, Government of India, Ahmedabad 1963, pp. 139.

50. Gandhi's anti-modernism, which drew on arguments of European pessimistic intellectuals such as Max Nordau, Edward Carpenter or Oswald Spengler, was a global phenomenon that informed several Occidentalist discourses in many parts of the world. See, among others, Dilip Menon, "An Eminent Victorian: Gandhi, *Hind Swaraj* and the Crisis of Liberal Democracy in the Nineteenth Century", *History of the Present*, Vol. 7, n. 1 (2017), pp. 33–58. On globally circulating visions of anti- Westernism, see Cemil Aydin, *The Politics of Anti-Westernism in Asia: Visions of World Order in Pan- Islamic and Pan- Asian Thought*, Columbia University Press, New York 2007.

51. For the making of the productive citizen in postcolonial India, see Anandita Bajpai, "Making the New Indian Citizen in Times of the Jawan (Soldier) and

the Kisan (Farmer), 1962–1965", *Comparativ*, Vol. 28, n. 5 (2018), pp. 97–120. See also the discussion in Srirupa Roy, *Beyond Belief: India and the Politics of Postcolonial Nationalism*, Duke University Press, Durham and London 2007, pp. 133–156. For the continuities and discontinuities in ideas, discourses and practices of citizenship from colonial South Asia to independent India and Pakistan, see the contributions in Taylor Sherman, William Gould and Sarah Ansari (eds.), *From Subjects to Citizens: Society and the Everyday State in India and Pakistan, 1947-1970*, CUP, Cambridge 2014.

52. Gandhi to Maganlal Gandhi, p. 139. On Gandhi's views on education, see also Parimala V. Rao, 'Compulsory Education and the Political Leadership in Colonial India, 1840-1947', in Rao, *New Perspectives*, pp. 171–173.

53. Gandhi, *Gokhale, My Political Guru.*

54. "Speech at Santiniketan on Gokhale's death", 20 February 1915, CWMG, Ministry of Information and Broadcasting, Government of India, Ahmedabad 1964, Vol. 13, pp. 26.

55. Wolpert, *Tilak and Gokhale*, p. 143.

56. Dilip Menon, "An Eminent Victorian", dealing with *Hind Swaraj*, provides important insights into this transitional phase of Gandhi's thought. Only from the 1920s onwards did Gandhi become more clearly against the British empire. His *ashram* practices and *satyagraha* campaigns represented alternative modalities of inhabiting the political world through a critique of liberal modernity and the state. See Ajay Skaria, "Gandhi's Politics: Liberalism and the Question of the Ashram", *South Atlantic Quarterly*, Vol. 101, n. 4 (2002), pp. 955–986; David Hardiman, *Gandhi in His Time and Ours: The Global Legacy of His Ideas*, Columbia University Press, New York 2004, pp. 66–93.

57. Manfred B. Steger, "Searching for Satya Through Ahimsa: Gandhi's Challenge to Western Discourses of Power", *Constellations*, Vol. 13, n. 3 (2006), pp. 332–353.

58. This appears both from CWMG and the SISP. His friendship and collaboration with A.V. Thakkar, prominent member of the SIS, especially in terms of 'uplifting' work targeting the 'depressed classes,' was lifelong.

59. On how Gandhi's moral and material uplifting programmes shared several similarities with the colonial 'civilising mission' and INC development schemes, see Ben Zachariah, 'In Search of the Indigenous: J. C. Kumarappa and the Philosophy of "Gandhian Economics"', in Harald Fischer-Tiné and Michael Mann (eds.), *Colonialism as Civilizing Mission: Cultural Ideology in British India*, Anthem Press, London and New York 2004, pp. 248–269.

60. *Account of the Servants of India Society (1905–1916).*

61. For an analysis of the SIS activities, see Watt, *Serving the Nation*, pp. 97–116.

62. On the AITA, see Colvard, "A World Without Drink", esp. chapter 3 and Lucy Carroll, "The Temperance Movement in India: Politics and Social Reform", *Modern Asian Studies*, Vol. 10, n. 3 (1976), pp. 417–447.

63. Carroll, "Temperance Movement in India." For a first-hand account, see W.S. Caine, 'The Temperance Problem in India', in C.Y. Chintamani (ed.), *Indian Social Reform*, Thompson & Co., Madras 1901, pp. 89–96.

64. This would become a key point for Gandhi's views of temperance and vice too. See Harald Fischer-Tiné, "Eradicating the 'Scourge of Drink' and the 'Un-pardonable Sin of Illegitimate Sexual Enjoyment': M. K. Gandhi as Anti-Vice Crusader", *Interdisziplinäre Zeitschrift für Südasienforschung*, n. 2 (2017), pp. 113–130.

65. *Res. Ill, Tenth Conference, Calcutta, 1896*, quoted in "Appendix", *Indian Social Reform*, p. 372.

66. "Diwan Sant Ram's Presidential Address, Lahore 1900", quoted in "Addenda", *Indian Social Reform*, p. 387.

67. Harald Fischer-Tiné, "Eradicating the 'Scourge of Drink'", p. 114.
68. On this, see Jessica Pliley, Robert Kramm and Fischer-Tiné, 'Introduction: A Plea for a "Vicious Turn" in Global History', in idem (eds.), *Global Anti-Vice Activism, 1890–1950: Fighting Drinks, Drugs, and 'Immorality'*, CUP, Cambridge 2016, pp. 1–30; Harald Fischer-Tiné and Jana Tschurenev, 'Introduction: Indian Anomalies? Drink and Drugs in the Land of Gandhi', in H. Fischer-Tiné and J. Tschurenev (edited by), *A History of Alcohol and Drugs in Modern South Asia: Intoxicating Affairs*, Routledge, Abingdon 2014, pp. 1–26; David M. Fahey, "Temperance Internationalism: Guy Hayler and the World Prohibition Federation", *The Social History of Alcohol and Drugs*, Vol. 20 (Spring 2006), pp. 247–275.
69. See, for example, Caine, "The Temperance Problem in India", pp. 87–88.
70. Colvard, "A World Without Drink", *passim*; Robert E. Colvard, "'Drunkards Beware!': Prohibition and Nationalist Politics in the 1930s', in H. Fischer-Tiné and J. Tschurenev, *A History of Alcohol and Drugs*, pp. 173–200. Western temperance activists were motivated more by the will to enhance the credibility of the British Empire rather than by the larger condemnation of imperialism. Caine, for instance, found unacceptable from the point of view of Victorian values and Christian morality, that a "Christian Government" obtained revenue from intoxicants sold to a people who were "by religious and social habits" opposed to the sale of liquor and drugs (Caine, "The Temperance Problem in India", pp. 92–93). See also Deana Heath, *Purifying Empire: Obscenity and the Politics of Moral Regulation in Britain, India and Australia*, CUP, Cambridge 2010.
71. Frederick Grubb, *Fifty Years' Work for India: My Temperance Jubilee*, H. J. Rowley and Sons, Ltd, London 1942, p. 16.
72. The *Times of India* was among the most prominent newspapers which criticised the temperance agitation (see *Oriental Review*, 1 December 1909).
73. Colvard, "A World Without Drink", pp. 104–105; Indra Munshi Saldanha, "On Drinking and 'Drunkenness': History of Liquor in Colonial India", *Economic and Political Weekly*, Vol. 30, n. 37 (1995), pp. 2323–2331.
74. "The New Mhowra Bill", *Quarterly Journal of the Poona Sarvajanika Sabha*, Vol. XV, n. 2 (October 1892), p. 38.
75. Caine to Gokhale, 7 October 1898, GP.
76. Caine to Gokhale, 18 February 1901, GP.
77. Caine to Gokhale, 23 July 1902, GP.
78. David Hardiman, 'From Custom to Crime: The Politics of Drinking in Colonial South Gujarat', in R. Guha (ed.), *Subaltern Studies* IV, OUP, New Delhi 1985, pp. 165–228, here 189.
79. "Bombay Abkari Act Amendment", Bombay Legislative Council 1901, *GSW*, Vol. I, pp. 403–413.
80. Gokhale to Joshi, 26 February 1901, GP.
81. "Bombay Abkari Act Amendment", p. 409.
82. *Report of the Indian Hemp Drugs Commission 1893–94*, Government Central Printing Office, Simla 1894. The quasi-judicial and quasi-scientific IHDC had been appointed by the secretary of state for India in 1893 at the request of the temperance leader Caine in order to consider the desirability of prohibition. Consisting of four British and three Indian members, the commission published a lengthy and fascinating report on cannabis consumption in the subcontinent. It concluded that the prohibition of hemp drugs was neither necessary nor expedient and established that the occasional use of hemp in moderate doses could be beneficial and was "practically attended by no evil results at all" (*Report of the Indian Hemp Drugs Commission 1893–94*, p. 264). Distinguishing between moderate and excessive consumption, the majority

of the commission members recommended a "control and restriction" policy to check on excessive use – a decision that would actually increase the Crown income through duties on the consumption of hemp products. See James H. Mills, *Cannabis Britannica: Empire, Trade, and Prohibition 1800-1928*, OUP, Oxford 2005, chapter 5 for hemp and broader colonial drug politics. See also Ronen Shamir and Daphna Hacker, "Colonialism's Civilizing Mission: The Case of the Indian Hemp Drug Commission", *Law & Social Inquiry*, Vol. 26, n. 2 (2001), pp. 435–461. For the shifting colonial attitudes towards narcotics, see James Mills, "Cannabis and the Cultures of Colonialism: Government, Medicine, Ritual and Pleasures in the History of an Asian Drug (c. 1800 - c. 1895)", *Zeitenblicke*, Vol. 9, n. 3 (2009) https://pureportal.strath.ac.uk/en/publications/cannabis-and-the-cultures-of-colonialism-government-medicine-ritu [accessed 22 April 2021].

83. "Financial Statement, 1901-02", Bombay Legislative Council, Poona, 22 August 1901, *GSW*, Vol. I, p. 453.

84. "Budget Speech, 1902", *GSW*, Vol. I, pp. 11–12. For similar reasons, Gokhale was in favour of the abolition of the Opium revenue, "derived from the degradation and moral ruin of the people of China" ("Budget Speech, 1907", *GSW*, Vol. I, pp. 116–117). On the campaigns in favour of the abolition of opium, see Maria Framke, 'Internationalizing the Indian War on Opium: Colonial Policy, the Nationalist Movement and the League of Nations', in Fischer-Tiné and Tschurenev, *A History of Alcohol and Drugs*, pp. 155–172.

85. "Budget Speech, 1904", *GSW*, Vol. I, p. 60.

86. "Budget Speech, 1904", p. 61.

87. See, for instance, for cannabis drugs, Mills, *Cannabis Britannica*, pp. 47–69 and for alcohol, Saldanha, "On Drinking and 'Drunkenness'".

88. See, among others, Hardiman, 'From Custom to Crime', and David T. Courtwright, 'The Rise and Fall and Rise of Cocaine in the United States', in J. Goodman, A. Sherratt and P.E. Lovejoy (eds.), *Consuming Habits: Global and Historical Perspectives and How Cultures Define Drugs*, Routledge, Abingdon and New York 2007, pp. 215–237.

89. National Temperance Society to Gokhale, 17 April 1911, GP.

90. Fahey, "Temperance Internationalism", p. 258.

91. *India*, 19 July 1912, Vol. 38.

92. See Colvard, "A World Without Drink", p. 133–152 for the activities of the PTA in the Bombay Presidency.

93. Report of Native Papers, Bombay Presidency, Vol. 18, 1908, p. 15.

94. Colvard, "A World Without Drink", pp. 137–138.

95. *Sind Journal*, 16 July 1908, in Report of Native Papers, Bombay Presidency, Vol. 30, 1908, pp. 16–17.

96. "Mr. R.C. Dutt, C.I.E., and the Hon. G.K. Gokhale, C.I.E., on Temperance Reform", *Abkari: The Quarterly Organ of the Anglo-Indian Temperance Association*, Vol. I, n. 73 (1908), p. 91.

97. *The Indian Social Reformer*, Vol. XIX, n. 35, 2 May 1909, p. 409.

98. Colvard, "'Drunkards Beware!'"; Fischer-Tiné, 'Eradicating the "Scourge of Drink"; Pliley, Kramm and Fischer-Tiné, 'Introduction: A Plea for a "Vicious Turn" in Global History', pp. 5–10; David M. Fahey and Padma Manian, "Poverty and Purification: The Politics of Gandhi's Campaign for Prohibition", *The Historian*, Vol. 67, n. 3 (2005), pp. 489–506.

99. *Kesari*, 7 April 1908, Report of Native Papers, Bombay Presidency, Vol. 15, 1908, pp. 16–17.

100. *Dinbandhu*, 25 April 1908, Report of Native Papers, Bombay Presidency, Vol. 18, 1908, p. 14.

101. Ambedkar's Letter to the Anti-Untouchability League, 14 November 1932, *Dr. Babasaheb Ambedkar: Speeches and Writings* (edited by Vasant Moon), Vol. 9, Education Department, Government of Maharashtra, Bombay 1991, p. 134, quoted in Srivatsan, *Seva, Saviour, and State*, p. 165.

102. For a discussion on this, see Srivatsan, *Seva, Saviour, and State*, pp. 163–181.

103. On Gandhi's view of the ideal citizen as "non-Dalit," see Joel Lee's contribution "Gandhi, Protestant Missionaries, and Dalit Labour: Northern parallels to The Pariah Problem" in "A Roundtable on Rupa Viswanath's The Pariah Problem: Caste, Religion, and the Social in Modern India and the Study of Caste", *Modern Asian Studies* (2021), pp. 41–49.

104. *Account of the Servants of India Society (1905–1916)*, p. 25.

105. *Account of the Servants of India Society (1917–1923)*, pp. 25, 30, 32. The Depressed Classes Mission in Mangalore, funded in 1897 by the social reformer Kudmul Ranga Rao (1859–1928), was taken over by the SIS in the 1920s.

106. V. Geetha, "Periyar, Women and an Ethic of Citizenship", *Economic and Political Weekly*, Vol. 33, n. 17 (1998), WS9–WS15. On Thakkar's perception of the 'tribal question,' see Saagar Tewari, "Debating Tribe and Nation: Hutton, Thakkar, Ambedkar, and Elwin (1920s-1940s)", NMML Occasional Paper History and Society, New Series 86, pp. 1–30.

107. *Speeches and Writings of Sarojini Naidu*, G.A. Natesan & Co, Madras 1925, p. 49.

108. See Bhattacharya, *The Colonial State*, pp. 36–37; Sabyasachi Bhattacharya, *Rabindranath Tagore: An Interpretation*, Penguin Books, Delhi 2011, esp. chapter 3.

109. See chapter 7 in Jon E. Wilson, *The Domination of Strangers*, Palgrave Macmillan, London 2008.

110. Nanda, *Gokhale*, p. 146.

111. On the subtle line separating voluntary and philanthropic work from political activities, see Watt, *Serving the Nation*, pp. 177–181.

112. Debates about the separation of civil and political society are ongoing among scholars of South Asia. Chatterjee, *The Politics of the Governed*, argues that the two domains are separate and correspond respectively to the realms of popular sovereignty and governmentality, with the latter being the violent negation of the former. Veena Das, for instance, rejects this binarisation claiming that civil society and political society "bleed into each other" ("State, Citizenship, and the Urban Poor", *Citizenship Studies*, Vol. 15, n. 3–4, pp. 319–333).

113. Sidney and Beatrice Webb, *Indian Diary* (edited by Niraja Gopal Jayal), OUP, Oxford and New York 1990, p. 193. For the visibility and influence of the SIS in Britain, see Georgina Brewis, "Education for Service: Social Service and Higher Education in India and Britain, 1905-1919", *History of Education Review*, Vol. 42, n. 2 (2013), pp. 119–136.

114. See Watt, *Serving the Nation*, p. 175, chapter 6.

115. Public health projects like clean water and adequate drainage systems had become particularly urgent after the spread of cholera and other gastro-enteric diseases in the Bombay Presidency, especially in Berar and in the Deccan, where the exportation of cotton had a dramatic impact on the general living conditions of the people, mostly in terms of food security. See Laxman D. Satya, *Cotton and Famine in Berar, 1850-1900*, Manohar, New Delhi 1997; David Washbrook, "The Commercialization of Agriculture in Colonial India: Production, Subsistence and Reproduction in the 'Dry South', c. 1870-1930", *Modern Asian Studies*, Vol. 28, n. 1 (1994), p. 131. For the role of Indian cotton in the global economy, see Christof Dejung, 'The Boundaries of Western Power: The Colonial Cotton Economy in India and the Problem of Quality', in idem et al. (eds.), *The Foundations of Worldwide Economic Integration: Power, Institutions, and Global Markets, 1850–1930*, CUP, Cambridge

2013, pp. 133–157 and Sven Beckert, *Empire of Cotton: A Global History*, Alfred A. Knopf, New York 2014.

116. Gokhale to Wedderburn, 29 April 1910, GP.

117. See, for instance, "Budget, 1912-13. Surpluses and Provincial Reserves", *GSW*, Vol. I, p. 254.

118. See "Budget Speech, 1906", *GSW*, Vol. 1, pp. 103–106. More generally, Gokhale's pleas for a greater role of government in society appear mainly in the Financial Statements presented in front of the Bombay Legislative Council and in the Budget Speeches in the Imperial Council. These are collected in volume I of GSW. Before the 1909 Morley-Minto reforms, the discussion of the annual budget was the only occasion when non-official members could criticise the colonial administration and advance their suggestions in terms of finances.

119. So, for instance, in the 1950s, Kunzru, member of the SIS since 1909, would protest that the voluntary sector was encroached upon by the independent Indian state. See Watt, "Philanthropy and Civilizing Missions", p. 297. It should be noted, though only in passing, that well into the first decade after independence, India's first rulers placed the responsibility for development both on state-led programmes and on popular action outside of the state (see Taylor C. Sherman, "From 'Grow More Food' to 'Miss a Meal': Hunger, Development and the Limits of Post-Colonial Nationalism in India, 1947–1957", *South Asia: Journal of South Asian Studies*, Vol. 36, n. 4 (2013), pp. 571–588). Although more research is needed, there are good reasons to believe that the Nehruvian state's reliance on popular initiatives also contributed to the clout of social service and voluntary associations in postcolonial India.

120. "Budget Speech, 1903", *GSW*, Vol. I, p. 39.

121. "Budget Speech, 1903", *GSW*, Vol. I, p. 40.

122. From 1898 and for the following ten years, Indian finances had seen large surpluses. Whereas according to the rulers, that was an undisputable sign of the prosperity of 'British India,' Gokhale pointed out that it was the result of the artificial appreciation of the rupee. Not per se a supporter of budget surpluses, which generally determined a greater taxation burden on the people ("Budget Speech, 1902", pp. 1–6), Gokhale repeatedly argued that they should be returned to the population through welfare programmes.

123. See Ahuja, "A Beveridge Plan for India", pp. 207–248.

124. Gokhale to Joshi, 24 January 1902, GP.

125. For the broader phenomenon of the ideology of reform of the poor, see Nandini Gooptu, *The Politics of the Urban Poor in Early-Twentieth Century India*, CUP, Cambridge 2001.

126. See Chatterjee, *The Politics of the Governed*, on how slum dwellers in Calcutta, who are otherwise at the margins of civil society and associational politics, have appropriated the language of governmental categories of welfare and needs to assert their political agency and make claims on the state. See also Arjun Appadurai, "Deep Democracy: Urban Governmentality and the Horizon of Politics", *Environment and Urbanization*, Vol. 13, n. 2 (2001), pp. 23–43.

127. On the role of non-state welfare in the Global South, see Melani Claire Cammett and Lauren M. MacLean, "Introduction: The Political Consequences of Non-State Social Welfare in the Global South", *Studies in Comparative International Development*, Vol. 46, n. 1 (2011), pp. 1–21. In the same issue, see Anirudh Krishna, "Gaining Access to Public Services and the Democratic State in India: Institutions in the Middle", pp. 98–117. See also Jean Drèze and Amartya Sen, 'Public Action and Social Inequality', in B. Harris-White and S. Subramanian (eds.), *Illfare in India: Essays on India's Social Sector in Honor of S. Guhan*, Sage, New Delhi 1999.

128. *Report of the National Committee on Women's Education*, Ministry of Education, 1959, p. 143, quoted in Sherman, "Education in Early Postcolonial India Expansion, Experimentation and Planned Self-Help", *History of Education*, Vol. 47, n. 4 (2018), p. 515. The report maintained that "The State in a true democracy is there only to help people to help themselves [...] Any extension of these self-help activities is an extension of democracy itself" (*ibidem*).

129. For an insightful discussion on this long-term phenomenon, see Watt, "Philanthropy and Civilizing Missions".

130. *Report of the National Committee on Women's Education*, p. 143.

131. Reliance on non-state actors for basic needs entails the risk – especially when non-state actors are sectarian and identity-based organisations that present themselves as substitutes of a state incapable of taking care of the welfare of its citizenry – that citizens may develop attachments to political communities whose views are at variance with a plural and democratic society. Some useful insights are given in Soundarya Chidambaram, *Welfare, Patronage, and the Rise of Hindu Nationalism in India's Urban Slums*, Ph.D. Dissertation, Ohio State University, 2011, pp. 158–227.

132. After all, the construction of the Welfare State in advanced economies was in general a compromise aimed at reducing the revolutionary appeal among the working classes. See, among others, Stein Kuhnle and Anne Sander, 'The Emergence of the Western Welfare State', in F.G. Castles et al. (eds.), *The Oxford Handbook of the Welfare State*, OUP, Oxford 2010 and Alan Brinkley, *The End of Reform: New Deal Liberalism in Recession and War*, Vintage Books, New York 1995.

133. T.H. Marshall's theory of social citizenship is perhaps the most famous example. See T.H. Marshall and Tom B. Bottomore, *Citizenship and Social Class*, Pluto, London 1992. For the broader ideological context of Marshall's social citizenship, see Julia Moses, "Social Citizenship and Social Rights in an Age of Extremes: T. H. Marshall's Social Philosophy in the Longue Durée", *Modern Intellectual History*, Vol. 16, n. 1 (2019), pp. 155–184.

134. *Elementary Education Bill. The Hon.ble Mr Gokhale's Speech and the Debate Thereon*, Aryabhushan Press, Poona 1911. 'Elementary education' was intended to mean "the courses in reading, writing and arithmetic, and other subjects, if any, prescribed from time to time by the Department of Public Instruction for elementary schools" (ibid., p. 1). See also Nanda, *Gokhale*, pp. 386–394 and Krishna Kumar, *Political Agenda of Education: A Study of Colonialist and Nationalist Ideas*, Sage, New Delhi 2005, 2nd edition, pp. 118–120.

135. "Education in India", Tenth Annual General Meeting of the Bombay Graduates' Association, 11 April 1896, *GSW*, Vol. III, p. 166.

136. "Elementary Education", Resolution moved in the Imperial Legislative Council, 18 March 1910, *GSW*, Vol. III, pp. 73–89.

137. Quoted in Nanda, *Gokhale*, p. 394.

138. Manu Bhagavan, *Sovereign Spheres: Princes, Education and Empire in Colonial India*, OUP, Delhi 2003.

139. See Nira Wickramasinghe, *Sri Lanka in the Modern Age: A History of Contested Identities*, University of Hawaii Press, London 2006, pp. 74–81.

140. Marius Jansen, *The Making of Modern Japan*, Harvard University Press, Cambridge, MA 2002, pp. 156–186.

141. *Elementary Education Bill*, pp. 85–86.

142. Gokhale's admiration of Japan as a part of the broader enthusiasm that the Asian nation's brand of modernity had kindled among Indian nationalists has been seen in chapters two and three.

143. *Elementary Education Bill*, p. 88.

144. *Elementary Education Bill*, p. 21.

145. *Elementary Education Bill*, p. 91

146. *Elementary Education Bill*, p. 89.
147. "Alexandra Prize-Distribution Ceremony", Alexandra Girls' English Institution, 3 April 1912, *GSW*, pp. 254–255. The institution, open to girls of all castes and communities, was founded in 1863 by the Parsi businessman and judge from Bombay Manockjee Cursetjee (1808–1887). Italics mine.
148. See chapter one for Gokhale's earlier take on female education.
149. Gokhale to Wedderburn, 6 October 1911, GP.
150. "Budget Speech, 1903", p. 40.
151. "Budget Speech, 1906", *GSW*, Vol. III, pp. 102–106. The colonial state, by the late 19th century, had established a number of government industrial schools aimed at training the children of labourers towards skilled employment as well as redressing the neglect of primary education. But Gokhale wanted a greater commitment. See Arun Kumar, "Skilling and its Histories: Labour Market, Technical Knowledge and the Making of Skilled Workers in Colonial India, 1880–1910", *Journal of South Asian Development*, Vol. 13, n. 3 (November 2018), pp. 249–271, esp. 251–260; Bidisha Dhar, "The Lucknow Industrial School c.1892–1918: A Case Study of Technical Education for the Artisan", *Global South*, Vol. 4, n. 4 (July 2008), pp. 8–10; Sumanta Banerjee, 'Educating the Labouring Poor in 19th Century Bengal: Two Experiments', in Sabyasachi Bhattacharya (ed.), *The Contested Terrain*, pp. 171–199; Aparna Basu, "Indian Primary Education, 1900–1920", *The Indian Economic and Social History Review*, Vol. 8, no. 3 (July 1971): 284–286; Aparna Basu, "Technical Education in India, 1900–1920", *The Indian Economic and Social History Review*, Vol. 4, n. 4 (October 1967).
152. See, among others, W. Norton Grubb & Marvin Lazerson, *The Education Gospel: The Economic Power of Schooling*, Harvard University Press, Cambridge, MA 2004; Martin Carnoy, 'Education and the State: From Adam Smith to Perestroika', in R. Arnove, P. Altbach and G. Kelly (eds.), *Emergent Issues in Education: Comparative Perspectives*, State University of New York Press, Albany, NY 1992, pp. 143–159; Jim Carl, 'Industrialization and Public Education: Social Cohesion and Social Stratification', in R. Cowen and A.M. Kazamias (eds.), *International Handbook of Comparative Education*, Springer International Handbooks of Education, Dordrecht 2009, pp. 503–518.
153. On Tews, the most comprehensive study is Andreas Pehnke (ed.), *Johannes Tews (1860 - 1937); vom 15-jährigen Dorfschullehrer zum Repräsentanten des Deutschen Lehrervereins; Studien über den liberalen Bildungspolitiker, Sozialpädagogen, Erwachsenenbildner und Kämpfer gegen den Antisemitismus*, Verlag, Beucha 2011. See also Andrew Lees, *Cities, Sin, and Social Reform in Imperial Germany*, University of Michigan Press, 2002, chapter 6, pp. 223–254; Forsell Håkan, "The City as a Curriculum Resource: Pedagogical Avant-Garde and Urban Literacy in Europe, c.1900 – 1920", *Social and Education History*, Vol. 1, n. 2 (2012), pp. 182–188.
154. "Budget Speech, 1903", p. 40.
155. "Financial Statement 1901-02, Bombay Legislative Council", *GSW*, Vol. I, p. 455.
156. The Bill was based on the Factories Commission Report of 1908, which was appointed in 1907 by the colonial government to inquire into the conditions of textile labour following workers' riots against harsh working conditions in Bombay.
157. "Labour in Indian Factories", 21 March 1911, *GSW*, Vol. I, p. 325.
158. See, for example, the *Report of the Indian Factory Labour Commission 1908*, Govt. of India, Ministry of Commerce and Industry, Simla 1908, pp. 20–21. The report recommended that in order to make the Indian 'peasant' a good and efficient factory worker, new technologies of labour management should be introduced.

159. For a discussion on this, see Peter Robb, "Labour in India 1860-1920: Typologies, Change and Regulation", *Journal of the Royal Asiatic Society*, Vol. 4, n. 1 (1994), pp. 52 ff. For changes in notions of time and shifts in technology in colonial India, see Sumit Sarkar, *Beyond Nationalist Frames: Relocating Postmodernism, Hindutva, History*, Permanent Black, Delhi 2002, pp. 10–37; Aparajita Mukhopadhyay, *Imperial Technology and 'Native' Agency: A Social History of Railways in Colonial India, 1850-1920*, Routledge, London 2018, chapter 1; see also Vanessa Ogle, *The Global Transformation of Time 1870 – 1950*, Harvard University Press, Cambridge, MA 2015.

160. "Education in India", p. 174.

161. "Mahadev Govind Ranade", 24 July 1904, *GSW*, Vol. III, p. 297. Gokhale also praised the British public schools, typically elite schools for their "manly influences" and "healthy discipline" ("Education in India", p. 174).

162. "Madras's Support to Bill", 22 July 1911, *GSW*, Vol. III, p. 218.

163. "Madras's Support to Bill", p. 218.

164. "Advice to Students", p. 187.

165. "Elementary Education Bill", *GSW*, Vol. III, p. 92.

166. "Elementary Education Bill", p. 131.

167. "Madras's Support to Bill", p. 218.

168. "Elementary Education Bill", p. 131.

169. See Rao, *Tilak's Nationalism*, pp. 251–280, on Tilak's views on mass education and Rao, "Compulsory Education and the Political Leadership in Colonial India, 1840-1947", pp. 151–175.

170. "Elementary Education Bill", 18 March 1912, *GSW*, Vol. III, p. 113.

171. "Bengal Support to Bill", p. 243.

172. "Elementary Education", p. 88.

173. "Elementary Education Bill", p. 138.

174. See Soni, *Famine Orphan "Rescue" Missions: Childhood, Colonialism and Nationalism in Colonial India, 1860s–1920s*, unpubl. Ph.D. thesis, ETH Zurich, 2020; Karen Vallgårda, *Imperial Childhoods and Christian Mission: Education and Emotions in South India and Denmark*, Palgrave MacMillan, Basingstoke 2015; Guoping Zhao, "The Modern Construction of Childhood: What Does it Do to the Paradox of Modernity", *Studies in Philosophy and Education*, Vol. 30, (2011); Satadru Sen, *Colonial Childhoods: The Juvenile Periphery of India, 1850-1945*, Anthem Press, London 2005, p. 115, *passim*; David M. Pomfret, *Youth and Empire: Transcolonial Childhoods in British and French Asia*, Stanford University Press, Stanford, CA 2015; and the less recent Judith E. Walsh, *Growing up in British India: Indian Autobiographers on Childhood and Education under the Raj*, Holmes & Meier, New York 1983. Childhood was increasingly perceived as a new, if negotiated, shared value. For changing notions of childhood, see Peter Stearns, *Childhood in World History*, Routledge, New York 2011, pp. 71–83.

175. Ishita Pande, *Sex, Law and the Politics of Age. Child Marriage in India 1891–1937*, CUP, Cambridge 2020, pp. 1-27.

176. "Labour in Indian Factories", pp. 320–325.

177. "Students and Their Duties", p. 225.

178. This view of education as beneficial for the spread of democratic values and fostering greater political participation has been embraced by theorists of modernisation since the 1950s (among others Seymour Martin Lipset, "Some Social Requisites of Democracy: Economic Development and Political Legitimacy", *The American Political Science Review*, Vol. 53, n. 1 (1959), pp. 69–105; Marion J. Levy, *Modernization and the Structure of Societies: A Setting for International Affairs*, Princeton University Press, Princeton 1966, 2 vols; Robert A. Dahl, *Polyarchy, Participation and Opposition*, Yale University Press,

New Haven 1971; Samuel Huntington, *The Third Wave: Democratization in the Late Twentieth Century*, University of Oklahoma Press, Norman and London 1991) and has continued to be influential in different postcolonial contexts and among contemporary scholars (see, among many others, Acemoglu et al., "From Education to Democracy?", *American Economic Review*, Vol. 95, n. 2, pp. 44–49; Ananya Basu and Elizabeth M. King, "Does Education Promote Growth and Democracy? Some Evidence from East Asia and Latin America", World Bank, Washington, D.C. 2001). Other intellectuals belonging to the left of the political spectrum like Gramsci (Antonio Gramsci, *Selections from the Prison Notebooks* [edited by G.N. Smith], International Publishers Co, New York 1971), Freire (Paulo Freire, *Pedagogy of the Oppressed*, Penguin, Harmondsworth 1972) and Fanon (Frantz Fanon, *The Wretched of the Earth*, Grove Press, New York 2005 [1961]) and the scholarship influenced by them focused on the content of education according to which education can be an expression of the cultural hegemony of the ruling elite, or liberating for the subalterns.

179. Taylor C. "Education in Early Postcolonial India", p. 505.
180. "Bengal Support to Bill", p. 244.
181. Regarding elementary education, Gokhale condemned crude teaching methods such as rote learning (a practice that is still common in India), whereas he believed that, like the West, instruction had to be made interesting to the child, supported by a variety of books and by constantly improving methods of teaching ("Education in India", p. 169).
182. "Elementary Education", p. 88. Whichever place was assigned to religion in a compulsory and state-sponsored educational system created nervousness among those that, for cultural or ideological reasons, saw it as an integral part of education. See, for example, the letter to Gokhale from Maulvi Mohammad Aziz Mirza, Honorary Secretary of the All-India Muslim League, 24 October 1911, and the letter from Annie Besant to Gokhale, 1 May 1907, both in GP. It appears that Gokhale was willing to give safeguards to the Muslim minority: following the apprehension of some Muslims in Punjab, where they were a minority, that the Bill might be used to compel boys of their community to attend Hindu schools and learn Hindi instead of Urdu, he conceded that a parent could object to sending his child to a school where the vernacular taught was not the vernacular of the parent ["Madras's Support to Bill", p. 214; on the communalisation of Punjab, see Harald Fischer-Tiné, "'Kindly Elders of the Hindu Biradri': The Arya Samaj's Struggle for Influence and its Effect on Hindu-Muslim Relations', in A. Copley (ed.), *Gurus and their Followers: Studies in New Religious Movements in Late Colonial India*, OUP, New Delhi 2000, pp. 107–127]. The idea that was taking ground was that each child had to be taught in their own mother-tongue. Given that Indians spoke around 1600 different mother-tongues, this concept was hardly realisable, and so the linguistic medium of education remained a field of contention in postcolonial India (Sherman, "Education in Early Postcolonial India"). What made the contest between Hindi and Urdu so vociferous was the fact that they were religiously identified. See Farina Mir, "Imperial Policy, Provincial Practices: Colonial Language Policy in Nineteenth Century India", *Indian Economic and Social History Review*, Vol. 43 (2006), pp. 395–427; Kavita Datla, *The Language of Secular Islam: Urdu Nationalism and Colonial India*, University of Hawaii Press, Honolulu 2012.
183. "Elementary Education Bill", p. 100.
184. "Elementary Education", p. 88.
185. "Elementary Education Bill", p. 143.

186. Jean Drèze and Amartya Sen, *An Uncertain Glory: India and Its Contradictions*, Allen Lane, London 2013, esp. chapter 5, pp. 107–142; Jayal, *Citizenship and its Discontents*, pp. 156–157.
187. Also, article 41 of the Constitution establishes that the state should, *within the limits of its economic capacity and development*, effectively provide for the right to work, the right to education, and the right to public assistance.
188. On the Indian welfare state from independence to the liberalisation reforms, see Anand Kumar, 'The Welfare State System in India', in B. Vivekanandan and Nimmi Kurian (eds.), *Welfare States and the Future*, Palgrave Macmillan, Basingstoke 2005, pp. 336–371.
189. See Jayal, *Citizenship and its Discontents*, chapter 6, "Social Citizenship in Neoliberal Times", pp. 163–196. Regarding the effects of non-state welfare on the state capacity to supply social services and public goods, scholars are divided in their opinion. See, for example, Geoffrey D. Wood, 'States Without Citizens: The Problem of the Franchise State', in D. Hulme and M. Edwards (eds.), *NGOs, States and Donors: Too Close for Comfort?*, Save the Children Foundation and Macmillan, London 1997, pp. 79–92; Michael Bratton and Nicholas van de Walle, *Democratic Experiments in Africa: Regime Transitions in Comparative Perspective*, CUP, Cambridge 1997; L. David Brown, 'Creating Social Capital: Nongovernment Development Organizations and Intersectoral Problem Solving', in W. Powell and E. Clemens (eds.), *Private Action and Public Goods*, Yale University Press, New Haven 1998, pp. 228–244; Derick W. Brinckerhoff, "Exploring State–Civil Society Collaboration: Policy Partnerships in Developing Countries", *Nonprofit and Voluntary Sector Quarterly*, Vol. 28, n. 1 (1999); Anirudh Krishna, *Changing Policy and Practice from Below: Community Experiences in Poverty Reduction*, United Nations Development Programme, New York 2000; Anirudh Krishna, "Gaining Access to Public Services and the Democratic State in India: Institutions in the Middle", *Studies in Comparative International Development*, Vol. 46, n. 1 (2011), pp. 98–117.
190. Jayal, *Citizenship and its Discontents*, p. 169.
191. On the question of social and economic rights in the Indian Constitution, also Jayna Kothari, "Social Rights and the Indian Constitution", *Law, Social Justice and Global Development Journal*, Vol. 2 (2004), available at https://warwick.ac.uk/fac/soc/law/elj/lgd/2004_2/kothari/; and Rohit De, *A People's Constitution: The Everyday Life of Law in the Indian Republic*, Princeton University Press, Princeton and Oxford 2018, pp. 5–9. It should not be forgotten that India's 1950 constitution was on the one hand shaped globally by other constitutions (including the Irish, Swiss and Australian) and on the other by the recently published Universal Declaration of Human Rights (UDHR). Javed Majeed, "A Nation on the Move: The Indian Constitution, Life Writing and Cosmopolitanism", *Life Writing*, Vol. 13, n. 2 (2016), pp. 237–253. The implicit hierarchy between political rights and socio-economic rights – the latter inserted in the Directive Principles of State Policy – fell in line with the discussions that were taking place at the UN General Assembly, which postulated a 'progressive realisation' of social and economic rights. This differentiation between rights reflected the Cold War divide, with each bloc appropriating its own version of human rights: whereas economic and social rights were believed to derive mostly from socialist ideologies, civil and political rights, seen as legacy of the Enlightenment, were considered more immediately applicable in democratic contexts. On the making of the Indian Constitution, see Madhav Khosla, *India's Founding Moment: The Constitution of a Most Surprising Democracy*, Harvard University Press, Cambridge, MA and London 2020.
192. Efforts in the socialistic direction have been celebrated, for example, by Francine R. Frankel, *India's Political Economy: The Gradual Revolution, 1947–77,*

Princeton University Press, Princeton 1978 and Partha Chatterjee, 'Development Planning and the Indian State', in P. Chatterjee (ed.), *State and Politics in India*, OUP, Delhi 1997, esp. pp. 271–297.

193. Christian Aspalter, 'Discovering Old and New Shores in Welfare State Theory', in C. Aspalter (ed.), *Discovering the Welfare State in East Asia*, Praeger, Westport 2002.

194. A.W. Little, "Access to Elementary Education in India: Politics, Policies and Progress", in CREATE Pathways to Access Series, Research Monograph n. 44 (2010); Jayal, *Citizenship and its Discontents*, pp. 185–189; Prachi Srivastava and Claire Noronha, "Institutional Framing of the Right to Education Act: Contestation, Controversy and Concession", *Economic and Political Weekly*, Vol. 49, n. 18 (2014), pp. 51–58.

195. Amartya Sen, "The Country of First Boys", *The Little Magazine*, Vol. 6, n. 1 and 2 (2005), pp. 7-17.

196. Aihwa Ong, *Flexible Citizenship: The Cultural Logics of Transnationality*, Duke University Press, Durham and London 1999.

197. Drèze and Sen, *An Uncertain Glory*, pp. 127–129. The Indian state of Kerala, which is formed by, besides Malabar, two former princely states of Travancore and Cochin with a history of advanced educational policies during the British *Raj*, retained the same pro-education outlook after 1947 and today it is significantly ahead in terms of educational development compared to the rest of India. Similarly, Bombay, later Maharashtra and Gujarat, which, as seen, was among the first provinces to enact compulsory education, and was one of the states which educated more children to a higher level (Sherman, "Education in Early Postcolonial India", p. 506).

198. Drèze and Sen, *An Uncertain Glory*, p. 113.

199. For the discourse of 'moral and material progress' in colonial India, see Michael Mann, "'Torchbearers Upon the Path of Progress": Britain's Ideology of a "Moral and Material Progress" in India. An Introductory Essay" in Fischer-Tiné and Mann (eds.), *Colonialism as Civilizing Mission*, pp. 1–26.

200. Sanjay Seth, "Rewriting Histories of Nationalism: The Politics of 'Moderate Nationalism' in India, 1870-1905", *The American Historical Review*, Vol. 104, n. 1 (1999), pp. 95–116.

201. A.B. Shah, 'Foreword', in A.B. Shah and S.P. Aiyar (eds.), *Gokhale and Modern India, Centenary Lectures*, Bombay 1966, p. v.

References

A Brief Account of the Work of the Servants of India Society, Poona (From June 1905 to December 1916), Aryabhushan Press, Poona 1917.

A Brief Account of the Work of the Servants of India Society, Poona (From 1st January 1917 to 30th June 1923), Aryabhushan Press, Poona 1924.

"A Roundtable on Rupa Viswanath's The Pariah Problem: Caste, Religion, and the Social in Modern India and the Study of Caste", *Modern Asian Studies* (2021).

Acemoglu, Daron et al., "From Education to Democracy", *American Economic Review*, Vol. 95, n. 2 (2005), pp. 44–49.

Ahuja, Ravi. "A Beveridge Plan for India? Social Insurance and the Making of the 'Formal Sector'", *International Review of Social History*, Vol. 64, n. 2 (2019), pp. 207–248.

Allender, Tim. "Understanding Education and India: New Turns in Postcolonial Scholarship", *History of Education*, Vol. 39, n. 2 (2010), pp. 281–288.

Ambedkar, B.R. *Dr. Babasaheb Ambedkar: Speeches and Writings* (edited by Vasant Moon), Vol. 9, Education Department, Government of Maharashtra, Bombay 1991.

Amrith, Sunil. 'Empires, Diasporas and Cultural Circulation', in Andrew Thompson (ed.), *Writing Imperial Histories*, Manchester University Press, Manchester 2013, pp. 216–239.

Appadurai, Arjun. "Deep Democracy: Urban Governmentality and the Horizon of Politics", *Environment and Urbanization*, Vol. 13, n. 2 (2001), pp. 23–43.

Aspalter, Christian. 'Discovering Old and New Shores in Welfare State Theory', in C. Aspalter (ed.), *Discovering the Welfare State in East Asia*, Praeger, Westport 2002.

Aydin, Cemil. *The Politics of Anti- Westernism in Asia: Visions of World Order in Pan-Islamic and Pan- Asian Thought*, Columbia University Press, New York 2007.

Bagchi, Barnita. "Connected and Entangled Histories: Writing Histories of Education in the Indian Context", *Paedagogica Historica*, Vol. 50, n. 6 (2014), pp. 813–821.

Bajpai, Anandita. "Making the New Indian Citizen in Times of the Jawan (Soldier) and the Kisan (Farmer), 1962–1965", *Comparativ*, Vol. 28, n. 5 (2018), pp. 97–120.

Banerjee, Prathama. "Between the Political and the Non-Political: The Vivekananda Moment and a Critique of the Social in Colonial Bengal, 1890s–1910s", *Social History*, Vol. 39, n. 3 (2014), pp. 323–339.

Banerjee, Sukanya. *Becoming Imperial Citizens: Indians in the Late-Victorian Empire*, Duke University Press, Durham and London 2010.

Banerjee, Sumanta. 'Educating the Labouring Poor in 19th Century Bengal: Two Experiments', in Sabyasachi Bhattacharya (ed.), *The Contested Terrain: Perspectives on Education in India*, Orient Longman Limited, Hyderabad, India 1998, pp. 171–199.

Basu, Aparna. "Indian Primary Education, 1900–1920", *The Indian Economic and Social History Review*, Vol. 8, n. 3 (1971), pp. 284 –286.

——. "Technical Education in India, 1900–1920", *The Indian Economic and Social History Review*, Vol. 4, n. 4 (October 1967), pp. 361–374.

—— and King, Elizabeth M. *"Does Education Promote Growth and Democracy? Some Evidence from East Asia and Latin America"*, World Bank, Washington, D.C. 2001.

Bayly, C.A. *Origins of Nationality in South Asia: Patriotism and Ethical Government in the Making of Modern India*, OUP, Delhi 1998.

Beckert, Sven. *Empire of Cotton: A Global History*, Alfred A. Knopf, New York 2014.

Bhagavan, Manu. *Sovereign Spheres: Princes, Education and Empire in Colonial India*, OUP, Delhi 2003.

Bhattacharya, Sabyasachi. *The Colonial State: Theory and Practice*, Primus Books, Delhi 2016.

——. *Rabindranath Tagore: An Interpretation*, Penguin Books, Delhi 2011.

—— (ed.). *The Contested Terrain: Perspectives on Education in India*, Orient Longman Limited, Hyderabad, India 1998.

——, Bara, Joseph and C.R. Yagati (eds.). *Educating the Nation: Documents on the Discourse of National Education in India 1880–1920*, Kanishka Publishers and Distributors and Jawaharlal Nehru University, New Delhi 2003.

Brewis, Georgina. "Education for Service: Social Service and Higher Education in India and Britain, 1905-1919", *History of Education Review*, Vol. 42, n. 2 (2013), pp. 119–136.

Brinckerhoff, Derick W. "Exploring State–Civil Society Collaboration: Policy Partnerships in Developing Countries", *Nonprofit and Voluntary Sector Quarterly*, Vol. 28, n. 1 (1999), pp. 123–147.

Brinkley, Alan. *The End of Reform: New Deal Liberalism in Recession and War*, Vintage Books, New York 1995.

Brown, Judith. *Gandhi: Prisoner of Hope*, Yale University Press, New Haven 1989.

Brown, L. David. 'Creating Social Capital: Nongovernment Development Organizations and Intersectoral Problem Solving', in W. Powell and E. Clemens (eds.), *Private Action and Public Goods*, Yale University Press, New Haven 1998, pp. 228–244.

Cammett, Melani Claire and Lauren M. MacLean. "Introduction: The Political Consequences of Non-State Social Welfare in the Global South", *Studies in Comparative International Development*, Vol. 46, n. 1 (2011), pp. 1–21.

Carl, Jim. 'Industrialization and Public Education: Social Cohesion and Social Stratification', in R. Cowen and A.M. Kazamias (eds.), *International Handbook of Comparative Education*, Springer International Handbooks of Education, Dordrecht 2009, pp. 503–518.

Carnoy, Martin. 'Education and the State: From Adam Smith to Perestroika', in R. Arnove, P. Altbach and G. Kelly (eds.), *Emergent Issues in Education: Comparative Perspectives*, State University of New York Press, Albany, NY 1992, pp. 143–159.

Carroll, Lucy. "The Temperance Movement in India: Politics and Social Reform", *Modern Asian Studies*, Vol. 10, n. 3 (1976), pp. 417–447.

Chatterjee, Partha. *The Politics of the Governed: Reflections of Popular Politics in Most of the World*, Columbia University Press, New York 2004.

——. 'Development Planning and the Indian State', in idem (ed.), *State and Politics in India*, OUP, Delhi 1997, pp. 271–297.

Chidambaram, Soundarya. *Welfare, Patronage, and the Rise of Hindu Nationalism in India's Urban Slums*, unpubl. Ph.D. Dissertation, Ohio State University, 2011.

Chintamani, C.Y. (ed.). *Indian Social Reform*, C. Y. Thompson & Co., Madras 1901.

Colvard, Robert E. "'Drunkards Beware!': Prohibition and Nationalist Politics in the 1930s', in H. Fischer-Tiné and J. Tschurenev (eds.), *A History of Alcohol and Drugs in Modern South Asia: Intoxicating Affairs*, Routledge, Abingdon 2014, pp. 173–200.

——. "*A World Without Drink: Temperance in Modern India, 1880–1940*". Unpubl. Ph.D. diss., University of Iowa, 2013.

Courtwright, David T. 'The Rise and Fall and Rise of Cocaine in the United States', in J. Goodman, A. Sherratt and P.E. Lovejoy (eds.), *Consuming Habits: Global and Historical Perspectives and How Cultures Define Drugs*, Routledge, Abingdon and New York 2007, pp. 215–237.

Dahl, Robert A. *Polyarchy, Participation and Opposition*, Yale University Press, New Haven 1971.

Das, Veena. "State, Citizenship, and the Urban Poor", *Citizenship Studies*, Vol. 15, n. 3-4, pp. 319–333.

Datla, Kavita. *The Language of Secular Islam: Urdu Nationalism and Colonial India*, University of Hawaii Press, Honolulu 2012.

De, Rohit. *A People's Constitution. The Everyday Life of Law in the Indian Republic*, Princeton University Press, Princeton and Oxford 2018.

Dejung, Christof. 'The Boundaries of Western Power: The Colonial Cotton Economy in India and the Problem of Quality', in idem et al. (eds.), *The Foundations of Worldwide Economic Integration: Power, Institutions, and Global Markets, 1850–1930*, CUP, Cambridge 2013, pp. 133–157.

Dhar, Bidisha. "The Lucknow Industrial School c.1892–1918: A Case Study of Technical Education for the Artisan", *Global South*, Vol. 4, n. 4 (2008), pp. 8–16.

Diener, Alexander C. 'Re-Scaling the Geography of Citizenship', in Ayelet Shachar et al. (eds.), *The Oxford Handbook of Citizenship*, OUP, Oxford 2017, pp. 36–52.

Drèze, Jean and Amartya Sen. 'Public Action and Social Inequality', in B. Harris-White and S. Subramanian (eds.), *Illfare in India: Essays on India's Social Sector in Honor of S. Guhan*, Sage, New Delhi 1999.

——. *An Uncertain Glory: India and Its Contradictions*, Allen Lane, London 2013.

Ellis, Catriona. "Education for All: Reassessing the Historiography of Education in Colonial India", *History Compass*, Vol. 7, n. 2 (2009), pp. 363–375.

Fahey, David M. "Temperance Internationalism: Guy Hayler and the World Prohibition Federation", *The Social History of Alcohol and Drugs*, Vol. 20 (Spring 2006), pp. 247–275.

—— and Manian, Padma. "Poverty and Purification: The Politics of Gandhi's Campaign for Prohibition", *The Historian*, Vol. 67, n. 3 (2005), pp. 489–506.

Fanon, Frantz. *The Wretched of the Earth*, Grove Press, New York 2005 (1961).

Farquhar, J.N. *Modern Religious Movements in India*, MacMillan, London 1924 (first published 1915).

Fischer-Tiné, Harald. *Muscling in on South Asia: Colonial Difference, American Soft Power, and the Indian YMCA (c.1890-1950)*, Bloomsbury, London forthcoming 2022.

——. "Third-Stream Orientalism: J. N. Farquhar, the Indian YMCA's Literature Department, and the Representation of South Asian Cultures and Religions (Ca. 1910–1940)", *The Journal of Asian Studies*, Vol. 79, n. 3 (2020), pp. 659–683.

——. "Eradicating the 'Scourge of Drink' and the 'Un-Pardonable Sin of Illegitimate Sexual Enjoyment': M. K. Gandhi as Anti-Vice Crusader", *Interdisziplinäre Zeitschrift für Südasienforschung*, Vol. 2 (2017), pp. 113–130.

——. *Der Gurukul Kangri Oder Die Erziehung Der Arya Nation: Kolonialismus, Hindureform Und 'nationale Bildung' in Britisch-Indien (1897-1922)*, Ergon-Verlag, Würzburg 2003.

——. '"Kindly Elders of the Hindu Biradri": The Arya Samaj's Struggle for Influence and its Effect on Hindu-Muslim Relations', in A. Copley (ed.), *Gurus and Their Followers: Studies in New Religious Movements in Late Colonial India*, OUP, New Delhi 2000, pp. 107–127.

—— and Tschurenev, Jana. 'Introduction: Indian Anomalies? Drink and Drugs in the Land of Gandhi', in idem, *A History of Alcohol and Drugs in Modern South Asia: Intoxicating Affairs*, Routledge, Abingdon 2014, pp. 1–26.

Framke, Maria. 'Internationalizing the Indian War on Opium: Colonial Policy, the Nationalist Movement and the League of Nations', in Harald Fischer-Tiné and Jana Tschurenev (eds.), *A History of Alcohol and Drugs in Modern South Asia: Intoxicating Affairs*, Routledge, Abingdon 2014, pp. 155–172.

Frankel, Francine R. *India's Political Economy: The Gradual Revolution, 1947–77*, Princeton University Press, Princeton 1978.

Freire, Paulo. *Pedagogy of the Oppressed*, Penguin, Harmondsworth 1972.

Gandhi, Mohandas Karamchand. *The Collected Works of Mahatma Gandhi, Vol. 13*, Publications Division, Ministry of Information and Broadcasting, Govt. of India, New Delhi 1964.

——. *The Collected Works of Mahatma Gandhi, Vol. 10*, Publications Division, Ministry of Information and Broadcasting, Govt. of India, Ahmedabad 1963.

——. *Gokhale, My Political Guru*, Navajivan Publishing House, Ahmedabad 1955.

Geetha, V. "Periyar, Women and an Ethic of Citizenship", *Economic and Political Weekly*, Vol. 33, n. 17 (1998), WS9–WS15.

Gokhale, Gopal Krishna. *Gokhale Speeches and Writings (GSW), Vol. I Economic*, in R.P. Patwardhan and D.V. Ambekar (eds.), Asia Publishing House, Poona 1962.

——. *Gokhale Speeches and Writings (GSW), Vol. II Political*, in R.P. Patwardhan and D.V. Ambekar (eds.), Asia Publishing House, Poona 1966.

——. *Gokhale Speeches and Writings (GSW), Vol. III Educational*, in D.G. Karve and D.V Ambekar (eds.), Asia Publishing House, Poona 1967.

——. *Public Life in India: Its Needs and Responsibilities*, National Literature Publishing Company, Bombay 1922.

——. *Elementary Education Bill. The Hon.Ble Mr Gokhale's Speech and the Debate Thereon*, Aryabhushan Press, Poona 1911.

Gooptu, Nandini. *The Politics of the Urban Poor in Early-Twentieth Century India*, CUP, Cambridge 2001.

Gramsci, Antonio. *Selections from the Prison Notebooks* (edited by G.N. Smith), International Publishers Co, New York 1971.

Grubb, Frederick. *Fifty Years' Work for India: My Temperance Jubilee*, H. J. Rowley and Sons, Ltd, London 1942.

Gupta, Charu. «'Hindu Communism': Satyabhakta, Apocalypses and Utopian Ram Rajya», *The Indian Economic and Social History Review*, Vol. 58, n. 2 (2021), pp. 213–248.

Håkan, Forsell. "The City as a Curriculum Resource: Pedagogical Avant-Garde and Urban Literacy in Europe, c.1900 – 1920", *Social and Education History*, Vol. 1, n. 2 (2012), pp. 182–188.

Hardiman, David. *Gandhi in His Time and Ours: The Global Legacy of His Ideas*, Columbia University Press, New York 2004.

——. 'From Custom to Crime: The Politics of Drinking in Colonial South Gujarat', in R. Guha (ed.), *Subaltern Studies IV*, OUP, New Delhi 1985, pp. 165–228.

Heath, Deana. *Purifying Empire: Obscenity and the Politics of Moral Regulation in Britain, India and Australia*, CUP, Cambridge 2010.

Hoyland, John S. *Gopal Krishna Gokhale: His Life and Speeches*, YMCA Publishing House, Calcutta 1933.

Huntington, Samuel. *The Third Wave: Democratization in the Late Twentieth Century*, University of Oklahoma Press, Norman and London 1991.

Jansen, Marius. *The Making of Modern Japan*, Harvard University Press, Cambridge, MA 2002.

Jayal, Niraja Gopal. *Citizenship and Its Discontents, An Indian History*, Harvard University Press, Cambridge, MA 2013.

Kapila, Shruti and Faisal Devji (eds.). *Political Thought in Action: The Bhagavad Gita and Modern India*, CUP, Cambridge 2013.

Khosla, Madhav. *India's Founding Moment: The Constitution of a Most Surprising Democracy*, Harvard University Press, Cambridge, MA, and London 2020.

Kothari, Jayna. "Social Rights and the Indian Constitution", *Law, Social Justice and Global Development Journal*, Vol. 2 (2004), available at https://warwick.ac.uk/fac/soc/law/elj/lgd/2004_2/kothari/.

Krishna, Anirudh. "Gaining Access to Public Services and the Democratic State in India: Institutions in the Middle", *Studies in Comparative International Development*, Vol. 46, n. 1 (2011), pp. 98–117.

——. *Changing Policy and Practice from Below. Community Experiences in Poverty Reduction*, United Nations Development Programme, New York 2000.

Kuhnle, Stein and Anne Sander. 'The Emergence of the Western Welfare State', in F.G. Castles et al. (eds.), *The Oxford Handbook of the Welfare State*, OUP, Oxford 2010, pp. 61–80.

Kumar, Anand. 'The Welfare State System in India', in B. Vivekanandan and Nimmi Kurian (eds.), *Welfare States and the Future*, Palgrave Macmillan, Basingstoke 2005, pp. 336–371.

Kumar, Arun. "Skilling and Its Histories: Labour Market, Technical Knowledge and the Making of Skilled Workers in Colonial India, 1880–1910", *Journal of South Asian Development*, Vol. 13, n. 3 (2018), pp. 249–271.

Kumar, Krishna. *Political Agenda of Education: A Study of Colonialist and Nationalist Ideas*, Sage, New Delhi 2005 (first published 1991).

Lees, Andrew. *Cities, Sin, and Social Reform in Imperial Germany*, University of Michigan Press, Ann Arbor 2002.

Levy, Marion J. *Modernization and the Structure of Societies: A Setting for International Affairs*, Princeton University Press, Princeton 1966, 2 vols.

Lipset, Seymour Martin. "Some Social Requisites of Democracy: Economic Development and Political Legitimacy", *The American Political Science Review*, Vol. 53, n. 1 (1959), pp. 69–105.

Little, Angela W. "Access to Elementary Education in India: Politics, Policies and Progress", in *CREATE Pathways to Access*, Research Monograph n. 44 (2010).

Majeed, Javed. "A Nation on the Move: The Indian Constitution, Life Writing and Cosmopolitanism", *Life Writing*, Vol. 13, n. 2 (2016), pp. 237–253.

Mann, Michael. '"Torchbearers Upon the Path of Progress": Britain's Ideology of a "Moral and Material Progress" in India. An Introductory Essay', in Harald Fischer-Tiné and Michael Mann (eds.), *Colonialism as Civilizing Mission: Cultural Ideology in British India*, Anthem Press, London and New York 2004, pp. 1–26.

Marshall, T.H. and Tom B. Bottomore. *Citizenship and Social Class*, Pluto, London 1992.

Menon, Dilip. "An Eminent Victorian: Gandhi, *Hind Swaraj* and the Crisis of Liberal Democracy in the Nineteenth Century", *History of the Present*, Vol. 7, n. 1 (2017), pp. 33–58.

Mills, James H. "Cannabis and the Cultures of Colonialism: Government, Medicine, Ritual and Pleasures in the History of an Asian Drug (c. 1800 - c. 1895)", *Zeitenblicke*, Vol. 9, n. 3 (2009), https://pureportal.strath.ac.uk/en/publications/cannabis-and-the-cultures-of-colonialism-government-medicine-ritu   [accessed 22 April 2021].

——. *Cannabis Britannica: Empire, Trade, and Prohibition 1800-1928*, OUP, Oxford 2005.

Mir, Farina. "Imperial Policy, Provincial Practices: Colonial Language Policy in Nineteenth Century India", *Indian Economic and Social History Review*, Vol. 43 (2006), pp. 395–427.

Moses, Julia. "Social Citizenship and Social Rights in an Age of Extremes: T. H. Marshall's Social Philosophy in the Longue Durée", *Modern Intellectual History*, Vol. 16, n. 1 (2019), pp. 155–184.

Muhammedali, T. "In Service of The Nation: Relief and Reconstruction in Malabar in The Wake of The Rebellion Of 1921", *Proceedings of the Indian History Congress*, Vol. 68 (2007), pp. 789–805.

Mukhopadhyay, Aparajita. *Imperial Technology and 'Native' Agency: A Social History of Railways in Colonial India, 1850-1920*, Routledge, London 2018.

Nagappa, Gowda K. *The Bhagavadgita in the Nationalist Discourse*, OUP, Delhi 2011.

Naidu, Sarojini. *Speeches and Writings of Sarojini Naidu*, G.A. Natesan & Co, Madras 1925.

Nanda, B.R. *Three Statesmen: Gokhale, Gandhi and Nehru*, OUP, New Delhi 2004.

Norton, Grubb W. and Marvin Lazerson. *The Education Gospel: The Economic Power of Schooling*, Harvard University Press, Cambridge, MA 2004.

Ogle, Vanessa. *The Global Transformation of Time 1870 – 1950*, Harvard University Press, Cambridge, MA 2015.

Ong, Aihwa. *Flexible Citizenship: The Cultural Logics of Transnationality*, Duke University Press, Durham and London 1999.

Pande, Ishita. *Sex, Law and the Politics of Age. Child Marriage in India 1891-1937*, CUP, Cambridge 2020.

Panikkar, K.N. *Against Lord and State: Religion and Peasant Uprisings in Malabar, 1836-1921*, OUP, New Delhi 1989.

Pehnke, Andreas (ed.). *Johannes Tews (1860 - 1937); Vom 15-Jährigen Dorfschullehrer Zum Repräsentanten des Deutschen Lehrervereins; Studien über Den Liberalen Bildungspolitiker, Sozialpädagogen, Erwachsenenbildner Und Kämpfer gegen Den Antisemitismus*, Verlag, Beucha 2011.

Pliley, Jessica, Robert Kramm and Harald Fischer-Tiné. 'Introduction: A Plea for a "Vicious Turn" in Global History', in idem (eds.), *Global Anti-Vice Activism, 1890–1950: Fighting Drinks, Drugs, and 'Immorality'*, CUP, Cambridge 2016, pp. 1–30.

Pomfret, David M. *Youth and Empire: Transcolonial Childhoods in British and French Asia*, Stanford University Press, Stanford, CA 2015.

Rao, Parimala V. 'Compulsory Education and the Political Leadership in Colonial India, 1840-1947', in idem (ed.), *New Perspectives in the History of Indian Education*, Orient Blackswan, New Delhi 2014, pp. 151–175.

——. *Foundations of Tilak's Nationalism: Discrimination, Education, and Hindutva*, Orient Blackswan, New Delhi 2007.

Report of the Indian Factory Labour Commission 1908, Govt. of India. Ministry of Commerce and Industry, Simla 1908.

Report of the Indian Hemp Drugs Commission 1893–94, Government Central Printing Office, Simla 1894.

Robb, Peter. "Labour in India 1860-1920: Typologies, Change and Regulation", *Journal of the Royal Asiatic Society*, Vol. 4, n. 1 (1994), pp. 37–66.

Roy, Srirupa. *Beyond Belief: India and the Politics of Postcolonial Nationalism*, Duke University Press, Durham and London 2007.

Saldanha, Indra Munshi. "On Drinking and 'Drunkenness': History of Liquor in Colonial India", *Economic and Political Weekly*, Vol. 30, n. 37 (1995), pp. 2323–2331.

Sarkar, Sumit. *Beyond Nationalist Frames: Relocating Postmodernism, Hindutva, History*, Permanent Black, Delhi 2002.

Satya, Laxman D. *Cotton and Famine in Berar, 1850-1900*, Manohar, New Delhi 1997.

Sen, Amartya. "The Country of First Boys", *The Little Magazine*, Vol. 6, n. 1 and 2 (2005), pp. 7-17.

Sen, Satadru. *Colonial Childhoods: The Juvenile Periphery of India, 1850-1945*, Anthem Press, London 2005.

Seth, Sanjay. *Subject Lessons: The Western Education of Colonial India*, Duke University Press, Durham and London 2007.

——. "Rewriting Histories of Nationalism: The Politics of 'Moderate Nationalism' in India, 1870-1905", *The American Historical Review*, Vol. 104, n. 1 (1999), pp. 95–116.

Shah, A.B. 'Foreword', in A.B. Shah and S.P. Aiyar (eds.), *Gokhale and Modern India, Centenary Lectures*, Manaktalas, Bombay 1966.

Shamir, Ronen and Daphna Hacker. "Colonialism's Civilizing Mission: The Case of the Indian Hemp Drug Commission", *Law & Social Inquiry*, Vol. 26, n. 2 (2001), pp. 435–461.

Sherman, Taylor C. "Education in Early Postcolonial India: Expansion, Experimentation and Planned Self-Help", *History of Education*, Vol. 47, n. 4 (2018), pp. 504–520.

——. "From 'Grow More Food' to 'Miss a Meal': Hunger, Development and the Limits of Post-Colonial Nationalism in India, 1947–1957", *South Asia: Journal of South Asian Studies*, Vol. 36, n. 4 (2013), pp. 571–588.

——, Gould, William and Sarah Ansari (eds.). *From Subjects to Citizens: Society and the Everyday State in India and Pakistan, 1947-1970*, CUP, Cambridge 2014.

Simonow, Joanna. *From Famine to Famine. Hunger Relief, Nutritional Reform and Political Mobilisation in South Asia (c. 1890-1955)*, Leiden University Press, forthcoming.

Skaria, Ajay. "Gandhi's Politics: Liberalism and the Question of the Ashram", *South Atlantic Quarterly*, Vol. 101, n. 4 (2002), pp. 955–986.

Soni. *Famine Orphan "Rescue" Missions: Childhood, Colonialism and Nationalism in Colonial India, 1860s–1920s*, unpubl. Ph.D. thesis, ETH Zurich, 2020.

Srinivasa Sastri, V.S. *My Master Gokhale: A Selection from the Speeches and Writings of V. S. Srinivasa Sastri* (edited by T.N. Jagadisan), Model Publications, Madras 1946.

——. *Life and Times of Sir Pherozeshah Mehta* (edited by S.R. Venkataraman), Bharatiya Vidya Bhavan, Bombay n.d. (first published 1945).

——. *The Letters of the Right Honourable V.S. Srinivasa Sastri* (edited by T.N. Jagadisan), Rochouse and Sons, Madras 1944.

——. *Life of Gopal Krishna Gokhale*, Bangalore Printing and Publishing Co, Bangalore 1937.

Srivastava, Prachi and Claire Noronha. "Institutional Framing of the Right to Education Act: Contestation, Controversy and Concession", *Economic and Political Weekly*, Vol. 49, n. 18 (2014), pp. 51–58.

Srivastava, Priyanka. *The Well-Being of the Labor Force in Colonial Bombay: Discourses and Practices*, Palgrave Macmillan, Cham 2018.

Srivatsan, R. *Seva, Saviour and State: Caste Politics, Tribal Welfare and Capitalist Development*, Routledge, Abingdon and New York 2015.

Stearns, Peter. *Childhood in World History*, Routledge, New York 2011.

Steger, Manfred B. "Searching for Satya Through Ahimsa: Gandhi's Challenge to Western Discourses of Power", *Constellations*, Vol. 13, n. 3 (2006), pp. 332–353.

Tewari, Saagar. "Debating Tribe and Nation: Hutton, Thakkar, Ambedkar, and Elwin (1920s-1940s)", *NMML Occasional Paper History and Society*, New Series 86, pp. 1–30.

Valdameri, Elena. "Debates on Citizenship in Colonial South Asia and Global Political Thought (*c.*1880–1950)", in Harald Fischer-Tiné and Maria Framke (edited by), *Routledge Handbook of the History Colonialism in South Asia*, Routledge, Abingdon and New York 2022, pp. 450–462.

Vallgårda, Karen. *Imperial Childhoods and Christian Mission: Education and Emotions in South India and Denmark*, Palgrave MacMillan, Basingstoke 2015.

van de Walle, Michael Nicholas. *Democratic Experiments in Africa: Regime Transitions in Comparative Perspective*, CUP, Cambridge 1997.

Walsh, Judith E. *Growing up in British India: Indian Autobiographers on Childhood and Education Under the Raj*, Holmes & Meier, New York 1983.

Washbrook, David. "Forms of Citizenship in Pre-Modern South India", *Citizenship Studies*, Vol. 23, n. 3 (2019), pp. 224–329.

——. "The Commercialization of Agriculture in Colonial India: Production, Subsistence and Reproduction in the 'Dry South', c. 1870-1930", *Modern Asian Studies*, Vol. 28, n. 1 (1994), pp. 129–164.

Watt, Carey A. 'Philanthropy and Civilizing Missions in India c. 1820–1960: States, NGOs and Development', in C.A. Watt and M. Mann (eds.), *Civilizing Missions in Colonial and Post-Colonial South Asia: From Improvement to Development*, Anthem Press, London 2011, pp. 271–316.

——. *Serving the Nation: Cultures of Service, Association, and Citizenship in Colonial India*, OUP, New Delhi 2005.

Webb, Sidney and Beatrice Webb. *Indian Diary* (edited by Niraja Gopal Jayal), OUP, Oxford and New York 1990.

Wickramasinghe, Nira. *Sri Lanka in the Modern Age: A History of Contested Identities*, University of Hawaii Press, London 2006.

Wilson, Jon E. *The Domination of Strangers*, Palgrave Macmillan, London 2008.

Wolpert, Stanley A. *Tilak and Gokhale: Revolution and Reform in the Making of Modern India*, OUP, New Delhi 1989 (first published 1961).

Wood, Geoffrey D. 'States Without Citizens: The Problem of the Franchise State', in D. Hulme and M. Edwards (eds.), *NGOs, States and Donors: Too Close for Comfort?*, Save the Children Foundation and Macmillan, London 1997, pp. 79–92.

Zachariah, Ben. 'In Search of the Indigenous: J. C. Kumarappa and the Philosophy of "Gandhian Economics"', in Harald Fischer-Tiné and Michael Mann (eds.), *Colonialism as Civilizing Mission: Cultural Ideology in British India*, Anthem Press, London and New York 2004, pp. 248–269.

Zhao, Guoping. "The Modern Construction of Childhood: What Does It Do to the Paradox of Modernity", *Studies in Philosophy and Education*, Vol. 30 (2011), pp. 241–256.

Conclusion

Rendering a deeper and more nuanced understanding of Gokhale's political thought and interweaving his political life with wider theoretical, historiographical concerns and debates were the two main stated aims of this book. Gokhale's political life has been used as a window on several important aspects of the history of 'British' India in the late 19th and early 20th centuries, with a view to better grasp the dynamics of nationalism in other colonial milieux, too. The centrality of liberalism in the "moderate" phase of Indian nationalism, the emphasis placed on modernity to claim India's power to control its own future, the sacralisation of politics to demonstrate India's superiority to Western materialism, the contradictions and complexities inherent in the attempt by Indian nationalists to envisage a 'progressive' nation in a colonial context, all are the foci of continuing debates. It is these debates with which this book has engaged and intends to make a further contribution. Here, I revisit my arguments and consider the future research agendas suggested by them. Finally, moving beyond historical analysis, I briefly consider – from a less academic and more political point of view – the long-term impact of Gokhale's national vision and the liberal discourse of rights he articulated.

Liberalism has been the *fil rouge* running throughout all the chapters. We have seen that liberalism was influential in Gokhale's intellectual formation and largely determined his social outlook; it was the foundation of his political ideology and the bedrock of the variety of nationalism he advocated; the belief in liberal values imbibed Gokhale's supranational feelings and gave him a sense of belonging to a cosmopolitan community; it was liberal ideas on which his civic constructions were substantially predicated.

As argued especially in Chapters 1 and 2, ideas and values like individual freedom, secularism, moral universalism and a belief in material and moral progress were considered by Gokhale vital in transforming Indian society and making it 'modern.' This transformation entailed liberating individuals from the 'constraining' social and cultural influences imposed by their belonging to a certain caste or religious community, as well as becoming aware of, and opposing, despotic and paternalistic views and practices of sovereign power such as those embodied by the colonial state.

DOI: 10.4324/9781003037422-6

It was individual freedom that preceded and made possible the sovereignty of the nation-state.

The state envisioned by Gokhale respected citizens' civil and political liberties but acted also as a catalyst of social change. In other words, the state was attributed the pedagogical role of transforming the 'social.' It functioned as the legitimate unifier of a multifarious nation like India, allowing individuals to primarily identify with the national political community beyond religious and caste affiliations. This understanding of the state is crucial to grasp why the Indian 'Moderate' leader did not perceive his programme of nation building to be at odds with the continuance of the British Raj. The colonial state, in fact, was portrayed by Gokhale as 'providential' exactly in view of its unifying agency that coalesced India's 'natural' diversity into a unity. Conditional upon a greater participation of Indians in its institutions, the continuance of the colonial state would contribute to holding together politically the nation while de-emphasising those 'objective' elements of divisions that, in colonial discourse, made India a geographical entity rather than a 'modern' nation. Overall, this tension in Gokhale's political vision is at least partially resolved if we consider that for him self-government in India was not something that could be attained immediately, but rather a long-term goal for which India had to be prepared.

It is important to note, however, that Gokhale articulated his idea of national project not only in state-centred terms. Of equal importance was the role of the 'educated classes' in the political education of the 'uneducated masses' – a frequently invoked dyad. The larger populace was depicted as 'passive' and lacking a sense of public spiritedness and therefore in constant need of tutelage and guidance from above. Besides the masses, Muslims and the so-called 'Depressed Classes' increasingly became the object of political concern. Indeed, the debate about a separate electorate for Muslims on the occasion of the Morley-Minto Reforms as well as the discussions provoked by the Gait Circular spurred anxieties among the Indian National Congress (INC) leadership. It was feared that Muslims and the 'Depressed Classes' would claim particular political interests vis-à-vis the 'universal' ones represented by the national polity on the basis of their historical specificity and oppression. Thus, these two symbolically and demographically salient sections of colonial Indian society were increasingly perceived as a threat to the unity of the 'national' Indian/ Hindu community. Gokhale's preoccupation with the 'emergence' of these minorities goes some way to further understand the ideological and political limits of his liberal nationalism. Gokhale's imagination of nationhood oscillated between the language of abstract universal equality and a perception of the broader population as being unprepared for membership of the envisaged nation. Also, the inclusivity of his national vision faltered under the logic of the 'modern' concept of nationhood, which unfavourably regards ethnic and cultural characteristics as legitimate bases for political claims and therefore as potentially threatening to national unity. It appears, in fact, that Gokhale did not acknowledge all identities as constitutive to the nation's unity in diversity: whereas the transformation of Indian Muslims' political identity was recognised and considered worthy of state safeguards to ensure this community's loyalty to the national project, the 'Depressed Classes' became the object of an effort of inclusion and homogenisation in the Indian/Hindu majority.

The question of Indian society's 'unpreparedness' for freedom explains the importance that Gokhale placed on civic activism and social service, as I argue in Chapter 4 in particular. This was epitomised by the creation of the Servants of India Society (SIS), aimed at the mobilisation of selected 'disciplined' and 'selfless' members of the lettered elite invested with the task of building the nation and 'making' its citizens. The empirical case studies analysed have made possible the further investigation of the hierarchies and conservative aspects that characterised Gokhale's national vision and its understanding of what it meant to be a citizen. In particular, Gokhale's civic construction implied the imposition of a code of 'good' citizenship based on a 'superior' morality that was portrayed as Indian but in reality corresponded largely with upper-caste social values as well as with global ideas. So, while the INC leader imagined citizens as political individuals beyond any particularity of interests, the civic virtues that became associated with 'good' citizenship, such as discipline, self-restraint service and sacrifice, largely belonged to the Hindu upper-caste ethos and were reinforced by the liberal belief in a teleological vision of progress through individual self-development and by globally circulating notions and practices of social service. As this book has made clear, the very process of inculcating such social norms and values to the lower orders of Indian society often perpetuated, rather than erased, the dichotomy existing between those few already deemed to be worthy (subject-)citizens and the others, whose future as members of the nation was on hold. Overall, from the ideas and practice of associations like Gokhale's SIS, we can observe the emergence of modes of political participation which had a lasting impact on the socio-political context in the following decades, well into independence. Initiatives within civil society aimed at 'improving' sections of Indian society that were considered 'backward' served the purpose of compensating for the limited responsibility of the (post-)colonial state for the welfare of its (subject-)citizens, to hold governments accountable and recommend changes in policies. Also, those same initiatives, which allowed citizens' participation in activities of social relevance that fostered inclusion and membership of a nation in the making, did not only confer a sense of moral superiority to those who took part in them vis-à-vis the 'needy' ones; on a broader level, social services and voluntary activities were presented as an expression of 'Indian' forms of social idealism, citizenship and moral justice that transcended politics and were often constituted in supra-political, if not anti-political, terms. A systematic investigation of the long-term trajectories of civic constructions promoted by non-state actors after independence, and a thorough analysis of how they were transformed by the logic of a nation state no longer foreign, as well as by development agendas, is an undertaking yet to be pursued by existing research. The prospects for such an investigation are promising.[1]

Chapter 3 has explicated the 'Moderate' leader's ability to exploit different border-crossing networks and platforms in the promotion of his political vision. It has demonstrated that, in doing so, Gokhale was facilitated by his prominent role in the INC as well as by his willingness to engage with cultural alterity and by a perception of human beings sharing fundamental values. Overall, it was his belief in liberalism's abstract equality and in the existence of a moral universalism that made Gokhale feel and think beyond the nation, giving him a sense of belonging to a cosmopolitan community. In this sense, national emancipation, although gradual, was part of a larger global tendency that Gokhale understood as driven by liberal forces while uniting the world through the same values. A free Indian nation, thus, was only a *tessera* of a global mosaic of free nations. Nevertheless, this discursive form of cosmopolitanism was never translated into a concrete political transnational programme nor in transversal acts of solidarity. While the tour in South Africa could have been a fitting stage on which to promote a similar agenda to unite those peoples that were victims of imperial discrimination, Gokhale failed to manifest any real interest in the conditions of the Chinese community or of the black South African population. Gokhale's epistemic and emotional enmeshment with the values of the British empire influenced him to reproduce its prejudices and hierarchies while rendering him unable or unwilling to imagine a world without imperialism. Gokhale, in fact, did not criticise the imperial order *per se* but condemned its discriminatory forms. At this point, the empire still represented – until its racialist nature became unjustifiable – a political opportunity for Indians as the space within which India could attain self-government on the basis of Queen Victoria's Proclamation.

Taking all these issues into account, this volume proposes to illustrate how the nationalist leader absorbed and reconfigured the liberal idiom, while shedding light on the specific ambivalences and political and ideological limits that resulted from this complex process.

All its weaknesses notwithstanding, Gokhale's national project aimed at promoting the creation of a fairer society and sought greater inclusion. The importance of such a stance becomes even more patent if today's Indian political situation, increasingly affected by the crisis of democracy and the rising tide of Hindu fundamentalism both at the ideological and political level,[2] is taken into consideration.

Gokhale's liberal nationalism looked to the future and was based on a project of common moral and material wellbeing to which all the inhabitants of India should contribute and from which they should benefit. The envisaged national emancipation was not only about modernisation, understood as techno-scientific and economic improvement, but also about modernity as a project involving societal and political liberation. Such a project entailed liberation from the oppressive colonial state and from any form of tyranny (whether exogenous or not), but also freedom from social discrimination on the basis of 'race,' religion and caste, and freedom from poverty. In other words, a free Indian nation was not only about the Indian elite taking the reins of power, but also – and perhaps more importantly – about the liberties and welfare of the Indian population in its entirety. Crucially, its realisation was significant – at least at the rhetorical level – beyond the Indian subcontinent, since it represented the *pars pro toto* of a more just global order, where 'West' and 'East' shared a more equitable distribution of power.

Gokhale's nationalism was far from being the exclusionary and chauvinistic ideology for which this term has acquired its pejorative connotation over time. It was a nationalism that, while not ignoring pre-political factors, did not celebrate a nation that had its roots in a 'golden' Indian or Hindu past and that had to be protected or purified from foreign contamination to preserve or restore its essential and pristine nature. In other words, it was a nationalism starkly and radically different from the one proposed by Savarkar from the 1920s onwards – and the more recent political configurations of the Hindutva forces. Gokhale's humane and nonsectarian vision, which saw India's cultural diversity as its strength and richness, was the same that animated the subsequent mainstream doctrine of the INC – Nehru *in primis*. That was a doctrine that embraced the concept of 'unity in diversity' and promoted a political culture committed to safeguard minorities and ensure social harmony.

The nation envisioned by Gokhale was not intrinsically more authentic or legitimate than other visions that defined the Indian nation in unchanging cultural/religious terms. As highlighted in this book, any notion of nation – and the one elaborated by Gokhale was no exception – entails a certain measure of oppression and considers some sections of society worthier members than others. This does not detract from the fact that, in plural societies like India, characterised by the presence of minorities of all kinds, a vision that emphasises the unifying factors of the national community and focuses on the building of a common future together is undoubtedly more conducive to democracy, social peace and the creation of a humane society.

Gokhale combined his idea of an Indianness capable of sheltering diverse identities equally with a political vision that was pervaded by the language of the mystic devotion of the nation. For him, politics represented something that, albeit differently, characterised Gandhi's view, too – an occasion for moral regeneration entrusted to the pedagogical action of the state, selfless social service and the cult of a civic religion. While considering individual dignity and the citizenry's freedom undisputable achievements of the modern age, Gokhale did not see the political mysticism of the national community as posing much of a threat to these principles. As a result, he did not see the two as actually incompatible. History, nonetheless, has shown that the sacralisation of politics – a phenomenon that stems from the tensions of modernity – contains the inherent potential for developing reactionary and authoritarian features, especially when severed from ideas of equality and freedom.[3] Narendra Modi in his 2014 maiden speech on Independence Day as India's Prime Minister – a speech that, due to its language, could have been given by Gokhale a 100 years earlier – defined himself 'the *pradhan sewak*' (first servant) of the nation.[4] This is yet another significant example of the multiple ways in which devotion for the nation can be appropriated, acquiring ideological connotations conflicting with democracy. It is an example that calls for further research on the historical trajectories and cultural specificities of civic and political religion in colonial and post-colonial India.

Another important element that this political biography has tried to illustrate is Gokhale's concrete vision of the state as the legitimate unifier of a highly diverse society and as the instrument through which modernity was to be realised. This modernity did not simply involve the creation of the liberal political individual,[5] as the state was also a crucial agent of socio-economic change. Its morality resided in bearing the responsibility for ameliorating the conditions and quality of life of the people. Direct state action – although supervised by civil society actors – was, in other words, expected to bring about economic development *and* social justice, and to have redistributive, if mild, effects. The need to combine economic development with the creation of a fairer society has remained a relevant objective – at least, but not exclusively, at the discursive level – in postcolonial India too. Although attacked from the left and the right, challenged by neoliberal views and often questioned by the so-called middle class, the significance of an ethical form of development centred on the well-being of people still determines the morality and legitimacy of the Indian state and informs the struggles and expectations of those organisations of civil society.

July 2021

Notes

1. Important starting points are the insightful discussions provided in Washbrook, "Forms of Citizenship in Pre-Modern South India", pp. 235–37 and in Watt, "Philanthropy and Civilizing Missions". Although focused on the process of nation-state formation in independent India and on the official discourses that accompanied it, Srirupa Roy, *Beyond Belief: India and the Politics of Postcolonial Nationalism*, Duke University Press, Durham and London 2007, offers an enlightening perspective on the activities that both state and non-state actors carried out in the transition from the colonial to the postcolonial period.

2. On the recent political developments, see Michelguglielmo Torri, "India 2020: The deepening crisis of democracy", *Asia Maior*, XXXI/2020, pp. 331–375 and Ramachandra Guha, "Uncanny Parallels", *The Telegraph*, 12 September 2020.

3. See Emilio Gentile, *Il culto del littorio. La sacralizzazione della politica nell'Italia fascista*, Laterza, Roma 1993, esp. pp. 5–33 and 269–281.
4. See "I'm your 'pradhan sewak': Modi tells nation", *The Hindu*, 15 August 2014, and Makarand K. Paranjape, "The Importance of being Narendra Modi", Mint, 12 September 2016.
5. Modernity actually unfolded in a way that was enormously more complex than Gokhale and more generally the liberals expected. This notwithstanding, the state has been a crucial reference point to dispense group rights and protect group interests as remedies for majoritarianism, discrimination and 'backwardness'. On this, see the discussion in Sudipta Kaviraj, *The Imaginary Institution of India*, pp. 210–233. See also Jayal, *Citizenship and its Discontents*, pp. 199–228.

References

"I'm your 'pradhan sewak': Modi tells nation", *The Hindu*, 15 August 2014, available at https://www.thehindu.com/news/national/im-your-pradhan-sewak-and-not-pradhan-mantri-modi/article6321514.ece.

Gentile, Emilio. *Il Culto del Littorio. La Sacralizzazione della Politica nell'Italia Fascista*, Laterza, Roma 1993.

Guha, Ramachandra. "Uncanny Parallels", *The Telegraph*, 12 September 2020.

Jayal, Niraja Gopal. *Citizenship and its Discontents, An Indian History*, Harvard University Press, Cambridge, MA 2013.

Kaviraj, Sudipta. *The Imaginary Institution of India: Politics and Ideas*, Columbia University Press, New York 2010.

Paranjape, Makarand K. "The Importance of being Narendra Modi", Mint, 12 September 2016, available at https://www.livemint.com/Opinion/lkLXc6b1v5 OyOqFxCiLLeO/The-importance-of-being-Modi.html.

Roy, Srirupa. *Beyond Belief: India and the Politics of Postcolonial Nationalism*, Duke University Press, Durham and London 2007.

Torri, Michelguglielmo. "India 2020: The Deepening Crisis of Democracy", *Asia Maior*, Vol. XXXI (2020), pp. 331–375.

Washbrook, David. "Forms of Citizenship in Pre-Modern South India", *Citizenship Studies*, Vol. 23, n. 3 (2019), pp. 224–239.

Watt, Carey A. 'Philanthropy and Civilizing Missions in India c. 1820–1960: States, NGOs and Development', in C.A. Watt and M. Mann (eds.), *Civilizing Missions in Colonial and Post-Colonial South Asia: From Improvement to Development*, Anthem Press, London 2011, pp. 271–316.

Index

Page numbers followed by n denote endnotes.

CPSIA information can be obtained
at www.ICGtesting.com
Printed in the USA
LVHW082046310123
738304LV00005B/341